Reconstructing Childhood

The Bucknell Studies in Latin American Literature and Theory
Series Editor: Aníbal González, Pennsylvania State University

The literature of Latin America, with its intensely critical, self-questioning, and experimental impulses, is currently one of the most influential in the world. In its earlier phases, this literary tradition produced major writers, such as Bartolomé de las Casas, Bernal Díaz del Castillo, the Inca Garcilaso, Sor Juana Inés de la Cruz, Andrés Bello, Gertrudis Gómez de Avellaneda, Domingo F. Sarmiento, José Martí, and Rubén Darío. More recently, writers from the U.S. to China, from Britain to Africa to India, and of course from the Iberian Peninsula, have felt the impact of the fiction and the poetry of such contemporary Latin American writers as Borges, Cortázar, García Márquez, Guimarães Rosa, Lezama Lima, Neruda, Vargas Llosa, Paz, Poniatowska, and Lispector, among many others. Dealing with far-reaching questions of history and modernity, language and selfhood, and power and ethics, Latin American literature sheds light on the many-faceted nature of Latin American life, as well as on the human condition as a whole.

The aim of this series of books is to provide a forum for the best criticism on Latin American literature in a wide range of critical approaches, with an emphasis on works that productively combine scholarship with theory. Acknowledging the historical links and cultural affinities between Latin American and Iberian literature, the series welcomes consideration of Spanish and Portuguese texts and topics, while also providing a space of convergence for scholars working in Romance studies, comparative literature, cultural studies, and literary theory.

Titles in Series

César Augusto Salgado, *From Modernism to Neobaroque: Joyce and Lezama Lima*

Robert Ignacio Díaz, *Unhomely Rooms: Foreign Tongues and Spanish American Literature*

Mario Santana, *Foreigners in the Homeland: The Latin American New Novel in Spain, 1962–1974*

Friis, Ronald J., *José Emilio Pacheco and the Poets of the Shadows*

Robert T. Conn, *The Politics of Philology: Alfonso Reyes and the Invention of the Latin American Literary Tradition*

Andrew Bush, *The Routes of Modernity: Spanish American Poetry from the Early Eighteenth to the Mid-Nineteenth Century*

Santa Arias and Mariselle Meléndez, *Mapping Colonial Spanish America: Places and Commonplaces of Identity, Culture, and Experience*

Alice A. Nelson, *Political Bodies: Gender, History and the Struggle for Narrative Power in Recent Chilean Literature*

Julia A. Kushigian, *Reconstructing Childhood: Strategies of Reading for Culture and Gender in the Spanish American Bildungsroman*

Reconstructing Childhood

Strategies of Reading
for Culture and Gender
in the Spanish American Bildungsroman

Julia A. Kushigian

Lewisburg
Bucknell University Press
London: Associated University Presses

Associated University Presses
2010 Eastpark Boulevard
Cranbury, NJ 08512

Associated University Presses
16 Barter Street
London WC1A 2AH, England

Associated University Presses
P.O. Box 338, Port Credit
Mississauga, Ontario
Canada L5G 4L8

The paper used in this publication meets the requirements of the American National Standard for Permanence of Paper for Printed Library Materials Z39.48–1984.

Library of Congress Cataloging-in-Publication Data

Kushigian, Julia Alexis.
    Reconstructing childhood : strategies of reading for culture and gender in the Spanish American bildungsroman / Julia A. Kushigian.
        p.   cm. — (The Bucknell studies in Latin American literature and theory)
    Includes bibliographical references and index.
    ISBN 0-8387-5522-4 (alk. paper)
    1. Spanish American fiction—History and criticism.   2. Gender identity in literature.   3. Bildungsroman.   I. Title.   II. Series.
PQ7082.N7 K77   2003
863.009′355—dc21   2002014969

PRINTED IN THE UNITED STATES OF AMERICA

To John and Francisca, my inspiration.

Contents

Acknowledgments

I WISH TO ACKNOWLEDGE A YALE/MELLON VISITING FACULTY GRANT that facilitated research in the final stages of completing the manuscript. I also wish to acknowledge various grants from Connecticut College in the form of a sabbatical, R. F. Johnson Faculty Research stipends, and a grant to participate in a CIEE International Seminar in Cuba, which, in total, enabled me to conduct research and present papers in development of this book. The opportunity to serve as Director of the Toor Cummings Center for International Studies and the Liberal Arts at Connecticut College, the Associate Director of the Holleran Center for Community Action and Public Policy, and co-Director of two conferences for the Connecticut College Initiative for Social Development, afforded me the opportunity to join an inspired public debate that placed my research in a global perspective.

Preliminary versions of some of the material contained in this book were previously published as essays in various journals and books. Parts of chapter 2 were published in *Revista Iberoamericana* (July–December 1987). Parts of chapter 3 were published in *Actas, IILI* (January 2000). Parts of chapter 7 were published in *Obra Completa. Severo Sarduy* (Paris: Colección Archivos 1999) and *Movimiento Actual* (September 2000).

The following publishers have generously given permission to use extended quotations or tables from copyrighted works: From *Statistical Abstract of Latin America*, James Wilke, editor, Eduardo Alemán and José Guadalupe Ortega, co-editors. Copyright © 1999 by The Regents of the University of California. Reprinted by permission of the University of California, Los Angeles Latin American Center Publications. From *La casa de los espíritus*, by Isabel Allende. Copyright © 1982 by Isabel Allende. Reprinted by permission of the literary agent Carmen Balcells. From *The House of the Spirits*, by Isabel Allende, translated by Magda Bogin. Copyright © 1985 by Alfred A. Knopf, A Division of Random House, Inc. Used by permission of Alfred A. Knopf, a division of Random House, Inc. From *The House of the Spirits*, by Isabel Allende, translated by Magda Bogin, published by Jonathan Cape. Used by permission of The Random House Group Limited. From *La ciudad y los perros* by Mario Vargas Llosa. Copyright © 1962. Reprinted by permission of the literary agent Carmen Balcells. From *The Time of the Hero* by Mario Vargas Llosa, translated by Lysander Kemp. Translation copyright © 1966 by Grove Press, Inc. Used by permission of Farrar, Straus and Giroux. From *The Time of the Hero* by Mario Vargas Llosa, translated by Lysander Kemp, published by Jonathan Cape. Used by permission of Faber and Faber. From *Hasta no verte, Jesús mío* by Elena Poniatowska. Copyright © 1969. Reprinted by permission of the publisher Ediciones Era. From *Here's to you, Jesusa* by Elena Poniatowska, translated by Deanna Heikkinen. Copyright © 1969 by Elena Poniatowska. Translation copyright © 2001 by Farrar, Straus and Giroux, LLC. From *Here's to you, Jesusa* by Elena Poniatowska, translated by Deanna Heikkinen. Copyright © 1969 by Elena Poniatowska. Translation © 2001. Reprinted by permission of Elena Poniatowska (U.K. and British Commonwealth). From *Conversación al sur* by Marta Traba. Copyright 1981 by Marta Traba. Reprinted by permission of the publisher Siglo XXI Editores. From *Mothers and Shadows* by Marta Traba, translated by Jo Labanyi, Copyright © 1985. Reprinted by permission of the publisher Readers International Inc. From *Las memorias de Mamá Blanca* by Teresa de la Parra. Copyright © 1988. Reprinted by permission of the publisher Association Archives de la Literature Latino-americaine/UNESCO. From *Mama Blanca's Souvenirs* by Teresa de la Parra, translated by Harriet de Onís, copyright © 1959. Reprinted by permission of the publisher of the UNESCO collection/OAS.

I wish to thank those friends and colleagues who read and critiqued portions of this manuscript and whose insights were invaluable: Carlos Alonso, Flora González, Fred Luciani, Doris Meyer, Robert Proctor, Alicia Rivero, and Roberto Véguez. A special debt of gratitude goes to Julio Ortega, Francine Masiello, and George Yúdice for their efforts in critiquing and supporting the entire manuscript, and to Rolena Adorno for her intellectual generosity during my fellowship year at Yale. I sincerely wish to thank both friend and mentor, Roberto González Echevarría, for his vision and commitment to excellence in scholarship and teaching in the true Liberal Arts tradition. I especially wish to recognize my parents, Rose and Jack Kushigian, and brother, Russell, who are always a source of inspiration to me. Finally, to my husband, Charles Secor, Jr., my undying gratitude for his support of this project and all of our endeavors together.

Reconstructing
Childhood

Introduction

I. RITES OF SELECTION

WHEN A PORTRAIT OF THE ARTIST/BANKER/POLITICIAN/DOCTOR AS A young man is altered to reveal a female and/or lesbian/gay/marginalized/middle-aged/insurgent paradigm, how do we adjust for the pushing of boundaries, emptying of symbols, and hybridization of forms? Clearly the superimposition of codes from the traditional model of self-realization and coming of age onto other forms of cultural production is ineffective and disillusioning. Why, ultimately, is the examination of one's life process in the making and molding of the self deemed beneficial? And to that end, how can one consider the *Bildungsroman*, the novel of growth and youthful development, an important tool to renovate and challenge cultural scripts despite its eighteenth-century roots and that contemporary criticism which dismantles its approach?[1] Finally, what strategies revive and value alternative forms of development? In effect, this study argues for a critique of the grand narrative of coming of age, namely the Bildungsroman, and its traditional paradigm of normative human development. Hence, my contention that childhood be reconstructed by rescuing the nuanced qualities of the *Bildung* process is predicated on the fact that access to this concept through culture and gender corrects the 'absolute' status of Bildung.[2] My goal, therefore, is to suggest answers to the questions above by advocating two theories: 1) the application of the concept of Bildung as a process that enhances growth and development, gender, and cultural patterning; and 2) the anchoring of the Bildungsroman in catharsis, which argues for the destiny of literature and against the finality of growth and maturity, death as an end point, or the loss of the Beautiful Soul. The Beautiful Soul, a cultural icon that personifies an interconnection between moral and aesthetic qualities, symbolizes the ultimate achievement of human endeavor when linked to potentiality. In essence, the objective of this study is to propose strategies for reading the Spanish American Bildungsroman based primarily on a reconfigured examination of gender and culture as

13

more satisfying and humanizing formational markers for development than the more common biological/psychological approach to
coming of age.[3]

In a comparative examination of works in English, French, German, and Spanish, many studies on the Bildungsroman begin with
a detailed genre classification as a defense of this class of novel.
The reason why the defense is considered necessary is because
while the concept works well historically, the underlying tension is
that most research takes the self-realized male as the central metaphor for the Bildungsroman—a Christian, middle-class, white male.
All other interpretations appear ill-conceived, forced, unfit, or extreme because they do not echo the white male experience as "normative human paradigm."[4] Here I have expanded Sidonie Smith's
evaluation of "the naïve conflation of male subjectivity and human
identity," so as to qualify it by race, because it is not accurate with
respect to the Bildungsroman to say that all male experience is reflected in the traditional model. To resolve this dilemma of focus,
various studies conclude that *all* novels are variations of the Bildungsroman, while others support a more suitable term: "Individualro-
man," the novel of development, awakening, or initiation, the
apprenticeship novel, the coming-of-age novel, the psychological
novel or *Entwicklungsroman*, the *Kunstleroman*, the *Erziehungsroman*, the anti- or failed Bildungsroman, among others.[5] While I do
not claim that every novel is a Bildungsroman, my theory is that
Bildung, for its nuanced, complex, and enlightening potential, is
conceptually the most significant, satisfying, and viable term.[6]

With this in mind, I caution against an oversimplification of Bildung.[7] Bildung views reality as a whole and all components (chem-
ical, physical, cultural, social, historical, philosophical, etc.) as
complementary ways of understanding the whole. By charting development from past actions to future potentialities, Bildung af-
firms life and celebrates human values. It inscribes the whole of
reality—life and death, memory and dreams, success and failure,
rebellion and acceptance—exploring the intervening stages as
markers for personal growth. What distinguishes the Bildung process is that it is a highly individualized exercise that encourages autonomy and the reaching of potentiality and personal goals in an
atmosphere that supports social and moral growth, unlike the
learned lessons of the narrowly pedagogic novel, the *Erziehungsroman*, or the programmable lessons of the more recent trend in character education; that is, teaching students to be "diligent, obedient,
and patriotic," by "planting the ideas of virtue, of good traits in the
young."[8] Frequently a discussion of the Bildungsroman does not

take potentiality into account, dismissing this form after a cursory glance at the literature to date and a nod to its definition as a coming-of-age novel. This approach, while perhaps helpful in its intent to translate complex material into everyday metaphors for the benefit of a general readership, avoids Bildung's compelling nature. A fully realized, philosophic insight into the Bildung process will help not only review historically the literature written, but, more importantly, revitalize the text and an understanding of the self, which is what Karl Morgenstern had in mind when he first coined the term Bildungsroman in the nineteenth century. In effect, Morgenstern said that this class of novel promotes the reader's Bildung to a greater degree than any other kind of novel. If it is true that literature helps us understand the symbolic manifestations of our inner dreams, then, I argue, it is especially true in the case of the Bildungsroman, which encourages self-reflection.

II. BILDUNG AND SPANISH-SPEAKING AMERICA

As the theory of the Bildungsroman—self-realization, identity, and development—would look different if you took the female or marginalized experience as the norm, I have developed strategies for reading that unpack the self-realization process for both women and men, the marginalized and the majority, rich, poor, and otherwise, valuing all experience as formational in the Bildung process. The novels of Spanish America or Spanish-speaking America are the focus of this study because of the strong personal and cultural identities of their protagonists in a world often plagued by alienation. Also significant is the multicultural nature and variety of works, confounded by their lack of representation in comparative literary studies.[9] Spanish America has revived the Bildungsroman by transforming self-realization into the service of something larger, that is, a universal social goal. One point that distinguishes the Spanish American Bildungsroman is its ability to exploit the full potential of the genre. It reinforces the goal of forming, cultivating, and developing the self through transcendence, to become, as Nietzsche would conclude, the self beyond the self, reaching potentiality and understanding life from universal points of view. It describes/inscribes those people who "come of age" and develop regardless of where they started, at what point they finish, and what the outcomes may be.[10]

An equally important point that distinguishes the Spanish American Bildungsroman is its celebration of issues of gender, race, class, and age, for a more complex and satisfying weaving of humanity. To achieve this stage it moves beyond the typical white male, middle class, adolescent protagonist to incorporate portraits of self-realization and development, both personal and economic, which center the poor, black, indigenous, female, elderly—in effect, marginalized experience. It also recognizes itself as hybrid, with respect to its cultural, social, economic, historical, and political matrices, and can be characterized as relational, that is, grounded in an understanding of the self in relation to the Other.[11] Spanish American Bildungsromane give a sense of a powerful process of self-awareness that is contestatory and complements the equally powerful social movements of individual and collective discovery taking place in these countries, particularly from the period of Independence to the present. It is frequently accompanied by a moral vision, owing to the intellectual and philosophical debt many Spanish American authors have with truth.

To what do we owe the contestatory power of this cultural project? In truth, the Bildungsroman's ability to represent anyone other than of middle or upper class status does not belong to this form historically. Its goal in the German formula was to inspire the middle class to a life of public service, with obvious benefits for the state (think later of Max Weber's assertion in *Economy and Society* that the bureaucrat is an inevitable byproduct of the modern state). The narrative formation of the English model foregrounds a social context, registering attainment of social status through growth, accommodation, and self-realization. I believe the uniqueness of the Spanish American model lies in its capacity to generalize human experience owing to the Bildung or developmental process of nations and social movements on the one hand, and the inevitable forming of an American identity, on the other. Its potential, furthermore, to serve as a bridge between modernism and post-modernism negotiates a sliding from individual strategies to collective consciousness, imbuing personal development with a collective charge.

Importantly, collective representativeness surfaces early in the testimonies of the chronicles of conquest, the colonial period, and again during the unique post-colonial period. The distinctiveness of Spanish American post-colonialism, which deviates from the norm of origins rooted in Western Europe, lies in its narrative of futurity through which the New World came to be identified, as Carlos J. Alonso forcefully argues.[12] That is, post-colonial nation-building does not seek to retrieve indigenous origins, and in its future-looking context serves as foundation for the modernist project. Modernism, however, with its reappropriation of linguistic power and exotic models,[13] inserts doubt into a progressive movement of development. The project of modernity uses generalized culture, drawing from science, morality and art for the enrichment of everyday life. But what happens contradicts this paradigm setting modes of thinking as specializations that no longer undercut each other. Alonso couches this contradiction in terms of Modernity's threat to its own discourse: ". . . the Spanish American text argues strenuously for modernity, while it signals simultaneously in a number of ways its distance from the demands of modernity's rhetoric as a mean of maintaining its discursive power."[14] But even the rhetorical slippage away from itself, as we shall see, constitutes its own rhetorical authority.

To a large extent, the Spanish American Bildungsroman distinguishes itself through its metahistory. For example, the role that national identity plays in the developmental process suggests an intertwining of aspirations that encourages the individual to act as a part of something larger, this relationship between national identity and aspirations having been explored first in the foundational fictions of the nineteenth century. Historically, as the developing nations first assigned their existence to independence and post-colonialism, they centered a quest for identity firmly in the national character (which is still open and fluid). Furthermore, as most of the Wars of Independence were fought between 1810 and 1825, with the exception of Brazil and Cuba, these fictions tended to reflect the creation of new nations rather than the recovering of indigenous cultures and glorification of past achievements. The intertwining of history and fiction seen by Djelal Kadir and Doris Sommer in their respective works reflects a shaping through mutual influence, which, Sommer argues, has a public, political function.[15] I would suggest on another level proposing a reading of nation-building fictions as foundational Bildungsromane in search of communal self-realization.

What I am saying is that the prospect of self-realization and identity should be measured metonymically: as the person grows and forms him/herself, so does the nation, feeling similar growing pains and struggles with rites of passage as the individual. What is provocative here is the development of a national Bildungsroman. From *Teresa la limeña* to *Biografía de un cimarrón*, *Hijo de hombre*, *La casa de los espíritus*, and *In the Time of the Butterflies/En el tiempo de las mariposas*, a cultural patterning emerges that forms and identifies an individual, not separate from but representative of a nation. This self-examination and search for identity is especially productive and fluid in moments of national crisis, a historical period when, as Francine Masiello signals, a shifting discourse on gender and family may insinuate doubt into the binary structures that inform official history.[16] The foundational fictions of the last two centuries struggled for the establishment of a national character or cultural identity unique to the political, socioeconomic, historical, linguistic, and natural conditions of their citizens. This process articulated at once a national and personal "I". James Romano concludes that those in a felicitous position to reconcile national and self-identity were and continue to be the authors who helped define the values and orientation of society in both individual and collective terms.[17] In other words, they interpret for us a national character, which, as an analogue of larger events in Latin America, is in a constant state of flux. Furthermore, it is complex, fluid, and flexible, and cannot be appreciated as realized even one hundred years after Independence.

Latin American literature does not belong to the individualistic tradition embodied by the literature of the United States and Europe. In essence, individualism is the patrimony of western tradition from the Declaration of Independence and the Bill of Rights in the United States, to the national, cultural, and linguistic unifications that make a citizen German, British, French, Spanish, or Italian. This does not mean, however, that it belongs to an eastern tradition where authorship is not central to creation, as the great books are written and rewritten throughout history. Writing the story of one's development in life is not a culturally neutral act. Therefore, what we see in Spanish American novels of growth and development is a communal and relational structure that frequently critiques the failures of individualism. For example, Mario Vargas Llosa's earlier novels through Severo Sarduy's postmodern novels underscore the failure of individualism and perhaps tangentially point toward the complexities inherent in superimposing a western market economy on a hybrid, baroque foundation. The characteristics, furthermore, that Jerome Buckley details of the English tradition (*Seasons of Youth: The Bildungsroman from Dickens to Golding*) and Martin Swales (*The German Bildungsroman from Wieland to Hesse*) of the German tradition do not lead us to search for a Paraguayan, Colombian, or Chilean tradition, because this would lead us to a conflictive colonial past that is not responsive to national identities or a "Latin American" selfhood. We rather explore a cultural tradition in transition that searches for new forms of articulation. That is, the goal is to discover who " I" am in relation to the other and Latin America. It reflects an exhaustion of the cultural resources of national identity and a restructuring of society, artistic form, and politics.

The voyage of discovery and encounter with the self assumes for the Latin American text the European, indigenous, African, or eastern past, but not so much out of reverence to this history as with a need to manipulate the aesthetic and political, and unsettle codes of identity. This would explain the enormous appeal of the Bildungsroman as a self-defining statement that overrides the need to identify solely with a canonical text or an accomplished author of renown. The point I wish to make is that the unique journey of discovery toward the making and molding of the self invites an examination of intersections where ethnic identities, cultural difference, and contextual otherness merge. Tapping into larger anxieties of Latin America's sense of self with respect to its heritage partners and neighbors to the north, these portraits of discovery and self-realization contain the seeds of a hybrid nature from the beginning. As alluded to earlier, we do not simply read a Mexican portrait of development and self-realization, for example, but rather one that reveals in all its complexity the rites of passage and issues for framing life within the context of the nation and larger goals of America.[18]

The Spanish American Bildungsroman, to paraphrase Fredric Jameson, is ideologically charged; hence, I believe, morally and culturally charged. Many Spanish American texts have a double mission: 1) to communicate human values in the endeavor to be the self beyond the self, and 2) to seek social justice. The goals of the Spanish American Bildungsroman include and frequently transcend those of the traditional Bildungsroman. That is, the individual's subjective goals of love, honor, and ambition do not always lead, as Hegel concluded, to the protagonist's getting the girl and some kind of job, marrying, and becoming a philistine just like all others.[19] These same subjective goals may lead in Spanish American literature to the goals of what we can now define as those of new social movements, which are foreshadowed in many early works: the defense of human rights, the quality of life and one's surroundings, and the redefinition of sexual and gender identities.[20]

The ideological dimensions of a narrative account reflect the ethics of its author. Therefore, when a position is broadened to include the disenfranchised, the narrator acts upon and argues, so to speak, a political position that pits a dominant culture against marginalized groups, or society's Others. The result of exploring the national "I" in this manner is an including or blending in of those who previously had been left out of the national portrait. Visually, the graphic design of a national portrait can be explored through Juan Dávila's image of Simón Bolívar, Liberator. This image, reproduced and circulated on a postcard, transgresses the margins of meaning, Latin American myth, politics, race, ethnicity, "good taste," and gender. Bolívar's mestizo features, female torso (transvestism?), and obscene gesture contaminate the official portrait of the hero of the Latin American independence movement. And yet, they bring to light a Latin American sub-identity that has long been censured by history.[21] This symbolic attack on the solemnity of a national portrait and the hero it represents suspends the edges of definition and repeats itself in both the Bildungsromane of national identity and the marginalized. In effect, the Spanish American Bildungsroman of the disenfranchised depicts the self-identity of those women, indigenous, blacks, mestizos, gays, lesbians, transvestites, poor, indigent, socialists, communists, and so forth, who struggle for self-development in a society that devalues their contributions but historically demands their participation.

Giving voice to these protagonists at the literary level lends an air of objective reality to their personal stories, which redeems the collectively marginalized through the telling of truth.[22] At the very least, it is a rare opportunity for their testimony to be heard and understood, relying on a relationship with a sympathetic reader/listener for the communication of some of the more humane values. At its fullest point, it is an invitation to understand the power of self-reflection and awareness in all traditions, as essential first steps toward "cultivating our humanity" (Nussbaum) and achieving "communal self-realization" (Tu Wei-ming).[23] In effect, the accomplishments of communal self-realization reveal that the growing movements of self-awareness including those of feminists, environmentalists, religious pluralists, human rights and multicultural rights advocates, are first rooted in a project of self-reflection and cultivation. Thus, the transformation of the world these movements seek is predicated on self-reflection and self-cultivation to their fullest potentialities. These diverse, narrative portraits of self-development encourage a capacity to reach our goals to reason logically and reflect with sound judgment on all experience as formational. They also help to dispel the false belief that one's own tradition is the only one that is capable of self-criticism or universal aspiration.[24] Simply put, these goals, like archetypes, enable us to comprehend ourselves more fully and participate in a larger, communal self-realization.

One final point that distinguishes the Spanish American Bildungsroman is found in its meta-literary history. The precursors of the Bildungsroman in Spanish America bring to light two narrative forms in which the voice of the disenfranchised position the Bildungsroman for its exploration of the self: the picaresque tradition, which originates in Spain, and testimonial discourse, which has its roots in the period of conquest. The picaresque presents a quality of enfranchisement for the disenfranchised that becomes evident as its protagonists form a part of the community through the writing or telling of their stories. Claudio Guillén in a classic study of the picaresque observes its autobiographical nature, concluding that the act of telling the story of one's life creates space for the illusion of life and the development of truths. The picaresque narrative blends with autobiography and permits, Manuel Durán suggests, *Don Quijote* to be read as perhaps one of the greatest Bildungsromane of all time.[25] Roberto González Echevarría insightfully argues that what distinguishes the picaresque in Latin America is the innovative mimicking of legal cases and documents that brim with the voice of authority from the New World.[26] Examples of the picaresque genre in Latin America include *El carnero* (1636) by Juan Rodríguez Freyle and *El Periquillo Sarniento* (1816) by José Joaquín Fernández de Lizardi. By framing the Latin American picaresque within the argument of notarial rhetoric, González Echevarría emphasizes the picaresque's narrative of individual existence, which is trapped in the network of daily life in fulfillment of its bureaucratic goals and its desire to underscore the text's/narrator's legitimacy. In the picaresque this observation of people, places and ideas looks to the future as it reinforces a journey toward self-realization that mocks authority and seeks social justice. The process of seeking one's own in the alien and returning to oneself from what is other enhances a narrative that is also a vehicle for social satire. Its journey toward truth or legitimacy opens a path to similar goals in the Bildungsroman.

Testimonial literature shares with the picaresque novel the device of narrator as subject who demands the reader's attention. We might consider Bernal Díaz del Castillo's *Historia de la conquista de la Nueva España* (1568), Fray Bartolomé de las Casas's *Historia de las Indias* (1559), Guaman Poma de Ayala's *El Primer Corónica y buen gobierno* (c. 1615), and, parenthetically, Miguel León Portilla's *El reverso de la conquista* (1961), among the first in a series of Latin American discursive examples that reflect testimonial literature's goal to uncover the truth of a people. Told in the first person by a narrator who is also a witness to the events, the testimonial narrative projects a need to communicate by covering significant life events (arrest, labor strife, etc., in the contemporary models or battles, attacks against moral and religious principles, and human torture, in the model of conquest), which lead to repression, poverty, marginalization, war, and exploitation. George Yúdice locates authenticity and urgency of situation within testimony's need to represent collective memory and identity,[27] suggesting, in this manner, the important concept of communal self-realization. Written with an eye on a future that envisions a transformed society, testimonial narrative distinguishes itself from those Bildungsromane that seek simply to present a bourgeois individual record, and enacts rather a formula similar to those novels that give voice to a collective self engaged in a common struggle.[28] While both picaresque and testimonial narratives are grounded from below, John Beverley reinforces the private nature of the pícaro's destiny and underscores the metonymical/representational function of the testimonial narrative.[29] I argue both summon the reader as sympathetic listener, and both relate to the Bildungsroman because of their revitalized personal journeys of self-awareness.[30]

Picaresque and testimonial narratives equally signal human relatedness, a value reconfigured in Spanish American literature. The interconnectedness of stages within the developmental Bildung process promotes a similar movement of human relatedness or connection to others, which in Spanish America underscores a hybrid structure of origins. This hybrid nature may explain why identity politics tends to absorb everything (like the Bildung process itself) including competing agencies of representation, to interpret and transform, for example, Uruguayan, Brazilian, Colombian, Peruvian, Salvadoran, and Ecuadorian cultures. It does not imply a new, improved version of the self that achieves a "higher" cultivation than in an earlier stage. Hybrid cultures are grounded in dissonance and harmonies that reinforce their connectedness to the world. As a compelling subject in the Spanish American Bildungsroman, everything is absorbed and vitally related.

III. BILDUNG AND CULTURE

Why is the Bildung process more compelling than a rite of passage, initiation, or lifestyle development? The answer is found in its organic ties to culture. Culture, if examined for its values, virtues, or truths, reveals an emancipatory potential not unlike that of the Bildung process. At stake in the culture wars is the idea that culture can establish consensus and make contemporary life less alienating.[31] Culture grounds the Bildung process in a humanistic concept of development and becoming, the latter being as Nietzsche interpreted it, ultimate and inexplicable, incorporating what has been achieved and those levels or stages that are only striving for realization in the making and molding of the self. Through culture and the acquisition of language, customs, and institutions, one has a given body of material with which to make his/her own place in the world. By emphasizing lasting human values and capabilities, Bildung thus engages the reader in a strategy for life that rejects particularity, dependency and narrow-mindedness. It suggests hope—a necessary ideal because, to paraphrase Hegel, it empowers a people to give itself its existence in its world. In theory, Bildung affects the entire human being—mind, body, and spirit—to "become" what he/she will be. Bildung moves from the outward self to interiority, and from the inward self out to the public sphere. It connotes a shaping and molding of the self, both of the body, as the individual passes through adolescence, reaches adulthood and ages, and of the mind, as ideas are explored, modified, and adopted. The complexity of Bildung is that it can be conceived of as being both static and fluid at the same time.

Wilhelm Dilthey's canonical definition of Bildung reinforces the concept of a process characterized by a linear progression toward harmony.[32] But we should not assume that harmony or a "happy ending" is the end product of the process. Bildung cannot be "achieved" as one would acquire practical knowledge through lessons in a process of lifelong learning. Self-cultivation leads to further cultivation or to cultural maturity, not to a goal outside of itself. By cultural maturity I mean the recognition and the allowing of what is different from oneself. This recognition is stressed to the point where one leaves the familiar and secure, opens oneself up to the Other, and returns with a greater understanding of the self and the Other without feeling threatened by contact with the unknown. This suggests the combination of dissonance and harmony at every level where everything is absorbed.

Another compelling example of the cultural persistence of Bildung is found in the hero's connectedness or interrelatedness within the stages of progression and to the world. The products of culture are with the individual from the beginning of life through cultural integrity—languages, customs, and so on—that are made one's own by raising oneself out of the natural being to the spiritual. That is, by acquiring a capacity or skill such as language use, man gains the sense of himself, or as Hegel determined in his *Phenomenology of Spirit*, by forming the thing it forms itself. Bildung and culture together enhance reflective powers by incorporating diverse, nonformal, and formal lessons. Bildung mirrors the Nietzschean ideal of self-transcendence, whereby one rejects the present self to aspire to a self beyond it.

The most powerful and irresistible force of Bildung as a tool is seen in its psychic persistence. It is cultural in the sense that it relates to the essence of childhood. Historically, we can look to European industrialization for the emergence of the idea of childhood in the West, the centering of the family on children, and an increasing concern with education. Child-centeredness, or the prolongation of childhood through the centering of the family on children and their education, produced the skilled laborers that society needed and the potential for a better life for everyone.[33] The obverse of this concept is the loss of the child. Probably the most traumatic experience imaginable in life is the death of a child. There are none more inconsolable, distraught, bitterly anguished, and angry than those who have lost a child or sibling. Quite significantly, Freud bases his heralded theory of mourning on the infant mortality he confronts at nineteen months of age, the death of his eight-month-old brother Julius. The child's death leaves Freud filled with self-reproach, which affects every friendship he sustains in life.

The link between the death of a child and Bildung is at once uncanny and ironic. The mysterious relationship between the two is most clearly evidenced in cultures where a high rate of infant and child mortality may exist (in eighteenth- and nineteenth-century Europe and twentieth-century Latin America). Latin America, with the exception of Cuba (which will be explored in chapter 3), demonstrates through 1995 high rates of infant and child mortality from birth through age five.[34] (See also Appendix, Tables 1.1 and 1.2). In cultures of this nature the Beautiful Soul is equal to the weaker form that Hegel ultimately envisioned at the point of madness and consumption:

> The "beautiful soul," lacking an *actual* existence, entangled in the contradiction between its pure self and the necessity of that self to externalize itself and change itself into an actual existence, and dwelling in the *immediacy* of this firmly held antithesis—an immediacy which alone is the middle term reconciling the antithesis, which has been intensified to its pure abstraction, and is pure being or empty nothingness—this "beautiful soul," then, being conscious of this contradiction in its unreconciled immediacy, is disordered to the point of madness, wastes itself in yearning and pines away in consumption.[35]

Following Hegel's logic, the Beautiful Soul or ultimate goal of Bildung would be the first to go; nevertheless, Laurence Rickels determines, in the *new* culture of Bildung she survives.[36] If you extend this to the narrative, the cathartic nature of literature enables the impossible—the survival of the "weaker" form. For example, the Beautiful Soul occupies the position of perennial mourning in Goethe's classic Bildungsroman, *Wilhelm Meister's Apprenticeship*, burying and mourning even her stronger siblings. As a metaphysical principle, the natural order of things understood in the Bildung process embodies a divine plan for the salvation of individual souls, that is, the Beautiful Soul. Hegel ultimately acknowledges that the Beautiful Soul does not vanish but remains an important moment in the development of Spirit, culminating in the self-awareness of God.[37] Bildung comes to represent a reconstruction of childhood grounded in hope, potentiality, access to life, and victory over death. It would seem natural that at the same time childhood was "literally" invented—given name, image, language, clothes, and games with the development of the printing press—the expression of Bildung in literature would also become of primary importance. This image of childhood also shocks, however, because with the advent of the printing-press culture, the child receives for the first time a proper name and image that can be shadowed by death. Childhood, ironically, is supposed to save one from death and the "powers of horror".

The resolution of this tension may be encountered in the following: as strong as this novel image of death is, a new desire for preservation surfaces that is first centered on the child. The resulting apotheosis of the child in print who is shadowed by death is the "Beautiful Soul."[38] We should link this apotheosis to Bildung's origin in the ancient mystical tradition according to which man carries in his soul the image of God after whom he is fashioned and must cultivate in himself.[39] In effect, Bildung symbolizes the triumph and survival of the Beautiful Soul over apparently stronger childhood illnesses and poor health. In a provocative study on the nineteenth-century novel Marianne Hirsch sets up a paradigm of the Beautiful Soul that separates inner psychological, spiritual and emotional development from a more complete Bildung process.[40] I argue, however, a strengthening of the exterior through the Bildung process of inner self-realization. The Beautiful Soul, the supposedly weaker figure represented by females, homosexuals, and mixed races, that is, the marginalized, is kept supernaturally alive. As an emblem of hope, it strengthens the reader's ability to cope with apparently indomitable circumstances, ranging from the specifics of poor nutritional, prenatal and general health care, impossible living conditions, and survival aids on the one hand, to the vagaries of fate, on the other. The Bildungsroman offers the platform for the Beautiful Soul to forever showcase its Bildung, that by which the Beautiful

Soul was formed and cannot be forgotten. It characterizes one's being-in-the-world, which for Heidegger is the appropriation of man's essence that is always understood as his possibilities. In effect, Bildung is a necessary ideal because it compellingly ensures the future.[41]

Another cultural component of Bildung is its cultural drive. In fact, it has been said that Bildung was instituted to respond to a cultural crisis of sorts, the Jewish question in Western Europe.[42] Correspondingly, the Bildung process in Latin America facilitates the assimilation of diverse cultures—of Jewish, Asian, Middle Eastern, indigenous, or African peoples, and gay or popular cultures, into mainstream culture by shaping, molding, and making the self, into what is ultimately recognized as "one of us." The disjoint in this challenge is that the other is us and is not us at the same time. 'Aberrant' behavior is molded into new stereotypical, acceptable behavior through cultural cross-referencing and/or cross-dressing.

If we were to chart the Bildung process, for some the representation would be a linear progression toward harmony in the form that Wilhelm Dilthey had set out. For others, the path to self-realization would take many turns, double back, advance, retreat, take the forking path and then advance again, as in the threads of return to oneself Hegel envisioned. This latter path echoes Susan Fraiman's conception of the way to womanhood, seen not as a single path but as "the endless negotiation of a crossroads."[43] Both paths lead to self-realization because their goal is personhood not perfection. Significantly, each path is grounded in the experience of the protagonists—be they women, men, indigenous, black, white, poor, and so forth, as the norm. Each aspires to the self beyond the present self—the reality is that some fight against greater odds than others in their social and cultural formations. The act of aspiring, however, keeps each one vital, intellectually curious, and open to the potentiality of development.

In reality, the inner form of Bildung represents a combination of the cultivation of talents and the cultivation of humanity and spirituality in us. Because of its cultural and philosophic grounding, it, in a Kantian sense, essentially dares the protagonist and reader to realize the potential self. Unlike a simple rite of passage to maturity, the Bildung process does not end with recognition of adulthood or independence. As human development cannot be ordered uniformly, Bildung may begin in adolescence or well into adulthood. Moreover, it may end with the passage into adulthood, or it may not end at all. Significantly, because full potential in some may not be reached until death, Bildung remaps childhood as a metaphor for development throughout life.

One final cultural component of the Bildungsroman is located in its metonymical quality for unveiling the abject and leading us, as Julia Kristeva understands the power of literature, to an "indefinite catharsis". Kristeva argues that literature, far from being a marginal activity in our culture, represents the ultimate coding of our crises, of our most intimate and most serious apocalypses. While she asks, "does one write under any other condition than being possessed by abjection," she allows literature to be a hollowing out of abjection through the Crisis of the Word.[44] What causes abjection is what disturbs identity, system, or order, and what does not respect borders, positions, or rules. This is all part of the Bildung process in that one abjects oneself from the edges in the same motion that one establishes oneself, formed by all experiences of fear and fascination by confronting the Other. Kristeva stresses that literature is rooted in the abject but by the same token purifies it, following an earlier Freudian theory of catharsis as therapeutics. Subject and object push each other away, confront each other, collapse, and start again. The Bildungsroman, in following this circuit, gathers in a single move the impure and the pure, perversion and beauty, strengths and weaknesses as one and the same economy of the Bildung process. Its cathartic qualities permit the reaching of potentiality even through death.

III. A STRATEGIC APPROACH:
THEORETICAL APPLICATIONS TO SPANISH AMERICA

This section presents four strategies for reading the Bildungsroman of Spanish America. The strategic approach animates a dialog and suggests an interconnectedness that stems from a plan to read and question the narration of the process of life. Its stratagems enable us to reread for gender and cultural patterning, in addition to political, social, racial, and economic values. Based on the always timely quality of Bildung, these strategies consider each form as a separate entity, not as a failed or incomplete version of a standard. They use and then paraphrase the Freudian question of what does a woman want, to the expanded question—what does a mestizo, gay, indian, black, poor, socialist, or white male want? The strategies also reveal the process through which culture and gender negotiate the complexities of self-realization. In effect, they sustain an open-ended dialog with the concept of personhood, reconceptualizing

Dilthey's "unified and firm form of human existence" to reference all forms of human existence. The strategies also recognize the cultural tension that is produced through the push toward assimilation and the pull toward self-identity.

1) Rites of Passage

The first strategy elucidates the reading of the traditional, male Bildungsroman. The plot development of this classical Bildungsroman is the following: the hero identifies with and emulates a tutor/father or father figure who guides and aids him to perform the tasks he could not accomplish without help. At a specified point the hero rebels against the father and all of the values he represents—social, religious, political, economic, philosophic, and cultural. Owing to the father's hostility to his ambitions, the boy moves away from the father figure (either emotionally or physically, or both) and declares his independence through an assertion of self in his education, way of life, career choice, selection of companions and partner, philosophic outlook, etc. In most examples his Bildung process advances through the various rites of passage that are markers for the movement to another stage of development. Ultimately, the hero inserts himself back within the rules of society determined to uphold society's values. He gets the job and girl, becoming, as Hegel asserted, a philistine like all others.

This strategy revolves critically around timing. It asks *when* the hero is prepared to move from one stage of development to the next in a linear progression toward self-cultivation and personhood. By asking *when*, this strategy illuminates those fixed, uncritical assumptions frequently made about gender and culture. Routinely, the male, middle-class hero possesses the free will, social conditions, and economic power to make the passage to other stages a conscious, organic decision. An overarching sense of purpose guides his development, to the extent that, ultimately, it is unimportant whether the purpose is frustrated or fulfilled in his process of becoming. No such claim can be made of the marginalized experience, where timing for the passage to other stages of development is periodically haphazard and controlled by exterior forces. What is especially true in this first strategy is that it appears we hold time constant and allow achievement to vary to a degree. That is, the making and molding of the self will take place within the childhood formative years and will be completed by adulthood where a form of education, profession, marriage, and so on, are markers for success. But the other three strategies I develop stress the holding of achievement constant and the variation of time; that is, the process may begin at any point on the human timeline and finish accordingly when personhood is achieved. In this first strategy, timing reveals what gender and culture can tell us about the exercise of translation of social, economic, and political conditions into self-realization. Examples of the Bildungsromane that reinforce the first strategy are Ricardo Güiraldes's *Don Segundo Sombra* (1926), Carlos Fuentes's *Las buenas conciencias* (1959), Mario Vargas Llosa's *La ciudad y los perros* (1963) and Gabriel García Márquez's *Cien años de soledad* (1967).

2) Models of Wholeness

The study of the female Bildungsroman has always been more polemical than the study of the male, traditional form. Indeed, for some critics (as discussed earlier), the concept of Bildungsroman is so emotionally and politically charged that they prefer to remove it from the sphere of critical theory altogether. They would replace it with the "female novel of development," or "novel of awakening," but these alternate terms appear circumspect and ambivalent. Difference cannot be understood, moreover, without a link between self and other. With reference to the terms themselves, is "development" or "awakening" as powerful a concept as "self-realization" or "self-cultivation," terms with which Bildung has long been identified? Do they not conjure up aspects of biology and psychology that would not have to be discussed in the traditional male context? In essence, the revival of interest in the Bildungsroman, as cogently discussed by Bonnie Hoover Braendlin, does not signal a return to an outmoded, unfashionable, historical genre, but rather an examination of "experiential phenomena and interpersonal relationships that figure prominently in the formation of personality."[45] It also calls for a unique journey of discovery toward the making and molding of the self, which invites an examination of *intersections* where those gender and ethnic identities merge. In effect, I will explore the hybridization of the Spanish American form and ask if the tools of distinct disciplines can be used to illuminate various portraits of growth and development. I infuse this examination of hybrid, interpersonal relationships with the reality of the female and marginalized experience.

With respect to the argument stated above, I conclude that the female or disenfranchised hero should not be removed from the critical sphere of the Bildungsroman. Neither should she/he be located in a less prominent position in the weaker arena of the novel of development, or the *Entwicklungsroman*, which registers mere passage from one stage to another. Rather, these figures could be viewed as dialoguing with the others including the conventional heroes, creating a process of self-realization and cultivation that is grounded in, because it is recognized as, their own experience—be it female, male, or marginalized. This normative approach rejects one identity as a central metaphor against which all other experience is measured in terms of what it lacks. It encroaches, as Shoshana Felman suggests, on the female resistance in the text (which can also be generalized to that of the marginalized), and presents itself as an enabling inspiration.[46] In effect, it supplements the other strategies, rescuing the hero from not being able to reach human potentiality.

I perceive the structure of this Bildungsroman to be the following: the female and/or disenfranchised hero, by virtue of gender, culture, religion, race, or socio-economic status, rebels against the father or mother, distances her/himself emotionally from the parent and the society the parent represents, and remains defiantly and ironically outside their rules. The female and marginalized Bildungsromane should be valued in the context of culture and gender, which, to expand upon Catharine MacKinnon's theory, are social categories.[47] They mean whatever they mean socially.

This strategy, therefore, recognizes the "failure" of the female or marginalized hero to live up to the standards ascribed to the more successful male hero. The result, frequently, is disillusionment or suffocation of ambition during the process of growth and development. This strategy revolves around survival. It asks *what* the Bildung process looks like when the lives of women and the marginalized are taken as the norm. It disputes the notion that faith in a coherent self is the purview of the "successful" hero (male, Christian, middle-class) reformulating coherence in terms of life experience. In fact, a more satisfying approach with respect to Bildung is the concept of *Werden*, becoming, and Judith Butler's theory that gender is something one becomes, but can never be. That is, there are ways of culturally interpreting the sexed body that are not limited to the apparent duality of sex.[48] This strategy rejects the notion that the traditional male protagonist's disconformities are character builders while the female's or disenfranchised's are failed aspects of personality development.[49] The process of becoming is the essence of survival, and this strategy underscores the *struggle for survival* rather than a failure to succeed.

By asking what the process looks like from the perspective of the female and marginalized protagonists, and giving voice to them, this strategy aids in illuminating the struggle for survival. For example, Jean Franco highlights the entirely original concept of feminist intellectuals or women who have found ways of aligning gender politics with other forms of struggle without sacrificing either, such as the Mothers of the Plaza de Mayo and Rigoberta Menchú,[50] her recent controversy notwithstanding. It is possible to translate this concept of feminist intellectuals to female and male literary heroes who align gender or cultural issues with political and social struggles, without sacrificing either. It is also especially evident in moments of national strife, destruction, and rebuilding. Examples of this nature are found in the following diverse texts: José María Arguedas's *Los ríos profundos* (1958), Augusto Roa Bastos's *Hijo de hombre* (1966), Elena Poniatowska's *Hasta no verte, Jesús mío* (1969), Isabel Allende's *La casa de los espíritus* (1986), and Mario Vargas Llosa's *El hablador* (1987).

3) Heroic Character

The next strategy redefines the concept of hero in the novel. In this strategy a rewriting of the definition of hero occurs that declares the new Bildungsroman a success in terms of the self-realization of the hero, viewing triumph even in tragedy, destruction, and death. This strategy revolves around the act of rewriting. It demonstrates *how* to reorder the Bildung process so that self-realization may be declared a success.

These novels perhaps function in a state of defiance. That is, they defy negativity by denying that a definition is negative or without truth. The negative is rendered positive; life is not an endless battle, but a celebration; death is not a negative force or failure since the hero accomplishes through death that which could not be accomplished in life. Lee Edwards in *Psyche as Hero* examines the boundaries of the old framework and social paradigms, suggesting first that the woman hero is an emblem of patriarchal instability and insecurity. Edwards concludes that precisely because patriarchy has assigned women certain characteristics that are other than those assigned to men, the female hero can make use of the culturally feminine traits to challenge the male definition of society. In other words, the model of hero must be redefined by providing a contrasting model that is blessed with unique, irreproducible qualities, which could force society to alter its structure.[51] This strategic approach puts into question aspects of gender and culture that contribute to misconceptions about failed lives and processes. By demonstrating how to reorder the Bildung process, it becomes a guide to positive outcomes. Examples of the Bildungsromane that exemplify this strategy are Soledad Acosta de Samper's *Teresa la limeña* ((1869); Teresa de la Parra's *Las memorias de Mamá Blanca* (1929); Ana Vásquez's *Abel Rodríguez y sus hermanos* (1981); Elena Castedo's *El paraíso* (1990); and María Luisa Puga's *La viuda* (1994).

4) Parody and Pastiche

The final strategy is perhaps the most unique because it incorporates a structure that counterpoises surface with submerged plots, linear development with weblike connections, totalities with pieces. This strategy revolves around identity and is the site par excellence for experimentation with culture and gender. It mixes myth and pieces as pastiche from different sources—sociological, psychological, aesthetic, and so forth—to create, in a disguised or ambiguous form, a self-actualized hero with a hybrid, Spanish American identity.[52] It explores behavioral traits and social acts that dissect and reconfigure friendships, marriage, work, and family. In rewriting the social text, the female and marginalized heroes are encouraged to establish new categories of success and to define themselves as independent of the traditional model. This final strategy suggests *who* can create her/himself as the self-actualized hero either a) relationally and/or communally, or b) through cultural exchanges in the form of parody or pastiche.

With respect to relationships, this strategy evaluates development in terms of who takes responsibility for the cohesive self and who successfully, and often, ironically, combines gender and culture to make the journey toward self-realization. It has been observed that women define themselves relationally while men define themselves independently. This is one of the many "differences" in the grand design. Carol Gilligan's study, *In a Different Voice*, concludes that women define themselves differently in terms of a context of male and female relationships, and judge their path to maturity in terms of their ability to care and ongoing attachments.[53] Eve Tavor Bannet suggests that the female Bildungsroman has made enormous strides in rewriting the social text by relying on newly developed relationships of care, support, and consent.[54] What in other strategies might be seen as a turning point in the hero's Bildung, that is, acceptance of self-sacrifice or death in order to be considered an adult, here raises the question of responsibility, choice, and alternative forms.

Significantly, women use power to advance their own development (Bildung) and enhance their relationships, but not to limit the development of others. The unresolved issues and pitfalls Nancy Chodorow sees as women seek to become the self beyond the present self,[55] need to be reevaluated in light of a woman's strengths and rights, which support her connections to others and her position in public discourse. This would reinforce Katha Pollitt's view that women should be admitted to the public discourse because they have a right to be there, not because they are morally superior and would improve it.[56] I very strongly second this perspective and see it as dismantling the traditional interpretation of woman's development in the Bildungsroman as interior, moral, spiritual, and reflective, whereas man's development is understood as exterior, active, creative, and physical. Many feminist critics hold that the female Bildungsroman offers the most logical forum through which contemporary women may write about women's experience.

Essentially, the feminist movement also paved the way for the opening of the gay text in Latin America to interpretation—in this instance, as relational Bildungsroman. This illuminates but does not make easier the clearing of the path toward a lesbian framing in Latin America because, as David William Foster reasons, lesbian culture is substantively different from gay male culture in Latin America and the United States, and has not yet had the room to experiment that the female or male text has enjoyed.[57] A nuanced reading of texts, however, will reveal a blending of both reflection and action in the female and marginalized characters who use exterior and interior, and the spiritual and physical to their advantage. These portraits of development are grounded in sexual, political, and dialogical relationships. In effect, we speak of sexual relationships that include but are not limited to the binary opposition supported by the Judeo-Christian tradition, many foundational political goals, and military regimes in Latin America. Rather, we step outside of prevailing sexual discourse to examine sexuality as social discourse.

Homoerotic themes of gay and lesbian literature provide, Foster contends, an ideology for sexual activity that inscribes it in a macrodiscourse of social acts, including both the public and the private. Any goal of sexual liberation must by definition, therefore, mean a reideologization of sexuality and a redefinition of social macrodiscourses, and not simply the renegotiation of putatively private acts with no regard for their transindividual social contexts.[58] Even though cultural nationalism may be marked as masculinist and heterosexist in certain Latin American countries,[59] the opening of social discourse to gendered acts is a logical move. It encourages Latin American critical thought away from examining homosexuality as illness and crime, and toward permitting a view of personal development in the Bildung process as social and political. This relational strategy demonstrates, therefore, that growing up female/marginalized requires vigilant demystification of an enigmatic world and the relationships sustained. The question of sexual identity to be explored here for its behavioral, relational traits points toward historic national identities in service of social transformation.

Finally, relationships should not exclude the communal variety. With respect to the narrative portrait, testimonial discourse also explores the role of interpersonal relationships in a process of communal self-realization. Testimonial discourse, which finds its roots in the chronicles of Conquest in both the works of the conquerors and the subjugated cultures,[60] reflects the protagonist's or protagonists' need to explain exploitation, poverty, injustice, repression, marginalization, violation of the right to life, and crime. As a struggle for truth, these foundational fictions read as testimony and Bildungsromane because they are grounded rhetorically in processes of self-definition and growth that inform larger issues of justice, social change, identity, and ethical choices. They also appeal to a representational quality through their protagonists who recreate the larger, historical struggles of a nation in birth, or who move from subject to object in the voicing/creation of their own story.

Examples of the Bildungsromane that reveal strength through a variety of foundational relationships explored above are Miguel Barnet's *Biografía de un cimarrón* (1968) and *Oficio de ángel* (1988); Manuel Puig's *El beso de la mujer araña* (1976); Marta Traba's *Conversación al sur* (1981); Reinaldo Arenas's *El palacio de las blanquísimas mofetas* (1980) and *Arturo, la estrella más brillante* (1984); José Agustín's *Ciudades desiertas* (1982); Rosamaría Roffiel's *Amora* (1989); Sara Levi Calderón's *Dos mujeres* (1990); and *Hijo de hombre, Teresa la limeña, Las memorias de Mamá Blanca, La casa de los espíritus, Abel Rodríguez y sus hermanos, El paraíso*, and *Hasta no verte, Jesús mío*, mentioned earlier.

Parody and pastiche are more prevalent in writing about women and the marginalized, because these groups increasingly find themselves in a world responsive to their needs for the first time, and are able to disapprove and subvert accordingly. The goal of pastiche is to effect a change, a dissolution of the present form through an interacting of cultural voices, similar to the dialogism characterized by Bakhtin as central to a world that privileges context—social, historical, or otherwise—over text. Annis Pratt suggests that textual inversions in the woman's Bildungsroman allow an author to inject some form of protest to the work, voicing objections while she drowns out their effect.[61] Literary inversions may be parodic, or ironic, or they may rest on pastiche, a piecing together from various sources. In sum, pastiche is not what it appears. In Latin America, parody and pastiche also undercut the cultural and social message surreptitiously communicated by the bearer. For example, the smiling, subservient *pongo* (*Los ríos profundos*) and the compliant, servile gardener (*Las memorias de Mamá Blanca*) mask irreconcilable and independent spirits in their everyday acts of resistance. Furthermore, it is not possible to separate pastiche from a political and satirical charge in the Latin American context.[62] The female and marginalized are redefined in a new context of culture, an area where the hero can potentially build consensus and achieve success. Due to the emancipatory potential of culture and its representations, culture, Yúdice concludes, logically steps forward to rethink modern life.

Latin American culture linked to identity must be understood as a postmodernist hybrid rather than a monolithic being, which, like the Bildung process and gender, is always in the process of becoming. The person, the place, the art form are all hybrid shapes. The challenge of accepting alternative, hybrid forms in the process of becoming is that self-determination appears diluted through the process of transculturation. Instead of seeking to emulate one model of the cultural market with its hegemonic power, a more diffuse Latin American model seeks to reach out to and join a global culture, already coopted by a modernism propelled by market forces.[63]

Following this trend, the female and marginalized pastiche effects a multi-voiced cultural translation bridging continents, politics, and cultural markets. In asking *who* can create themselves as self-actualized heroes in the Spanish speaking Americas, pastiche points toward hybrid forms. The Bildungsromane that exemplify this strategy span the spectrum from picaresque to parody and pastiche: Severo Sarduy's *Cobra* (1972), *Colibrí* (1984), and *Cocuyo* (1990); Sylvia Molloy's *En breve cárcel* (1981); Diamela Eltit's *El cuarto mundo* (1988) and *Vaca sagrada* (1991); Tununa Mercado's *En estado de memoria* (1990); Cristina García's *Dreaming in Cuban* (1992)/ *Soñar en cubano* (1993); Julia Alvarez's *In the Time of the Butterflies* (1994)/*En el tiempo de las mariposas* (1995); Angeles Mastretta's *Mal de amores* (1995); and Esmeralda Santiago's *América's Dream* (1996)/*El sueño de América* (1996).

IV. The Bildungsroman—a Summation

The Bildungsroman demonstrates in literature a quest for life's meaning, and a desire for self-articulation, realization, and cultivation. In some examples it traces the Bildung, or the making and molding of the self, from childhood to adulthood and maturity. In others, the process does not begin until adulthood and demonstrates no obvious closure in life. In the classical male form, the hero leaves his family after rejecting the constraints of home, and sets out on a journey to explore the world and his own soul. He is influenced by opposing world views, but ultimately chooses a world view that incorporates a philosophy of life, vocation, education, family, and so on that reflects society's views. In the final passage the hero goes home in order to demonstrate his newfound philosophies and socialization skills. In the classical form there is a basic identification with the hero, while this may or may not be true of the other forms.

The female or marginalized Bildungsromane may reject society's rules in an effort to redefine society through culture and gender. By accepting a reevaluation of society's structure, she/he (the author and/or hero) rejects life as a disconnected series of events and relationships, and develops a model for change. The renovation of childhood through the Bildungsroman foregrounds reconstructed theories of culture and gender, the relational and collective, and signals an acceptance of new models of being that are characterized by wholeness, heroic character, relationships, or hybrid exchanges. These heroes seek to establish a new social model through a hybrid subtext. The understanding of Bildung as a necessary ideal and the development of strategies to analyze the hybrid text are, hopefully, the most unique contributions this book may make to the study of Spanish American literature and its class of novel, the Bildungsroman.

1
The New Mother

Self-development is a higher duty than self-sacrifice.
—Elizabeth Cady Stanton

IN FREUD'S FAMILY ROMANCE THE CHILD FANTASIZES GRANDER AND more perfect parents. But what is the role of the mother in this fantasy? In literature the answer to this question is grounded in the category to which the novel belongs. For example, in the classical Bildungsroman the role of the mother is traditional, that is to say, that of a highly invisible support. The mothers in the Bildungsromane with traditional male heroes fulfill what are seen to be conventional female tasks in the care and running of the family and home within her domain. Consequently, the mother is little able to affect the hero's developmental process, either to facilitate his being-in-the-world, that is, aiding him in reaching his potentiality, or to establish the norms against which the hero must rebel outside of the home. Ultimately, the woman is a standard-bearer, not creator, of those norms.

One example of the classical role of mother is found in the limited normative development of women in Mario Vargas Llosa's *La ciudad y los perros* (1963) [*Time and the Hero*]. That is, Vargas Llosa succeeds in plotting the failure of liberal individualism in Peru based on individual autonomy, but fails to go beyond shadow representations of women as victims. In this novel, the mothers of the young cadets are either a source of embarrassment because of their weakness and inability to stand up to men, or bothersome because of their insistence on making their sons feel guilty. In the extreme, they are practically invisible to those around them. This role, furthermore, is not necessarily limited to the biological mother. It may be generalized to any woman who takes on the traditional role of mother, nurturer, and guardian, such as the aunts in Güiraldes's *Don Segundo Sombra* (1926) and Fuentes's *Las buenas conciencias* (1959) [*The Good Conscience*]. Their motives appear suspect

37

and self-serving, but are never questioned as such because that is what is expected of them. In many Bildungsromane with either female or male heroes the mother is either killed off by the author before the narrative begins, as in Arguedas's *Los ríos profundos* (1958) [*Deep Rivers*] and Fuentes's *Las buenas conciencias*, or shortly after that point as in Poniatowska's *Hasta no verte, Jesús mío* (1969). Therefore, in her traditional role the mother demonstrates little influence over her child either owing to her untimely death or personal frailties.

The role of mother in Latin America, nevertheless, can be seen as radically legitimizing her position because its underlying structure anchors the desire to recover the founding father, the conquering Spaniard, whose absence de-legitimizes his sons and daughters. Beyond the abundantly researched issues of matrilineal societies in Latin America, Sonia Montecino points in *Madres y huachos* to a historical and economic centering of the mother in the familial structure of the New World after the conquest. In her illuminating study, Montecino offers the metaphor of the huacho, who embodies a cross of blood lines, lineages, and linguistic codes, to explain a hybrid, Latin American identity. Carefully tracing the institutions that by design (or not) centered the mother in the family model, the practices of *amancebamiento* (illicit cohabitation) and *barraganía* (concubinage) emphasize ties to colonial, social stratification, which reinforce complex contemporary social problems. That is, the demographic composition of colonial society (more women than men), legal obstacles, and prohibitive fees to the clergy discouraged many from seeking marriage. Curiously, the promulgation of the ideal of the legitimate, Christian family did not suffer alongside the practice of concubinage at times within the same family space legitimized by marriage. Today, we note, the prohibition or expense of divorce, the release of moral obstacles, latent macho instincts, and the overwhelming economic and social challenges of raising a family again encourage the centering of mother in the family ordeal.

Historically, indigenous women often came from societies where polygamy was a standard practice, so concubinage and cohabitation were not unreasonable impositions of will. Polygamy also proposed the gestation of *mestizos*, who, in effect, were solely dependent on the mother. The model of the family centered on the mother embraced all social classes in colonial society (Spanish colonists and soldiers, Indians and mestizos, etc.). Quite often it was the women who took control of homes/ranches and families while the men migrated for the purpose of conducting battle or improving economic conditions by travelling to mines and more favorable, fertile lands. Montecino argues that the mestizo Latin American culture made possible, in a sense, a family model in which generic identities could not be ascribed to an Indigenous or European structure, but rather to a structure in which the nucleus of mother and her children prevailed.[1] This nucleus endorses an image of the new mother who parents the child, and advocates a more nuanced reading of the Bildungsromane of Latin America, also parented by the mother in many instances.

The role of the new mother embraces an ideal. She stands alone or guides her husband through the process, and radiates an acceptance of bonds that is foundational to the development of Bildung. In effect, she defines a new concept of family. As Elaine Showalter wisely states: "If a man's text, as Bloom and Edward Said have maintained, is fathered, than a woman's text is not only mothered but parented; it confronts both paternal and maternal precursors and must deal with the problems and advantages of both lines and inheritances."[2] Franco Moretti reinforces the role of family in the Bildungsroman by underscoring its potential to create a reassuring atmosphere of 'familiarity' midway between the intimate and the public sphere.[3] But his interpretation speaks to the social pact of the family as a traditional, "familiar" unit, which is capable of sustaining happiness. As this is frequently not the case, it appears necessary to reconfigure the family portrait and rewrite the social text to displace "normal" family constraints, either replacing them with alternative forms of familial relationships based on care, support, and consent,[4] or developing social organisms that respond to the evolving family. One could achieve this rewriting of the social text through the displacement of the traditional mother with the new mother and the reading of family as a parented text.

The new mother is the grander parent that the child has fantasized. In contrast to the mother of the conventional Bildungsroman, the new mother is able to affect developmental elements of the Bildung process, which lead to the necessary and coveted stage of independence. The father's role in traditional Bildungsromane is to mold his son in one example, *La ciudad y los perros*, into his own image of wealth, flamboyance and success, and to protect in another, Don Segundo's example, which destines Fabio to *become* his hero in *Don Segundo Sombra,* as Christopher Leland argues. One could suggest that the homoerotic quality of the novel *Don Segundo Sombra* explored by Christopher Leland in his work, *The Last Happy Men*, would remove this novel from the category of traditional Bildungsroman. I contend, however, that the strategy of this novel leaves it within the conventional scheme of growth process, namely, the rejection of the father and his values (patricide), the election of a male tutor and study at his feet, and the ultimate return to the core values of the father. Politically, the shadowy foreboding of the father of a Liberal reality foregrounds the inevitability of a free enterprise/ market economy, and implies a rejection of a spiritual, national patrimony, which was mired in class distinctions and economic hierarchies.

In contrast, the strategy of the new mother tends toward individuation. The method requires a reading of the heroic character she creates in her "offspring" as a pattern of how to reorder the Bildung process so that self-realization may be declared a success, tragedy a triumph, reality an acceptable illusion. Isabel Allende's *La casa de los espíritus* [*The House of the Spirits*] explores relationally the dimensions of the concept of "new mother". The central characters of this novel are women from the same family but distinct generations. They rebel against the rules respected by their mothers and society and remain defiantly isolated by their struggles. There is no triumphant return to the values of family and society, and occasionally disillusionment is so strong they are left ambivalently in limbo without clearly won gains. And yet these women are exemplary models of wholeness because of their vision of the self as a coherent being developing in stages, still becoming the self beyond the present self. The triumph is in how they conduct themselves during the struggle for survival.

The first generation "new mother," Nívea del Valle, is a woman who fights during numerous pregnancies for the right of women to vote. Defying the social reasoning of generations, Nívea is the first suffragette in her family. She attempts to level hierarchy's ranking and view woman as man's equal, even though religion, in the name of her parish priest, sees evil in the Pharisees who sought equal footing for women and men. In later years, Nívea is thought of as the first feminist in the country. She begins her own political career by chaining herself to the gates of Congress and the Supreme Court, hanging suffragette posters, calling for equal rights and the right for women to vote and study at the university. Nívea and her affluent friends visit factories to make speeches about equality, oppression, and rights, and take food and clothing to the poor on the outskirts of the city. She is not dissuaded by the obvious social-class distinctions between her social group and the women they attempt to help, even though it appears absurd to her daughter Clara that women in furs would speak of oppression to poor factory workers. While outside her cultural and social heritage, Nívea as new mother wills to future generations of new mothers a double inheritance: a capacious imagination and a clear conscience of social justice.[5] In effect, the new mother's inspiration is critical to the Bildung impulse of the child to develop the self and cultivate mind and body.

Nívea's daughter, Clara, also participates in activities that challenge the social order. Her challenge, however, manifests itself through effective periods of silence and communication with spirits and the supernatural. Clara marries Esteban Trueba, her sister Rosa's fiancé, after Rosa, the beautiful, is mysteriously poisoned with a doctored brandy meant for her father. The engagement and impending marriage is announced by Clara after nine years of silence brought on by her sister's death and frightening autopsy. This long period of silence chosen by Clara as a mode of action serves at this time as an apprenticeship for her work as a clairvoyant.[6] It is, curiously, one of the stages in her Bildung process that will later be used to fight oppressive, patriarchal structures in society. Julia Kristeva recognizes this power in the "socialized" woman: "A dark, abominable, and degraded power when she keeps to using and trading her sex, woman can be far more effective and dangerous when socialized as wife, mother, or career woman. The unbridling is then changed into crafty reckoning, hysterical spells turn to murderous plots, extreme masochistic poverty becomes a commercial triumph."[7] This powerful danger of the socialized woman is glimpsed vigorously in Clara and, to be explored later, in Jesusa Palancares (*Hasta no verte Jesús mío*) on economic, social, and cultural levels.

Following their marriage, Clara lives in a world in which she communicates with the spirits, is listless, and pronounces everything "lovely". It is not until their arrival one summer at Tres Marías, the ranch inherited from Esteban's family, that Clara discovers her mission in life. At Tres Marías she is drawn irrepressibly to the looks and murmurings of dissatisfaction among the workers and discovers her own role in trying to reinvent society. By supporting a flurry of activities, Clara attempts to change the social order. She is a witness to the struggle of the subordinate group against the dominant group her husband Esteban represents. At sundown, after Férula gathers the women and children to say the rosary, which they attend as an act of kindness not faith, Clara preaches to them with the same slogans her mother had used during her suffragette days in the capital. But her audience, again listening politely, laughs at her message of equality that Clara curiously does not think as absurd as her mother's. Esteban, as a member of the

dominant group, clearly rejects the goals of these meetings. Generally speaking, the dominant group suffers because it is denied an
essential part of life, the opportunity to acquire self-understanding
through knowing its impact on others.[8]

In contrast, Clara's self development aids her to understand that
she is fighting, ironically, to change the lives of those who were
hired to serve her and whom she loves, because of that contact. The
psychological experience of creating a new self is central to this
female-centered novel.[9] This experience becomes for Clara not simply a barrier against which to fight or become entrapped, but a point
that propels her to another level of growth and development. Her
experience is not exclusionary or judgmental. Her Bildung process
absorbs everything through which she is formed.

Curiously, Clara is incapable of performing the ritual of caring
for her daughter Blanca's hair that is the grounding of the mother/
daughter relationship in *Las memorias de Mamá Blanca*, but she
does share the same love of language and firing of imaginations
through stories so prevalent in both novels:

Clara no era capaz de hacer las trenzas a Blanca para ir al colegio, de
eso se encargaban Férula o la Nana, pero tenía con ella una estupenda
relación basada en los mismos principios de la que ella había tenido
con Nívea, se contaban cuentos, leían los libros mágicos de los baúles
encantados, consultaban los retratos de familia, se pasaban anécdotas de
los tíos a los que se les escapan ventosidades y los ciegos que se caen
como gárgolas de los álamos, salían a mirar la cordillera y a contar las
nubes, se comunicaban en un idioma inventado que suprimía la te al
castellano y la remplazaba por ene y la erre por ele, de modo que queda-
ban hablando igual que el chino de la tintorería.[10]

[Clara was incapable of braiding Blanca's hair for school, a task she
entrusted to Férula or Nana, but she had a wonderful relationship with
her based on the same principles as the relationship she had with Nívea.
They told each other stories, read the magic books from the enchanted
trunks, consulted family portraits, told anecdotes about uncles who let
fly great amounts of wind, and others, blind, who fell like gargoyles
from poplar trees; they went out to look at the *cordillera* and count the
clouds, and spoke in a made-up language with no t's and with r's instead
of l's, so they sounded just like the man in the Chinese laundry.][11]

Unlike the figure her husband had come to know, detached, in another dimension where he could not reach her or withdraw into her
silence, Clara anchors herself in her active life through language,
through stories both spoken and written in her notebooks that bear

witness to life. They serve to sustain her relationship with her daughter and her daughter's daughter, and so on, through time to reorder the world. Clara raises her daughter's consciousness through example, but then more powerfully through words: "Igual como ella lo había hecho con su madre en tiempos de la mudez, llevaba ahora a Blanca a ver a los pobres, cargada de regalos y consuelos. —Esto sirve para tranquilizarnos la conciencia, hija— explicaba a Blanca—. Pero no ayuda a los pobres. No necesitan caridad, sino justicia (124) [Just as she had gone with her mother in the days when she was mute, she now took Blanca with her on her visits to the poor, weighed down with gifts and comfort. 'This is to assuage our conscience, darling,' she would explain to Blanca. 'But it doesn't help the poor. They don't need charity; they need justice' (117)]. While characterized occasionally by silence and "negative" personal qualities such as occult interests and communing with spirits, the various stages of Clara's Bildung process respond to Clara's need to challenge and defy patriarchy's structure and redefine the roles imposed by society. Through self-formation and self-articulation (speaking, not speaking, writing) Clara escapes the limitations imposed on her sex by others.

As a protagonist whose self-realization is grounded in personal choice, Clara is perhaps the clearest example of Bildung as a life-long process of coming into being. She adds to her mother Nívea's sense of justice, strength, and determination, a dimension of mysticism or communion with the spirits, which will be perfected well into middle age. Matriarchal lineage is the narrative texture of A-llende's *La casa de los espíritus* that enables women to act upon their culture and history.[12] Clara's cultivation of the spiritual is one of the many points in her development that suggest her possible other selves.[13] An example of this openness toward being other possible selves is found in Clara's premonitions. Clara first predicts an earthquake that kills thousands of people in her country. Her premonitions return Clara to a childlike state in which the advances of modern science and technology are purposefully forgotten or disregarded.

By forgetting, to paraphrase Georg Gadamer, Clara's mind has the opportunity to see things with fresh eyes so that the familiarity of the quakes in a country accustomed to the periodic, systematic shaking of the earth, combines with the new, in this case almost total destruction, into a many leveled unity and reality.[14] By opening herself to universal viewpoints such as the ability of the mind to will or control actions, or the possibility of interpreting premonitions as predictors of reality, Clara heightens all of her senses universally. Her enhanced sense appeals quite ironically to her more practical side, to the material instead of the spiritual. It is after the earthquake that Clara "forgets" her distraction, apparitions, three-legged tables, and cards that read the future, and develops her more practical side. Clara's openness to all facets of her personality, especially the alternating between the spiritual and practical, will be adopted as practice throughout all of her life.

As is consistent in human nature, Clara will use personal and natural tragedies to engage in the process of Bildung and extend beyond her naturalness, beyond her non-speech and inaction, so as to concentrate on remembering and forming another aspect of herself. For example, after the earthquake Clara awakes from a protracted childhood to the needs of those around her. Curiously, Clara's activity is referred to as an awakening after her husband is badly injured during the earthquake, Nana dies of fright at the earth's rumblings, and her sister-in-law Férula dies of loneliness prior to the catastrophe. But we could speak of Clara's *struggle* for self-definition, self-articulation, and survival prompted by an upheaval in her personal life. Her struggle is adjusted, finely tuned, and rehearsed in the making and molding of herself.[15] The process could be interpreted as sensing the possible others present to her throughout life and keeping herself open to all possibilities. Everything that Clara receives is absorbed and acted upon, manifesting itself in one form or another throughout her process of formation.

Clara's formation is grounded in human impulses and moral strength. By changing her relationship to the men around her from passive and inconsequential wife of the patrón to leveler of differences, she endows her impulses with a value that prior to this was debased by restrictions of gender. By calling on this strength, she defies the conventional associations of gender and behavior. While on the surface it may appear that Clara is replacing justice with charity, her inner development provides a framework from which to build the new social order. Her heroism subverts patriarchal structures and exposes the cracks in a social ideology that privileges aggressiveness and conquest over equality and moral justice. As her mother had before her, Clara rewrites the social order, exposing the cracks in the present order and reinterpreting her role as hero and mother. Significantly, what prior to this in Clara was distraction and non-recognition, now becomes impulse and moral imperative.

Ultimately, Clara presents a competitive model of heroism. She confronts institutions forcing them to recognize their weaknesses, be they political, economic, social, or philosophic. For example, she recognizes she has been inadequately prepared to provide for her formation by these institutions, but, nevertheless, her actions suggest her own future transformation. Her transversal approach to self-education and coming-of-age connects her to what Nelly Richard comprehends as a hybridization of cultures. This is where modernity and tradition, vanguard and folklore, urban aesthetics and popular culture meet to challenge the model of Latin American identity. Nelly Richard, as mentioned earlier, gives the imposing, visual example of Dávila's postcard image of Simón Bolívar and contemplates a crossbreeding, feminization, and popularization of culture that transgresses a long censured, sublimated model of Latin America.[16] The striking element of this equation is that in the example of Clara there is little evidence of a physical transformation to signal a blending of opposites; the changes are rather more subtly revealed. As incapable as Clara was before the earthquake of running the household or making simple decisions with respect to its daily routine, afterwards she is empowered to make decisions about the entire estate and ranch and carry them out on her own. Quite evidently, Clara is transformed as she transforms everything around her. Her grasp of economics, social and labor policy, and health and cultural codes speak to a realignment of sexual representations, social classifications, identity theory, and geopolitics. A year and a half after the earthquake, Clara's will revives Tres Marías from almost total destruction to the model estate it had been when Esteban brought it back from abandonment, and centers her as moral compass of the family when back in the capital.

Through these efforts Clara finds solace in her own moral code and rises above self interest by throwing herself into work that benefits society. While her son Jaime studies to become a doctor in order to help the poor, Clara does everything she is capable of to aid the poor and challenge social restrictions: "Clara se convirtió en una experta en beneficencia social, conocía todos los servicios del Estado y de la Iglesia donde se podía colocar a los desventurados y cuando todo le fallaba, terminaba por aceptarlos en su casa" (197) [Clara became an expert in social benefits. She was acquainted with all the services the state and the church provided for taking care of the disadvantaged. When all else failed, she took them into her own house (189)]. Clara transforms herself into an agent for social change both before and during the years of political unrest. She employs her culturally feminine traits of caring and concern for others to challenge a hierarchical structure of society that is grounded in divisions, oppositions, and open warfare between classes.[17] She accomplishes this task from behind Gilbert and

Gubar's looking glass imagery, while agreeing to play the part of the loving and respectable Senator's wife in public.

Precisely because these are the characteristics assigned to women from the patriarchy, Clara uses them from within to challenge patriarchy's dogma, and present society with alternative structures or archetypes for reading women's reality. Her bold design to rewrite patriarchal injustice that forces divisions in society is a heroic ideal. But it is not necessarily matriarchal justice that substitutes itself for patriarchal injustice. Clara seeks to dissolve distinctions in an effort to provide justice for *all*. Therefore, she will not replace patriarchal structures with other divisions that separate men from women. In effect, Clara reconfigures relationships by creating a crisis of category that refuses to be oppositional.

Clara's need to confront the constraints of culture (taboos included) and her need to confront submission to codes—wife/husband, mother/child—lead to decisions that on the surface appear to support the patriarchy. One example would be her consent to Blanca's marriage to satisfy the constraints of culture and society. However, if viewed as a mode of articulation of the third space where the child no longer confronts the mother or the father but is her/himself, it becomes the space of self-realization and selfhood. Perhaps Clara knew that this seemingly conservative decision to marry Blanca to a man she did not love would evolve into a situation in which Blanca would be forced to take charge of her life for her own sake and for that of the baby she was carrying. In the spirit of what her granddaughter admits Clara's role to be,[18] her role is not to promote hatred occasioned by the creation of more divisions.

The various stages of the Bildung process respond to Clara's need to challenge and defy patriarchy's structure and redefine the roles imposed by society. But Clara's formation is grounded in human impulses and moral strength. By changing her relationship from passive wife to leveler of differences, she endows her impulses with a value that prior to this was debased because of gender restrictions. In effect, Clara's making and molding of the self transforms her into an agent for social change. Ultimately, Clara's actions represent human and humane impulses that are imbued in her through the new mother's goal to parent the child and to affect the Bildung process of the child.

Blanca's desire to level distinctions is perhaps not as pronounced as her mother Clara's, but Blanca too, in smaller measure, seeks to change society. The Bildung process that overtakes Blanca embraces all of her senses and guides her also to independence. Joining the private to the public sphere, Blanca's art of inspiration does not draw attention to itself. It is, however, enabling and empowering, satisfying her movement of spirit as the process of Bildung continues. Despite her father's protests, her aunt's indignation and disgust, and Nana's class-conscious concerns, Blanca falls in love with a member of the working class. Her relationship with Pedro Tercero is an attempt to oblige her family and society to recognize the unnatural oppositions of classes and to challenge their structures. The fruit of their union and leveling of distinctions is Alba, who, curiously, is the only person completely loved and accepted by Esteban Trueba, a symbol of unyielding patriarchy.

Blanca's desire to reach out to others is shared with her daughter Alba in their work in the studio teaching mentally handicapped children to make ceramic figures. In reality, what they teach the children about is the love they feel for them. This generalized, unconditional love has passed from new mother to daughter through three generations, anticipating its continuation in a fourth. It is a love, however, that is not restricted to mothers and daughters because it is also given from mother to son (Clara to Jaime), grandmother to granddaughter (Clara to Alba), and new mother to pupils and all in need. In a line of linguistic tradition, Blanca tells Alba her stories, which are transformed because of Blanca's poor memory. By forgetting, Blanca sees the events in a new light, bringing familiar and unfamiliar in close contact through a unity that privileges neither. The new mother passes on her ennobling, creative power to stay open to all, more universal points of view. The daughter, in gratitude, records the stories the mother forgets as soon as they are told. The new mother encourages Alba to develop a world view, which she develops like Clara, recording the things that seem important to her.

After a military coup and the death of the President of the country, Alba sets out to help the victims of the persecution by seeking asylum and finding food for them. As in the days of her grandmother, Alba replaces justice with charity hoping to use this culturally feminine trait to shock and challenge the social order to change, but this time it is even more difficult since charity is frowned upon during the military regime. Of course, it is a cause so drastic that even her grandfather Esteban Trueba is forced to admit for the first time in his life that he has made a mistake. The women's contributions in forcing society to reinvent its foundations, removing them from war and conquest and replacing them with charity and concern for all, precipitate a social revolution that is unfortunate simply because its effects are not felt immediately and completely. When Alba is no longer able to challenge the social order through her actions because she has been taken prisoner and brutally tortured per orders of Esteban García, she receives a message from the spirit of Clara that suggests she write in her mind a testimony of the horror many pretend not to see.

While her country is at war with itself, Alba redoubles her efforts to remove war as the metaphor for their existence. Alba is ultimately released by her captors in a poor neighborhood and told to wait until dawn to move because of the curfew. She is taken in and given a cup of tea by a poor woman who, in effect, symbolizes the role of the new mother in their country:

> Era una de esas mujeres estoicas y prácticas de nuestro país, que con cada hombre que pasa por sus vidas tienen un hijo y además recogen en su hogar a los niños que otros abandonan, a los parientes más pobres y a cualquiera que necesite una madre, una hermana, una tía, mujeres que son el pilar central de muchas vidas ajenas, que crían hijos para que se vayan también y que ven partir a sus hombres sin un reproche, porque tienen otras urgencias mayores de las cuales ocuparse. Me pareció igual a tantas otras que conocí en los comedores populares, en el hospital de mi tío Jaime, en la Vicaría donde iban a indagar por sus desaparecidos, en la Morgue, donde iban a buscar a sus muertos. Le dije que había corrido mucho riesgo al ayudarme y ella sonrió. Entonces supe que el coronel García y otros como él tienen sus días contados, porque no han podido destruir el espíritu de esas mujeres (377).

> [She was one of those stoical, practical women of our country, the kind of woman who has a child with every man who passes through her life and, on top of that, takes in other people's abandoned children, her own poor relatives, and anybody else who needs a mother, a sister, or an aunt; the kind of woman who's the pillar of many other lives, who raises her children to grow up and leave her and lets her men leave too, without a word of reproach, because she has more pressing things to worry about. She looked like so many others I had met in the soup kitchens, in my Uncle Jaime's clinic, at the church office where they would go for information on their disappeared, and in the morgue where they would go to find their dead. I told her she had run an enormous risk rescuing me, and she smiled. It was then I understood that the days of Colonel García and all those like him are numbered, because they have not been able to destroy the spirit of these women (365).]

The role of the new mother is generalized to an entire country breaking boundaries of generations and classes. *La casa de los espíritus* can be read, therefore, as a foundational novel of growth and development of a culture, an entire country, or people. And, significantly, this is inspired by the mother's condition unadorned and unmodified, which is one proof of equality in the new social order. Francesca Miller speaks engrossingly of the "different mission" of women in Latin America, as she draws distinctions between the goals of Latin American feminist movements and those of Great Britain and the United States where equality with men is the goal, and gender differences are denied or at least played down: "In the Latin American context, the feminine is cherished, the womanly— the ability to bear and raise children, to nurture a family—is celebrated. Rather than reject their socially defined role as mothers, as wives, Latin American feminists may be understood as women acting to protest laws and conditions which threaten their ability to fulfill that role. Moreover, there is an explicit spiritual or moral content to the declarations of Latin American feminists which has strong parallels with feminist thought as it developed in Catholic Europe."[19] Latin American women, as do all other heroic women according to Lee Edwards, challenge the compulsions of aggressiveness and conquest, subvert patriarchy's structures, and level hierarchy's endless ranks. It is their spirit that obliges them to question the cracks in the surface of reality in order to reinvent it. The role of new mother therefore signals in *La casa de los espíritus* another rite of passage for that country whose future movement to a level of development in its economy is signaled by a collapsing of differences through globalization. The image of Nívea, wrapped in furs to deliver speeches of universal suffrage, identifies codes of belonging to a social order that later cedes to a universal youthful culture embodied by Alba, which Beatriz Sarlo conceives of as a leveler of differences within the context of social identity.[20]

Alba writes as her grandmother did before her to reinvent reality because "memory is fragile" (367), and she writes purposefully, because memory must be formed and is part of her Bildung. She learns to value her memory for some things but not for others. Alba's Bildung process is advanced by piecing together the parts of the puzzle that resemble life. In acquired Bildung everything is absorbed, which has the positive effect of encouraging the necessary separation of the self from the self. In this manner, Alba is able to forget her hatred even when she purposefully looks for it. Her need to overcome the desire to seek revenge to avenge her torture and humiliation along with the torture and humiliation of thousands of others, is a desire to overcome patriarchy's structure of society as war and conquest, whether it is categorized as social, political, or economic. Alba breaks the chain and rewrites the social text. Her struggle for survival turns remorse into satisfaction and hatred into abidance. Significantly, Alba awaits the birth of her child and the chance to enter another stage of her formation as she begins to comprehend the enormity of her role as new mother. Perhaps the fruit of her role is visible in Esteban's conversion of spirit toward women from Tránsito Soto to his granddaughter. Alba leads her grandfather to the threshold of memory and Bildung, so that the forgetting and healing process may begin.

As evidenced by these two groundbreaking novels in their depiction of heroic character, *Las memorias de Mamá Blanca* and *La casa de los espíritus* embrace the ideal of a new mother who defines a new concept of family. The strategy in reading these novels is to read the heroic character the new mother creates in her "offspring" as a pattern of how to reorder the Bildung process so that self-realization may be declared a success, tragedy a triumph, and reality an acceptable illusion. The new mother in *Las memorias de Mamá Blanca*, for example, teaches Blanca Nieves to barter the cultural code of beauty for everlasting moral value. She turns the metaphor of beauty inward and demonstrates that the female hero can make use of culturally feminine traits—beauty and submission to its power—to subvert and change the male definition of the social text. By cautioning the female hero to renegotiate the social contract, take what she needs and pursue self-development, the daughter is inspired to re-inscribe the new social order with terms of triumph. The child learns to use language as a tool for change, which can be used to fight the patriarchal structure of society.

We may encounter the rebirth or reincarnation of the new mother on several occasions within the same novel. This is the case when the biological mother, Mamá Blanca, becomes the new mother to the narrator. It illuminates the Bildung process of an elderly woman whose vitality postulates an evolving need for self-formation and realization. Her mature status is less programmed by ego and, therefore, facilitates the developmental process of the narrator. Curiously, the role of new mother that Mamá Blanca assumes is empowering because it conveys all the rights and privileges specific to a mother/child relationship, including the legalistic aspect of inheritance, bequeathing her memoirs to her "adopted daughter", the narrator. The narrator's inheritance enables the reader, through the literary contrivance of a lost or newly recovered manuscript, to enter into Mamá Blanca's narrative and ultimately witness her Bildung process, where each stage contains the elements of the next stage.

As if to underscore the potentiality of the role of new mother in *Las memorias de Mamá Blanca*, the narrator makes it known in both thesis statements of the first two paragraphs in the foreword that they are in no way related by blood. In fact, Mamá Blanca's maternal instincts tend toward caring and protecting everyone she comes into contact with, especially those who really need her, excluding those of her biological family. Mamá Blanca filled the narrator, a young girl of twelve, with joy through her special ability to tell stories and play the piano. As one who had always wanted to have a little girl, she rejoices in the attention of her little friend. Her sons, of course, want her to go and live with them especially after their father's death and subsequent depletion of funds, but Mamá Blanca refuses their offer. She wears her newfound poverty like nobility to the embarrassment of her family.

To the young girl she teaches to play the piano, Mamá Blanca bequeaths her memoirs (written, ironically, for her sons), asking her to read them but not show them to anyone. As literary device, the narrator cannot resist the temptation to publish the memoirs, and begins the process of organizing and editing the stories to create *Las memorias de Mamá Blanca*. Mamá Blanca, the new mother adopted by the young girl in the foreword, becomes the child in the following chapters until the ending, an aporia that sends us back to the foreword for closure. Significantly, the aporia provides an opening for the introduction of the "new" mother into the body of the novel.

Upon telling the story of Mamá Blanca or Blanca Nieves as we meet her in her childhood, it becomes obvious that the role of new mother passes to Blanca Nieves's biological mother. What distinguishes this figure and makes her "new" is her influence in her daughters' Bildung process toward selfhood. Blanca Nieves's mother, having the soul of a poet, is credited with or blamed for the ironic naming of her dark-skinned, dark-eyed, dark-haired daughter, Blanca Nieves, "Snow White". The reference to the mother's soul of a poet is to a poetic temperament that: ". . . despreciaba la realidad y la sometía sistemáticamente a unas leyes arbitrarias y amables que de continuo le dictaba su fantasía. De ahí que Mamá sembrara a su paso con mano pródiga profusión de errores que tenían la doble propiedad de ser irremediables y de estar llenos de gracia[21] [. . . scorned reality and endeavored to rule it by the pleasant and arbitrary laws dictated by her imagination. But reality refused to submit to them. As a result, Mama's generous hand broadcast a profusion of errors which had the twofold quality of being irreparable and funny[22]].

It is from this early encounter with the mother's play with artifice that we discover her willful blending of reality and illusion that forms Blanca's life, encourages her process of becoming, and empowers her to create her own reality. The new mother magnifies Adrienne Rich's dictum: "the most important thing one woman [a mother] can do for another [her daughter] is to illuminate and expand her sense of actual possibilities."[23] The mother embues Blanca Nieves with the qualities to overcome ironic reality, to change, through supplementation, a loss into a gain. Irony is paramount in the creative mind of de la Parra, and it is one of the most crucial elements of her work that is misunderstood.[24] Hoover Braendlin suggests that there is a distinctive use of irony at work in the Bildungsromane by female authors.[25] True irony in this novel begins with Blanca Nieves's symbolic naming that inheres the legalistic with ritualistic creativity, and reveals the complexity of her quest for self identity. The act implies a sympathetic listener who will subscribe to the ritual and call her by her given name, despite the obvious irony.

The overarching goal of Blanca Nieves's mother is to guide her daughters' education. The mid-nineteenth century's localization of the novel suggests that it was more fashionable for those of this social class to learn French, and, in fact, de la Parra grew up under the tutelage of a French nanny. Carmen María, however, hires Evelyn, a Trinidadian nanny, to teach her daughters English. The nanny becomes known as the mother's solace and the young girls' drill sergeant. It soon becomes evident that she is bringing to bear a discipline and an order that the mother deems necessary for her daughters' development, because the parents are incapable of providing this training for a variety of reasons. The girls dominate the center of the cosmos at Piedra Azul, their sugar plantation, house, and world. In this cosmos, the mother is perceived as a delight and one of the advantages bestowed upon her daughters. Their relational world centers on the mother. While the father, Juan Manuel, is viewed as a supreme authority for which they feel a mysterious terror, he might be considered less influential because he is more a symbol that is present by definition in language. He serves to remind the girls of their original sin, the mistake they made at birth of not being the desired male heir. Conversely, the mother in this setting is able to provide her daughters with a kind of security through the quality of their relationship and the daughters' identification with her.[26]

Blanca Nieves's description of her mother as told with the distance and aid of time in her memoirs, thrives on the union of the insignificant with the admirable. The child's legitimization of the mother is perceived through her contact with the world of literature: the mother's soul is pure poetry, her affectations are not grounded in pride or vacuousness like those of the futurists; her imitators are the Romantics. The almost imperceptible shift as the narrator describes the infecting of Napoleon with Romanticism, allows the drawing of the following parallel: "Digan lo que quieran, búrlense o no, yo aseguro que Mamá y Napoleón se parecieron mucho" (24) [They can laugh at me as much as they like, but I firmly believe that Mama and Napoleon were very much alike (22)]. The connection drawn through the immoderate pleasure that both her mother and Napoleon achieved in celebrating and rewarding their relatives, is but a sense of the success and power that is subtly suggested by the comparison.

The only criticism raised by her children against their mother is with reference to her vanity and their own complicity in her vanity. The mother reinscribes the negative with the positive, forming her own truth and making her daughters accomplices to this "truth". In response to her visitors' glowing appreciation of her enchanting children the mother responds: "Sí. Es verdad que tienen el pelo sedoso y crespo. Y han de saber ustedes que es enteramente natural. La única que lo tiene un poco menos rizado es Blanca Nieves, aquélla, la más trigueñita . . . , pero sus crespos . . . ¡también son naturales! La primera frase era verdadera. En la última mi querida Mamá mentía de un modo descarado y enternecedor" (30) ["Yes, they all do have pretty hair. And it is naturally curly. The one whose hair is a little straighter than the others is Blanca Nieves, that one, the darkest of them . . . but her curls are natural too." The first part of the statement was true. The last was a brazen, touching lie (27)]. On the surface it appears we are subjected to the mindless chatter of a superficial and delightfully charming but unscrupulous personality. This is the impression held by many critics including José Carlos González Boixó, who interprets the mother's role as that of an adornment who accepts with pleasure her submissive role, limiting herself to decorating her house and arranging her daughters' hairstyles. It is this interpretation of the role of mother that traps critics into a conclusion signaling *Las memorias de Mamá Blanca* as an ideologically conservative work whose feminism is extremely moderate, similar to the life of Teresa de la Parra.[27]

But far from accepting the social paradigm in which woman represent the symbolic essence of beauty, Blanca's mother turns the metaphor inward and demonstrates through deceit and conceit that the female hero can make use of the culturally feminine traits, beauty and submission to its power, to subvert and change the male definition of the social text. In essence, the allegiance to the cause and promotion of beauty assigned to women by patriarchal society insures its systematic destruction from within as unnatural artifice is exposed through parody. This pastiche, the "portrait" of mother and daughter glimpsed and held in the frame of a mirror, is also framed linguistically through stories on each occasion as the mother sits her daughter down to struggle with injustice—the straight hair that should be curly, a symbol of natural beauty—and asks her daughter, "Pero de dónde sacarías tú el pelo tan liso, Blanca Nieves, mi hijita querida?" (31) [But where in the world did you get such straight hair, Blanca Nieves, my darling daughter? (28)]. The rhetorical question reinforces the mockery evident in the patriarchy's view of nature. The irrationality of the molding of women to meet the male standard of beauty is echoed and intensified by Blanca's equally gentle question "¿Y de dónde lo sacaría de verdad, Mamaíta?" (31) [Where *did* I get it, Mummy? (28)]. Interpret this as either an allusion to the irreconcilability of reality and the supreme being, or as the ironic aside "what difference does it make?", but we are left with the impression that quite literally the issue of beauty is a cover up for what is cultivated and emerging below.

In effect, the new mother and Blanca Nieves realize that the making and molding of the self is far more important than the molding of the female to meet the male standard. That is to say, self-definition is more important than self-sacrifice. The new mother parents the child, accepts the problems of the ideal of beauty passed down by paternal and maternal precursors, and encourages the Bildung process of the child by expanding her knowledge and promoting a creativity for which she would never have reason to apologize. As Blanca Nieves refers to their shameless use of artifice she reminds the reader that rather than pleading for their sympathy, she is in an enviable position:

He querido brillar por el sufrimiento y exaltarme en la compasión de ustedes. En el fondo no merezco tal exaltación. Mi pelo liso me imponía sacrificios, es cierto, pero si me los imponía, era para regalarme luego ratos de exquisito coloquio con personajes interesantísimos llenos de belleza física y de encantos morales. Andando por los ásperos senderos de mi pelo liso, fué como encontré al amanecer a Nuestra Señora, la amable poesía. Aunque ni entonces ni después debía yo cubrirme familiarmente con su propio manto, ella me sonreía ya, bondadosa, desde lejos, y en contestación, desde lejos también, yo le sonreía. La mutua y discreta sonrisa dura todavía. He aquí como ocurrían las cosas y cómo a la amargura de la privación sucedían las dulzuras de una escondida abundancia (32).

[I have wanted to hold your attention by my sufferings and win your sympathy. The truth of the matter is that I don't deserve it. To be sure, my straight hair occasioned certain sacrifices; but in return it afforded me opportunities for delightful conversation with interesting persons of exquisite physical charms and moral attainments. Traveling the rough road of my straight hair, I had an early encounter with Our Lady of Poetry. Even though neither then nor later was I able to find refuge beneath her cloak, nevertheless she smiled pleasantly on me, from a distance, and in reply, I, from a distance, too smiled at her. The discreet, mutual smile still endures. You shall hear how things happened, and how the bitterness of privation was followed by the delights of abundance (30).]

Blanca Nieves goes beyond making the best of a bad situation. Rather, the protagonist affords a glimpse of her introduction to the pleasure of the text, which metaphorically and literally smiles on her through the joy of creation.

The physical arranging of Blanca Nieves's hair is framed in a long mirror. The mother sits before the mirror in a high-backed chair, while Blanca Nieves is positioned in front of her mother on a stool. Blanca Nieves rests her back up against her mother's knees, using her mother as her support and strength. To talk to each other they speak to their reflected images in the mirror, in effect to the image behind the looking glass, out from behind which they could dance if they desire, out of the field of male superiority, to reflect again on Gilbert and Gubar's looking glass imagery. This imagery asserts that while the woman is a prisoner of the mirror/text's image, she is filled with a sense of her own autonomy and interiority. As the work progresses of unwrapping Blanca Nieves's hair and ironically laying bare the deceit, illusion gives way to the movement of lips accented by voice that issues the mother's story for the day.

The figures, Blanca Nieves and her image, are distinct. The mother's audience for the stories is Blanca Nieves and her image reflected in the mirror. Blanca Nieves herself is the social "I" and her reflected image, the specular "I". The function of the imago, or identification, is found in Lacan's distinctive use of mirror imagery, which is to establish a relation between the organism and its reality. It facilitates a dialectic that links the "I" to socially elaborated situations. Blanca Nieves assumes an image and the image precedes language. The mother positions her before the mirror in a stage-like fashion, unadorned aesthetically, spiritually, or linguistically. This is performed so that identification might take place before the "I" is made social, that is to say, before the "I" is objectified in the dialectic of identification with the other.[28] It is the totality that permits the social "I" to move toward maturity. Natural maturity must be mediated by culture, Lacan argues. Cultural mediation for intellectual and cultural maturity is the Bildung process, the molding of the self or the quest for selfhood. Lacan realizes, however, that it is beyond the power of practitioners to bring the subject to the point where the real journey begins.[29] In other words, we may facilitate the Bildung process of others, such as in the role of the new mother with respect to the child, but we cannot take them there. The protagonist alone must find the essence of spirit to reconcile herself to herself and others.

The new mother becomes a facilitator for the learning of Blanca Nieves's role, that of "excelente lector o complemento" (35) [unique reader or collaborator (32)]. What makes her role unique is Blanca Nieves's unusual perspective and combinatory will, which enables her to mold the stories culled from her mother's reading of mythology, fables, novels, and Biblical history so as to enrich the desires of her own spirit. In fact, her favorite story, that of Paul and Virginia or the two children, is re-staged to take place at her home, Piedra Azul. The familiarity of the setting leads to a veneration that supports her self-esteem and maturation from inside out. Blanca Nieves's self-reflection, through becoming the characters she has her mother create, connects her with a more complete intellectual and moral endeavor vis à vis her relationship with the people she has sought after, those of "high moral attainments". Everything Blanca Nieves absorbs from her creations becomes an acquired element of her Bildung, which is preserved as a sign of her formation. Her rebellion against her mother in refusing to present herself and cooperate with the daily grooming that flows into the storytelling hour, is Blanca Nieves's demonstration of authority that leads to independence. The independent spirit is more readily understood from the male perspective, whose social orientation is hierarchical or positional and rewards independence and individual achievement. Traditionally, the female perspective has rewarded self-sacrifice for the greater good of relationships. But the new mother cautions the female hero to renegotiate the social contract, take what she needs from both lines of inheritance, and pursue self-development. Blanca Nieves realizes she must enter a new social contract with the mother in order to shrug off the barriers and limits the patriarchal structure has determined for her. And it is a mutually beneficial bargain between Blanca Nieves and her mother even while appearing to be a temporary annoyance: "Era un malhumor arrogante lleno de autoridad. Mientras mi persona se sentaba en el taburete, él dictaba sus leyes y si consentía en entregar mansamente a Mamá la posesión material de mi cabeza era a trueque de asegurarse la posesión moral y absoluta de la de ella" (35) [It was an imperious annoyance that needed to show its authority, and if it consented to hand over to Mama the material possession of my head, it was at the price of the absolute and moral possessions of hers (33)].

Blanca Nieves supports her mother's goals in order to witness her mother's mind at work. Bartering or exchange in the above scene (beauty for moral maturity and intelligence, one head for another) permits a re-appropriation of presence, and appears to be a fair price to pay for the return to speech and the empowering of the female voice. While we are not privy to the mother's thought processes, we may conjecture that the unmasking and further ritualization of beauty before witnesses (their mirrored images) is designed to awaken her daughter to a social impulse and related issues of gender. The daughter, then, may take the contrasting model a step beyond this and oppose other institutions that defeat equality. The mother will be faithful to these impulses to the end, insisting that the girls attend school for their education over the father's belief that there is time for that later on in life. Blanca Nieves develops into Mama Blanca in the Introduction, who not only confronts and opposes the social institutions that divide men from women, but also those that divide social classes, economic groupings, and races. She re-inscribes the terms of triumph within a new social order, showing how to reorder the Bildung process so that self-realization may be declared a success in her mature years. Clearly, we have more information about the developmental process of Blanca's youth, which prepares her to remain open to lifelong learning, basing her cultural and moral maturity on her acquired Bildung. Her life's passages including marriage and raising children, reveal an independent spirit not tempered or truncated by social pressures in fulfilling her role in a patriarchal society. The insinuated social awareness of the child Blanca transforms her into a woman of character who defends the poor and disenfranchised and whose growth and development refuses to be limited to her youth.

Writing has always been a supplement to speech, which is the most natural expression of thought. Writing is representation, an artificial way to make speech present. But in supplementing speech it is replacing speech, positioning itself in the place of speech. What is added, however, may also be subtracted, permitting us to return to disclose the natural state. This is the direction taken in the activity between mother and daughter. First, for obvious pedagogical

and natural reasons, a five-year-old child is more inclined to follow
a tale told to her than a reading. Her education, designed to recon-
stitute her natural being, is grounded in speech. The literature read
by the mother is significantly male: fables by Samaniego, ballads
by Zorrilla, the Bible, novels by the elder Dumas, and a poem by
Saint-Pierre. These works were then reordered, and, in effect, rewritten by the demands of the daughter and the imagination of the
mother through speech. Mama Blanca recalls in her memoirs:

> "Yo me encargaba luego de imprimir unidad al conjunto. En mis ratos
> de ensueño, al hacer revivir con entusiasmo los más notables hechos,
> invitaba a mis torneos espirituales a aquellos personajes que juzgaba
> más nobles o interesantes. Como nadie decía que no, en mis libres
> adaptaciones se veía por ejemplo a Moisés vencido por d'Artagnan o a
> la dulce Virginia naufragando tristemente en el arca de Noé y salvada
> de pronto, gracias a los esfuerzos heroicos e inesperados de la Bella y
> la Fiera" (35)

> [I later gave unity to the whole. In my hours of dreaming, as I recalled
> the more thrilling incidents, I invited those personages I thought most
> novel or interesting to appear at my spiritual jousts. As nobody ever
> refused, Moses was at times defeated by d'Artangan, or sweet Virginia
> was shipwrecked in Noah's ark, and rescued just in the nick of time by
> the heroic efforts of Beauty and the Beast (33)].

A completely new story added to the repertoire or a familiar
story with "tyrannical changes" might be requested or—passive
listener/reader to active participant/creator: "Pero ya sabes, Mamá,
que la Fiera se quede Fiera con su rabo, su pelo negro, sus orejotas
y todo y que asimismo se case con la Bella. ¡Que no se vuelva Príncipe nunca! ¿Ya lo sabes? Mamá tomaba nota (37) ["You remember, Mama, the Beast is to remain Beast, with his tail, his black
hair, his ears and everything, and he is to marry the Beauty like
that. He is never to become a prince. You won't forget?" Mama
took due notice (34)]. It propels the mother and daughter to further
levels in their development where the female voice may be valued,
and patriarchy's prohibitions cast aside as capricious. Once she has
overturned the code of female beauty, she is inclined to liberate the
male code as well in a symbol of new social order. Doris Sommer
interprets this motivation for active creation as an act of disobedience.[30] In this manner, female disconformities are ultimately understood to be character and culture builders.

Not surprisingly, the universal nature of Bildung beckons Blanca
Nieves. As she strives to become whatever she can become, she

blends the human and the heroic. The familiar setting of their plantation permits Blanca Nieves a spirit of veneration that never leaves her, even in her memories. Death and destruction alternate with happily ever after in these stories that become part of Blanca's emotional life from which she barred the intrusive and unappreciative, namely the nanny Evelyn. Curiously, it is Evelyn who reverts to a more traditional role in order to assign vices and virtues to her charges. She views Violeta's independence, rebelliousness, and conventionally masculine traits, as signs of great intelligence. Conversely, she views Blanca's contemplative attitude (especially after daily encounters with her imagination) as a sure sign of feeble-mindedness.

Blanca's weak nature embarrasses Evelyn, so much so that she feels obligated to conceal this characteristic from others. But neither Evelyn's humiliations nor Violeta's indifference diminishes Blanca's creativity. Just as her uncurled hair comes to represent in her mind a kind of nakedness, so too the untrained mind symbolizes a representation of the subaltern text. Ironically, the father understands this and leads by example of rationality and modernity. The urgency to curl her hair becomes a need to avoid the shame of her "nakedness". Correlatively, the urgency felt to fill the mind staves off the inadequacy of not having a voice, of being left in silence. The previously upstaged female hero is no longer in darkness. The new social and cultural order questions conventional associations of gender and activities, and promotes culturally feminine traits that reorder women's contributions to society. The new mother has empowered Blanca Nieves to dance out of the looking glass (reflection of beauty) to the health of female authority, which needs a healthy male authority for mutual support. Her image no longer needs to conceal its self-definition or acquiesce to another's definition, male or female.

The new mother encourages the child to seek self-articulation and to form her ideology and audience. This is accomplished when Blanca is rejected by Evelyn, Violeta, and her father, and pursues instead the appreciative and attentive Estrella, Rosalinda, Vicente, and Daniel. Parenting the text, as the new mother does initially and in the Foreword, is an act that confronts both paternal and maternal precursors. It engages Blanca in a dialogue of social justice and national identity to be explored further in chapter five. The new mother guides by example without limiting life's experiences. She also takes the child to that point where the real journey begins, recognizing that the rest is the enterprise of the child. The new mother gives her the tools along the way for the child to reinvent herself, become her own moral compass, turn tragedy into hope, and discomfort into solace up to and including the mature stages of her life.

One final protagonist who rewrites the Bildung process to remap the developmental process and reprogram it for the mature stage of her life is Verónica, or Vero, in María Luisa Puga's *La viuda*. After almost fifty years of marriage and the death of her husband, Vero is left to determine the course of her life. She ultimately is able to put family priorities in perspective and seek to fashion and mold herself building on her truncated growth since high school that yielded to uncritical rites of passage. What appears to others to be the beginning of Vero's life after her husband's death is, in reality, her refusal to accept another uncritical rite of passage into widowhood. Her Bildung process revives itself in the form of an apprenticeship of life through reading and learning to view critically people, culture, history, and images of Mexico previously commodified and legitimated. Here she concentrates on her intellectual and emotional growth rather than on the needs of others. Vero's insecurity about her inability to function in her new situation transforms into a discovery of inner strength that defies the incredulous with respect to growth and development at her age: "Soy una viuda y tengo tanto derecho como cualquiera a descubrir el mundo"[31] [I am a widow and have as much right as anyone to discover the world, *my translation*]. This strength contradicts the person she was before who let her husband do all the talking because she did not have anything to say. Learning to be with herself, she can open herself to other challenges such as searching for her authentic self by yielding to her entrepreneurial spirit. This goal of self realization inspires her in her late sixties to open a café-bookstore that blends her newfound freedom of expression with the written word. Carefully, Vero reinforces her awakening to culture and gender. Having asked herself countless times why she could not simply learn to be a widow, the answer becomes her refusal to accept widowhood as a culminating point in her life and Bildung process.

2

Private Lives/Public Spheres

It is true, there is little real culture among men; there are few
strong thinkers and fewer honest ones; but they have still some
advantages. If their education has been bad, it has at least been
a trifle better than ours.
                    —Catherine Crowe, *The Story of Lily Dawson* (1852)

THE ABOVE, PROSCRIPTIVE QUOTE BEGRUDGINGLY REINFORCES THE
benefits men have, which are mirrored in the coming-of-age narrative and novel of formation. In essence, the education of males,
whether it be in public or private, has always been "a trifle better"
than that of females, owing to the strength derived from the opposition of public/private. Significantly, the staging of publicity, or
stark division of public and private, is more completely accomplished throughout history in the male world. Personal attributes
circumscribe male status, dress, and address in the public sphere
and have done so since the early Middle Ages with respect to battle,
religion, and exterior courtly (public) ritual Jürgen Habermas argues. They supercede those attributes of the more delimiting world
of a female counterpart, or that of an ancient Greek correlate whose
public representation is the political sphere. Significantly, the code
of conduct in all its normative features of dress (badges, arms,
clothing, insignias) and speech (greetings, address, formal discourse) signals authority and status in the male sphere. The code
provides norms for conduct both in the public and private spheres,
both constantly and everywhere.[1] Furthermore, its influence is so
great that the code of the public sphere, albeit transformed, still exists as an indication of social status today.

Characteristically, the dichotomy of public and private defines
the male sphere. It is impermeable and influences the role of the
male hero in the traditional Bildungsroman. Nevertheless, and this
is the point I wish to make, however the public sphere by definition

may be structurally transformed through the ages, the opposition of public and private is always present to the male sphere. Mario Vargas Llosa's *La ciudad y los perros* (1963) [*The Time of the Hero*] is the traditional Bildungsroman that I will examine to demonstrate the structural dichotomy in this hypothesis. Varga Llosa's novel responds to the first strategy of rites of passage discussed in the introduction and plots when the various hero/protagonists move toward the next stage in pursuit of the goal of self-realization or selfhood in the Bildung process.

The improbability of a dichotomy between public and private existing in the female plot is the subject of the second half of this chapter. The female sphere explodes the dichotomy with the very clear rationale that women's lives have always been public and political—their status, economic independence, and reproductive rights being a matter of public debate.[2] The female Bildungsroman reflects the permeation and transformation of reality concordant with the female's view of public and private. This is "life as an open book" as evident in Elena Poniatowska's *Hasta no verte, Jesús mío* (1969), a fine example of testimony and literature that reinforces the interconnectedness of public and private. *Hasta no verte* demonstrates who can become the created, self-actualized hero through a fusion of public and private. It is a picaresque novel that evolves from the centering figure of the first person that creates herself by fusing with the community and giving her story as testimony. Her relationships with those of the community explore new socio-political models that collapse hierarchical forms by engaging the individual and the larger community in a determined process of becoming. The pícara/protagonist is more deeply enfranchised in the narrative because this is also a testimonial novel, adding another figure as witness and sympathetic listener, in addition to a community to whom she is responsible. The centering metaphor of this chapter will be space—the dichotomy of public and private space in the traditional Bildungsroman and the fusion of public and private in the new Bildungsroman.

The public domain is transformed when what previously has been held private, such as decisions on education, family health, and economics, becomes a subject of public interest. This is most readily seen today in the debate on health care, or it may be understood historically in the seventeenth century as the coming together of private people as a bourgeois public to debate, through the use of reason, for the common good. But the divisions between public and private remain clearly enforced in the military and, by extension, military academies such as the Leoncio Prado, which is the setting of Mario Vargas Llosa's novel *La ciudad y los perros*. The barriers between public and private are administered structurally in this novel by the division of chapters and sections between the outside and the inside world, the military vs. the private self, authority vs. the private sector, the adherence to rules vs. the use of reason. Routinely, the divisions are physical and linguistic. Sharon Magnarelli argues this point, "What strikes the reader about *La ciudad y los perros* is the fact that not only is the world reduced to signs recognized as such, even within the fiction, but that the fictitious world is founded (overtly so) on a system of dichotomy and difference. The boys' world is set up on an either/or basis. From the linguistic perspective of the characters, the world comes to be reduced to that inside the academy and that outside—the two ways of life demand different language and different behavior."[3] The barriers that divide the two worlds seem insurmountable, although the influence of the public sphere reverberates subconsciously in the private lives of the cadets even from without the walls of the military institution.

Most importantly, the narrative voice in *La ciudad y los perros* shifts continuously from public to private. It demonstrates a tension as the cadet within the walls strives for the development of all faculties that mark the independent man. It then lays the groundwork for the emotions that will become the foundation for community outside the walls, which is instrumental to the cultivation of the individual or hero. The reader is at the mercy of the narrative voice because the chapters have no identifying titles, nor is the narrative "I" identified. That is, the reader must follow a narrative told from a variety of unidentified perspectives. In addition, the narrative voice will shift from the public to the private within the same chapter providing only a visual marker of difference in the blank space between narratives. Furthermore, there is unceasing pressure on the private to change and open up more to the public. This is in contrast to the absolute need of the private to maintain those divisions or be subsumed by the public.[4] Vargas Llosa's traditional Bildungsroman, brilliantly portrays the dichotomy of public and private in its plot development and linguistic strategies.

The chapters identifying the narrative voice belong to the world of the military, whose task it is to aid youth in the process of self-development in a practical sense. The hero's self-development ultimately permits independent thought and maturity through incremental stages. Ironically, a conflict arises because the public sphere wishes to have too much control over the private. Its absoluteness, which ensures its future existence and prosperity, needs to curb the emancipation and self-formation of the individual that it inspires. However, the more the public sphere identifies its goal as the independence of its charge, the more it must continue to retreat and impose the impenetrable barriers that support its survival and the hero's dependence. In the past, the private sphere gave over the propagation of personal cultivation, freedom, and even love to the rules of the public. But if it wishes to reclaim its role in guiding the hero beyond immediate experience, it must appeal to the uncertainty it holds in its favor. That is, Bildung, unlike professional or occupational requirements, may not be foisted upon or demanded of another individual. The concept of Bildung emphasizes the conflict between the mere training of an individual (public sphere) and the cultivation of that person (private sphere), which ultimately leads to self-formation, and builds on further self-formation. In sum, it is open to everyone who pursues it but cannot be taught or imposed by another.

Ironically, the certainty of the public sphere is enhanced by the uncertainty of the private and its goals (relationships with women, family, etc.). The staging of publicity in the first section of the first chapter of La ciudad y los perros follows the guidelines of the public sphere and is linked to names the protagonists are given and wear like insignias to communicate rank and class of rhetoric, or the manner in which they should be addressed: Jaguar, Cava, Boa, el poeta, el Esclavo. It is possible to replace their names with military or social codes that would reveal their military/social status, but these are not the reigning codes used to inform the narrative. Jaguar takes command of the narrative structure through priority—he speaks first and has the most imposing, self-authored name. To reinforce their distinctions, the cadets are divided by sections and years and share their public sphere with noncoms, soldiers, and officers, whose roles are separate from their own. The father figure against which the young hero rebels in the public sphere belongs to the patriarchal social structure represented by the military. The military's seemingly inalterable rules and regulations instruct the cadets in two conflicting lessons: 1) survival—however brutal or violent—of the fittest, and 2) power—however irrational or arbitrary—of social rank. The father figure against which the young hero rebels in the private sphere belongs to the patriarchal conjugal family, and is represented by the father, whose values are upheld even after the father abandons the family.

The narrative voice introduces each protagonist and recounts each individual Bildung process, from the successful to the uncertain, toward cultivation of capabilities and strengths in the private sphere. The process may begin in childhood and end in adulthood (career, marriage) as, for example, the narratives of Alberto and Jaguar, which end with a core of uncertainty indicating further Bildung and self-development. The process may also be a truncated one, abruptly halted by tragedy after its childhood commencement, as exemplified by the life of Ricardo. It may also begin in adulthood and indicate no closure, as is the experience of Lt. Gamboa. In their private lives the protagonists are identified by their given names, not by nicknames or rank, one touch of humanity denied in the military school. The use of the nickname "Richi" demonstrates the affection Ricardo's mother holds for him. But when they meet in the military academy they become the other, wearing their names like an insignia, indicative of their position and others' esteem (or lack thereof) for them. The new director of the military school imbues the cadets with the magnitude of publicity's staging in the military: "En el Ejército, cadetes, hay que respetar los símbolos, qué Caray"[5] [In the army, Cadets, you have to have respect for symbols, damn it[6]]. The army's respect for symbols demands the cadets become in their personal attributes, dress, demeanor, and rhetoric, that is to say, in their public display, the soldier they ironically do not wish to grow into in their private lives.

For many, the Academy—part military, part correctional institution—is their punishment for poor grades or for behavior uncharacteristic of men in the private sphere. Once inside the military academy their civilian or private life ends for three years during which time they are taught obedience, courage, and hard work, to fulfill the objective of making them into men. In other words, the public sphere provides the skills and training to set in motion the Bildung process. But the process of Bildung and the making of a man are uniquely necessary ideals. They involve getting beyond the hero's naturalness and discovering what is different from himself in order to find more universal viewpoints from which to grasp life without selfish interest. In either case, nothing is achieved conclusively. There can be no singular guideline from which to draw conclusions about the recognition of self-realization or manhood. The concept and definition of manhood as the hero reaches each stage in the passage through life changes and builds on previous accomplishments and formations of the self. In fact, the process may never achieve closure.

The function of the public sphere crystallizes in the idea of "public opinion". Public opinion separates virtues from vices, and relies on the tacit consent of a sympathetic audience for its continuation. Public opinion also validates public performance, which in turn influences the private sector. For example, the third year cadets are initiated and treated in the most degrading, vile, humiliating, and violent form possible by the upperclassmen within the academy, with the tacit approval of the officers. Ironically, they are lectured by the same officers before their first pass-day on the proper conduct of a uniformed cadet in public, outside the academy. Public opinion may sway the staging of publicity because dress, demeanor, and rhetoric are altered by opinion. In effect, it sets the stage for contradiction. This is why the army cannot tolerate insubordination, but will tacitly approve of the inhuman harassment of students to remake them into men, as long as it is able to second the definition of manhood held privately in each home. Public opinion is the consent of private people who do not have the authority to put their beliefs into law. Anyone is capable of contributing to it regardless of education or status.[7] Furthermore, and this is where I believe Bildung of the private sphere clashes with the public, it is public opinion that decides whether making a cadet a man in the public sphere also contributes to his humanity or cultivation in the private sphere. It must also be remembered, however, that what is established by public opinion as habit may later be critically opposed as prejudice by the same group.

Public opinion is dynamic, capricious, and volatile, and must be courted cautiously for public consumption. Curiously, the same cadets the officers belittle, despise, and insult, are ironically entrusted with representing the military outside the academy. The cadets symbolize the power of the Army in the hearts and minds of the people, an opinion held in the privacy of their own homes. The cadets also convey the military's autonomy, which must never be challenged. In an example of stream of consciousness a cadet recalls: ". . . qué es eso de exhibirnos como monos, evoluciones con armas ante el arzobispo y almuerzo de camaradería, gimnasia y saltos ante los generales ministros y almuerzo de camaradería, desfile con uniformes de parada y discursos, y almuerzo de camaradería ante los embajadores, bien hecho, bien hecho" (65) [what's this about exhibiting us like monkeys, armed drill in front of the archbishop and a lunch for everyone together, gymnastics and field events in front of the ministers and generals and a lunch for everyone together, a full-dress parade and speeches, and a lunch for everyone together in front of the ambassadors, well done, well done (74)]. The repetition of the phrase "y almuerzo de camaradería" [and a lunch for everyone together] reinforces in the cadet's mind the ironic nature of the staging of publicity that brings everyone together in the spirit of a communion, but under false pretenses. It also recalls the hypocrisy of dress as a staging of publicity: monkeys dressed as soldiers who dine with Ambassadors, ministers, and generals. At this point the staging is mere artifice because the cadets have not succumbed to the seductive call of public opinion. They feel neither more fulfilled nor more cultivated or sensible because of their affiliation with the military. Only later when they read the pleasant reaction in the faces of others (women, family, friends, etc.) upon inspecting them in uniform, will they understand the symbolism and power of publicity and public opinion.

By necessity, the private sphere in this culturally Latin American novel is grounded in the power of the patriarchal conjugal family. The father wields ultimate power even in his absence due to abandonment, as is the case of Alberto's family, or through his abusive presence owing to an uneasy reconciliation, as in Ricardo's family. Alberto's father has left his household to pursue other women, but wishes to maintain control of his family through the economy of support. Alberto's mother, a shadow of the person she was before her husband leaves her, is anxious, clinging, and destitute emotionally and economically, but too proud to accept anything from her estranged husband. Her presence becomes a weight for Alberto because of her ability to instill guilt in him at every turn:

Se había sentado a la mesa con hambre y ahora la comida le parecía interminable e insípida. Soñaba toda la semana con la salida, pero apenas entraba a su casa se sentía irritado: la abrumadora obsequiosidad de su madre era tan mortificante como el encierro. Además, se trataba de algo nuevo, le costaba trabajo acostumbrarse. Antes, ella lo enviaba a la calle con cualquier pretexto, para disfrutar a sus anchas con las amigas innumerables que venían a jugar canasta todas las tardes. Ahora, en cambio, se aferraba a él, exigía que Alberto le dedicara todo su tiempo libre y la escuchara lamentarse horas enteras de su destino trágico (77).

[He had been hungry when they sat down at the table, but the meal seemed endless and tasteless. Every week he dreamed about his pass, but the moment he got home he felt irritable: his mother's overwhelming attentions were as hard to put up with as the Academy. Also, there was something new to get used to. Before, she sent him out of the house on any pretext whatsoever, in order to gossip with the flock of women friends who came to play canasta every afternoon. But now she clung only to him, begging him to give her all his free time, and Alberto spent hours listening to her complain about her tragic fate (87).]

Alberto's sympathy and affection for his mother dissolves into aggravation and irritation, while his hatred of his father ultimately becomes reconciled anger and respect, because his father has the ability to manipulate public opinion through the money he offers as necessary financial support for his family.

In essence, the mother cannot aid in the Bildung process of the child because she negates the patriarchal social structure (patriarchal conjugal family, hierarchical Catholic church, etc.). The author depicts a mother's shadowy existence that does not offer alternatives to the son. On the contrary, far from offering alternatives, the mother forces the son to reject her affections and return to the patriarchal social structure of the Academy to seek the approval of his father:

> Sin el menor embarazo, el hombre cerró la puerta, arrojó a un sillón una cartera de cuero y, siempre sonriente y desenvuelto, tomó asiento a la vez que hacía una señal a Alberto para que se sentara a su lado. Alberto miró a su madre: seguía inmóvil.—Carmela—dijo el padre, alegremente—. Ven, hija, vamos a conversar un momento. Podemos hacerlo delante de Alberto, ya es todo un hombrecito. Alberto sintió satisfacción. Su padre, a diferencia de su madre, parecía más joven, más sano, más fuerte. En sus ademanes y en su voz, en su expresión, había algo incontenible que pugnaba por exteriorizarse. ¿Sería feliz? (80)

> [His father closed the door without the slightest embarrassment, tossed his leather briefcase on a chair and then sat down, still smiling, still casual, and motioned to Alberto to sit down beside him. Alberto looked at this mother; she had not moved. "Carmela, come here, girl," his father said in a breezy voice. "Let's have a little chat. We can talk in front of Alberto, he's a man now." Alberto felt pleased. His father, unlike his mother, seemed younger, healthier, stronger. There was something irrepressible in his voice, his expressions, his gestures. Was that because he was happy? (91)]

Alberto attends the Academy because his father, angered by Alberto's poor grades, accuses him of "trampling on the family traditions," meaning unequivocally those of *his* family. His father's pleasure with Alberto's progress at the Academy and offer to send him to the United States to study engineering when he graduates, reconciles for Alberto the disgust he feels for his military schooling, and the resentment he has felt in the past toward his father.[8] Slowly he is able to discern approval in others for his educational choices, even though he is unable to distinguish the military from the detention center he knows the Academy to be. He knows from Teresa's comments on their first date that he and his fellow cadets stand apart from the other boys: "—Ustedes, los del Leoncio Prado, son muy peleadores. El enrojeció de placer. Vallano tenía razón: los cadetes impresionaban a las hembritas . . ." (89) ['You cadets from Leoncio Prado, you all like to fight.' He reddened with pleasure. Vallano was right: the cadets really impressed the girls . . . (102)]. However, the code of conduct of the public sphere (dress, insignias, address) is instantly rendered ineffectual when the symbols are removed or simply disappear.

One example of the negation of code entails Alberto's visit to the prostitute who has become, by her own admission, the mascot of his section at the Academy. Appearing naked before her, all objects and symbols disappear, permitting her to write his story of inexperience on the blank form that is his virginity. For Alberto, it is his rite of passage toward self-development in the Bildung process. It is part of the unwritten code of the Academy forced upon him that makes the cadet a man. Significantly, his body rejects this prescription of manhood dictated by the public code, and his Bildung process is further advanced through his self-determined development.

Rituals abound in the rites of passage of the Bildung process. The relationship with the opposite sex is the focus of various stages of development. Here the Bildungsroman's narrative through flashbacks reviews the passage from antagonism between young boys and girls to mutual attraction. For boys, separation and individuation are markers of their maturity and identity, an identity grounded in single-generational contact that is threatened by relationships. Conversely, for girls, ongoing attachments or relationships are the criteria that inspire maturity. Boys continue to evade intimacy with girls even as they pursue them. In addition, they fight intimacy with other boys through the manipulation of degrading insults that reinforce the distance between them. Sharon Magnarelli explores the male/female as well as the male/male separations, and concludes that the distance in the male relationship must not lead to a uniqueness that is totalizing.[9] Magnarelli suggests that the result of total uniqueness is overcompensation in an effort to be "NOT FE-MALE", but I argue it points here to evidence of a third space that goes beyond binary opposition.

The third space is characterized in Vargas Llosa's novel by linguistic acts, the repeated insults of "queer" or "fairy", cast throughout the novel that enrage through fear. The disconcerting question of transvestism, that is, that underneath the social codes of publicity one might encounter a woman dressed as a man in the public sphere, only inadvertently touches upon an irreconcilable issue—in the private sphere a man might dress or act as a woman. The meaning of this transgression is examined by Marjorie Garber:

"To transgress against one set of boundaries was to call into question the inviolability of both, and of the set of social codes . . . by which such categories were policed and maintained."[10] For the boys in the novel, it leads to an unspeakable attraction.

Curiously, once the familiar social codes are removed from the staging of publicity, one is at a loss to know how to qualify what is seen. It creates a crisis of category that alternately terrifies and seduces. The crisis of category does not represent the public or private sphere, and results in the creation of a third space filled by people who are powerful agents of destabilization and change. It signals the "ungroundedness of identities on which social structures and hierarchies depend."[11] It is a place where culture can be changed and the impossible made possible. It is threatening for that reason. A crisis of category puts into question the concept of self-knowledge and self-development that is taught in the binary opposition of public sphere (Academy) and private lives (home, neighborhood). It is the reason that el Esclavo is an enigma and a threat, an interruption in the accepted codes. His hatred of fighting—allowing himself instead to be beaten and urinated on, and his food to be contaminated with the spit of his defilers—is perhaps the reason he does not respond when the cadets brand him as the lover of el poeta. If not read as a homoerotic quality, perhaps it demonstrates a sensitivity that is admissible only in the third space of possibility, where love and admiration for a member of the same sex are permissible. After the cadets have become excited by the reading aloud of an erotic novel in the barracks: "el Jaguar se lanza como un endemoniado sobre el Esclavo, lo alza en peso, todos se callan y miran, y lo lanza contra Vallano. Le dice: "te regalo a esta puta." El Esclavo se incorpora, se arregla la ropa y se aleja. Boa lo atrapa por la espalda, lo levanta y el esfuerzo le congestiona el rostro y el cuello que se hincha; sólo lo tiene en el aire unos segundos y lo deja caer como un fardo. El Esclavo se retira, despacio, cojeando" (127) [Jaguar leaped at the Slave, picked him up bodily while the others watched in silence, and threw him against Vallano, saying, "You can have this whore as a gift." The Slave got up, straightened his clothes, and began to move away. Then Boa caught him under the shoulders and lifted him up. The effort made his veins bulge and his neck swell out. He held him in the air for only a few seconds and then let him fall like a rag. The Slave limped out of the barracks (147)]. The third space is as inexplicable to el Esclavo as it is to the other cadets because it mystifies and explodes the conventional dichotomy of public and private as the female does, but yet it is not female. In effect, it stymies the rules of self-realization that are complementary in the public and private spheres. It therefore seals el Esclavo's fate at the hands of the other cadets.

The redefinition of public and private takes place as the youths mature, lose their antagonism for girls, and find themselves open to more universal viewpoints, that is, those outside their neighborhood. The neighborhood symbolizes an intimate extension of their private lives. A special bond unites its inhabitants who will fight to ward off invaders of their boundaries. But as they mature the restless tug of the unknown causes the barriers to be overwhelmed by outsiders: "En efecto, desde hace algún tiempo, el barrio ha dejado de ser una isla, un recinto amurallado. Advenedizos de toda índole—miraflorinos . . . muchachos de San Isidro e incluso de Barranco—, aparecieron de repente en esas calles que constituían el dominio del barrio. Acosaban a las muchachas, conversaban con ellas en la puerta de sus casas, desdeñando la hostilidad de los varones o desafiándola. Eran más grandes que los chicos del barrio y a veces los provocaban. Las mujeres tenían la culpa; los atraían, parecían satisfechas con esas incursiones" (144) [For some time the neighborhood had ceased to be an island, a walled fortress. Outsiders—boys from Miraflores . . . boys from San Isidro and even from Barranco—had suddenly appeared in the neighborhood. They were after the girls, and talked with them in the doorways of their houses, ignoring or defying the resentment of the neighborhood boys. Also, they were older, and sometimes they even threatened them on their home ground. The girls were to blame, because they encouraged these invasions (168)]. It is precisely the male dichotomy that is in jeopardy when the private sphere is invaded by the public. It is the female perspective that denies the divisions and purposefully pursues the blending of opposites, the more universal viewpoints, to go beyond what she knows and experiences immediately. The boys ultimately understand disloyalty as the motivating factor for the girls' actions: "Y Ana, justamente, no se distinguía por su celo, su espíritu de clan era muy débil, casi nulo. Los advenedizos le interesaban más que los muchachos del barrio" (145) [Ana was especially disloyal, her feeling for the neighborhood was very weak if she had any at all. She was more interested in the outsiders than she was in the boys who lived near her (169)]. The "protecting of one's turf" is not part of the female rite of passage because, from the very beginning, she does not view this as a conflict or competition. Her relational identity pursues a more complete web of relationships and an interconnectedness of public and private. For the female it is a turning point—it represents a marker for one stage that forms the basis for another stage in the Bildung process.

The Bildung process of Ricardo Arana, known as el Esclavo, takes many unexpected turns in its progression. His father had asked him to enroll at the Academy to make a man out of him, and Ricardo agreed in order to please his father and move away from him at the same time. The father understood Ricardo's agreement to convey a tacit approval of the theory that the public sphere would be able to accomplish what the private sphere could not—to change him, give him backbone, a strong body and personality, and make him into a man. However, Ricardo's agreement contextualizes his desire to move from one patriarchal structure to another hoping for salvation through anonymity; he will no longer be the unfortunate, only son. Ultimately, the Military Academy takes to an extreme its role *in locus parentis*, redefines freedom and independence for the cadets, and subsumes the parents' control over the child, deciding when and if Ricardo's parents may visit their gravely ill son. The father, embittered by his son's condition and lack of information from the Military Academy on the cause of the accident, eventually supports the military's position over his own convictions: "Pero yo tengo mis dudas. Yo pienso que la bala se escapó por accidente. En fin, uno no puede saber. Los militares entienden de estas cosas más que uno" (206) [I don't know. It may have been an accident. It's hard to tell. The Army knows more about these things than I do, its part of their job (242)]. The enemy for the father is not the Army that has taken control of his son's life, but his wife and the boy's Aunt who raised him since birth. Rather than confiding in the private sphere to promote a leaving behind of the invulnerability of childhood for the independence and responsibility of adulthood, the father assigns his son's development to the public sphere because it upholds a more definitive code of conduct. Curiously, with Ricardo's death, the blame is placed on the child's shoulders. His assumed responsibility manipulates and transfers back the child's development and lack of preparation to the private sphere, his personal life, that had prevented him from becoming a man and caused his death. Of course, the Military knows that it would have been impossible for Ricardo to have died in the way they describe, but it shifts the blame, nevertheless, from itself to the family in this staging of publicity.

Ironically, it is the staging of publicity during the Academy's maneuvers, with insignias and divisions for sections to reflect social status, which draws Ricardo's Bildung process to a close. Thus both patriarchal forces, the father (private sphere) and the Military Academy (public sphere), realize their culpability in Ricardo's death over their own protestations. The Academy is concerned about their reputation and that of the army as well. The father is concerned about an image of manhood that he would use as justification for sending his son to the Military Academy. Ricardo, on the other hand, belonged to a third space, neither public nor private, which could not be tolerated by the dichotomy. Upon relating the cadets' many indiscretions to Captain Garrido as a way of explaining that Ricardo's death was not accidental, Alberto concludes: "Todos éramos todo . . . Sólo Arana era diferente. Por eso nadie se juntaba con él" (255) [We're all guilty, Sir, . . . Of everything. The only one who wasn't was the Slave. That's why he never had any friends (301)]. Alberto, in fighting to bring out what he believes is the truth, searches through his actions to underscore Ricardo's virtues in comparison to his own vices. It is a necessary separation of himself from himself to understand for the first time how Ricardo views reality. It is a point that projects Alberto forward in his own Bildung process toward maturity and independence, but his "confession" is only the beginning of the process.

The knowledge Alberto acquires of human nature promotes an intellectual and moral maturity that inspires sensibility and character development. Alberto necessarily refuses to yield to the pressure of his superiors to forget his theories on Ricardo's death: "—¿Entendido?—dijo el capitán y su rostro insinuó una sonrisa. —No, mi capitán—dijo Alberto. —¿No me ha comprendido, cadete? —No puedo prometerle eso—dijo Alberto—. A Arana lo mataron" (257) ["Do you understand?" the captain said, trying to smile. "No, Sir." Alberto said. "You don't understand me, cadet?" "I can't make that promise," Alberto said. "They killed Arana." (303)]. Alberto has not sought this development of his character but accepts and is formed and transformed by it. Alberto is one of the many characters in the novel who build on the stages of Bildung. As a hero of a traditional Bildungsroman, Alberto chooses a masculine figure to emulate, his father, and accepts his father's values including his selection of school and profession, and his relationship with women. He briefly rebels against society and the societal values his father and, by extension, the Academy represent, and becomes a poet and writer in love with a woman from the wrong social class, in addition to a virtuous seeker of truth. But confronted with his indiscretions, Alberto has to choose between virtue, which could lead to his professional demise, or acquiescence to the values of the public man. He has as a model his friend Ricardo Arana, who is a decent person that is brutally attacked by the other cadets and is eventually killed. His other model is Lt. Gamboa, whose ideals of discipline and responsibility force him into a conflict between truth and survival.

The one officer who appears to support Alberto's theory is Lt. Gamboa. Lt. Gamboa is a virtuous representative of the public sphere because he truly believes in the Army's responsibility to further its charges Bildung process by making men out of them through discipline and regulations. His superior, Capt. Garrido, on the other hand, believes in the survival of the fittest, so that his definition of Bildung incorporates virtues and vices and disqualifies the weakest, but not the least virtuous: ". . . lo primero que se aprende en el Ejército es a ser hombre. Los hombres fuman, se emborrachan, tiran *contra*, culean. Los cadetes saben que si son descubiertos se les expulsa. Ya han salido varios. Los que no se dejan pescar son los vivos. Para hacerse hombres, hay que correr riesgos, hay que ser audaz. Eso es el Ejército, Gamboa, no sólo la disciplina. También es osadía, ingenio" (262) [. . . the first thing you learn in the army is to be a man. And what do men do? They smoke, they drink, they gamble, they fuck. The cadets all know they get expelled if they're discovered. *If*, Gamboa. We've already expelled quite a few. But the smart ones don't get caught. If they're going to be men, they have to take chances, they have to use their wits. That's what the army is, Gamboa. Discipline isn't enough. You've got to have guts, and you've also got to have brains (310)]. Gamboa cannot reconcile the staging of publicity (dress, manner, discourse), for the purpose of deception—to feign manhood because the cadets are not capable of taking responsibility for their actions. That is, if there is a cover up of the murder, the guilty party will be protected because, not yet being a man, he cannot accept responsibility for his actions. Gamboa's goal is to make "better men" of the cadets because the Army promotes a version of manhood that oscillates between virture and vice in order to escape scandal. Owing to this choice, he is sent at great personal and professional loss to a post in the jungle of Peru and away from his bride and newborn child.

Lt. Gamboa also seeks self-realization in his pursuit of truth. He begins his Bildung process as an adult questioning the wisdom of his blind allegiance to authority, order, and discipline: "El orden y la disciplina constituyen la justicia—recitó Gamboa, con una sonrisa ácida en los labios—, y son los instrumentos indispensables de una vida colectiva racional" (313) [Justice is constituted of order and discipline, he recited to himself with a wry smile, and these are the indispensable instruments of a rational collective life (372)]. Indeed, the public sphere is made up of private people come together as a public. It is their responsibility to establish general rules that govern the public sphere made up of private people. The public's use of reason regulates the rules relevant to the public interest. But reason, as Gamboa learns, is impossible to regulate, and needs to be protected from public domination, because it may not include the faculties of cultivated, rational, human beings. Then, too, the demands of labor and the teaching of skills run contrariwise to the cultivation of the self that emancipates the inner realm from the goals of the exterior. That is, the quest for the perfection of skills in the public sphere (instruction to become a soldier/man) contradicts the goals of the private sphere (freedom, love, development of all faculties): "The old contradiction continues on today in the conflict between a cultivation of the person, on the one hand, and a training that provides mere skills, on the other."[12] As the family has relinquished its productive functions in its structural transformation over the centuries, it converts from producer to consumer, allowing the public sphere to dictate the rules of labor (skill acquisition)—a tradeoff for the family to be publicly protected. This opens the individual family members, Ricardo, Alberto, Jaguar, and his brother, to socialization by extra-familial authorities, that is, by society directly. In fact, pedagogical functions had been relinquished almost completely by the families to society beginning in the nineteenth century. Therefore, the student acquires socialization skills outside the home.

The regulations of the Academy firmly reinforced the dichotomy of public and private. The cadets are allowed to drink and smoke in their homes or their neighborhoods but not at the Academy. They are expected to gamble and have sexual intercourse within the private sphere but not in the public sphere. The irony of expecting young men to witness their rites of passage in the private sphere, such as their initiation to sex with highly frequented, neighborhood prostitutes, but not to engage in sexual acts, whether reading or writing about or performing them in any form at the Academy (public sphere), seems to escape the officers. In fact, the officers use Alberto's "pornographic novels" against him as proof of his degenerate nature, and oblige him to conform to the codes of the public sphere or risk expulsion and humiliation. During Alberto's interview with the colonel, the highest ranking official at the Academy, the colonel asks Alberto if he is a real cadet—sensible, intelligent, and educated. Ironically, these attributes cannot be drilled into a charge but are accessible to those who pursue the goals of the Bildung process. The attributes grow out of the inner process of formation and cultivation and reflect Alberto's Bildung process in the private sphere that is complemented by a practical process in the public sphere. Alberto chooses to withdraw his accusation for lack of concrete evidence in order to graduate and pursue his life interests. Rather than basing his developmental process on a goal of individualization, Alberto reinforces his identification with normative structures of the society he had previously spurned, and finds solace in its conventional goals.

The loss of ground in the private sphere is evident in *La ciudad y los perros* in the parents' apparent inability to affect the child's development after making the crucial decision to intern him in the Military Academy. The reduction of privacy in the home, the lack of space therein or the interpersonal problems that spill out onto the street, puts more pressure on the private to conform with the public. However, what the public sphere cannot replace is the interconnectedness of the private sphere, regardless of the outside pressures brought to bear. The section in the Academy acts like a family but disintegrates when cadets accuse each other of being traitors, faggots, squealers, and cowards. The community of love identified within the conjugal family is constant, nevertheless, and encourages the development of all faculties that marks the cultivated person—in this instance the cadet whose inner process of formation and cultivation remains in a continual process of Bildung. Therefore, it is against the values of the conjugal family in the private sphere that the hero rebels, and it is to these same values he returns in his maturity within the traditional Bildungsroman.[13]

Alberto returns to his reunited parents after graduation and is rewarded with a gift of a valuable watch from his father for his good grades. The watch's other purpose is to impress his friends, and it has just that effect as it becomes the topic of conversation one evening with his friends in the park. Alberto remarks thoughtfully: "Mi padre conoce la vida" (327) [My father knows what life's all about (389)]. This is an indication that Alberto has returned to the values of his family: image and social status. Alberto, therefore, rejects Teresa for Marcela, a girl from his own social class. His actions echo his sentiments about his formation in life learned from his parents: "Alberto pensó: "estudiaré mucho y seré un buen ingeniero. Cuando regrese, trabajaré con mi papá, tendré un carro convertible, una gran casa con piscina. Me casaré con Marcela y seré un don Juan. Iré todos los sábados a bailar al Gril Bolívar y viajaré mucho. Dentro de algunos años ni me acordaré que estuve en el Leoncio Prado" (335) [Alberto thought, I'll study hard and be a good engineer. When I come back, I'll work with my father, and I'll have a convertible and a big house with a swimming pool. I'll marry Marcela and be a Don Juan. I'll go to the Grill Bolívar every Saturday for the dancing, and I'll do a lot of traveling. After a few years I won't even remember I was in the Leoncio Prado (399)]. Contrary to this statement, in Bildung everything that is received will be remembered, absorbed, and preserved. That by which Alberto is formed becomes completely his own and will remain with him forever.

It is important to note that the Bildungsroman is written for the sake of the process, the Bildung process, which illuminates the hero's all-around self-development. Self-development may lead to or include uncertainties, inconclusive endings, or possibly the death of the hero. Martin Swales determines the goal of the genre to be the sake of the journey not a happy ending awaiting the hero at the end of the process.[14] In other words, the movement toward self-culture may include actions that defeat positive outcomes because in Bildung everything is absorbed and preserved. Jerome Buckley points to the difficulty of ending a Bildungsroman with conviction and decision,[15] the subgenre avoiding the expected happy ending that its autobiographical nature appears to demand. These theories call into question the insistence upon a collusion of naturalness and the perfected self in order to guide the successful hero. Moreover, they do not reveal an "optimistic genre,"[16] which is not a useful interpretation of the subgenre that Román Soto underscores. Nevertheless, Soto distinguishes La ciudad y los perros as Bildungsroman and not parody in his conclusion that Alberto, after surmounting a series of trials in his rite of passage, arrives at positive, self knowledge, only to return to the world of lies and deceit.[17] But lies and deceit are absorbed into self-knowledge, the stuff of which we are made. They are precisely the values of his parents' world that will remain with Alberto and be transformed into his mold of self-development.

Finally, the Bildung process of Jaguar, seemingly the most individualistic of all protagonists, is grounded in isolation, in having those in public and private turn against him including his mother, el círculo [the Circle], Lt. Gamboa, and Ricardo. But through alienation he upholds society's most conventional goals and also returns to the values of the conjugal family. Jaguar pursues Teresa, the female figure in the novel who represents a desire to regress to lost paradise and to origins.[18] The lost paradise in question is grounded in family and society's values to which the hero returns in the traditional Bildungsroman. But the values are further elaborated by the hero's Bildung process. For example, Jaguar's church wedding symbolizes the community of love, which is the basis of the conjugal family that inspires him to a decent life and a decent job. This is an unexpected narrative turn given Jaguar's upbringing and comportment throughout the novel. Jaguar's highly original improvisation, his "creation" of a personage to embody the individuating symbolism and singularity of the name, has as its underpinning, curiously, one of society's more traditional goals, an officially sanctioned marriage. In essence, for Jaguar as well as Alberto, the pressures—religious, familial, societal, and economic—that provoked their rebellion as adolescents, support and propagate the values of private life in the public sphere, and draw them to the communal norm of the traditional Bildungsroman. While the adversity and pressures the protagonists of *La ciudad y los perros* confronted and endured were seemingly insurmountable, the fact is that their conventional backgrounds made it possible to decide when to face misfortune, change whenever feasible, reinsert themselves back within rules of society, and move to the next stage of their lives. Such is not the case of the protagonists of the new Bildungsroman.

A contrasting depiction can be found in the new Bildungsroman, *Hasta no verte Jesús mío*, by Elena Poniatowska. This text dialogues with the reader/listener in order to explain what the Bildung process looks like when the lives of women and the marginalized are taken as norm. This strategy pushes the hero closer to what Diamela Eltit identifies as a method of constructing a way out of marginality.[19] The technique of giving testimony to one's life makes the acceptance of the one who has come into being and her development appear deceptively easy. The picaresque figure centers herself in the narrative through the telling of her story and her subsequent fusion with the Mexican community that she examines critically, socially, and culturally. Her voice seduces, overwhelms and mystifies the reader. Jesusa is the marginalized hero who becomes the disguised self-actualized hero by forming a self-identity in the actual life of the narrative and in her previous lives through reincarnation. The novel begins with a reference to her third reincarnation, which is the one in which she has suffered the most because in her previous life she was a queen. Jesusa envisions the process as one, long, continuous Bildung, reconstructing the boundaries of growth from one life to the other, in that she cultivates her inner self throughout all of her experience, one stage being indebted to the accomplishments of another in another life: "¿Por qué vine de pobre esta vez si antes fui reina? Mi deuda debe ser muy pesada ya que Dios me quitó a mis padres desde chica y dejó que viniera a abonar mis culpas sola como lazarina"[20] [Why did I come back as a poor woman this time if last time I was a queen? My debt must be really heavy, for God took my parents away when I was a child and left me alone to pay for my sins like a leper[21]]. As a testimonial novel it echoes the development of an autobiography, or an anthropological study such as Óscar Lewis's *The Children of Sánchez*, on which Poniatowska worked with the author. What distinguishes *Hasta no verte* from those works, however, is point of view—it follows a single protagonist who is not the author herself. Curiously, the early death and burial of the mother has resonance with the mother's death in Lewis's work, but in *Hasta no verte* it is told from the female perspective so as to bring the private tragedy into the public sphere. In contrast with Roberto in *The Children of Sánchez*, who internalizes the pain of his mother's death, Jesusa externalizes the pain and uses it in public. Rather than a negative complement of the male Bildungsroman or an anti-Bildungsroman where the journey toward maturity is rooted in failure or death, this is the journey of a picaresque figure, grounded in an interacting of cultural voices and thriving on a mixing of elements including public and private, tragedy and survival, present, past, and future lives.

Jesusa's education is formed in the private sphere, unlike the cadets in *La ciudad y los perros*. Therefore, her education is informally gleaned from answers to questions asked of everyone with whom she comes into contact. Her intellectual curiosity favors those who are most capable of inspiring her. In fact, Poniatowska suggests in our unpublished interview that the seeds of Jesusa's Bildung process are evident in her childhood. The seeds will be nurtured and developed as she grows but the essence of who she will become is evident in the child Jesusa.[22] In childhood, Jesusa's relationship with her father is uniquely close even before her mother's death. As they are very poor, the father has no money to buy her toys with which to play, so he makes them from whatever he finds. He makes her a doll from a squirrel that he stuffs and sews together. Her father presents Jesusa with the results of his labor: "—¿Por qué está dura, papá? —Por el relleno. —Pero ¿con qué la rellenaste, con tierra? —No, con aserrín. —¿Y qué cosa es aserrín? —¡Ay, Jesusa, confórmate, juega con ella! (19) [—Why is it so hard, Father? —Because of the stuffing. —Did you fill it with dirt? —No, sawdust. —What's sawdust? —Ay, Jesusa, don't ask so many questions, just be content and play with it! (13)]. Jesusa's inquisitiveness and persistence permits her to take what she needs for selfhood realizing innately that that through and by which one is formed becomes one's own.

Because her mother never scolded or beat her, Jesusa expects to be treated as an equal even by those mother figures who take the place of her mother emotionally. These "new" mothers have the task of encouraging Jesusa spiritually, mentally, physically, and emotionally in her Bildung process. But Jesusa's formation and cultivation are not limited to her relationships with women. Her interconnectedness balances a weblike alliance between men and women, privileging whomever helps Jesusa gain a greater sense of herself. At times it is the men in her life who teach her to acquire developmental experiences. For example, her father takes care of and nurtures her when Jesusa's mother's patience is exasperated: "Y él me peinaba con mucho cuidado porque nunca me ha gustado que me agarren los cabellos. Siento muy feo que me jalen y él tenía su mano suavecita, muy suavecita. Cuando mi mamá me peinaba parecía como que me caía lumbre. Sólo de él me dejaba peinar" (21) [He had very gentle hands, really supple, and he was careful. I hated to have my hair pulled, it felt like sparks falling on my head, I'd only let him comb my hair (15)]. Her father also instructs Jesusa in personal hygiene, nutrition, and in the searching for and preparation of their food for their meals. The metaphor of hunger is pervasive throughout the novel and unites Jesusa in a weblike relationship with others: Ignacia, her brother Efren's girlfriend, and her stepmother both attempt to teach Jesusa how to make tortillas, a staple and utensil in the Mexican diet.[23] But this is a lesson she never learns despite a lifetime of practice. Jesusa also becomes so accustomed to the male instructional component in the relationship that she frequently rejects women. For example, the idea of putting herself into her sister Petra's care after their mother's death is anathema to her : "Como yo no me crié con la hermana, no la quería, ni decía que era mi hermana. Yo ya estaba acostumbrada a mano de hombre, a la mano de mi padre" (31) [Since I wasn't raised with my sister, I didn't love her. I didn't even call her sister. I was used to a man's touch, to my father's touch (27)]. Significantly, that by and through which Jesusa is formed becomes completely her own. Jesusa acquires abilities that are wholly her own and molded to her needs after she dares to take what is needed in lessons from others.

In an analysis of Jesusa's actions it becomes clear that she is working out her existence in the world. Jesusa goes out from herself in a movement of alienation from what she is naturally in order to appropriate in the alien what will later become her own. The acquisition of Bildung is based on Jesusa's learning to allow what is different from herself and her nature, to store this information in her

stepmother, children she takes in, and friends. Her husband Pedro, on the other hand, varies his behavior according to a particular staging of publicity—his public demonstration of care and concern for her versus his private beatings of her, his public allegiance to machismo and the defending of his honor versus his private interest in Jesusa's cultivation of the mind. This may be explained by the Mexican masks used to separate private from public. Octavio Paz engages readers in a review of the works of Ruiz de Alarcón and the colonial period to discuss authenticity and clarify the contemporary use of masks, gestures, and lies.[25] Masks, gestures, and lies, we note, are the tools that support disjunctures between public and private morality. But Jesusa is always one in the same. Her status as caregiver and nurturer since childhood endows her actions with a sense of the public.

For Jesusa, not only are the barriers removed between public and private but the fourth wall of the stage and/or temple altar is also missing. The audience and congregation (public sphere) are not separated from Jesusa (private sphere) by the wall of representation. She is precisely that person she appears to be and occasionally her unadorned figure holds sway in a fundamentally threatening way. Defiantly she refuses to become anything or anyone else. Significantly, in her theatrical representation of the apache dancer Jesusa is Jesusa. While the male dancer depicts emotions of pride, jealousy, and anger representative of male, French society, Jesusa curiously is herself, receiving blows and beatings for some unknown reason but rising to receive more because she could be herself and refuse to recognize the dichotomy of public and private. In comparison to Wilhelm Meister's theatrical mission in the prototypical Bildungsroman, Jesusa's succeeds because it is purely an extension of her and does not rely on representational divisions of the staging of public and private.

In truth, Jesusa does not understand the motives for the dichotomy of public and private. She cannot fathom why her husband would want her for a wife and then believe her unfaithful because another women claimed it to be true. She also cannot comprehend her husband's simultaneous distrust of and concern for her. When he is anxious for her to learn to interpret life through literature, she is baffled. She questions his motives, attributing his questions intended to spark her intellectual curiosity to boredom or tiredness:

Ya volvía él a leer y le inteligenteaba yo mucho muy bien, aunque le dijera disparates que se me venían a la cabeza, y es que él nunca me enseñó a platicar y de repente le dio por hacerme preguntas. El se ponía a leer, bueno, pues que leyera. Luego me preguntaba, pues seguro se aburría de estar hable y hable solo como loco, hable y hable fuerte, y yo allí, amoscada, nomás mirándolo, esperando a que me pidiera su café. Decía yo: "Bueno, pues que siga hablando." Pero lo que sea de cada quien sí leía bonito, o yo le entendía o sabe Dios, pero hay cosas que se me grabaron y que nunca se me van a olvidar (115).

[And he'd continue reading and I figured it out pretty good, even if I said whatever came into my head. The thing is, he never taught me how to talk, and then all of a sudden he decided to ask me questions. He'd start reading, and he probably got bored with talking to himself all the time like a crazy person, talking out loud, with me there real quiet, just watching him, waiting for him to ask for his coffee. But I do have to give him credit, he did read real nice, and I did understand what he read, because there are things that are engraved in my mind, and I'll never forget them (114).]

For Jesusa there is no division between reality and illusion, public and private. Her husband's need for domination (public) is incongruous with his desire for intimacy (private) within her realm of understanding. Her moral stance molds a behavior grounded in equality that reinforces her interconnectedness with the stages of her Bildung, within her relationships, and with public and private activities. If Pedro's moral stance is indefensible to her, she does come to appreciate what she can take from him to further her Bildung such as the lesson of the readings she will never forget.

Pedro is killed in battle with Jesusa at his side, and once again Jesusa ignores the divisions between public and private to take command of the troop, because the major is incapable of any coherent response to Pedro's death. Jesusa scolds the general who surrenders to the North Americans as if he were a child, ignoring the codes of rank, privilege, and address. She explains to him what she would have done to avoid her husband's death and the troop's capture. The general accepts what appears to be a willful crossing of boundaries between private and public and orders the command of her husband's troop to Jesusa because she has taken responsibility for it. Jesusa meets his offer with a refusal because she knows this to be one division the men would never respect. She returns the command to a male officer and travels to Mexico City where she finds herself one of many widows filling the Presidential Palace awaiting an audience with President Carranza to request their pensions. When it is her turn to speak to the President of the Republic, Jesusa again disregards government regulations, privileges, and protocol.

Jesusa purposefully transgresses the barriers between public and private to speak to the President as a common man, because he refuses to respect the rationality that supports what is just and right, declared in the public sphere and supported in private. That is to say, rationality indicates the support and defense of the widows of the Revolution. Jesusa's insistence that rule converge with reason lays claim to a private trust in the public basis for action. If the trust is broken, the public sphere refusing to pension the private after the loss of a spouse, the private must register distrust to protect the inseparable public and private (". . . es usted, más que grosero, ladrón, porque le quita el dinero a los muertos" (136) [. . . You're even ruder, worse than rude, you're a thief, because you steal from the dead" (136)]) and remove its support, leaving public service to return home.

The manner in which the separation between public and private most naturally collapses is in the observation of how society in general affects women in the private sphere. The mention of society as a whole gives the public sphere the moral imperative to invade the privacy of women. One example in this novel is the passage of women from the role of wife to widow, and the re-negotiation of a contractual or moral commitment to pension them. Since the care of the conjugal family had been removed from the private sphere in the nineteenth century, the expectations of care and support were assumed by the public as a form of recompense for the removal of labor and land from private wealth. But the concept of privacy, which leaves men alone to decide in which sphere an issue belongs, does not equally shield women who have their livelihood or support removed on the whim of a public official. Jesusa's audience with the President leads to the following rationality offered by the nation's leader: "Si estuvieras vieja, te pensionaba el gobierno, pero como estás muy joven no puedo dar orden de que te sigan pensionando. Cualquier día te vuelves a casar y el muerto no puede mantener al otro marido que tengas" (136) [If you were old, the government would give you a pension, but since you're young, I can't give the order for them to continue paying you. You could remarry and there's no reason for the dead man to support your new husband (136)]. The issue of one man supporting his wife and her new husband is redolent with concerns of cuckolding and abuse of male pride. It disregards the fact that the pension is a right or, at the very least, a privilege that has been fought for by women in public so that it might be handled respectfully in private. In other words, her dignity demands that it be kept a private issue while the concerns of the "society as a whole" force it into the public. But one does not have to look solely at the end of the relationship of Jesusa and Pedro to understand the collapse of public and private. The very reason why Jesusa and Pedro marry is a public concern. Jesusa is obliged to marry against her will because the Captain cannot guarantee her safety (freedom from abuse) to return home. He then consigns her as public chattel to Pedro (given to abuse) without having either the moral or legal obligation to do so, as he neither respects her right of eminent domain nor represents her father. For his part, Jesusa's father is capable of establishing or denying her existence through the evocation in the public sphere of a simple phrase "es mi hija" (61) [—My daughter (60)] or "no tienes para qué venirme a buscar porque tú no eres ni mi hija (56) [—There is no reason for you to come looking for me, because you are not my daughter (55)], making her visible or invisible at whim.

Although Jesusa would not recognize self-cultivation as a personal goal, it is a continuation of the process of Bildung begun much earlier in life. Her love of freedom and independence implies self-deprivation and hunger frequently, but she is her own guide and controls her fate in the public and private spheres. When her independence is threatened, she is free to leave and look for another path that will take her to the next level of her Bildung. Jesusa accepts all manner of work and performs the lowliest of tasks to the best of her ability. She accepts and performs well the jobs that require experience she does not have because her strength lies in her interconnectedness and her return to herself. Jesusa's honesty and openness work in both directions—requesting and accepting help/instruction when needed, and giving freely to anyone who asks. Her sense of equality knows no boundaries: Jesusa cares for stray animals, children, and disenfranchised adults alike, and with people she refuses to make distinctions. Two interesting and dissimilar elements of the pastiche of her Bildung reinforce her sense of equality. First, a man appears at the restaurant where she works and states he is in love with her but her response leaves her safely independent because even in love she demonstrates complete equality: "¿Y yo qué culpa tengo de que me quieras? Yo quiero a todo mundo sin distinción. Si te conviene, bueno, si no, salúdame a nunca vuelvas" (152) [—Is it my fault you love me? I love everyone the same way. If you can live with that, fine. If not, say goodbye and don't come back! (154)]. Second, the owner leaves the responsibility of running the restaurant to Jesusa in order to follow her husband during the Revolution. Jesusa performs the impressive task with such success, making money, raising salaries, and opening more businesses, that the owner begs her to continue in her position. Jesusa declines the offer, preferring freedom and equality to money, power, and responsibility/leadership.

Freedom is the impetus of Jesusa's Bildung process. Perhaps because her father was a free spirit who left one place for another whenever he tired of where he was, Jesusa desires that freedom, which to her signifies lack of responsibility. But because she is a woman, the freedom she seeks to propel her to the next stage of her Bildung is evasive and intangible. The reason behind this is that the collapse of public and private in her provides no respite from which to contemplate an exchange of duties and relief of responsibilities. Perhaps it is that life seems less complex if contemplated from the opposite perspective: "Para todas las mujeres sería mejor ser hombre, seguro, porque es más divertido, es uno más libre y nadie se burla de uno. En cambio de mujer, a ninguna edad la pueden respetar, porque si es muchacha se la vacilan y si es vieja la chotean, sirve de risión porque ya no sopla" (186) [It's better for all women to be men, for sure, because it's more fun, you're freer, and no one makes fun of you. A woman isn't respected at any age, because if you're a girl they tease you and if you're old they mock you, everything sags and you're the butt of jokes (191)]. Even though Jesusa recognizes that she did everything she wanted to as a young girl, she would have preferred to have been a man. She innately perceives that the division of the male staging of publicity between public and private facilitates his coming and going. The man is not obliged to give account of his actions in either sphere, because each sphere respects the power of the other. In contrast, women's lives do not distinguish those divisions. In effect, they mutually contaminate each other and women are accountable to everyone at all times in both spheres. Ironically, this is in contradiction to Jesusa's declaration: "Como a nadie le tengo que rendir cuentas, nomás me salgo y adiós" (238) ["Enough of this, I'm going to the capital" (236)]. But in reality, her interconnectedness leads to further responsibilities and emotional indebtedness. She takes in children off the street who respond to her kindness by stealing and leaving without notice. Nevertheless, she is incapable of chastising them for desiring to enter the public sphere when she is always grounded in both. The interdependence she creates empowers her and the others to develop a way of life out of marginality, but neither at the other's expense. In truth, she gives them the strength to be more like her, willful and fiercely independent. Jesusa's independent identity adds a moral dimension to life that breaks down the barriers between public and private.

The central metaphor for identity formation in *Hasta no verte* is the dialogue that ensues between public and private. The narrative strategy itself explodes the dichotomy giving voice to the most private, intimate details of one life in a very public forum; it is the voice of the disenfranchised pícaro attempting enfranchisement through the telling of her story. Jesusa does not simply mirror her own life, she gives voice to her Bildung process through her dialogue with the author, the reader, and those who are a part of her world both in this life and in others. Jesusa is very strong willed, "cosa que decido que nunca voy a volver a hacer, nunca la hago" (254) [If I decide not to do something ever again, I never do (249)] and is capable of giving up whatever may be harmful to her. Her will also balances her responsibility in the public and private spheres. In private she becomes "mother" to children she never bore out of responsibility to the public sphere: "A mí, los niños nunca me han gustado. Son muy latosos y muy malas gentes. A Periquito lo tuve no porque me gustara, pero ¿qué hacía ese escuincle sin madre y acostumbrado conmigo? ¿Qué hacía yo? ¿Lo echaba a la calle? Lo tenía que torear como si hubiera sido hijo mío, propio, muy propio . . . (280) [I've never liked kids. They're really annoying and mean. I had Periquito not because I liked him, but because he was a child without a mother. And he was already used to me. What could I do? Throw him out in the street? I had to fight with him like a bullfighter, just as if he were my child, my very own . . . (270)]. The child's mother makes a request of Jesusa that she take care of her children when she dies and Jesusa complies, taking more responsibility for them than the children's father. Jesusa's sense of responsibility ties her irremediably to the public sphere, performing acts of kindness and devotion that eluded her personally but come to represent her in private life: "Yo represento a su madre y soy de la obligación" (288) [I represent his mother and I have that responsibility, *my translation*] is her response to others who intend to undermine her authority as new mother. Her authority in public endures as long as the pact is maintained, but once Perico leaves, Jesusa feels no obligation to or sadness for him. The conduct of the father appears inexplicable after Perico's arrest because he advises Jesusa to look after her son. But Jesusa no longer recognizes her responsibility since Perico broke the pact and left her. The effectiveness of her devotion determines the extent of her responsibility as Jesusa deems it: "Pero no lo crié para que me durara toda la vida. Nomás hasta que se formara y se supiera defender" (312) [I didn't raise him so he would be with me my entire life. No, just until he grew up and knew how to defend himself, *my translation*]. The echoes between her relationship with her stepmother, who instilled in her survival skills, and the present relationship with her "stepson" are remarkable. Perhaps this is why Jesusa is able to shift between public and private with ease and, importantly, without guilt, which is a posture she personally believes only men are capable of sustaining.

Curiously, Jesusa displays neither masculine nor feminine character traits exclusively. She is rather a mixture of both as are we all, and it is for this reason, as Jean Franco advises, that Jesusa may not be representative of anyone in particular.[26] I would agree that Jesusa is not representative, but argue that her actions are gender-specific in that she advocates the equality of basic rights in the intimate sphere of the home as well as the public, political sphere without distinctions. This should not be confused with an act to deprivatize the private. Jesusa is uniformly and uniquely a private person who never wishes anyone to see her sick or to have to care for her in her old age. Her world is the objectification of a realm that is publicly and privately controlled. Her actions, then, are the actions of all women who, viewed as a social category, may or may not have the very same experiences as Jesusa but are driven by the same dominant social tendency. The tendency eradicates the dichotomy of public and private. Jesusa through her brazenness, intolerance, and true courage, permits a reading of *Hasta no verte* that demonstrates subtly that society could be other than it is. In fact, *Hasta no verte* should be read as the social critique that *La "Flor de Lis"*, Poniatowska's later novel, is.

The social context with which to explore Jesusa's Bildung process, therefore, is through the failure of Mexican society. The government's abusive relationship with the poor, stealing from and betraying them, creates a definition of Mexican society in Jesusa's mind that is grounded in economics. The definition develops an inseparable relationship between money and nationality: "Al fin de cuentas, yo no tengo patria. Soy como los húngaros: de ninguna parte. No me siento mexicana ni reconozco a los mexicanos. Aquí no existe más que pura conveniencia y puro interés. Si yo tuviera dinero y bienes, sería mexicana, pero como soy peor que la basura, pues no soy nada" (218) [After all, I really have no country. I'm like the Hungarians, the gypsies: not from anywhere. I don't feel Mexican nor do I identify with the Mexicans. If I had money and property, I'd be Mexican, but since I'm worse than garbage, I'm nothing (219)]. But she also criticizes the government's inability to educate, provide for, and inspire its people. Jesusa is openly critical of politics, religion, and popular myths of Mexican culture such as its popular revolutionary heroes.[27] Carlos Monsiváis emphasizes the role of hero in Mexican cultural consciousness concluding that even though the "contemporáneos" were able to situate Mexico within international or western development, the ties to national experience and the mythical structure of family and heroes did not fade.[28] Jesusa's critique of revolutionary heroes and social class warfare is nevertheless grounded significantly in the metaphor of hunger. It is within the moral domain of the rich and powerful to feed the poor who contribute to their power by working more than the value of their labor, but it is this moral imperative that the rich and powerful lack. Jesusa ultimately rejects the rotting and decayed food and work offered by her employers preferring hunger because it is her individual choice. She removes the power of fear over her that the rich might hold, because she selects hunger and freedom as an alternative to inhumane treatment. But Jesusa is also able to examine the situation from more universal viewpoints—she complains bitterly of *all* human weaknesses, those who cannot control their sexual appetites, desire for alcohol, or need for material goods.

The freedom that Jesusa exhibits is that she never claims to be representative. Rather, Jesusa is an agent for change between the patriarchal society of pre-revolutionary Mexico and the modern confusion of roles that is contemporary Mexico. To the degree that the Revolution and the family permeated each other, uprooting entire families in the service of a ruling charismatic figure or ideology by creating "soldaderas" who fought with or served the soldiers, the woman's role was changed forever in Mexico. Jesusa's strength of character molds her process of becoming perhaps more during her association with the Revolution than at any other point in her life, and is the reason she returns, if briefly, to the battle once more during her lifetime. But if she were to be representative of the soldaderas, she would have accepted the command of her husband's troop upon his death. Moreover, Jesusa's life is not meant to be exemplary. She is one of the countless marginalized members of society, expected to contribute their labor but willfully rejected by the same society that had vowed to support and pension them, and cast aside to survive as they see fit. In this case the new mother becomes the new hero, that is, an agent for social change, reinforcing the collapsing of public and private.[29]

Jesusa embodies the "radical loneliness of the subaltern classes,"[30] a loneliness that is occasionally but never completely assuaged by her father, husband, a friend, a child she takes in, or a stray animal. This view should not remove "subaltern" from its otherness, or as Patrick McGee concludes, "it means that the subaltern *as subaltern*—the subject of the oppressed constructed through the mirror of production—cannot really be thought outside the economy of the ethnocentric European subject. This latter is an imaginary construction like the ego (*moi*) which appropriates the other *as a whole self or identity* through its own reflection or image."[31] Jesusa as production views life, nevertheless, as a fusion of elements and opposites. Where others see an absence, such as an absence of sexuality, Jesusa sees a fusion of roles that is confusing but existent. She does not condone the weakness of the human spirit and is quite unforgiving in her descriptions of lesbians and, to a lesser degree, gay men, but she is compassionate in her interconnectedness in that she never turns her back on anyone. Her individuality is radicated in her humanity, the largest common denominator. Jesusa does not identify herself as Mexican, which she characteristically describes in economic rather than cultural terms. Neither does she identify herself through biological differences or categories of labor. But the actions of her humanity are gender specific and provocative. There is no moral to be drawn from the social, cultural, economic or philosophic tensions at work in Jesusa's life, but that is precisely what is at issue in the Bildungs-roman. Jesusa keeps herself open to more universal viewpoints of caring, spirituality, and survival in her Bildung process, never expecting cultivation to be a goal but becoming, nevertheless, "cultivated", after a fashion.

Jesusa's Bildung process is an outgrowth of her authority as a weaver of life's experiences and teller of life's tales. In reality, it matters very little if the entire narrative is rooted in verisimilitude. What matters is Jesusa's self-authorizing voice that empowers her self-actualization. Her authority in arranging her life story thrives on circumspection. She is concerned with individual activities and experiences but is open to observe what else is possible or necessary. She is cautious about her feelings for others and does not build her life experience around these attachments, an action that leaves her less vulnerable to pain and more open to other possible attachments. This approach reinforces a centrifugal force that reaches out and builds on relationships from the patriarchal conjugal family to the "extended" family of friends, spiritualist believers, co-workers, and companions in life.

Jesusa puts aside the notion of "perfect" Bildung as an ideal. Furthermore, perfect Bildung is an ideal that is central to the traditional Bildungsroman not to the novel of the marginalized. The traditional notion of the autonomous, rational, and unified self gives way to a critique by Jesusa of authority, truth, and self-presence. Jesusa, in this manner, "talks back" to the dominant culture, forcing her own story of hardship and resistance on the oppressor. Jesusa is free to criticize everything from education to immoral excesses, just as Diego Rivera satirizes false learning and the self-indulgence of the rich, to force others to see themselves as they are. *Hasta no verte* succeeds as a collaborative narrative because both Jesusa, the subject/hero, and Poniatowska, the interviewer/editor, negotiate the subject's responsibility for setting purposes and evolving the narration. The work becomes an intersubjective and transcultural project, which fixes the form of personal narrative to their own purposes without privileging one story over the other.[32] Jesusa negotiates the cultural and social discourses of Mexico as an agent of change by resisting and remaining independent. Significantly, her goal is not to have others imitate her person because she provides no model to emulate or plan to imitate. Rather, she embodies the need for change by means of a presence that is self-articulated, regardless of the diverse elements of her story.

One question that will always remain after reading *Hasta no verte*, is the issue of authority in the collaborative effort. The questions of to whom the authentic voice of the narrative belongs, and if there is a loss of agency implied in the co-optation of authorship, are successfully explored by Lucille Kerr and Debra Castillo in their critical studies on Spanish American literature. Castillo raises the disturbing spectre of the author as cultural translator who is on the outside observing and invoking however well-intentioned mistranslations and misapplications of theory.[33] The danger here is that Poniatowska as author and sympathetic listener could appropriate the stories of the marginalized and oppressed. In fact, when presented with the completed story the authentic narrator, Josefina Bórquez, who is replaced by the protagonist Jesusa, rebukes the author Poniatowska: "Usted inventa todo, son puras mentiras, no entendió nada, las cosas no son así"[34] [You invent everything, it's all lies, you didn't understand anything, that isn't the way things are]. But what Josefina does not comprehend are Poniatowska's assumptions about subjects and storytelling, that is, the narrative goal of communicating Jesusa's Bildung process as literary creation. This authorial intention is commented upon by Poniatowska in her "Testimonios". Poniatowska's intention is to give chapters and some sequence to Jesusa's story, and, I would argue, to make this more of a Bildung process than a biographical act. Nevertheless, author, critic, and reader do have the responsibility to be vigilant against what Gaytri Spivak calls appropriation and violation in the cultural translation from a colonial to a metropolitan context.[35] In truth, the fact that Poniatowska's "cultural translation" of Jesusa's life provides a forum for Jesusa to talk back to the dominant, colo-

nial culture, makes the politicization of this issue a further compli-
cation that is not easy to resolve.

The Bildung process facilitates Jesusa's talking back to the dominant culture in order to negotiate social and cultural contexts. Jesusa is an anti-nativistic creation—one that explodes the essence of
one absolute and essential identity for everyone. She perpetuates
a moral domain and philosophic sophistication that contradict her
oppressive upbringing and set her apart by rejecting the social, racial, and political divisions that colonialism imposes. Jesusa's role
as female hero is unique not because it locks itself into a play of
essential difference but rather because it pushes boundaries and enters both public and private, male and female worlds at once. In
other words, Jesusa insists on her voice and her identity to employ
the narrative for her purpose—social change through her perspective—achieved by a critique of social policy issues from one end of
the spectrum to the other. If she were in dialogue with Padre Teufel
in La "Flor de Lis", Jesusa might agree that social classes should
be abolished, but not biologically as he suggests, wherein women
would represent change by having children anywhere with whomever they please. Perhaps Jesusa would respond that women have
leveled the threshold between the staging of publicity and the revelation of private acts, because of the constraints that survival requires of them in both spheres, regardless of social class. In other
words, there's no place to hide and nothing to lose. But there is
everything to gain from the interconnectedness of social classes, the
public, and the private spheres.

The public sphere becomes the sphere for publicizing private
lives, and for women, regardless of social class, this has always
been true. Women objectify the need for a relativization of structural conflicts in the social context. This point is made subtly in
Hasta no verte. To the author's credit we only hear Jesusa's responsive voice of authority, and forget the questions posed by the inter-
viewer and sympathetic listener. The readers to whom the
commands are addressed at the end of the novel, are asked to focus
on the plight of this mestiza woman as a symbol of the millions
living in poverty, and work toward social change, but then to leave
the "hero" in peace: "Ahora ya no chingue. Váyase. Déjeme
dormir" (316) [Now fuck off! Go away and let me sleep (303)].
This is the voice of the woman who does not want to be a mythical
hero but, rather, an agent of change. Her cultural capital has been
reconverted, she has made the most of what she has, and is trying
to say something more and different.[36] Jesusa has placed readers on
their journey to personal development and Bildung. It is time for
the rest to begin the journey.

3

The Logic of Identity:
Self, National, and Cultural

ALTERNATIVE FORMS OF SELFHOOD INVERT, UNDERCUT, AND UNSETtle the message of identity in Spanish American literature owing to its culturally hybrid nature. This may be due to the complexity of the process of self-realization, which compares in intricacy to the formation of national (political, historical, regional) and cultural (linguistic, social, religious, ethnic) identities. In fact, each system of identity appears so relationally intertwined with the others that separate codes do not satisfy. With Bildung, the formed person turns her/his gaze toward something universal from which his/her own particular being is determined; hence, Bildung is raised to the universal. This could be understood as the other side of Socrates's pronouncement "know thyself," interpreted by Eric Auerbach as separate from the "real," in order to transcend the immediate and ultimately appreciate one's own culture in relation to the Other, and by Hans-Georg Gadamer as only through others do we gain true knowledge of ourselves. Essentially, the universal calls for an understanding of the viewpoints of possible others to achieve cultivated consciousness.[1] This means that through language, customs, and institutions one is able to seek one's own in the alien, return to oneself, and gain a sense of the self, a working consciousness. In accordance with gaining a sense of the self, the Spanish American Bildungsroman turns to formational and cultural identities to emphasize a narrative that ruptures boundaries and order. The strategy to be explored in this chapter suggests *who* can create themselves as self-actualized heroes through relationships that combine aspects of national character, self potentiality and cultural expression in search of social justice. This strategy grounds self, national, and cultural understanding in a quest for wholeness over uniformity.

Writing against the "master discourse" in a subversive manner often requires trying to identify the enigmatic "enemy". Pastiche and parody explore through anger and humor the demystification of a perplexing world dominated by global market economies and hegemonic cultures. Developing a historical consciousness relationally, the following four Bildungsromane to be examined in this chapter interweave personal and collective histories: *Oficio de ángel* (1988) by Miguel Barnet, *El paraíso* (1990) by Elena Casteda, *Conversación al sur* (1981) by Marta Traba, and *Abel Rodríguez y sus hermanos* (1981) by Ana Vásquez. The first and last explore male self-definition for the politically marginalized, and rely on political rituals and historical consciousness to forge identities. The other two novels examine the tensions and challenges inherent in transcending the self from the female, ethnic, religious or refugee perspective.

The strategies explored in this chapter suggest who can create themselves when impelled by an interaction of cultural voices. *Oficio de ángel* examines male self-definition, in addition to Cuban cultural and national identity through rites of passage including death, celebrations of life, education, and love. Collective and individual stories unite so that the narrative voice belongs to another, made strong by its obligations and responsibilities to others. Similarly, Ana Vásquez reveals the historical consciousness of the Chilean people in general, and a family of protagonists, in particular, through their social and psychological ills. Vásquez works toward a confrontation of the two groups so as to begin the process of reconstruction of national identity. The Bildungsroman of the marginalized relies on newly developed relationships of care as evidenced in the cultural patterning of two brothers.

Another Chilean example, *El paraíso*, reveals relationships that are socially, philosophically and politically charged. The web of relationships woven in this novel explores feminine, immigrant, socio-economic, and political identities. They determine a test of wills, courage, and inner strength, which require vigilance and adjustments to understand the other and benefit from the relationship without losing the self. The final example, *Conversación al sur*, explores the Southern Cone and relationships of the disenfranchised through dialogue and other forms of communication. In this final novel, Traba exposes the essential structure of relationships through a dialogic clashing of emotions. Traba's clever movement between public and private underscores the web of relationships that promote self-realization and encourage development in others.

Oficio de ángel (1988) and *Abel Rodríguez* (1981) are grounded in their familial relationships. Miguel Barnet creates in *Oficio de ángel* a superb character evolution (and parody of a manual for political edification) dominated by males of three generations. We know that Barnet adheres to the theory that a rescuing of history inspires literary creation. Consequently, Roberto González Echevarría wisely signals "conversion" as the theme and phenomenon that inspire and appear insistently in Cuban literature after 1959, including the works of Miguel Barnet.[2] The fast pace of political, historical, and economic changes the first years after the Revolution made the conversion of intellectuals and, more significantly, of all "non-believers," a political and moral imperative. Literature became a stimulating way to know the self through an examination of the other, and yet one more approach that reinforced key dogma. Significantly, both William Luis and Elzbieta Sklodowska offer politics as the impetus for Barnet's testimonial project. Luis underscores political expediency as governing the inclusion and exclusion of certain themes in Barnet's texts and Sklodowska focuses on Barnet's search for his own style of political commitment that permits him to cope with prevailing ideological demands.[3] If we can conceive of conversion as the dominant theme of Cuban literature of the 1960s and 1970s, the literature of the 1980s should reflect a slippage toward the evolving socio-political imperatives of a government struggling for economic survival. It is for this reason that I suggest a reading of *Oficio de ángel* in light of the late 1980s campaign in Cuba to "rectify errors and negative tendencies."

The "Rectification Program," which marked a government shift in development strategy, was a moral campaign to correct the trends toward mercantilism and economism. It represented a return to Marxist-Leninist principles and revived Che Guevara's philosophical ideas in that moral incentives, an expansion of the state's role in the economy, and collective and voluntary labor were put into practice. Susan Eckstein forcefully argues that the justification for this seemingly irrational policy shift at a time when open markets seemed the rule of the day (*glasnost* and *perestroika*), was the result of emergent government concerns, not primarily renewed ideological fervor. Ideology, it will be seen, can help legitimate policies driven by macro economic development that might seem risky politically without linkage to the core values that drew the people initially to its charismatic leader. The campaign centered on a clampdown on certain market features and profiteering.[4] In effect, it strove to minimize the loss of income and freedom many were destined to feel by reemphasizing the virtues of rising above self-interest and working for the common good.[5] "Rectification" and other experiments to shape human behavior failed, however, because they could not "convince" people to do otherwise than look out for themselves.

Viewing *Oficio de ángel* through the lens of the socio-economic policy of rectification permits a reading that proclaims the novel a testimony to revolutionary ideals. In effect, this is a subterfuge or aporia that seeks to reintroduce the revolution twenty years after the fact in an effort to revitalize and justify its foundational political principals. Furthermore, this novel may be read as a foundational Bildungsroman that links Spanish speaking communities in the Americas. That is, the cultural linkages among Havana, Tampa, New Orleans, New York, and Miami afford a view into a dialog that privileges collective urgency in conjunction with the upheaval of a master discourse. In addition, Barnet's work underscores the power of Latina literature in the United States, which will be discussed further in the final chapter. González Echevarría contends that Barnet's political sketches, like his observations of everyday life, are filled with reflections, memories, and feelings that fill in the interstices of a reality that is well known but not well comprehended.[6] His political sketches, I would add, lead to a powerfully subtle portrait of personal development and national identity that contradict and unsettle official portraits through the hint of an autobiographical working out of the self. Moving from the role of gestor (Barnet's term for author of documentary novels) of collective memory to an examination of self, Barnet concludes, "In this relationship between author and protagonist or researcher-informant one has to look for an unfolding [*desdoblamiento*], becoming the other by prying apart one's self."[7] The protagonist's features and motives frequently elude the reader because this is not a progressive march toward self-realization. On the contrary, in *Oficio de ángel* Barnet circles back to set the historical stage for the Cuban Revolution so as to provide economic, social and political evidence and justification for the revolt, the protagonist's politics, and perhaps his (the author's) own being-in-the-world. As history is the absolving force, it will also justify the push for and retreat from socialism that occasioned a program of "rectification." Furthermore, it will prove the moral need for a correction of course.

The protagonist in *Oficio de ángel* is indebted to rituals passed on to him by his father and grandfather that appear devoid of messages but are rich in meaning. From the beginning of the novel Proustian memories paint the portrait of a dreamlike childhood framed by the sea. In fact, the boy recalls that while he remembers his grandfather's voice, it is impossible to recall any of the stories he sat down to tell him. The grandfather, a figure of strength and order, reminds us of an earlier period after Cuban political independence at the end of the nineteenth century. The father, on the other hand, personifies the students who were able to play a decisive role in bringing down an initially popular president turned dictator, Gerardo Machado, in 1933. The father and grandfather's rituals that he is able to remember are lessons for respecting and forming the self in the image of God, one of the goals of the Bildung process: "Una noche, junto al cantero de florecillas rojas, mi abuelo— obligó a escuchar el mar. Años más tarde, presionando con sus grandes manazas sobre mis orejas, mi padre cumplía otro ritual similar. —Ahora verás a Dios"[8] [One night, next to the flowerbed with red blossoms, my grandfather compelled me to listen to the sea. Years later, pressing his great big hands over my ears, my father completed another similar ritual—Now you will see God].[9] The need to return to the self after raising the self to the universal is the working consciousness the boy must seek as exhorted by his father and grandfather. The male influence will permit him to confront his fears and an ambiguous attraction to the sea, and seek to create himself. The women in his life—tía Conchita, tía Agata, his other aunts and mother—on the other hand, will aid in facilitating the distinct cultural rites of passage (through which he will understand sexual impulses, learn to smoke, and appreciate material things). These experiences, however, will not hold the political symbolism imparted by the relationship with his father and grandfather. Men unite him to all that is nature and symbolically Cuban while women live for the foreign catalogues of a global economy that substitutes for nature. In effect, a male sense of order and justice permeates his memories of nation, the progenitors, and a dying race.

The goal of the father is to take his son to the beginning of his journey and away from the security of the family. He stands in defiance of the Batista period, which returns in 1952 after the general seizes power with military support from the United States. Economic conditions had improved in Cuba during the 1930s and 1940s owing to the opportunities for Cuban sugar as world production fell. But post-war economic opportunities were squandered by corruption, graft, mismanagement and miscalculation. Consequently, the effects of nearly a decade of corruption and scandal paved the way for the return of military rule with Batista in 1952.[10] But high rates of malnutrition, corruption, illiteracy, infant mortality, and repression were also hallmarks of the Batista regime. To put this in perspective, the need to purify the country is personified in and justified by an unlikely hero in *Oficio de ángel*, the protagonist's father. He serves as a mentor to aid in making judgments and supporting moral values: "Al subir hacia veintitrés y elegir un raro camino que le aleja de Paseo, mi padre se detiene un minuto. Sobre la calzada húmeda, un mar de gente con los ojos pegados y sombrillas negras sigue un cortejo fúnebre en cuyo centro va el escueto sarcáfago de un joven muerto en una reyerta con la policía. Es el primer mártir de la dictadura batistiana. El lento paso de la caravana hace reflexionar a mi padre, quien con irritación espeta unas malas palabras" (75) [Upon going up Twenty-third Street and choosing a block that takes him away from Paseo, my father stops the car a moment. On the wet road a sea of people with eyes tightly shut and black parasols follows a funeral procession in whose center is the plain coffin of a young man killed in a fight with the police. This is the first martyr of the Batista dictatorship. The slow movement of the caravan makes my father reflect on it, who with irritation spits out some bad words].

In addition to his father, the young man also forms casual relationships with other male/tutor figures that instruct him in the Bolshevik Revolution, the previous battles against the Dictator Machado, and life in the brothels of Havana. His uncle forces the protagonist into an apprenticeship of life as he interprets historical and cultural Havana on their Saturday excursions from bars to brothels, historical sites to the docks. In effect, the relationships formed by the young man are traditional, privileging, and even glorifying male relationships in an idealization of the goals of Revolution over the demoralized female characters. They are intended to justify the "future" revolutionary stance toward women. Ironically, one goal of the Cuban Revolution through the Family Code intended to present women with distinct, new possibilities and a more equal role in life. The results demonstrate, however, how difficult it is to legislate social and human development. It is obvious through Barnet's humorous descriptions that this is a man's world where machismo leaves its imprint from male privileges to female acquiescence. As is often the case, the female characters are confused as to who the true enemy is, blaming each other frequently, as seen in the relationship of la abuela, her daughters, and daughter-in-law.

Perhaps this confusion is attributable to the role of Bildungsroman in Spanish America addressed in the Introduction. The concept of Bildung is most powerfully exercised in cultures where there is a correlation between a high rate of infant and child mortality (in eighteenth- and nineteenth-century Europe and twentieth-century Latin America) and the desire to preserve childhood. Latin America, with the exception of Cuba, demonstrates as late as 1993 high rates of infant mortality (Table 1.1, in the Appendix and note 34 in the Introduction), which support portraits of childhood that preserve life and defy the finality of death. The rates in Cuba, on the other hand, drop from 38.4 deaths per 1,000 live births in first year of life in 1965 to 9.4 deaths per 1,000 live births in the first year of life in 1993 and 8.0 in 1996. This figure rates Cuba a number one ranking in Latin America and compares favorably to Western industrialized nations (see Tables 1.1 and 1.2 in the Appendix). On the other end of the spectrum in Cuba, life expectancy rises from 59 years of age in 1950 to 76 years of age in 1992. While life expectancy was already impressive by Latin American standards before the Revolution, in the early 1990s men tended to die younger in the United States than in Cuba.[11] These phenomenal measures of success in preventive health fields and medicine, coupled with innovative socialist theories of life that revolutionize gender roles, lead to unexpected results, however, in the social experiment.

Women in Cuba after the Revolution were encouraged to join the workforce as an underutilized group that could aid in the furthering of economic goals. The government, however, realized that moral suasion alone would not be enough to bring women permanently into the workforce (women's participation in the labor force barely increased in the 1960s), so with an emphasis on gender equality it developed a series of programs and fiscal commitments that facilitated women's participation. The 1976 Constitution codified the government's new concern with women's equal rights in marriage, employment, earnings, and education. An expansion of public day-care facilities, semi-boarding schools, maternity and child-care leaves, and the guaranteed support of a mate at home who was bound by the Family Code to share housework when the woman was gainfully employed, led, surprisingly, to a decline in fertility and henceforth a drop in birth rates in Cuba in the 1980s. Furthermore, readily accessible contraceptives and abortion services at low or no cost contributed to this result. That is, women chose and continue to choose to have fewer children. The "revolution within the revolution" and its success in advancing gender equality ultimately undermined the government's ability to count on future generations to generate the resources to finance the welfare state, even after women were driven from the workforce in the 1980s because of economic and political events.[12]

Given the Cuban example, the safeguarding of childhood and the Beautiful Soul becomes a tool for preservation, which also translates into an issue of choice promoted and propagandized by social justice in many Cuban Bildungsromane of this period. It affords the Cuban Bildungsroman the space to unite opposing forces and focus on collective action as participants in the larger struggles of all Cubans. Unlike those Latin American countries where health conditions made it difficult to assure the survival of all babies, Cuba after the Revolution could eliminate infant survival from the list of threats to national security, so it could concentrate, at least intellectually, on the quality of life of its society. I offer two theories to explain this counterindication that rely on gender and culture as mechanisms to respond to the fear of unchecked threats to society. The first is related to gender and the switching of power, however unintentionally, to Cuban women. Fearing economic pressures, an effort was made to assure future generations that could support the socialist state by giving women in the 1970s and 1980s, with the blessing of law if not religion, an enabling power to control their reproductive destinies. The "assurance" of survival was shared among all women, whereas before it had been the purview of the bourgeois household (e.g., the survival of the protagonist in *Oficio de ángel* and the death of Milagros's and Juan's son).

The second theory of difference demarcates Cuba's cultural differences based on race. Aline Helg argues that Cuba's social construct of race is remarkable in Latin America and the Caribbean because for almost one hundred years Cubans have perpetuated the mid-nineteenth-century notion of a *raza de color* (race of color) or *clase de color* (class of color) without differentiating mulattoes from blacks and have often referrred to both *pardos* (mulattoes) and *morenos* (blacks) as *negros* (black). Such classification differs from the three-tier or multitier racial systems prevailing in many countries of the region.[13] The fear of a racial class with counterideologies not held in check, of a revolt of Blacks similar to the Haitian Revolution, fueled the fear of an Afro-Cuban uprising and an Afro-Caribbean conspiracy to make Cuba a black republic, or one such as South Africa where Blacks rule. Related to this fear is the fear of African religions and culture, which Helg sees as beginning in the nineteenth century and continuing at least through the first half of the twentieth. I would argue this mistrust adheres to present-day thinking also. It was originally personified in caricature form of the black *brujo* (male witch) and the black *ñánigo* (member of a secret society of African origin). These caricatures conveyed the idea that Afro-Cuban culture was beholden to magic, witchcraft, criminality, and even anthropophagy. By implying that any white person, particularly small children, could be the victim of a brujo or a ñánigo, the caricatures stressed the threat that the latter represented to innocent human beings and to the institution of the family. It mobilized the general population against expressions of African culture. It brought the "black threat" into white Cuban homes.[14] The need for preservation in the Cuban case, therefore, is a backlash against culture and gender's potential to nullify the Beautiful Soul.

Oficio de ángel resolves in a complex fashion these issues of gender and culture. The unresolved tensions of this novel, a Bildungsroman that is also read as a documentary/testimonial, begin with the protagonist's choices in the making and molding of the self. The novel itself is grounded in the subterfuge that it is written in the late 1980s, a rectifying period of the revolution, but it portrays the prerevolutionary period, while the revolutionary slate was still clean. Another significant tension is located in the author's struggle to give voice and independence to the marginalized—women, laborers, and the working class—while never betraying the Cuban cultural balance or revolutionary ideals. This tension is grounded in determining for whom Barnet writes when forging a Cuban identity. While it is obvious that Barnet is working out his own being-in-the-world similar to the task he undertakes in *La sagrada familia*, his memories expose Cuban cultural inadequacies and social injustice. The protagonist's Bildung process reflects historical consciousness that begins in the nineteenth century and emphasizes the decades of the 1940s, 1950s and 1960s in its contextual reading but also the 1980s in its ideological, rectification drive. The question presents itself as the following—does Barnet's aesthetic representation unpack the goals of consciousness raising for the middle class, represented by the family of the protagonist, or does he claim to speak for the marginalized, women, and/or the dispossessed, a case in point being the servant Milagros and her husband Juan? The strategy of employing revolution and armed struggle as a metaphor for social change creates an important illusion of presentness and resolution in this cultural history, as distinguished by Roberto González Echevarría in his study of the documentary novel.[15] In *Oficio de ángel*, the triumph of the personal blends with the collective urgency of the present located in testimonial discourse. The increasing importance of the marginal figure in addition to the rejection of the master discourse privileges personal freedom over an oppressive external power in this relational Bildungsroman that is also testimony.[16]

As testimonial novel, Barnet underscores the urgency of a narrative that challenges the status quo from below. To this end he lends the voice of Milagros to the narration of a chapter of her own, rededicating a rhetorical device employed by Villaverde over a century earlier in *Cecilia Valdés*. In the latter novel the narrator's voice of whiteness cedes space to only one other voice, that of the black slave María de Regla. Milagros's chapter in *Oficio de ángel* mixes in and upsets social categories and human values ranging from the advice of a nosy neighbor who informs Milagros that she is being exploited by the boy's family, to the reasons for leaving her job out of fear of being sexually harassed by her boss, and her love for the young boy for whom she cares. It reveals a Euro-Hispanic power structure against which Milagros is seemingly powerless. The story of Milagros, while not as complete or powerful as the story of Esteban Montejo (which will be explored in chapter six), reinforces the tension behind the question of whose cultural identity the author is defining, especially given the fact this is another foundational Barnet narrative that privileges an Afro-Cuban voice.[17] Milagros's statement "Yo nunca fui otra cosa que una criada" (87)[I never was anything but a maid] reveals the contestatory power of the subaltern whose form of resistance against the dominant group is to leave her job after fifteen years. This seemingly innocuous behavior can have profound consequences for the shape of social order and can unravel the strategies of domination. In short, it is the context and the consequences that render certain actions contestatory, and these do not have to be dramatic or informed by conscious ideologies of opposition to seriously affect relations of domination.[18] James C. Scott contends that these everyday forms of resistance demonstrate that "the struggle between the rich and poor . . . is not merely a struggle over work, property rights, grain, and cash. It is also a struggle over the appropriation of symbols, a struggle over how the past and present should be understood and labeled, a struggle to identify causes and assess blame, a contentious effort to give partisan meaning to local history."[19] In fact, it can be an unexpected abandonment such as Milagros's action that sets the dominant/subaltern equation on its end in order to reinvent history. Barnet's purposeful preservation of Cuban history through a questioning of race and middle-class values, therefore, returns the reader to the values and organizing principles of a revolution gone astray.

In Cuba the integration of African and oriental strata into the historically Spanish culture is at once politically correct and without meaningful support. In essence, the fate of Afro-Cubans had not changed significantly since the War of Independence. Fought with a predominantly black army, the 1895–1898 independence war against Spain was led by the intellectual radical wing of the nascent Hispanic Cuban middle class. Its symbolic chief was José Martí, but when the United States intervened in the war, power within the independence movement shifted to the most reactionary sectors of the white creole bourgeoisie. It was this class that inherited command of the neocolonial republic. When the nationalistic black middle class formed its own political party (*Partido Independiente de Color*, or *PIC*) and rose in revolt in May 1912, several thousand Afro-Cubans were massacred and lynched throughout the island in the biggest blood-letting in centuries. After 1912, radical middle-class Blacks aligned themselves with the politics and ideology of the Communist party, but Black Cuba's efforts were brought to a halt when Batista took control in 1952. A blanket of silence has covered race issues since the massacre of 1912,[20] and determines racial relations in Cuba to the present. It was Castro's ideal when coming to power to rally everyone's support by frowning on racial segregation even while tacitly condoning white supremacy. After openly discussing race on separate occasions, however, Castro discovered it more politically expedient to remain silent on the issue so as not to offend the many power bases whose support he needed. Hence, a push for intellectuals to explore the history of blackness in Cuba and to understand its anthropological and social values without emphasizing its political content as empowering.

But the enemy is also enigmatic for the Cuban middle class—it is evil personified in dictators such as Machado and Batista, and the U.S. cultural invasion that puts pressure on the Cuban, cultural balance. The consciousness-raising of the middle class in *Oficio de ángel*, therefore, is not only social and political but also cultural in its fight against U.S.-inspired imperialism and globalization. After all, it is a nationalistic white bourgeois elite in Cuba that will eventually impose its revolutionary philosophy upon the Cuban people, an ideology and a strategy that leads to Marxism and a Soviet alliance.[21] This middle class consciousness raising must fight off the desire for sleds and Santa Claus in tropical Cuba, and air conditioning so frigid as to make the return to the "natural" climate impossible, unpleasant, or unhealthy.[22] It also rebels against the invasion of the English language and new Christian sects, and must look the other way when the government exempts itself from rectification, punishing entrepreneurial endeavors while aggressively pursuing Western economic ties. The blending of Bildungsroman with testimony through a strategy to define who can declare themselves self-actualized heroes, explores the identity of a class whose goal is social justice and collective victory grounded in historical consciousness.

In *Oficio de ángel*, the boy's political awakening is concurrent with that of the father's. An awakening, sexual or political, is an action taken in response to stimuli, and reflects an important rite of passage in the developmental process: "El grito de un torturado es como el aullido de un ángel. Yo siento rabia y deseos de apretarles el pescuezo a esos salvajes. Para Ana y Michel es el recuerdo de la guerra y para mis padres el del Machado. Para mí todo eso es nuevo. Siento un asco terrible y ganas de salir a vengar la muerte de tantas víctimas" (134) [The scream of someone tortured is like the wail of an angel. I am angry and feel like strangling those savages. For Ana and Michel it is the memory of the war and for my parents the Machado period. For me everything is new. I feel terribly disgusted and want to go out and avenge the death of so many victims]. As a symbol of his rebellion against the enemy, the protagonist's father, Richard, decides to hide Milagros's husband Juan from the police. This act endangers his own life, but Richard accepts the challenge of rising above self-interest to search for himself in more universal viewpoints. The act of solidarity renews Richard's sense of self: "Era presa de una mezcla de pavor y orgullo. Primera vez que hacía algo heroico" (138) [He was filled with a mixture of terror and pride. It was the first time that he was doing something heroic]. Richard's first act of historical and working consciousness is guided by his relationship with Juan, who initiates the contact and suggests the commitment. This notwithstanding, the act redeems and advances Richard's movement toward self-cultivation. The son, in turn, gives up attending classes at the University and commits himself politically to the cause by aiding a friend, Omar, who symbolizes the revolutionary movement and Cuba in its potentiality. After Richard's arrest and subsequent exile to Miami, the son turns to the Revolution as the only hope—revolution as salvation.

Father and son possess cultural maturity and are able to separate themselves from the familiar to understand themselves in the alien. In Miami, Richard begins to understand the need for the armed struggle. The protagonist carries on in the father's place, aiding the cause clandestinely even as he watches his closest friends die. The father as tutor takes his son figuratively to the place where the journey begins, but then the son must rebel against the father and establish new relationships in his process of individualization: "Felicidades papá. En vista de su ausencia prefería ser lacónico. Otro mensaje no podía articular. La distancia nos borraba toda posible comunicación" (205) [Congratulations, Dad. In view of his absence I preferred to be laconic. I could not articulate any other message. Distance was erasing any possible communication between us]. In order to further reject the father, the son performs a conscious act as developmental impulse to forget the father's face. Not until the protagonist is sent into hiding, a form of interior exile that underscores the autobiographical nature of this novel, is he able to return to the values of the father and forgive him completely upon his return. Ultimately, the protagonist reaffirms his values through the Revolution, learning to consider every act as if it were his last. He finally attains the historical and working consciousness he seeks as he desires to leave the particular and see life and the Cuban collective through universal viewpoints. His Bildung process parallels the founding of a "free" nation in his eyes: "En mis ojos cabe ahora mismo la historia del país. Soy depositario de su imagen" (292) [In my eyes you will find the history of my country. I am the trustee of its image]. The narrative, a pastiche of memories, styles, literature, sports, commercials for the newest products, and radio and television programs, is a cultural market that reflects the roots of Independent Cuba in the nineteenth century and its penetration into the twentieth. The cultural and national identity of Cuba also passes through developmental stages of life, death, and celebration that compete with those of the protagonist's self realization through education, love, acceptance and rejection of the parent's and society's values. The protagonist's memories mix in opposites not privileging one over the other. If he could, he says with the voice of a child, he would choose nature (Cuba/male values) and grow trees in his house, and reject materialism (the system of globalization through the market economies he critiques/female values). Seeking at another level to transform memory into imagination, this liberation enables the young man to realize that he carries within him from childhood the core of that which he will be. His ability to move beyond the natural and understand the other, be it through his readings or his relationship with Milagros or Omar, projects the protagonist's being-in-the-world. Collective and individual stories unite so that the narrative voice belongs to another, made strong by its obligations and responsibilities to others. The protagonist through a relational Bildung process becomes a self-actualized hero, as do, ultimately, the collective, Cuban people. In effect, the Revolution annuls all possibility of forgetting; an intellectual commitment demands, even of Miguel Barnet, growth, molding, and an adjustment to its evolving needs.

Ana Vásquez, author of *Abel Rodríguez y sus hermanos* (1981), is a Chilean psychologist living in exile since the Pinochet dictatorship. Vásquez specializes in relationships—the relationship of the self to self-identity, of children to exiled parents, and of those tortured to those left behind. Memory plays an important role in the developmental relationship because it determines whether one is ready to move beyond the previous level and view the Bildung process as incorporating all aspects of life. The title of this novel by Vásquez suggests a biblical, sibling relationship that as rivalry is destructive. The author reveals the historical consciousness of the Chilean people through their social and psychological ills, made real through images of destruction, torture, and death. While there are three brothers in the novel—Abel, el Cachorro, and Ramón— the relationship between Abel and Ramón is striking in its echoes of sibling rivalry but also in its symbolism of a country divided against itself, and between the haves and have-nots.

Ana Vásquez works toward a confrontation of the opposing groups so as to begin the process of reconstructing national identity. Because Vásquez is so much a part of the Chilean historical experience, being an author/psychologist who for political reasons seeks exile in France, she produces a narrative that rejects the socio-economic framework of power, in order to secure a new model. That is, the author speaks neither in favor of nor against capitalist interests (the threatened middle class of Chile), in favor of nor against social revolution (the working-class and poor), but points, rather, to the innate potential of relationships. In fact, each central character curiously appears to contain elements of the opposing groups: Abel sympathizes with the cause of the Left but follows a destructive, bourgeois lifestyle abusing alcohol and relationships. Furthermore, he takes on the purely middle-class obligation of running the family business, a gas station/service center whose practicality clashes with the aesthetic freedom needed to produce his art. The father's role is also paradoxical in that, on the one hand, his personal objective is economic independence in the free market system through his Esso station (the precursor to Exxon), while on the other, he is politically affiliated with the communist party. Ramón, the brother who betrays Abel, is also conflicted because he imitates bourgeois values on the one hand, which are foreign to the values of the family whose approval he seeks, and despises his wife, on the other, for obliging him to take on a powerless economic role in the family structure in order to secure the material things she wants. In effect, no one wins because in order to defend the transnational economic structure represented by a Chilean family running an Esso station, limits must be imposed. Curiously, these limits are visible only when the structure is threatened. Such threats to the structure involve workers who demand equal rights, or international corporations that write contracts benefiting only themselves. James Romano refers to this destabilizing arrangement in Chile as a "maintenance mechanism", which, while purported to be a doctrine of national security, becomes, in reality, a doctrine of national insecurity.[23] The concept of national insecurity can be understood through the analysis of sociologist Tomás Moulian: whereas national security allies with the fascist policy of defense of the national markets through intervention, national insecurity is the result of trying to insert the country into the current of globalization in a world market regardless of the interests of the nation-state. Moulian pursues this logic referencing an example of the Chilean dictatorship: "Fue, sin duda, una dictadura terrorista. Pero no fue fascista, porque la inserción en el mercado mundial tenía prioridad sobre la defensa del capitalismo *nacional*. Ella fue profundamente apátrida frente el gran signo universal de la época, el dinero[24] [It was, without doubt, a terrorist dictatorship. But it was not fascist, because the insertion into the world market held priority over the defense of national capitalism. It was profoundly a-national with respect to the great universal symbol of the times, money, *my translation*]. The limits imposed from the outside are not only of the "made in the USA" variety but also those of multinational corporations in a system of globalization and free markets that erases cultural and national boundaries.

The economic market relationships as well as the cultural, familial relationships, speak of outside pressure brought to bear on the developmental process of identity—self, national, and cultural in *Abel Rodríguez y sus hermanos*. The author navigates these competing interests while putting into question the identity of hero and enemy in the Chilean historical consciousness. While *Oficio de ángel* integrates individual memory and collective conscience through supporting cultural documentation on literature, style, economic markets, and so forth, *Abel Rodríguez y sus hermanos* does not alternate nor integrate cultural voices or levels.[25] The goal is not to defeat one enemy, be it Ramón, Esso (globalization), or the Captain. Rather, the goal is to understand the self in relation to the Other for preservation of the Beautiful Soul (literature as catharsis) and enactment of a more just society. Vásquez's experiments with the developmental process in the novel are characterized by ambiguities, that hidden form that guides one through a labyrinth of undefined desires. Once defined it gives identity to the individual/hero and connects her/him to the world. It is within the pre-definition or process rather than in the result that Vásquez works her narrative experiments, which present her characters "como protagonistas y como víctimas de un determinado proceso histórico" [like protagonists and victims of a determined historical process[26]].

The relationship between Abel and el Cachorro, brothers united by leftist tendencies and their desire for social justice, remains strong even when Abel drifts away from politics. Abel's relationship with Ramón, however, is more complicated. Ramón, a former student in the School of Aviation, commands respect from others owing to this relationship: "Las Fuerzas Armadas representan el honor de Chile: el orden, la disciplina"[27] [The Armed Forces represent the honor of Chile: order, discipline], but not from his own family, including, ultimately, his wife and son. Contrary to popular belief, the order and discipline he displays in school are not lessons of lifelong learning and do not aid him developmentally in the Bildung process. In effect, they do not help him overcome his personal and economic failures after leaving his studies to marry la Betty.

As occurs in many uneven relationships and dysfunctional families, Ramón always feels inferior to Abel and jealous of Abel's easy relationship with the family and la Gringa, Ramón's ex-girlfriend. But it is not enough that the father prefers Ramón's seriousness and sense of responsibility over Abel's bohemian life. Ramón consistently frustrates both his parents by mismanaging the funds of the Service Center and demanding a bourgeois lifestyle that is beyond their means. Ramón speaks of being bored by Abel's endless stories and Abel's insistence on treating him like a child, but there is an underlying tension and paranoia that suggests that he rejects Abel to avoid being rejected himself: "Pobre Abel, yo no quería rechazarlo. Después de un tiempo él también evitaba conversar conmigo y en el taller acabé hablando sólo lo estrictamente necesario con mi familia. Yo pensaba que la mamá y Abel se juntaban a hablar de mí cuando yo no estaba. Les tenía desconfianza, serían los últimos a quien les podría pedir un consejo" (77) [Poor Abel, I did not want to reject him. After a while he also avoided talking to me and in the shop I wound up speaking about only that which was strictly necessary with my family. I thought that Mama and Abel were getting together to talk about me when I was not around. I did not trust them, and they would be the last ones I would turn to for advice]. If la Betty's petit bourgeois aspirations are incomprehensible to Ramón, they are at least reaffirming because she has selected him to accompany her in her world. What he cannot comprehend is Abel's squandering of his intellect and talents on a cause that will not advance him socially or monetarily. Abel, for his part, believes in the value of a commitment to goals of righteousness and compassion, and is therefore incapable of believing his brother to be a traitor to the family, the cause, or social justice.

When informed of his brother Ramón's connections to the intelligence wing of the Air Force, Abel cannot comprehend the significance. He worries, rather, about what has happened to Ramón, who was taken prisoner with him. He also worries about not going crazy and being brave enough to withstand the pain of torture, and finally he worries about not betraying his family: "Se aferraba a su barreta y aun con los correntazos de la picana no lograron que se contradijera. Y Ramón ¿dónde estaba? ¿Qué le habían hecho? Aunque no recordaba nada, estaba seguro de que no había dado a los compañeros del Cachorro. Cuando hacía un esfuerzo por evitar una idea, la obsesión de la locura lo invadía todo. Se estaba volviendo loco, los torturadores lo dejarían encerrado hasta que ya no supiera nada de nada" (134–35) [He was holding on and even with the large jolts of electricity they could not get him to contradict what he had said earlier. And Ramón, where was he? What had they done to him? Although he did not remember anything, he was sure that he had not given them the names of Cachorro's companions. When he made an effort to avoid an idea, the obsession of craziness invaded his whole being. He was going crazy, the torturers would leave him locked up until he did not remember anything about anything]. In extreme cases like these, one understands the process of self-transcendence, how one can become the self beyond the self, or conversely, how one confirms his/her worst fears of inadequacy and weakness. To Abel, his desire to give value to his existence encourages him to make himself into a protagonist and victim of history.

When faced with the evidence of Ramón's betrayal, Abel still refuses to believe that his brother could also have been a protagonist and victim of history: "Podría tal vez aceptar que Ramón, en un estallido de rabia, después de una de las innumerables discusiones a gritos, lo amenazara, incluso lo denunciara en un momento de ira, pero esa declaración premeditada, en frío, le parecía imposible. Ramón no podía haberlo hecho. El Capitán estaba bluffeando para quebrarlo . . . Tenía que ser una trampa, no podía ser cierto" (147) [He could perhaps accept that Ramón, in a burst of anger, after one of their innumerable shouting matches, would threaten him or even denounce him in a moment of anger, but that premeditated denunciation, in cold blood, seemed impossible to him. Ramón could not have done it. The Captain was bluffing in order to break him . . . It had to be a trap, it could not be true]. Ramón had always been jealous of Abel's relationship with the family, and their mother in particular, who appeared to prefer Abel over Ramón. When El Cachorro turns up at the Service Center frequently, Ramón's paranoia leads him to think that his brothers are plotting to betray him and force him out of the family business. It becomes evident, however, that without each other's influence, Abel and Ramón could not have developed and become independent of the forces of society, politics, economic markets, and style that intended to rule them. Ramón needed to save the family business and learn to return to himself after finding universal viewpoints from which to view the world. Ultimately, Ramón's Bildung is perfected in a movement of alienation and appropriation, in which to master the situation and view it as selflessly as possible he has become independent of everyone, getting beyond his naturalness. In order to accomplish this, he rejects loyalty to the capitalist values and communist ideology of his father, the leftist leanings of his brothers, the fascist ideals of his son, and the bourgeois values of his social-climbing wife, and seeks refuge in a world of mental instability of his own making.

Abel also tries to see reality through more universal viewpoints, to understand Ramón's needs and motivations, and comprehend the father's capitalist values of stability, order, and honest work. The values they acquire do not permit either brother to continue life in its previous stages. That is, their development has taken them to the point where everything in their life that has formed them, particularly in relation to each other, has released them from the object of desire. Ramón had desired money and approval, and, after betraying Abel, suffers a nervous breakdown for which electric shock is applied in order to lead him back to himself. Abel, who, ironically, had had very little training as a militant, establishes his own code of ethics that he will not betray. After numerous tortures during which electric shock also is applied to bring him back to himself and the truth, Abel could have told the truth without fear of retaliation for himself and his companions, but chooses not to do so.

Ultimately, Abel chooses a hero's end that underscores the narrative's complex questioning of values and call for a new social order, for which no clear suggestions are made. The experience of self with other is fully explored in the cultural patterning of the story of the two brothers. Similar to the female Bildungsroman, the Bildungsroman of the marginalized relies on newly developed relationships of care. In *Abel Rodríguez y sus hermanos* the relationship of care is characterized by how one brother is responsible to and for the other. The choices made and alternative forms of development and maturity sought, lead to a complex rewriting of the social text. In the end Abel's daughter symbolizes the fusion and fission of power in her person by planting, in an act of revenge, the bomb that destroys the Service Center. This act signifies the explosion of hierarchies created by a patriarchal system to which the men of the narrative belong, in order to make way for a new order of social justice.[28]

The relationships explored in *El paraíso* (1990) by Elena Castedo are socially, philosophically, and politically charged. Although not identified, the country the Chilean novelist appears to be describing is Chile, with a particular fascination for the summer estates of the Chilean elite. The family of Solita, the protagonist, are refugees from Spain who are exiled for political reasons. Solita is the object of racist and class conscious "attacks" in "el paraíso," the name given by her mother to her friend's country estate. Solita's father, a union organizer and socialist, is not accepted for his physical appearance, deformities, leftist ideas, and lower class comportment. *El paraíso*, therefore, is a subtle, nuanced narrative of modes of cultural interpretation, where nothing is at it appears.

As a Bildungsroman, *El paraíso* rests on cultural differences because the link between the self and the other depends on differences. Solita's relational web is anchored by her mother's projects in the capital. That is, Solita aids in her brother's care and in the preparation of food for the family in order to feel a bond with her mother who is busy with other projects. But in *El Topacio* (el paraíso) the mother's projects are incomprehensible to the child and create a breach in relations between them. The relationship Solita is obliged to develop successfully by her mother is with the daughters of the owner of the country estate. This relationship with the Other is a test of wills, courage, and inner strength, which requires constant vigilance and adjustments so as to understand the other and benefit from the relationship without losing the self.

Unlike the traditional male narrative that is grounded in actions that propel the hero forward and compel the reader to simply question when the advancement will take place, the female and disenfranchised heroes must create themselves through a seemingly benign weaving of relationships toward a new reality. "El paraíso" is a site that constructs an invisible reality for women in order to break down the patriarchal system. Witness the absence of male figures of authority. It employs socio-economic hierarchies but only in defense of guaranteeing a woman's future. It is neither revolution nor complete submission but we should not expect either. That is, as Sumit Sarkar states, "What one needs to keep in mind is a vast and complex continuum of intermediate attitudes of which total subordination and open revolt are only the extreme poles."[29] It is a way of fighting the boredom of subservience and everyday, domestic life even for rich and important women. Through a close reading of the text, a social and cultural critique appears of a country long recognized, ironically, for its equal treatment of women and "inexistent xenophobia."[30] In *El paraíso* Solita compiles through her relationship with her mother, Tía Mercé, the owner, and her daughters, cultural discourses regarding the "feminine" and the regulation of class in a society governed by materialistic and nationalistic values.

Coming to terms with one's personal limitations is never easy, but for Solita it is especially difficult since the owner of El Topacio, her guests, and particularly her three daughters, Patricia, Graciela, and Gloria, reinforce class restrictions. The girls who declare themselves superior in everything make it clear, through their efforts to manipulate Solita in a series of master/slave games, that everything belongs to them and that Solita owns nothing but the imposed role of subaltern. Solita's Bildung process as an accumulation of all previous experience rests on a reversal of the traditional movement from country to city by taking her from the capital to the countryside. This reversal of directions, and in her mind, fortune, adds an air of sophisticated irony to Solita's declarations. Solita notices the more democratic nature of life in the city from the perspective of a child, noting that in the city you have independence and may play with others only when you want while at the country estate everything is done in groups. She learns quickly she cannot refuse to play with the girls who control all the elements of the game. Solita learns to identify with her difference, that is, her status as refugee even though her mother seeks to place that status strictly in the past. Solita finds her self worth linked inexorably to a process of becoming that incorporates her past. "En Galmeda nadie esperaba que hicieras lo que no podías hacer. Los refugiados no estaban a la altura de los del país, pero no se encontraban por debajo de nadie. En el Topacio, aunque no fueras refugiado, estabas bajo otros, lo que era odioso"[31] [In Galmeda people didn't expect you to do what you couldn't. Refugees weren't as good as other people, but they weren't *under* anybody. Being under others was hateful].[32] Solita's attention to details of social rank or mobility contradicts the promise of utopia in the New World, and destroys any universal notions of equality. It obliges her to see that neither the ideology of her mother or father is seamless in that there will always be voices disputing the dominant view.

Clearly, one of the most resonant voices is Solita's own, rendered more effective because of its childlike innocence. What is so striking about the novel is that it demonstrates an open-ended dialogue between Solita and the dominant views she interrogates. These are the voices of the subtext that we hear above the exchange of platitudes and pleasantries. The hierarchy of el Topacio governed by Tía Mercé and her daughters, owing to an ironic absence of male members of the family, joined by exotic guests and refugees, and grounded by an underclass of servants manipulated by the hostess,

provides the social conflict and uncertainty against which to measure one's process of growing up. Solita is despised by the nannies,
who complain of the extra work and participate in a filtering-up
technique of social belittlement, since as refugees the family members represent interlopers in a society that maids and nannies can
only hope to serve. Solita finds herself without a guide to aid her
through the treacherous turns in her Bildung process: "De modo
que me encontraba en un mar lleno de rocas ocultas y vorágines
inesperadas. Y sin piloto . . . Había que pensar mucho, para ayudar
a que las cosas sucedieran como debían ser" (87) [There I was, in
a sea full of hidden rocks and unexpected vortexes without a pilot
. . . you had to work harder, you had to *plan* for things to happen
(73)]. Of course, this thought process is one that will lead Solita
from one level of the Bildung process to another, surviving and sur-
passing one rite of passage after another.

One specific model to be changed in a new order is the feminine
model. The issue of the feminine appears to be the territory of Solita's mother who trades on the feminine to guarantee an acceptable
identity. She holds illogical and at times class-specific notions
about women, and about girls becoming women. This explains the
competing ideologies of being feminine that are available to Solita
from women, girls, and occasionally, men, in the novel. Her mother
reminds her of the benefits of being a well-mannered girl who does
not offend her hostesses and does what she has to in order to accomplish this goal even if it means risking her life on a runaway
horse. The unexpected heroics of Solita prompted by her mother's
lesson on being a proper young lady and guest translate, in Solita's
words, into a primer on how to grow up properly female: "Si no
tenías otra cosa, lo que había que hacer en las grandes casas de
campo era ser valiente. Todo el mundo hablaba de mí, era una gloria" (140) [In Country Estates the thing to do was to be brave. All
the grown-ups talked about me. It was glorious (118)]. But this information has to be measured against the price to be paid for appearing feminine: her father's admonition for the gaudy, hand-me-
down dress and gloves she is wearing to welcome him, Mlle.
Vicky's desire that the girls at the country estate dance the role of
princesses, and Tía Mercé's interest that the girls speak French.
Clearly the most disconcerting lesson for Solita about the feminine
appears at the conclusion of the novel. Her mother Pilar's examples
of femininity, her artifice, posturing, preening, examples of grace,
witticisms, and recitations of poetry form a strategy to capture the
fancy of a wealthy guest who would marry her and assure their future.

The issue of gender is experienced in this novel as a social but not a biological category. Through a reading of Foucault, Judith Butler arrives at the conclusion that cultural values are inscribed on the body and in order for this inscription to signify, the medium or body must be destroyed, because "gender is a complexity whose totality is permanently deferred, never fully what it is at any given juncture in time."[33] The final passage we witness in the novel is Solita's thrust into adulthood, to pursue her own model of the feminine, which is different from the one her mother pursues. After being told that there will be no room for her father in their lives owing to his selfish pursuit of labor issues and younger women, and that they would go to live in the city in tío Armando's mansion, Solita gives in to a scene of tears and sobs to which Pilar counters: "Me decepcionas, profundamente; no puedo creer que puedas ser tan egoísta, tan ingrata, tan falta de consideración por tu hermano, por mí y por tu futuro . . . después de todo lo que he hecho por ti; después de tanto trabajo . . ." (380) [I am deeply embarrassed at you. I can't believe you can be so selfish, so ungrateful, so lacking in consideration for your brother, for me, for your future . . . after all I've done for you, all the sacrifices . . . (326)]. The diversions from and definitions of happiness that concern some women do not pertain to all women—that is, the rewards of the mother are not the rewards of the daughter. For Solita the totality of gender is permanently deferred. But it goes even deeper than this. While the mother's posturing may appear deceptive and immoral, akin to a form of prostitution, "the sacrifices" to which she alludes are real. In effect, she chooses to opt out of an existing lifestyle and substitute it with a distinctively different one. This is a muted form of protest but one that is real nevertheless. Veena Talwar Oldenburg recognizes this form of protest and I would paraphrase her study of the courtesans of Lucknow to read the rebellion of women against patriarchy:

> It is futile to use conventional analytical tools and look for a full-blown 'class struggle' or a women's movement in progress. One does not use a hammer to prune a rose bush. Their struggle obviously cannot be a collective, revolutionary 'class struggle', for the gender divisions are vertical, not horizontal, and cut through class lines. The validity of their struggle cannot be refuted on the grounds that it is engaged in a private, unobtrusive level. Their will to resist existing gender relations and reproduce the radically reordered social relations within their ambit is as self-conscious and intractable as it is undeniable."[34]

Whether we adhere to the philosophy of the mother or not, we cannot deny these small, everyday forms of resistance that attempt to tip the balance of power in her favor.

Solita reveals confidence and anxieties about becoming and maturing as a female, but significantly, she is not limited to the prevalent code or binary opposition of gender. She will come to represent a third dimension of symbolic order in Lacanian analysis as examined by Marjorie Garber. The third element is a mode of articulation, a way of describing a space of possibility. Three calls into question the idea of one, of identity, self-sufficiency, self-knowledge. The third dimension or symbolic order in Lacanian psychoanalysis, is the register of language, hierarchy, law, and power to which the hero/protagonist must come to relate through immersion in the codes and constraints of culture. Solita will come to understand her power to develop and form herself through the cultural constraints of her mother's well-bred Castilian views and her father's role as "exception refugee" who is accepted for his intelligence but not his physical appearance or working class ideals. She is formed in the subtler discourses of power through her relationship with the daughters of the estate's owner, and realizes that to her surprise, she and the girls had been fighting for the same objectives, even if it had been for different reasons. She is quick to appreciate the value of her opponents and recognize that "algunas veces los enemigos podían trabajar juntos" (378) [sometimes enemies could work together (324)]. Ultimately, this register of admiration for her opponents and her newly adopted country releases her from her past status of refugee into a relationship with the new world, a world more vibrant, and hopefully more just than the one her mother would know.

The relationship established in *Conversación al sur* (1981) [*Mothers and Shadows*] by Marta Traba, is through dialogue, informal conversation, and other forms of communication. The narrative weaves elements of terror and disappearance through Uruguay, Argentina, and Chile, in a channel of communication that is outside language and inside historical time.[35] The title signals the historical and symbolic importance placed by the author on engagement as a means to reclaim the experience of the marginalized. The goal of the oppressive military regime (the patriarchal society) is to wrest power and voice from the oppressed (the marginalized), whose primary strength is found in relationships—the controlling of symbols through conversation and mutual consent. In contrast to *Abel Rodríguez y sus hermanos*, where the marginalized brothers fight for identity against the authoritarian discourse of economic and political power, which they coincidentally are a part of and seek to manipulate, Dolores and Irene fight for identity against a patriarchal system that had never admitted them into the natural order. The authoritarian desire to control women socially, physically (reproductively), and culturally is countered by the author's goal of illuminating the female experience as a signifying process of growth and development. In this relatively short, brilliant novel, the last published before her death, Traba exposes the essential structure of relationships through a dialogic clashing of emotions including love, desire, and fear. As the self seeks to emerge into the symbolic, it demands that the space of identity be readjusted to admit women and the marginalized. The self-realization process of Dolores and Irene maps an exchange of ideas that affords them the strength to seek survival and self-transcendence. And, curiously, their survival is ambivalently sought by the patriarchal system because without the marginalized the self-identity of authority is also threatened.

Dolores and Irene fight to control their own meaning in a time in their lives when they are struggling with questions of self-development, identity, sexuality, and motherhood. Their conversations and thoughts revolve obsessively around the need to make sense of their lives, a need complicated beyond the familiar workings of self-identity by the fear of torture, persecution, and death.[36] It is important to note that through conversation and engaged dialogue the two protagonists oblige each other to question their personal developments, suggesting an uneasiness of spirit that is confronted through reflection on the Other's experience. It is clear that this is no ordinary or superficial, social conversation sustained over time but rather one built on a relationship of trust and confidence.[37]

The significant development and passage through levels of growth and formation in the Bildung process for Irene is evident in mid-life at age forty when the novel begins. Dolores, the younger friend who visits Irene unexpectantly in her summer home outside of Montevideo, is twenty-eight. Their first encounter had been when Irene was invited to give a performance at the University, which evolved into a night of political demonstrations and terror. The irony of Irene's behavior rests, as true irony does according to Kenneth Burke, on her fundamental relationship with the enemy (the patriarchal system) as she needs it and is indebted to it.[38] Irene therefore presents herself as they see her, a silly, middle-aged woman dedicated to a frivolous profession, who runs around in miniskirts and high heels in hopes of endlessly appearing alluring. She also presents, however, an interior view in which she grows into the self beyond the self and is politically committed and sympathetic to the needs of others.

> De veintitrés a veintiocho años, sigue siendo la misma mientras que yo, no sé en que momento de estos cinco años, he dejado de parecer joven. Digo parecer, porque hace rato que no soy joven, pero conseguía parecerlo. De otra manera no hubiera aguantado la minifalda y además . . . No, es grotesco pensar que ocurrieron cosas tan graves a partir de una minifalda; pero lo cierto es que está, brillante fetiche en medio de las catástrofes. La visualizo, no hay remedio; la visualizo más a la minifalda que a mí cuando estaba en mitad de la calle y la gente se largó a correr a la desesperada. Sería porque ni me iba ni me venía lo que estaba pasando, (¿qué diablos estaba pasando?) y me había visto de lejos, de cuerpo entero, en una vidriera hasta el suelo, pensando que era increíble que uno saliera así a la calle, como los pajes del Renacimiento. Sentí rabia de verme metida en un lío.[39]

> [She looks virtually the same at twenty-eight as she did at twenty-three, while in the course of the last five years I've stopped looking young. I say 'looking' because I stopped being young a long time ago, but managed to go on looking it. Otherwise I'd never have tolerated the miniskirt I was wearing the day it all happened. It seems embarrassing in present circumstances to remember a miniskirt but then . . . No matter how grotesque it seems to associate such terrible things with a miniskirt, it's there, like it or not, standing out like a fetish in the midst of the horror. The image is lodged in my mind, I can't get rid of it; it's the miniskirt rather than myself I see in the middle of the street, when everyone started running for their lives. Perhaps it's because I had nothing to do with what was happening—and what in God's name was happening?—and I'd caught sight of my distant reflection, full-length, in a shop window that extended to the pavement, and had thought how amazing it was that people should walk around in public like that, like a Renaissance pageboy. I was furious that I'd got mixed up in something.[40]]

The logic of Irene's self-identity is indebted to her relationship with the enemy, the fact that men desire women in miniskirts, and is tied to her relationship with Dolores, because the miniskirt makes her feel as young and impressionable as Dolores. The miniskirt as "fetish" elicits unquestioning reverence for its erotic, symbolic power. It becomes a metaphor for Irene's personal and political awakening. The startled revulsion she feels at seeing her reflected image in a miniskirt is the direct result of awakening to a new stage of her life that absorbs previous selves and rejects the unformed. She would have never been open to this movement to another stage in her life had it not been for her unexpected relationship with Dolores and a cause she previously had not claimed as her own.

The anguish Irene feels in catching a glimpse of herself reflected in store windows as she runs from a chaotic clash with police, springs from a sense of spiritual emptiness in being outside time, place, and self. If, ultimately, the enemy decides she does not exist in their eyes, she must exist for herself. It takes the enemy's stinging recrimination, however, to bring her to this point of self-realization: "Usted es una vieja . . . debería darle vergüenza andar enseñando así los muslos . . . Una estafadora descubierta en falda, eso era" (52) [You ought to be ashamed of yourself . . . An old woman like you going around showing your thighs like that . . . I'd been found guilty of being an imposter and had been exposed in public (48)]. Traba's clever movement between public, exterior space/conversation and private, interior reflection/monologue underscores the protagonist's need to form a web of relationships (Traba refers to dialogue as "tejido" [weaving] and "entretela"[interfacing]) to promote self-realization and encourage development in others including the enemy. After all, an ignorant enemy will resist logic and change, and will destroy the peace of self-cultivation.

As focused as Irene had been on her acting career and exteriority—projecting outward through words, emotions, and physical appearance—she must now return to unpack the metaphor of awakening relying on self-reflexivity and interiority to project her toward a constant state of further Bildung. Her plot of awakening carries her to perhaps the novel's most unforgettable scene in the Plaza de Mayo where Irene seeks to support her friend Elena, whose daughter Victoria, a leader of the resistance, has "disappeared." Startled by the depth of her emotions, Irene opens the web of relationships to become another voice of the madres against the silence of the enemy.[41] This is accomplished through exteriority— the donning of white scarves and pictures of the disappeared, and screams of defiance—and through interiority—an interiorization of the loss, a loss of trust, and the agony of not knowing the truth. It is a rare moment in the novel when art mixes with and becomes life. The novel is a powerful illustration of Irene's development of her reflective powers and stature. She grows through her own deliberate observation of people (both in and outside the movement), places (both in the public sphere and the private world), and ideas (the divisions between self and non-self, space and non-space, alienation and engagement).

Once again Irene feels like an imposter. Her motives do not correspond to the enormity of the situation. Irene has come from Bogotá, not to accompany her friend in what she terms a "futile ritual", but rather to feel relief from the tension that was choking the life out of her. In reality, what she seeks is relief from fears and insecurity that come from relating to others who feel the same tension. Her self-identity is articulated through the reality of the group, as much as she tries to deny it: "Le molestó que le dijera 'compañera' y que se metiera en lo que no le importaba . . ." (86) [She felt annoyed with the woman for calling her 'sister' and poking her nose into what was none of her business . . . (86)]. Irene is overwhelmed by emotions, sounds, and chants that invade her space and force a second stage of awakening. By seeking relief in the primal screams of the mothers whose indescribable pain is released through piercing howls, Irene becomes one more "crazy woman" from the Plaza de Mayo.[42] Ana Vásquez in "Boca cerrada" makes a statement about the bold efforts of the women who fought the patriarchy. She explains that women who were accustomed to having their voice negated, were able to turn the military's further efforts to deny their voice by calling them crazy into a linguistic and political advantage. The reason why this is a poignant, explosive commentary in Traba's Bildungsroman and in literary history is because it recognizes how women can continue to realize their reflective powers even in the shadow of death. The image of women waving, smoothing out, clutching, and shielding the photos of their disappeared—the Beautiful Souls in organdy dresses or at the beach—serves as a powerful call for engagement that promises access to life, human potentiality, and victory over death. Irene's Bildung process exemplifies the triumph and survival of the Beautiful Soul over death, even while it confronts impossible images:

Me pareció oír de vez en cuando '¿dónde están?' '¿dónde están?' pero a lo mejor me lo imaginé. Sin embargo debían preguntar algo que movilizaba la cólera general, porque la masa de mujeres se movió hacia adelante, como una marea. Avanzaba, nos entrechocábamos, tropezábamos unas con otras. La confusión era inenarrable mientras se echaba al aire centenares de hojas de papel. Yo hacía lo mismo que las locas, y no te puedo decir lo que sentía; como si me estuvieran por arrancar las entrañas y me las agarrara con una fuerza demencial para salvarlas. Pero, ¿qué digo? No sé si fue así (89).

[Every now and then I thought I heard the words 'Where are they?', 'Where are they?' but it may have been my imagination. And yet they must have been voicing some demand that served as a focus for the general mood of anger, because the crowd of women surged forward like a tide. They continued to advance, we knocked into one another, stumbling over each other's feet. The chaos was indescribable as hundreds of sheets of paper were tossed into the air. I did exactly the same as the madwomen, and I couldn't begin to tell you what I felt; it was as if someone was trying to rip my insides out and I was clinging on to them for all I was worth. But that's not it either. I can't be sure it was really like that (89–90).]

The questions asked demand recognition of the status of all those who form part of the webbed relationship, and further Irene's process of self-realization as she locates her becoming in relation to all those caught up in that space between anguish and hope.[43] Irene's final brutal question: ¿Cómo hay que tomarlo, carajo, cómo hay que tomarlo?" (91) [How am I supposed to feel, for Christ's sake, how am I supposed to feel?" (92)], requires they recognize her pain but it also forces her to become more self-aware and seek the answers for herself.

The link between Dolores and Irene depends on their differences. Dolores is the focus of the second half of the novel, which contrasts with Irene's story found in the first half. It also demonstrates the unique acceptance of development timed by internal and external forces—while Irene is a late bloomer in launching her pattern of development, Dolores had been preparing for self-realization and cultivation since childhood through a rejection of her family's and society's values, an ambivalent attitude toward her sexuality, her self-definition through poetry, and so forth. Dolores, a poet and revolutionary, puts all categories into question including sexuality and motherhood. She struggles against overwhelming odds and certain death to explore self-identity, without losing herself in the process. Her refusal to relegate the exploration of sexual identity to a nonspace of corrupted emotions emphasizes Dolores's will against an authoritarian regime determined to deny her significance. One of the greatest achievements of the novel is to view Dolores's and Irene's experiences as female and human, underscoring the exceptional nature of human life.[44] Dolores keeps the relationship alive with Irene in the intervening five years they are apart by sending her letters containing the poetry she writes even as she carries out her responsibilities for the cause. The correspondence represents more than a casual exchange of daily events. Her personal narrative correspondence and her poetry further her process of self-realization. In fact, another woman friend, Luisa, inspires Dolores to write poetry even in the midst of political chaos. From this relationship Dolores concludes that self-cultivation is the purest force for the creation of a better world: "¿A quién se le ocurre hablar de poesía

cuando en cada cuadra te para una patrulla para pedirte los docu-
mentos y a partir de ahí puede pasarte cualquier cosa? Pero fue
asombrosa la velocidad con que Luisa comprendió que la imaginación, la invención de la vida estaba en otro campo, en pocas palabras, la habían agarrado los muchachos para usarla en cosas
concretas. Nada más y nada menos, ¿viste? que para imaginarse
otro país y no la mierda en que vivían" (115) [Who wants to talk
about poetry when you can be stopped on any street-corner by an
army patrol asking to see your papers, with the power to do whatever they want with you? But it was amazing how rapidly Luisa
adjusted to the realisation that imagination, the ability to create new
worlds, had passed into another camp; that's to say, it had been ap-
propriated by young people for practical purposes. For no less a
purpose than that of inventing a better country than the one they
were living in (117)]. The practical use of imagination grounds creativity in a movement toward accomplishment and realization. Solutions are sought that allow for self-cultivation and personal
identity, on the one hand, and promote social justice and reconciliation, on the other.

The narrative pretext of a frightful bus ride through Montevideo
sets the stage for the exploration of Dolores's imagination through
interior monologue. She reviews details of her "miserable life" including her relationship with her parents. Her emotional exile from
her home is a rite of passage rooted in the rejection of her parents's
values. While logically the growth process of the young Dolores
would be the one to explore for its traditional characteristics of rebellion against society's values (of exchange and worth), hers is
also the more difficult to comprehend in terms of self-realization.
While Irene appears to mature in her political and life views, there
is a tension in Dolores's development that erases her images: "El
viejo, ella, su hija; una línea completa de gente invisible" (156)
[Her father, herself, her daughter, three generations of invisible
people (162)]. This obliges her to realize "¡Oh Dios, no hay límite,
no hay descanso para la imaginación desesperada!" (156–57) [Dear
God, is there no end to it, no rest for the disturbed imagination?
(162)]. Dolores's developmental process must continue to accumu-
late all that was learned, felt, or imagined in order to create the
whole person she seeks. The goal is to save the Beautiful Soul even
in light of the pain this causes. One by one, as she presents individual memories that begin to form a larger picture, Dolores takes
stock of her process of development critically analyzing the beliefs
she is fighting for as well as her own identity in relation to that of
the others—Irene, Luisa, Victoria, Andrés, Enrique. Dolores's need

to grow in relation to others is fundamental to the role women take on in developing self-awareness in order to be able to imagine and contribute to a greater change in the social order. Ultimately, her goal, as in most relationships fostered by women in general, is a cultivation of her being-in-the-world through the support of others.

4

The Transitional State of Truth and Moral Maturity

Men cannot live by truth alone; they also need lies—those they invent of their own accord, not those foisted on them by others; those that emerge undisguised, not those that insinuate themselves through the trappings of history.

—Mario Vargas Llosa

CONTEMPORARY JUDGMENTS, BEING MORAL OR EVALUATIVE BY nature, rely on expressions of attitude or feeling that are neither true nor false. Hence the reference made to the "transitional" state of truth. Since it is impossible to agree upon a moral judgment through a rational method of discernment, the arrival at the "true" answer at the end of debate appears to be an implausible goal. There will always be other possibilities, hypotheses, conjectures, and arguments to consider because contemporary moral debate, unlike its ancient counterpart, is not a highly ordered philosophic form. Upon arrival back at rival premises from rival conclusions, it is clear that the array of assertions and counter-assertions reflect an interminable quality. According to Alasdair MacIntyre, this quality is present because our contemporary society provides no established way of deciding between rival moral claims. We interpret no argument to be more compelling than another, and so we remain stubbornly rooted to our original premise.[1] Ultimately, what is missing is moral certitude and closure. Locked in a shifting contemporary battle over truth are the desire to rationally select a moral judgment based on certain objective standards, and the need to rely on historical origins as a bellwether of human culture. The result is a state of disorder in contemporary moral utterance.

Literature in general, and the Bildungsroman in particular, have always been successful in the communication and interpretation of the nature of moral debate. In fact, Vargas Llosa believes that literature even lies (through deceits, devices, and hyperbole) in order to

124

best express deep-seated and disturbing truths.[2] For example, Soledad Acosta de Samper's *Teresa la limeña*, (1869) José María Arguedas's *Los ríos profundos* (1958), and Carlos Fuentes's *Las buenas conciencias* (1959) lucidly contextualize the angst of moral judgment from distinctive periods and geographic and cultural settings. In doing so, disturbing truths insinuate themselves as hybrid cultural reference points or cultural markers. If moral incertitude (or uncertainty in general, for that matter) is interpreted as cultural loss, it makes Carlos Alonso's argument that Latin American narrative is grounded in the "myth of permanent cultural crisis" as the "narrative of cultural identity," even more pertinent.[3] Because of the irresolvable clash of cultural codes, the issue of truth or identity has been called into question permanently. What the authors cited above demonstrate in their work is a faith in a coherent but hybrid self.

Soledad Acosta de Samper is known for her skillful positioning of nineteenth-century female protagonists so as to be at the center of moral dilemma. The purpose is to have them confront the effects of choice, that is, solitude, [dis]ease, psychological violence, trust, distrust, and unfulfilled dreams. Unlike a discourse on origins that explains where the protagonist is by how she got to be that way, *Teresa la limeña* (1869) attempts to totalize synecdochically the formative events in Teresa's process of development in order to explain how the symbolic and cultural codes became readable. The quality of readability of codes is important from the perspective of interpretation. It reinforces how the protagonist, whose topological characterization is resolutely established in the title, displaces her center both psychologically and physically from the capital, Lima, to a home in the town of Chorrillos, thereby leaving doubt and uncertainty to the inconstancy of the city. This is not to say that she achieves the goals of harmony and happiness in her life. But unlike other protagonists in Acosta de Samper's works who die for love, Teresa seizes life and tries to create for herself an existence where creativity and sexuality may coexist.[4] Jean Bethke Elshtain offers an important insight into the contribution of culture and gender in the recovery of texts, which we may expand to read *Teresa la limeña*, "There is no way *out* but there may be several ways *in*: by going back to the texts and offering readings that track the ambiguities and ironies of our gendered identities rather than reincoding them for whatever purpose . . ."[5] Clearly, this is not an insignificant feat for a nineteenth-century female author or protagonist.

Rooted in the precursor genre of those eighteenth- and nineteenth-century novels that explore society and the question of education for women, *Teresa la limeña* goes beyond their scope to explore the moral unpacking of subverted codes for women. Teresa does not acquiesce to the female melodrama—she rejects deceit and disloyalty as the method to achieve her goal, which is generally considered for female protagonists the man of her dreams. While it is important to remember that love and companionship or marriage are significant rites of passage in the Bildung process regardless of gender, it is crucial to uncover Acosta de Samper's subtle reconciliation of female realities, from "mother" in madre patria to independent being.

Teresa la limeña enriches the category of Bildungsroman in Latin America that is grounded in a quest for identity—an identity that is firmly rooted in the national character. The author herself is the embodiment of a unique national character. Soledad Acosta de Samper was born in 1833 in what was then called the Republic of New Granada, and died in 1913 in the then Republic of Colombia. During her lifetime her country changed names/identities five times. Her father, a general, politician, and historian of the Independence, and her husband, an author whose work was more widely read than her own, encouraged her to contribute to the body of work that the young republic was producing. Unfortunately, very little of her work is read or analyzed today, even though in general it delves into the most recurrent themes of eighteenth- and nineteenth-century Latin American literature: education, society, solitude, love, ambition, marriage, envy, and intrigue. Acosta de Samper's lack of readership reveals a familiar trend in nineteenth-century historiography, even though women made extraordinary advances according to Adriana Méndez Rodenas by expanding the concept of historiography to include private genres like letters, diaries, travelogues, or personal memoirs. The memoirs, she notes, were similar to male public texts in that they too were concerned with affairs of state, but the difference was in their public reception.[6] Acosta de Samper's work is reflective of fin-de-siècle Spanish America, in that, as Sylvia Molloy interprets this period in general, it paradoxically evokes degeneration and regeneration at the same time.[7] This subtle, contradictory quality is evidenced in *Teresa la limeña* and Acosta's later Bildungsroman, *El corazón de la mujer*.[8] The author's purpose in getting women to think rather than accomplishing the thinking for them is striking. Acosta uses her novels as a platform to question through discomforting and disquieting doubts. It is a more effective tool for change and self development than her direct articulation of women's intellectual capabilities in "Aptitud de la mujer para ejercer todas las profesiones" (1893). The approach toward a cohesive self in Acosta's Bildungsromane, to paraphrase Molloy, is an appeal to regeneration, even while viewing decadence and decay.

The collapse of Teresa's world gives rise to an unusual relationship of equals between protagonists and friends—Teresa and Lucila. The author elevates the relational focus of the woman's Bildung to the point of equality by alternating between the letters and stories of the two friends. Teresa and Lucila meet in a French convent school where they form a lasting and profound friendship reinforced by love and mutual respect. Significantly, they are able to respect their differences. Lucila's spirit is passive, sweet, and gentle, waiting for the love that would fill and fulfill her dreams. In contrast, Teresa's spirit is active, adventuresome, and independent, as she dreams of a daring life through which would pass a disgraced, romantic young man whom *she* would subdue after a thousand dangerous adventures. The difference in focus inspires Teresa to an uncritical interpretation of cultural codes that allows her to aspire to a "male" quest for adventure, independence from common social and familial roles, and escapades of love. She wills this into being by turning tragedy into triumph.

The cultural code that suggests Teresa's independence, singularity, and triumph in the world is the language of music. As stated earlier, many of Acosta's female protagonists die in her stories and novels, but Teresa maps the path of development with a self-critical form that propels her to another stage of development. Even the ending of the novel in its metaquestion signals movement toward another stage, and indicates that the process, while on track, is not complete. Teresa creates for herself an existence where memories and the past are used to encourage the process of self-cultivation. She learns through her mistakes, especially after agreeing to an arranged marriage designed to provide economic solvency for her father, that a woman is significant on her own. The moral dilemma of obligation to her father regardless of his inordinate demands drives Teresa into a loveless marriage.[9] Teresa's marriage, a rite of passage that is ironically marked by grave thoughts and feelings of loss, is heralded by a cultural marker—a musical piece: "Ella se levantó inmediatamente y después de un momento entonó con voz conmovida el ADIOS de Schubert . . . Era un adios supremo a su vida de niña, a sus aspiraciones y esperanzas, al Manfredo de sus ensueños, a la Teresa, amiga de Lucila, que iba a transformarse en la esposa de León"[10] [She rose immediately and after a moment intoned with a moving voice Schubert's FAREWELL . . . It was a supreme farewell to her life as a child, to her hopes and aspirations, to the Manfred of her dreams, to Teresa, Lucila's friend, who was going to transform herself into León's wife[11]]. Teresa has established herself on a plane equal to that of others, including Pablo, an acquaintance also obliged to marry for money to rescue the family fortune. The moral ambiguity confronting Teresa manages to muddle her instincts with respect to truth in love and a loving relationship. Nevertheless, she holds onto an aspiration to solve her moral dilemma through a persistent questioning of woman's reality. Teresa calls into question the abandonment of hope in love, a hope symbolized by her friendship with Lucila, thereby providing herself with a strategy for reevaluating moral choice. Teresa marries León, giving in to a cultural patterning of familial loyalty to secure her father's financial future. Nevertheless, she purposefully lays bare her unresolved feelings about the sacrifice of entering a loveless marriage. Curiously, it is not until Teresa is called to the deathbed of her husband that she realizes in some measure she had loved León.

The tension that shapes Teresa's development underscores a disjunctive between the surface plot and the underlying moral codes that guide her. It is a tension of identities. It is apparent in Teresa's balance between societal pressures to enter into a social/economic pact for the purpose of providing financial security and future heirs, and the increasingly irrepressible desire for independence and self-autonomy. In effect, these tensions mirror the politically unsettled climate in Colombia from colonial rule through Independence, when women faced these challenges both politically and legally. Perhaps Teresa could be faulted, following the narrative line, for her facile solution to her dilemma—the realization that there exist many forms of love so that she has not betrayed her own beliefs by substituting her father's for her own. In reality, her questioning of the convenience of the traditional marriage for women, a central theme in nineteenth-century women's writing, is an important stage in her development. Teresa acquires the material necessary to mold herself into the independent, cohesive being she is in the process of becoming by the novel's end.

In the Bildungsroman of the nineteenth century and before, the modes of learning are easy to categorize: learning through example and imitation, observing and reacting to people and events, exposing oneself to the arts, and so forth. Learning through the senses is not as important as it is in the contemporary Bildungsroman. Nevertheless, we do witness a movement in Teresa toward resolving the contradictions between intellectual and sensory experience. This movement may precipitate change because as Lucila writes in her letter from France: "en ese país nuevo se debe de pensar de otro modo" (113) [in that new country one should think differently].

Perhaps both women are constructing the framework for the autonomy of their development, which should be absent from suffering
because they call for harmony and happiness: "la felicidad consiste
en la armonía que guardan nuestros sentimientos y afectos con las
personas y objetos que nos rodean . . . Donde no haya armonía no
habrá felicidad!" (120) [happiness consists of the harmony that our
feelings and emotions hold for the people and objects that surround
us . . . Wherever harmony does not exist there will be no happiness!]. Harmony is the spiritual goal of the self-cultivated individual to transform and be transformed by her/his environment.
Harmony for Teresa accommodates all of the values by which she
forms herself.

Teresa's environment instills a lack of serenity in her, but this
underlying tension and her awakened emotions, which refuse to
leave her in peace, cannot be explained away as part of a "female"
problem. On the contrary, by reinitiating gender with a deferred
quality, the complexity must actually destroy the uncritical theories
written on the "male" and "female" bodies. The cultural values
communicated by Teresa are neither female nor male. They stand
independent of the gendered body. Specifically they are: the prizing
of autonomy in the development of self-cultivation and self-realization, the possibility of the blending of intelligence and the senses
(as in music), and the praising of individual potentialities. In a
sense, it is a desire to go beyond gender, beyond the masculine or
feminine qualities forever associated with either sex. Judith Butler
reinforces this potentiality in her assessment of gender as ways of
culturally interpreting the sexed body that are not restricted by the
apparent duality of sex.[12] Gender, therefore, is something that one
becomes, a corollary of *Werden* or process of becoming that is the
mainstay of the Bildung process. Gender, like Bildung, reflects a
series of actions that ultimately define us beyond binary oppositions.

To this discussion of gender, Marjorie Garber introduces a
"third" element that questions binary thinking and introduces crisis, as discussed earlier. The transitional state of truth for Teresa
registers a willingness to marry someone she does not love over her
desire for creativity and sexuality embodied in Roberto Montana, a
young man of mysterious origin. Greatly influenced by the Romantic period, Teresa is destined to suffer her losses in love. From these
experiences she concludes that "su vida era siempre un tejido de
equivocaciones" (161) [her life was always a weaving of mistakes],
one that is woven with broken promises and deceptions designed to
help others at great personal expense. Teresa believes she has
reached harmony through self-cultivation and declares Roberto to

be her agent of change, "bajo su influencia he procurado mejorar mi carácter, corregir mis defectos" (210) [under his influence I have endeavored to strengthen my character, correct my defects]. Their love, a moral causality in an economic battle, is frustrated by Teresa's father who fears financial ruin if they are permitted to marry. When Teresa threatens to marry Roberto for love, ignore her father's needs, and become independent of him, her father sets into motion a web of deceptions that drives the lovers apart. Teresa's father enlists Rosa, a social-climbing friend, who repents her misdeeds in the end and sends Teresa a letter revealing the deception: "Esta carta le causó mucha pena a Teresa, al pensar con cuanta facilidad se había dejado engañar Roberto, también le satisfizo la idea de que él no era tan despreciable como ella había creido, pues eso era lo que más la entristecía; pero no cambió en nada su vida" (232) [This letter caused Teresa much pain, thinking about how easily Roberto had let himself be tricked, the idea also satisfied her that he wasn't as despicable as she had thought, since that was what saddened her the most; but it didn't change her life at all]. The description of Teresa's pain and sadness precedes an abrupt break in tone registered by the declarative statement "pero no cambió en nada su vida." The statement marks the movement to another stage in her development because it signals the underlying tension that is Teresa's need for the self beyond the self. That is, the conjunction divides the woman who needed and would have been satisfied with the explanation of the deceit perpetrated so as to remedy the lost love, and the woman who has left all that behind so as to become independent and self-directed. Teresa's education and life experiences have permitted her access to a realm of interior strength and freedom. The failure of the male role models—that of her father, her husband León, and her lover Roberto—to enrich her life, demonstrates to Teresa the need to work on her own imperfections and improve her own personality rather than looking to someone else as her guide and support.

Teresa grows into her autonomous role, returning as does the narration full circle to the autonomy symbolized by her house in Chorillos. Chorillos is the only possession that truly belongs to Teresa without encumbrance, because she inherited it from her mother. Cautiously Acosta de Samper makes clear that education represses women because of its function in communicating bourgeois and Christian values. But, Acosta concludes, while education does repress women, women without education are even more oppressed. The independent individual, who is seen by Doris Sommer as combining Romanticism and Nationalism in classical nineteenth-century texts, is also at work in the Bildungsromane of Acosta de Samper. Acosta unsettles the notion of truth for women through a subversive narrative that reveals female independence as woman's choice—a choice that may include failure or disappointment. This unsettling is accomplished through a displacement in *Teresa la limeña*. Teresa removes herself socially, politically, and culturally from the capital to the town of Chorillos. The move from city to town contradicts the movement of the traditional Bildungsroman narrative that sends the hero to the city from the countryside to seek education, culture, love, social contacts, and life experience. Teresa rejects the doubt and inconstancy of the city to search for a new tradition that [dis]orders the one she knows. In Teresa the anxiety of rupture and the intense desire for autonomy and identity combine to reflect both the Bildung process and the foundation of a nation in their various stages. Perhaps the displacement of desire in Teresa is a displacement of desire for political peace and stability; the *new* country and the *new* woman threatening to live their own lives. The success of the enterprise is left without closure and as an open question. The question is raised in the end as to whether Teresa will go down the road to love again by which she has suffered so much in the past. The "road to love" is the subversive myth or metaphor for woman on the road to life. The answer is unsettling because it again reveals a tension for women—in this instance between the desire for independence and self-sufficiency, and the need for relational commitments, both male and female. The question is left unanswered: "Hasta ahora no lo hemos sabido" (233) [For now we just don't know]. More important than the answer is the act of questioning engaged in by both women and men. It is a struggle on which Acosta de Samper builds her narrative, the questioning of the male influence in Teresa's life from father to lover, which perhaps reveals the author's own struggle for an independent light far from the shadow of a revered father and a more famous husband.

Similar issues of independence, education, moral character, truth, and self-development ground Carlos Fuentes's novel *Las buenas conciencias* (1959) [*The Good Conscience*] and its traditional protagonist, Jaime Ceballos. Fuentes's cultural history of Guanajuato, Mexico, and the Ceballos clan is most powerful in its critique of social issues and moral stances.[13] The discussion of hypocrisy, suffocating traditions, and failed philosophies overrules a rational justification of an accomplished family who claims a historic role in the founding tradition of Mexico from the colonial period through the Mexican Revolution. Jaime Ceballos begins his Bildung process by questioning the moral values of his family and extricating himself from that moral culture. Viewing moral certitude as an attainable goal, Jaime signals failure and hypocrisy in everyone that touches his life in order to distance himself from their mistakes. This coming-of-age novel follows the development of the traditional Bildungsroman in its rebellion against patriarchal values. In effect, Jaime attempts to produce certain non-rational effects on the emotions of his priest, aunt, and uncle, to dissuade them of their hypocritical beliefs and persuade them of his life's philosophy. Clearly, this youthful self-interest gone awry does not aid the common good. After his family and mentors are awash in imperfect standards that fold back on them as metaphors for the good gone bad, Jaime realizes that moral judgments are interminable forms of debate. This less than satisfying conclusion for Jaime is undoubtedly the first significant step toward a cohesive self. It facilitates an introspection that guides his faith in his own development.

In *Las buenas conciencias* Carlos Fuentes illuminates the breakdown of moral standards by holding them to the test of cultural history. Specifically, quite early in the novel, Fuentes introduces a truth-bearing analogy for the historically class-conscious families of Guanajuato: "Guanajuato es a México lo que Flandes a Europa: el cogollo, la esencia de un estilo, la casticidad exacta"[14] [Guanajuato is to Mexico what Flanders is to Europe, the very core of a distinct style of life, and the preservation in all purity of tradition[15]]. This Mexico of the purest tradition, founded ironically on the cosmographies of the indigenous peoples, then europeanized through Spanish and French conquests, and converted through miraculous epiphanies of the Virgin and French philosophical theory, is a metaphor for complexity itself. It is similar to a pyramid superimposed on the base of an earlier one, whose cultural layers permeate each other through waves and echoes of sound. The underlying cultures are revealed regardless of a superimposed standard that seeks to suppress prior history. In practice, it demonstrates the intractability of other truths that are pervasive, not easily hidden, and difficult to define.

The mix of cultures brings about a colonial experiment that fails after centuries of Spanish rule over disparate cultures and vast geographic distances, an experiment unequalled by Roman or Napoleonic conquests. Mexican Independence achieved in 1810, and Napoleon's colonizing in the form of a Hapsburg Mexican Empire 1864–1867, are further stages in the exchange of cultural, social, and political values grounded in Mexico's history. Almost one hundred years after Mexican Independence, the Ceballos family looks back on their Mexico of the purest tradition, which they hope reflects the "purity" of their family tradition, and ironically, it does. Curiously, this ironic moral stance exemplified by the Ceballos family, should be understood as an access to wisdom, in this case wisdom being the reasons behind their selection of moral views and the exchange of cultural codes that explain their history. Specifically, in the case of Jaime, his motivation is the access to wisdom that leads to a cohesive self. A cohesive self is the goal rather than an irreconcilable, pessimistic world view, which is what you have if you simply examine the boy's rebellion against family values and his subsequent failure to exchange them for more "acceptable" values.

Fuentes unpacks the concept and practice of truth for the reader through the example of Guanajuato, the overarching symbol of pure tradition. The author underscores for us the strategy of this study of reading the Bildungsroman as a story of culture not as the story of a specific character. In essence, the traditional nature of truth is most powerfully rendered through a negative critique of Guanajuato and its inhabitants: "Así, el guanajuantense es un mocho calificado. Un mocho laico (como todos los eficaces) capaz de servir a la iglesia más oportuna y que, en su concepto, garantice la mejor administración práctica de la 'voluntad general' teórica . . . lo que en el capitalino, en fin, es afirmación o reticencia, en el guanajuatense es puro compromiso" (14–15) [The citizen of Guanajuato is, in other words, a practiced, talented, certified hypocrite. He is a lay hypocrite, as are all the best, and will serve whatever church seems in his opinion most likely to provide an efficient carrying-out of the theoretical "general will" . . . what in a native of Mexico City is enthusiasm or reluctance, is pure compromise in the Guanajuatan (4)]. The historical origins of hypocrisy and compromise have roots in pre-conquest Mexico while the origins in the twentieth century may be traced to the activities of Mexican progress. In Mexico, progress produced wealth and stability for some during the presidency of Porfirio Díaz, but fomented distrust, poverty, and ultimately revolution in the exploited. The ruthless reign of Díaz from 1876 to 1910 symbolizes a classic shift in the modes of perception of reality from the nineteenth to the twentieth century. In the nineteenth century one learned through example, imitation, and observation as stated earlier. In the twentieth one learns to view the world through a persistent clash of intellectual and sensory experience. During the Mexican Revolution Guanajuato is invaded by the troops of Pancho Villa and then overtaken by the troops of Obregón. In Las buenas conciencias principles of right and wrong conduct blur with each successive wave of invading troops. Jaime is caught in a vortex of competing interests, reasons, and desires that ultimately force the protagonist to move beyond criticism of others in order to mold himself. If ultimately Jaime does not satisfy readers as a protagonist, it is because the novel reflects the molding of a culture not a hero. The cohesion of intellectual and sensory experiences Jaime reaches is grounded in cultural hypocrisy. That is, Jaime possesses the will to frustrate hypocrisy by cataloguing every example of hypocrisy he encounters in society, including religious and social hypocrisy. But he lapses into a paradoxical state in which his own hypocritical nature makes the argument interminable and hinders Jaime's "escape" from the past. Jaime discovers himself to be like all other young people—while all youth believe fervently in the uniqueness of their experience, their reasons, sentiments, and desires have been thought, expressed, and felt by others before them as they too came of age. The cultural patterning Jaime believes he has "discovered" has been etched on the body or into nature since the beginning of time, awaiting a contextual reading.

Curiously, the contextual reading quite often confuses the protagonist because he is unable to decipher the cultural codes presented to him. For instance, Jaime learns to call his aunt "mother" because of the mysterious absence of his biological mother. But the presence of both his father and his uncle, the husband of his "mother," produces both intellectual and sensory experiences that confuse the boy: "Una de las grandes confusiones del niño era saber cómo dirigirse a uno y a otro. ¿Por qué el esposo de su mamá era su tío y su papá dormía en otra parte? ¿A quién debía obedecer más: al señor elegante, autoritario, o al señor gordo, complaciente?" (37) [That confuses the boy. Why don't his mamá and papá live together? Why is his uncle where his father should be? And to which of them should he be more obedient: to stern Uncle Balcárcel, or to fat and drowsy Papá Rodolfo? (27)]. Jaime's conundrum is symbolic of the paradox of truths written on the "body" that is Mexico: to whom does one owe allegiance—political, emotional, and social—to the obliging, indigenous people who conceived the pre-Columbian nation or to the authoritarian, European ancestors (Benito Juárez aside), who created the modern nation? The narrative yokes together oppositions in uneasy alliances such as sterility and fertility, wealth and poverty, faith and hypocrisy, to make obvious the opposition of "las buenas conciencias" (a good conscience) and las malas conciencias (a bad conscience). Jaime confuses the figure of the martyred Christ with the miner and union organizer, Ezequiel Zuno, whom he aids by hiding him from his enemies and offering him food. In the molding of himself Jaime's fervent desire is to drop everything, reject family values, and follow Ezequiel. Upon approaching Ezequiel, who is later turned over to authorities by the uncle, or Juan Manuel Lorenzo, an Indian friend who shares socialist ideals with Jaime, Jaime learns to fight against life's disturbing truths that envelop and absorb him. The truth that race and social class matter in a frivolous, irreverent society causes Jaime to explode emotionally. As he comes of age, Jaime realizes the necessity to strip away the values that support racism, poverty and the denial of another's worth: "Lucha contra el rencor, el odio y la rebeldía. Lucha contra toda la vida provinciana, contra los chismes y las buenas intenciones y los sanos consejos, contra el cura Lanzagorta, contra el que entregó a Ezequiel Zuno, contra la señorita Pascualina, contra su padre, contra sí mismo (94). [He fights against his rancor, his hatred, his rebelliousness, against all that is provincial in his life, against the priest Lanzagorta, against the man who betrayed Ezequiel Zuno, against Señorita Pascualina, against his father, against himself (71–72)]. It is another fundamental stage in Jaime's Bildung process because as he strips away the bourgeois values of his family and an indifferent religion, he finds he has nothing with which to replace them. Jaime is neither prepared nor willing to show humility and accept his mother and friends for what they are. His struggle is one that paradoxically embodies the racial inequities of Mexico.[16] But Jaime's struggle is significant because the development of his own talents or capabilities, namely, the development of culture of the individual, is intimately associated with the development of the culture of Mexico. Therefore, Jaime's inner process of formation and cultivation remains in a constant state of further Bildung or becoming, echoing Mexico's process itself.

Jaime's anguished, moral endeavor leads to a sensibility that is higher than his impoverished view of Mexican politics, society, and religious ethos. It is as if Jaime has planned the stages of Bildung in order to arrive at sensibility and development of character by returning to the values that have formed him. That is, his desire to be a man reads like a manual for the traditional Bildungsroman: "Ser hombre: otra idea que lo atarantaba. Fugarse de la casa. Amar a una mujer. Descubrir un tesoro. Regresar a vengarse. Ser hombre . . ." (127) [To be a man. To leave home, to love a woman, to discover buried treasure. To return and avenge himself. To be a man . . . (98)]. Significantly, the desire to be independent, experience love, discover wealth, and return to assert oneself in the society one had previously rejected reflects the traditional protagonist's connection with life. Jaime discovers in this hybrid form, however, a manner of reaching up to humanity by recognizing and acting on his own weakness: "Un canal de luz se abre en su mente. No debía recriminar al tío. Era él, Jaime, quien debía hacer algo, algo por Ezequiel, algo por Adelina. Algo en nombre de Asunción, de Rodolfo y de Balcárcel" (132) [A ray of light opens in his mind. He no longer needs to ask others to do anything. He ought not to blame even his uncle. He must ask of himself alone; himself alone must act and do something for Ezequiel's sake, for Adelina's sake, in the name of Asunción, in the names of Rodolfo and Balcárcel (101)]. Even though Jaime confuses this epiphany with a religious revelation, he is incapable of asking his father's forgiveness for treating him shamelessly before his death, or to approach his mother and identify himself. The self-awareness Jaime acquires in the end is a fulfillment of significance. That is, Jaime finds in himself his own significance. He learns to allow what is different from him and view life unencumbered by the selfish interest of perfection. Jaime moves toward a mature state of development upon realizing: "No he tenido el valor. No he podido ser lo que quería. No he podido ser cristiano. No puedo quedarme solo con mi fracaso; no lo aguantaría; tengo que apoyarme en algo. No tengo más apoyo que esto: mis tíos, la vida que me prepararon, la vida que heredé de todos mis antepasados. Me someto al orden, para no caer en la desesperación" (190) [I haven't had the courage. I couldn't be what I wanted to be. I couldn't be a Christian. And I was too weak to stay alone with my failure, I had to find some kind of support, and the only one I have is my aunt and uncle, the life they have prepared for me, the life I inherit. I shall submit myself to established order, in order not to fall into desperation (147)]. Jaime moves in stages from alienation to appropriation. The material he acquires is not new, but is written in nature. He learns to get beyond his own naturalness by first rejecting the pre-given body of cultural material and then by appropriating it. Through the various stages Jaime keeps himself open to more universal points of view. The imperfect hero returns, nevertheless, to himself, to his own spirit, and in the end, to the culture in which he was formed.

Another important example of a hybrid text, one that intersperses the process of self development and belief in a cohesive self with issues of race, gender, social class, and culture, is *Los ríos profundos* (1958) by José María Arguedas. Recognized as an autobiographical novel that also embodies an important anthropological study, *Los ríos profundos* is the Bildung process of both author and protagonist, Ernesto. The textualization of interactive voices insinuates the language of youth, innocence, and foundation—Quechua—within the world of Spanish, Colonial, and Baroque Peru. Cultural patterning imprints the narrative with tension—linguistic, political, economic—which, with the weight of history, steeps the novel in conflict. It is an attempt to bring the story of El Inca Garcilaso into modernity in Cuzco, the land of origins.

The narrative represents a dialogue with oneself, within oneself, for cultural survival. But if language is power, how do the historically mistreated have their say without becoming acculturated? This is a conflict that is left unresolved by the novel and certainly incomplete by the author's suicide. Julio Ortega argues that the exclusion of the servant in the process of communication points to the fact that social stratification sanctions the speech of some while manipulating the speech of others.[17] Nevertheless, *Los ríos profundos* reveals Ernesto's reaching up to humanity by educating himself in the ways of the Other. Self-formation means that that by which Ernesto is formed becomes his own. The paradox for Ernesto is that both sides are the Other. He is not wholly or truly in the world of the Indian or the minority, ruling class. He is not able to measure himself in either community, so his role of observer of cultural norms, while satisfying to the reader for its wealth of information and inspiration, displaces Ernesto and grounds him in the process of becoming.[18] The strategy for interpreting the novel is in the rhetorical strength of its dialogic technique, examining what Ernesto receives and absorbs in the process of becoming. Ernesto overwhelms the traditional definition of coming of age and closure by reinforcing the struggle in the process of becoming, a victory in spirit if not in reality.

The structural problem for Ernesto, as stated earlier, is that his dialogue does not root him in one world or the other. Clearly, his sympathies are with the Indians as example after example reveal mistreatment and oppression, ironically paralleling a poetic, mystical reality. The opposition between Old World and New, indigenous and Spanish, Quechua and Spanish, poverty and wealth, repression and oppression, is continually reinforced throughout the novel. In the opening paragraphs the reader is introduced to the older relative, El Viejo, who embodies the evil oppressor in his comportment in both Cuzco and his Apurímac hacienda: "Desde las cumbres grita, con voz de condenado, advirtiendo a sus indios que él está en todas partes. Almacena las frutas de las huertas, y las deja pudrir; cree que valen muy poco para traerlas a vender al Cuzco o llevarlas a Abancay y que cuestan demasiado para dejárselas a los colonos. '¡Irá al infierno!' decía de él mi padre"[19] [From the mountaintops he shouts with the voice of the damned, letting his Indians know that he is everywhere. He stores up the fruit from his orchards and lets it spoil; he doesn't think it's worth taking to sell in Cuzco or in Abancay, and says it's too dear to leave for his colonos. 'He'll go to hell,' my father said of him[20]]. Arguedas's overarching theory in both his anthropological studies and his literature is that Andean conditions domesticate and interiorize the dominant culture, incorporating European features into Andean institutional forms.[21] The European features here evident in the Christian damnation of one who believes he is omnipresent and omnipotent, serve to distance one world from another. The distance makes possible another goal of Arguedas's writings, that of making obvious the idea that the Indians were endowed with "a world view of their own, in which people, mountains, animals, the rain, truth, all had dimensions of their own, powerful, revealing, and utterly unlike the Iberian ones."[22] The quality of being unlike the Spanish is especially important because it speaks of unique origins, destinies, and guiding principles that liberate in principle if not in reality. This is the reason for the continuing allusion to animism—the belief that natural objects and the universe possess souls or consciousness—without even referencing the term. Ernesto longs to discover the Cuzco his father and possibly the Indians who have raised him have described. Ernesto understands that the stones speak, move, and sing there and that the Inca Roca's stones that form a wall can walk and swallow up the evil.

Los ríos profundos then is a yoking together of joyful celebration of discovery and sorrowful revelation of humiliation. For as much as the father chides the son about thinking like a child in his poetic attempts to explain the origins of the world, the son demonstrates a mature, sagacious, and soulful understanding of the power of humiliation in oppressing the Indigenous. It is this attempt to go beyond the self and self-interest that demonstrates Ernesto's need for Bildung. He is able to turn away from blind anger in order to gain a sense of universal points of view, which cause some to be joyful and others sorrowful. Ernesto learns to allow what is different from him in order to find universal viewpoints from which to grasp the dimensions of the Indian world without self-interest, without the need to transform it, rather allowing himself to be transformed by it. The father is unable to get beyond self-interest, the personal affront he has suffered at the hands of the old man, but the son anchors himself in the process of Bildung in order to pursue understanding.

Ernesto's journey suggests not only the familiar subaltern text speaking out against the dominant culture, but also a reverse acculturation—Spanish institutional forms incorporating Andean features. For example, the statue of Christ with Indian-like features, the musical blending of themes and instruments, and the Jesuit Church whose foundation is constructed with Incan stones, represent a blending that neither overwhelms nor obliterates either contributor or party. It is the former example, however, of the tension between the subaltern and dominant culture that grounds the novel. The representation is not an irresolvable opposition of good versus evil or European versus Indian, for Ernesto also documents the curses he offers for the irresponsibly poor treatment they receive in the pueblos at the hands of Indians who hate outsiders, and the savage treatment others practice on animals, outsiders, and women. The lesson Ernesto learns from his father is that no matter how much one personally may suffer, it is not sufficient cause to inflict pain or humiliate another.

The stages through which Ernesto passes in his Bildung process are clearly delineated—imitation of father and his values through an educational journey through two hundred towns in Peru, and independence of son through father's "abandonment" in Abancay to pursue studies until he is ready to enter the university, respecting his father's wishes. Many stages are indicated by cultural reference points or linguistic markers in the depiction of the huaynos, songs and popular dances of Incan origin, in both Quechua and Spanish. The flowing of Quechua into Spanish to translate the long words into expressions of emotions, nature, and life, aid Ernesto in remembering his journey: "Después, cuando me convencí de que los colonos no llegaban al pueblo, iba a las chicherías, por oír la música, y a recordar. Acompañado en voz baja la melodía de las canciones, me acordaba de los campos y las piedras, de las plazas y los templos, de los pequeños ríos adonde fui feliz" (53) [Later, when I had become convinced that the *colonos* never got to town, I went to the *chicherías* just to listen to the music and reminisce. As I accompanied the singing in a low voice I would think about the fields and stones, the squares and churches, and the streams where I had once been happy (46)]. For Ernesto, memories bring happiness because the present is uncertain. The cultural oasis that the protagonist finds in the huaynos is a fortress against the sterility of the landscape and the school where he had interned. The boarding school in Abancay, perhaps serving as precursor model to Vargas Llosa's novel *La ciudad y los perros*, is run, however, by authoritarian, Spanish-speaking priests rather than by the military. As Ernesto had passed through many towns where only the priests and town officials were non-Indians, it is yet another cultural clash to be taught in the language of the dominant culture. Roberto González Echevarría underscores the magnitude of the clash: "It is a deeply troubling experience because for Ernesto to learn from the Spanish-speaking priests and his classmates means to forget, or worse, to scorn the life of those who raised him."[23] It is significant that many of the students gathered frequently to play, sing, and judge the huaynos sung by others. The songs, as well as the games in competition, such as the contest of spinning tops, demonstrate the humanity of the young boys. However, the inhumanity is equally and carefully demonstrated including brutal games whose goal is to draw blood and make the young ones cry. Perhaps the cruelest of games employs punishing techniques that reflect general attitudes toward gender and race.

The most symbolic questioning of values in the young men is the treatment of la Opa, a young woman with mental deficiencies, who is brought by the priests to the school to work as a cook's aide. Taking advantage of the woman's mental illness, the older boys fight each other for the chance to assault her: "La propia demente me causaba una gran lástima. Me apenaba recordarla, sacudida, disputada con implacable brutalidad; su cabeza golpeada contra las divisiones de madera, contra la base de los excusados; y su huida por el callejón, en que corría como un oso perseguido. Y los pobres jóvenes que la acosaban, y que después se profanaban, hasta sentir el ansia de flagelarse, y llorar bajo el peso del arrepentimiento" (71) [I even pitied the feeble-minded woman; I grieved to remember how she was beaten and fought over with implacable brutality, how they banged her head against the board fence and the base of the toilets, and how she fled down to the passageway, running like a hunted bear. And the poor young men who pursued her, and then defiled themselves to the point of feeling the need to flagellate themselves and cry out under the weight of repentance (63)]. Ernesto realizes, as do the young men who feel the need to repent, that the sexual act being performed with the woman is not a simple rite of passage in the process of self-realization or coming of age. Rather, it is a humiliating act that signifies power over and degradation of the woman attacked. Ernesto bears witness to this debasing act as well as to others because it is within the power of the narrative voice to reveal the disturbing truths residing in the process of becoming. More striking is Ernesto's reaction: "La propia demente me causaba una gran lástima" [I even pitied the feeble-minded woman]. What is there not to pity in her portrayal? And yet pity empties out into fear, which brings about a need to repent and pursue forgiveness. Curiously, following Shoshana Felman's lucid argument on mental illness, rather than a protest or self-affirmation, madness in women produces an impasse, "a manifestation both of cultural impotence and of political castration. This socially defined help-needing and help-seeking behavior is itself part of female conditioning, ideologically inherent in the behavioral pattern and in the dependent and helpless role assigned to the woman as such."[24] In this novel, the woman's mental illness is symbolic of cultural impotence in general, but also, nonetheless, of her independence, in particular; she has no need of others for support or aid, mental, physical, emotional, political, or otherwise. She cannot be described as "help-seeking," and perhaps this is the source of her attraction, which goes beyond the purely physical as she is not the only female with whom the young men have contact. The disturbing truth is that the more independent her role becomes, the more need—physical, psychological, and emotional—the young men have of her.

It is also within the power of the narrative voice to present the world as it should be. Ernesto aside, the only other person who does not take advantage of the woman is Palacios, the only one to come from an *ayllu*, a community of Indians. Palacios's humbleness diminishes the brutality of the others, just as Ernesto's animistic descriptions of smiling, conquering rivers and material images of the world serve to ameliorate a brutal reality. Mario Vargas Llosa has brilliantly analyzed the impulse of Arguedas's work in general, arriving at the conclusion that it constitutes a beautiful lie, a radical negation of the world that inspires it.[25] This suggestion of a radical negation makes clear to us that Ernesto and Palacios are formed in the pre-existing cultural norms that are given to them rather than by a pre-existing, "truthful" or traditional model of reality.

Los ríos profundos seeks to correct misguided representations by forcing reality out of a recreation and invention of truth. Arguedas modifies reality to make the dominant narrative voice reflect difference, and power and beauty in diversity. The dominant narrative voice belonging to the son of a blue-eyed, blond Peruvian, communicates, nevertheless, the pure joy of the indigenous world view, based on molding oneself in awe and service of nature. The defiling of nature, curiously, is completed as an issue of gender. It is seen in the execution of unnatural acts such as the abuse of the young woman, abhorred by Ernesto and Palacios for its lack of natural respect. It also chronicles one of the key, formative experiences of the novel with respect to the stages of development. What is not clear to me, however, is what Arguedas is saying about the feeble-minded woman as a woman. Contrary to the Felman argument that mental illness is a sign of political castration, the woman in this novel seems to hold extreme power through fascination, not only for the male characters but for the author himself. In order to diminish this power, the woman is not named until the end of the novel, but then her name is uncovered by Ernesto in conjunction with the term doña, a title of respect whose usage even the priest finds curious. What purpose do the many references to the repugnance of her body or the filthiness of her physical features serve? In fact, why are the novel's vilest, most invidious descriptions that mark the readers' minds (including that of Vargas Llosa) made with reference to this woman and another poor young Indian girl during the plague? The plague itself is thought of by Ernesto as arriving like an "old woman." Why is it that the only positive female images are caricatures of women—the kindly mother replacement figure of the blue-eyed lady (European ancestry) who takes care of Ernesto after the confrontation between the chicheras, the priests, and the townspeople, or the Indian peasant women who sing and dance huaynos celebrating life and nature? Even Ernesto's biological mother has been curiously forgotten. Why is it that Ernesto is able to collapse nature into mother earth but is unable to reason the role of women in this world vision? Arguedas has singled out the enemies—the cruel power of the church, the brutal problem of feudalism—but is generally speechless in giving voice to women. Ultimately, Felman's argument about mental illness being a request for help and a manifestation of cultural impotence and political castration may better reflect the condition of the author than the characters themselves. But it is this sense of impotence that fuels the "correction" of reality in Arguedas' novel.

Other formative experiences that correct reality through Ernesto's process of self development are the zumbayllu rivalries, the confrontation with the chicheras, and the treatment of Brother Miguel. The zumbayllus, or tops, have a magical power that separate or unite the boys, whose mistrust of each other is rooted in their origins and the mysteries of race. Ernesto masters the zumbayllu but is berated by his classmates for being Indian even though he looks white. He is considered an outsider because of where he comes from, but also because he is white with Indian qualities. But Ernesto is able to correct that impression of him as an outsider by grounding his actions in culture—mastering the zumbayllu and communicating his belief in its spiritual powers to the nonbelievers.

Ernesto also matures through his support of the chicheras, who attempt to correct the historic injustice of the treatment of Indians by redistributing the wealth. The cultural and economic correction of the subalterns of the distribution of salt or economic power is welcomed by Ernesto, and then later mourned as the government forces restore the goods to the original owners. The narrative examines the angst of moral judgment from the side of political power, the view of the church, and the position of the subalterns, whose contributions are not respected but who are forced to supplement the agricultural prosperity of the haciendas. Arguedas does give the *chiceras* a voice and identifies their leader by name and physical description while the owners of the haciendas remain faceless and nameless, imposing a correction of reality rarely seen from the perspective of the indigenous. Ernesto is formed in these triumphs, defeats, and issues of power.

The final, formative experience to be discussed involves issues of race. Race is an undercurrent in the novel in that the students are identified by their birthplaces and the color of their skins. Race underscores the complexities of a nation where the minority (European descent) rule the majority (Indigenous). Once again the narrative voice modifies reality and highlights the subaltern text, forcefully examining racism in its brutal manifestations: "¡Auxilio, Padre!—Chilló el Añuco. ¡Auxilio, Padrecito! El Director vino. Hubiera querido correr, pero se contuvo. Lo vi claramente. Apresuró el paso.—¡Sin levantarse!—ordenó el Hermano. Pero el Añuco corrió, se lanzó sobre el Padre, lo abrazó.—¡El negro, Padre, el negro abusivo!—gritó, enfurecido" (132–33) ["Help, Father!" shrieked Añuco. "Help, Padrecito!" The Rector came. He would have liked to run, but he held himself back. I saw him clearly. He quickened his pace. "Don't get up!" ordered Brother Miguel. But Añuco ran, threw himself upon the priest, and clung to him. "The nigger, Father, the black bully!" he shouted angrily (119)]. This outburst followed by other abusive remarks encourages Palacitos to defend Brother Miguel and condemn Lleras for his incorrigible behavior. Ernesto, unlike the other students, does not preach his beliefs but rather rewards and encourages others who hold the same world view that he does. It is his battle against the myth of race that implies violence and degradation. It is the battle that grounds the revolt by the chicheras and the altercation between Brother Miguel and Lleras. Ernesto maintains his belief in the cosmographic vision of the world even when his friends demonstrate ignorance toward the Indians and Brother Miguel. Ernesto absorbs these impressions to cultivate his consciousness but vows never to be conquered in spirit: "¡Que quiere vencerme el mundo entero! ¡Que quiere vencerme! ¡No podrá! . . . Ni el sol ni el polvo del valle, que sofocan; ni el Padre ni el regimiento . . . Iré, iré siempre . . ." (153) [Let the whole world try to overcome me. Let it try. It won't succeed . . . Nor shall the sun, nor the choking dust of the valley, nor the Rector,

nor the regiment. I will go; I will go in spite of everything (139)].
Ernesto maintains his belief in the purity of the natural order including race and culture, even as he faces death in the end.

On facing his mortality, Ernesto survives another test or rite of
passage. As the plague sweeps through the surrounding towns and
approaches Abancay, Ernesto prays over Marcelina, the feeble-
minded woman, so that her spirit may be purified in death, and asks
her forgiveness in the name of all of the students at the school. With
the threat of plague and death, Ernesto's father sends word for him
to seek safety at his uncle's hacienda, the home of the despised Old
Man. This decision brings closure to another stage in the boy's development. Ernesto must learn to put his life in the hands of someone he has been taught to hate. He agrees to the solution
remembering he would find solace in the company of the Indians
working for his Uncle. Perhaps it is the fear of death or the priest's
admonitions that enable Ernesto to view his uncle as anything other
than evil encarnate, but he is willing to correct even this view of the
Old Man: "El pongo que permanecía de pie, afuera, en el corredor,
podía ser aniquilado si el Viejo daba una orden" (254) [The pongo
who had remained standing outside on the balcony could have been
destroyed by the Old Man's command (233)]. The fact that the
smiling, subservient pongo in his everyday acts of resistance had
not been destroyed by the Old Man or the Old Man annihilated by
the pongo's hatred suggests for Ernesto a movement toward understanding occasioned by forgiveness. Having lived with a sense of
community and the greater good he is now able to abandon his unformed particularity, that is, his anger toward the Uncle, for the
sake of the universal, that is, survival from the plague. Ernesto returns to his duty to himself to continue his process and remain open
to other possible versions of the self, already complicated by double
origins and multiple cultures. Ernesto endures hopefully as if beginning another journey to another stage of the Bildung, the process
he skillfully describes before entering the community of the school:
"exploraría palmo a palmo el gran valle y el pueblo; recibiría la
corriente poderosa y triste que golpea a los niños, cuando deben
enfrentarse solos a un mundo cargado de monstruos y de fuego, y
de grandes ríos que cantan con la música más hermosa al chocar
contra las piedras y las islas" (44) [I would explore the great valley
and the town inch by inch; and I would feel the force of the sad and
powerful current that buffets children who must face, all alone, a
world fraught with monsters and fire and great rivers that sing the
most beautiful of all music as they break upon the stones and the
islands (38)].

In essence, the most convincing aspect of Ernesto's process of development and self-cultivation is his formation of memory. He admits at the end of the novel to being "más atento a los recuerdos que a las cosas externas" (243) [more attentive to memories than to external things (222)]. His memory is grounded in a double, cultural heritage at once melancholy and beautiful, which permeates the novel.[26] While his mind and spirit identify with the Indians, his physical features link him to those of European descent. His formation is an outward and inward struggle, a battle to remember his origin but to live in the moment. Ernesto's is a struggle he takes on "all alone" to face evil, represented by mankind, and goodness, which he locates in nature. But contingent to the formation of memory is the ability to forget. By forgetting, Ernesto gives his mind a chance for total renewal, to see things with fresh eyes by allowing what is different from oneself. In this manner, Ernesto is able to "forget" what he remembers about the Old Man's treatment of the Indians, the Rector's duplicity in ministering to the Indians and the chicheras, and his classmates' unjust attitudes toward Indians. In *Los ríos profundos* the story of culture aids Ernesto in finding himself again so as to further his formation. The story of culture explains through magic the existence of the Indians, because it is difficult for Ernesto to believe in the logic of reality: "Reality can hardly be 'logical' for the exploited Indian peasant, scorned and humiliated all his life and defenseless against disease and poverty; nor can the world be rational for the outcast child, rootless among men, forever exiled."[27] Ernesto, the outcast child, is a marginalized figure who symbolizes the powerlessness of the subalterns, the majority who play the minority role in power and are subject to the brutal violence of nature and humankind. His tragic, personal journey is punctuated by exquisite joy and examples of beauty as well as violence, human violations and degradations, and unspeakable suffering. In the end, Ernesto's angst of moral judgment propels him to another stage in the developmental process, while the author inscribes himself within an interminable moral crisis that ends with his suicide.

5

The Forming of the Self and Nation: The Bildungsroman from Collective Urgency to Foundational Narrative

> The moral imperative of humanism is the endeavor alone, whether successful or not, provided the effort is honorable and failure memorable.
>
> —E. O. Wilson, *Consilience*

TESTIMONIAL NARRATIVES AND FOUNDATIONAL FICTIONS SHOULD also be read as Bildungsromane, because they convey the development of identity, be it self or collective, from within the social structure. Rhetorically they are grounded in processes of self-definition and growth that inform larger issues of justice, social change, identity, and ethical choice.[1] They also appeal to a representational quality through their protagonists who recreate the larger, historical struggles of a nation at birth, or who move from subject to object in the voicing/creation of their own story. I believe, therefore, that the journey of self discovery and enlightenment also reflects a collective journey, a journey of a people moving in a forward direction, confronting challenges, adversity and great odds, and rising to meet its potential by developing its capabilities.[2] As with the Apostle Paul's entreaty of the Philippians to be on the journey and press forward to the goals ahead, the desired response in this development of identity is a collective yes.

Testimonial narrative springs from collective urgency. This urgency is grounded in the first person who narrates the exploitation, violence, marginalization, and anguishing poverty of or against a group the "I" represents and for whom a structural, social change is demanded.[3] John Beverley suggests that testimony's purpose distinguishes it from the private destiny of the picaresque, autobiographical, or Bildungsroman hero. I also interpret duties toward one's ethnic group, tribe, culture, or founding nation as being born

146

in and enhanced by duties toward oneself when Bildung is raised to the universal. The relational quality of opening oneself to the viewpoints of possible others through circumspection and by not giving in to particular needs or personal anger, demonstrates a 'public' or cultivated consciousness within the Bildung process.

Cultivated consciousness, synonymous with growth and activity in all directions, parallels a search for identity in nation-building projects and testimonial narratives. Significantly, an active questioning of self promotes an empowered view of one's group or nation. Djelal Kadir discerningly points out that literary tradition in Latin America, as in all national literatures, moves toward an encounter with a self-definition that might constitute a homecoming. The Latin American model is more problematic, however, because "Latin America" itself is an artificial and debatable construct.[4] In addition, a homecoming for some reflects a nightmare for others, which demands social change but may potentially lead to a richer, socio-political fabric and liberating, literary strategies. Problematic and revolutionary, three foundational Bildungsromane unsettle normative patterns of growth and development through pluralities of cultural meaning: Miguel Barnet's *Biografía de un Cimarrón*, Teresa de la Parra's *Las memorias de Mamá Blanca*, and Augusto Roa Bastos's *Hijo de hombre*.

Miguel Barnet informs in the Introduction to *Biografía de un cimarrón* (1966) [*The Autobiography of a Runaway Slave*, 1968] that the strategy for writing his book reflects a desire to recover Cuba's past after reading a newspaper article dedicated to the stories of men and women in Cuba over 100 years of age. He states that two of these stories caught his eye: a woman ex-slave, *santera* and spiritualist, and a man who was a runaway slave who spoke of certain aspects of slavery and the War of Independence of Cuba. Barnet dedicates a total of 14 words to the woman, ignoring one of the fundamental anthropological goals of his study to explore African religions in Cuba, and dismisses her with "[o]lvidamos a la anciana . . .[5] [we forgot about the old woman[6]] while turning his attention to Esteban Montejo.[7] Elzbieta Sklodowska attributes this arbitrariness to the political rather than the ethnological objectives of the book. Ironically, Barnet looks to Esteban for a spiritual side that must be drawn out, in order to reconstruct a portion of Cuba's history that will be instrumental in defining the conversion to Cuba's "new" national character. Fidel Castro in his "Palabras a los intelectuales" (1961) challenges and demands intellectuals to explore the strength of the Cuban character. In addition, the prestigious prize awarded by *Casa de las Américas* under a new category for testimonial narrative (after Barnet writes *Biografía de un cima-rrón*) legitimizes the process of self reflection as supranational, that is, as a significant aspect of identity, regardless of nation.

There has been much discussion of why Miguel Barnet was encouraged shortly after the Revolution to explore the African core of Cuban society, for rhetorically, the narrative opportunities align themselves once more with the postcolonial founding of new nations. Perhaps this was made possible, as Carlos Alonso might argue, through an uneasy arrangement that permitted the coexistence of the narrative of futurity and the conservative, backward glance of the nation model:

> . . . each country would engage in the formulation of a national myth of origins that would identify and locate its presumed beginnings somewhere in the colonial period, while it would also be possible for each country to assert simultaneously that the final configuration and image of that national identity would be revealed only at an unspecified yet certain future date. In this way the monadic and static European model for the formulation of a national identity was infused in its Spanish American acceptation with a chronological dimension that made for a contradictory but nonetheless ideologically useful discursive space.[8]

Curiously, Barnet does elide the Spanish American postcolonial model of futurity and look to an autochthonous past, which had grown increasingly irrelevant, not instead of but because of its relationship with the future.

When Castro came to power in 1959 he assumed control over a population estimated at 6,700,000, of which conceivably about 50 percent were of African descent. Racial segregation both in public and private establishments was still pervasive when the Revolution overthrew Batista, who decidedly had the support of many Afro-Cubans owing to his own mixed background. Some Afro-Cuban soldiers who had risked their lives alongside Castro encountered discrimination, however, in the workplace and in hotels and restaurants where their white counterparts were welcomed. Castro nonetheless pointedly minimized the racial question in Cuba in those early weeks of euphoria, and remained silent for decades following a well-established pattern of Cuban ethno-politics. What we do know is that Castro saw the need to appeal to as broad a base as possible and maintain the support of the powerful Cuban upper and middle classes. Therefore, testing the waters once with the encouragement of military heroes and noted sociologist Juan René Betancourt, Castro delivered a statement that studiously avoided the political and cultural implications of the racial question, limiting it to two forms, "the one practiced in cultural and recreational resorts and that practiced in workplaces." This alone, however, was enough to cause fury among the Hispanic Cubans who brought Castro to power, and was the impetus for the almost constant silence on race experienced since that moment.[9] The struggle against the self that ensues at least impels Castro to reflect on social change, open the "case" of the Blacks in Cuba, and encourage Barnet's study among many others.

Beyond filling in the empty space of history with respect to slavery, the abolition of slavery, and independence from Spain, and beyond the descriptive details of architectural and social space within the *barracones* [barracoons], *Biografía de un cimarrón* opens the literary canon to the inclusion of the Other. Here the marginalized, poor, runaway slave and mixed-heritage hero explores and defines himself, the development of his moral code, and his "life choices." It is an analysis of life that reflects a complex dialectic of identity for subject and author grounded in "la manera de nuestro informante acercarse a las cosas, de tratar a los hombres, su actitud de grupo, parcial a su raza" (11) [the way in which our informant approaches things, deals with men, his group's attitude, which is common to those of his race]. One successful review of Esteban's attitudes could be explored through a social or racial prism. Another could be accomplished by returning to the foundation through a series of gestures backward, toward those textual origins of the novel vigorously argued by Roberto González Echevarría.[10] I believe, in addition, that yet another could be accomplished through the narrative potential of the Bildungsroman, which creates a vital, new space for the exploration of developmental tensions and imagination.

Far from the anthropological dilemma of how to know the other and remain the self, in literature and specifically in the novel of growth, development, and self-cultivation, we witness a dedication to knowing the self because of and through a relationship with the other. It projects a Hegelian concept of the spirit that seeks one's own in the alien, and becomes at home in it, in a basic movement whose being is the return to itself from what is other. For example, it is enlightening to analyze in *Biografía* how the seemingly consistent development of the qualities of an individualist would permit outstanding contributions of personal satisfaction made, nevertheless, in collective situations such as in war and in the preservation of Afro-Cuban cultural history through oral histories.

Similar to a picaresque novel, Esteban begins his narration with an identification and situation of the first person singular, his birth, family relations, and other important rites of passage. One element that is key to Esteban Montejo's self journey is his identification with a moral code. For this Esteban associates the senses with truth in his moral code. For example, if it is something that he has seen or heard, he can accept it as positive and with value. He describes his birth, his parents, and his mother's slave owner whose last name he bears with a demonstration of faith in the veracity of the account: "Claro que yo no vide a ese hombre nunca, pero sé que es positivo ese cuento porque me lo hicieron mis padrinos" (15) [I never saw him, of course, but I believe this story because my godparents told it to me, and I remember every word they told me[11]]. Esteban's mother was a slave of French origin, and his father was a *lucumí*, which is a Cuban term for a Negro slave who came from Nigeria or the Gulf of Guinea. He never knew his parents: "La verdad es que yo hubiera querido conocerlos, pero por salvarme el pellejo no los pude ver. Si llego a salir del monte ahí mismo me hubieran aga-rrado. Por cimarrón no conocí a mis padres" (15) [I would very much like to have known them, but if I had left the forest to find them I would have been seized at once. Because of being a runaway I never knew my parents (17–18)].

The Bildungsroman like autobiography narrates the life of the protagonist from its completion; that is, it communicates the devel-opment of the central character from birth onward as if in real time when in reality it is recalling a full life from an advanced position. Esteban, González Echevarría convincingly argues: ". . . lives on the far side of all change, of all upheavals, because he has already endured the most difficult trials and is in possession of the special knowledge that such a journey confers on him . . . He can incarnate both the child, the Messiah, and the old-man prophet: Jesus and Moses at once."[12] This is the power of the Bildung spirit to com-bine beginning and ending at once in varying degrees throughout a lifetime. The final statement "because of being a runaway slave I never knew my parents" is the first aporia of the text. It indicates a developmental process guided by a personal code of values that in-form his choices. Esteban clearly prefers this explanation of being a runaway slave, which elides or erases the earlier period of his life, because it is definitive and actionable, and recalls in a forward di-rection the memories in which he wishes to ground his identity.

The inner strength, independence of thought and action, union with the pureness of nature, and moral endeavor that does not be-tray him or anyone else are elements of Esteban's process to find in himself his own significance. In a sense it would have been less dangerous to remain the slave he was sold at birth to be, as the majority do. But Esteban is searching for those exit points and threads to return to himself, as a form of survival but also as a way of creating himself. This is why memory makes a powerful statement here. Esteban is *forming* his memory, memory for some things and not for others, slipping by memories rather than confronting those "he would have liked" but that would have violated the formation he has chosen for himself. The key point is what has come into being for Esteban, which he would have us believe was a part of him since birth, "Yo era cimarrón de nacimiento" (18) [I was a runaway from birth (21)], and leads him to choose the life of the runaway slave.

Esteban recalls other formative rites of passage beyond birth such as his first job in a sugar mill and his education through oral history, so as to be able to understand himself and the other: "Al negro le gusta el árbol, el monte. ¡Todavía el chino . . . ! Africa estaba llena de árboles, de ceibas, de cedros, de jagüeyes. China no, allá lo que había más era yerba de la que se arrastra, dormidera, verdolaga, diez de la mañana . . ." (20). [The Negro likes trees, forests. But the Chinese! Africa was full of trees, god-trees, banyans, cedars. But not China—there they have weeds, purslaine, morning-glory, the sort of thing that creeps along (22)]. Esteban struggles toward a cultural construction of himself that relies on an examination of the self with respect to the other, even if these constructs are once removed and based on geographic areas that are foreign to the principal speaker. The return to Africa throughout the novel as a space of potentiality underscores the Bildung process by which all experience is absorbed through the senses and nothing lost. It also reveals Esteban's belief in the impossibility of returning to Africa spiritually even after death (119), and to the exclusion of everything else. In acquired Bildung the reaching up toward the potential self includes all past experience and all past relationships that have created Esteban's knowledge of Cuba, Africa, China, the Philippines, or Spain.

Repeated references to slave owners continually reinforce the rigidity of life in the barracoons from whippings to a military-style religious life, the latter reminiscent of life for the Guaraní indians under the Jesuits in Paraguay. Esteban speaks proudly of his education from the elders of the community, from philosophic issues reflecting African religions and his African roots to nutritional training: "Yo aprendí de los viejos a comer vianda, que es muy nutricia" (23) [I learned to eat vegetables from the elders, because they said they were very healthy food (24)]. In this context there is a development of spirituality through a conversation on religion, which the author signals in the introduction as not flowing easily. Esteban's strength is in a clear access to identity that promotes further self-reflection. In effect, his categorization of distinctions aids in forming the self. With respect to religions he concludes: "Los dioses de Africa son distintos aunque se parezcan a los otros, a los de los curas. Son más fuertes y menos adornados" (31) [The African gods are different, though they resemble the others, the priests' gods. They are more powerful and less adorned (33)]. He makes distinctions between Jewish congo and Christian congo religions, while always defending Africa as the site of pure origins authenticated by the elders.[13] Perhaps his individualist spirit, his self reflection that propels him forward, and his openness to others who respect his separate nature, encourage a greater sense of tolerance in Esteban with respect to religious and sexual preferences.[14] Or perhaps the greater task of staying alive in the face of illness and forced labor permits a sense of freedom others find unimaginable.

Esteban's need to do something just because he feels like it leads him to a life in the mountains that few others would choose. González Echevarría reinforces the rebirth and renewal effect of this portion of Esteban's development: ". . . each flight into the bush is a flight into silence, into a sort of erasure that will allow him to convert, to start anew, to shed the trappings of society, to run naked back to Mother Earth."[15] The liberating potential of nature and the symbolic rebirth in the cave encourage in Esteban, ironically, a power to survive within society also. They propel him to the next level in his personal development. The solitude he finds in the mountain increases when his individual impulse for freedom requires a further separation from other runaway slaves in *palenques* to live for a year and a half in a cave: "Ni de los propios cimarrones me dejaba ver: cimarrón con cimarrón, vende cimarrón" (47) [I did not let the other runaways catch sight of me: 'Runaway meets runaway, sells runaway' (49)].[16] Esteban prizes the solitude and the healthy life he leads, and does not lament the price paid for the lack of human dialogue or comforting acts such as whistling to scare away the bad spirits.

A man of great personal strength, Esteban stays away from all human contact so that he will not lose his power to run his own life, an ironic attempt to dictate his own Bildung process. This affects his complex opinion of women also. While hiding in the mountain he does not have female companionship so he keeps himself from the pleasure of female company. He recognizes women as "the greatest thing", but even after the abolition of slavery when he returns to the towns and life at the sugar plantations, women come to represent for him (as do all relationships) the same handcuffing or loss of freedom through slavery. Significantly, his dialogue with nature, the animals and trees that talk to him, sustains and gives him companionship in addition to a sense of his own spirit, but requires nothing in return: "Por eso de cimarrón no estuve con nadie. Nada más oía a los pájaros y a los árboles y comía, pero nunca conocí a nadie" (56) [That was why I stayed on my own as a runaway. I did nothing except listen to the birds and trees, and eat, but I never spoke to a soul (59)]. With the abolition of slavery Esteban may discard his identity as runaway slave and, although he spends years without speaking to anyone, ironically push himself to another level in human relations.

Esteban's quest of self exploration after the abolition of slavery takes him to many towns to conduct a search for his family, during which time he never goes hungry because people always take care of him. His sense of self worth guides him, however, to a decision to seek work cutting sugar cane instead of living off the generosity of others. The next, complex level of development involves a transference of values from the mountain to the plantation workplace. Esteban works extremely hard and wastes little on gambling or women, thereby maintaining his economic independence. He also almost mysteriously and mystically develops a sense of dialogue, understanding the power of language and, therefore, varying his answers depending on his needs and those of his interlocutors. For example, understanding the fascination some have with him and his experience he answers: "Yo soy Esteban y fui cimarrón" (58) ['My name is Stephen and I was a runaway slave' (63)], opening a floodgate of questions that we presume he answers. On other occasions he simply replies that he has worked at such and such a plantation and that he has not found his relatives. This inspires his listeners to empathy and care. For someone who has spent years without speaking or hearing human sounds, associating only with the sounds made by bats, owls, and trees, he develops a profound confidence in his conversational abilities: "Yo era muy atrevido; a cualquier prieta linda le sacaba conversación y ellas se dejaban enamorar" (66) [I was very bold; any pretty dark-skinned girl I met I got talking to, and they used to fall for me (71)]. At this time Esteban recognizes women as equals and has no difficulty asking them for money in exchange for his friendship. Esteban develops this side of his personality in order to remain faithful to his understanding of a virtuous self: "El buen carácter es importante en todo. Cuando uno vive solo no hace falta. Pero como uno siempre está rodeado de gente, lo mejor es ser agradable; no caer mal" (95) [A good character matters in everything. If you live alone, it isn't necessary, but since we live surrounded by people it's better to make oneself pleasant, not fall out with them (103)].

The distinction between being alone and in others' company is most profoundly clear to Esteban, who has spent a year and a half listening only to sounds of nature. His decision to know the self through relationships with others should not be underestimated. Furthermore, by struggling toward a cultural construct of himself he also promotes a goal of good character for the Cuban nation. Yet Esteban's relationships are not without conflict. With women and children, for example, he demonstrates a superior, macho stance that he is reluctant to relinquish even after realizing the "equality" of women and stating that, in effect, women work harder than men because they have no 'down' time for themselves. He also demonstrates little interest in knowing the offspring he may have engendered because they represent the same kind of problems for him that women do. Curiously, Esteban mimics the constitution of the "new" Cuban state under Castro, proclaiming equality (by law) for women but promoting a very distinct reality.

With the War of Independence Esteban continues his process of coming into being, blending already realized acts with a potency still awaiting its realization. His moral code determines his course of reflection and action: "Nadie obligaba a nadie a robar. Lo malo se le pega al que es malo. Yo estuve en la guerra con unos cuantos degenerados y salí limpiecito" (103) [No one forced anyone else to steal. Evil sticks to evil. I went through the war with a bunch of degenerates, but I came out with my hands clean (112)]. The only person he truly respects is the national hero José Martí, because he is exceedingly honest and does not steal money to support revolutionary causes. Significantly, Esteban does not respect those men who lack character, that is, who sleep with women and want to give details of their encounters: "Yo nunca fui partidario de contar mis cosas. Cada hombre debe aprender a ser reservado . . . A mí esos chismes nunca me han gustado" (114) [I wasn't given to talking about my own experiences. A man should learn to keep certain things to himself . . . I don't like that sort of gossip (125)]. One who is true to himself is also true to others, to the collective. With this Esteban appears to communicate to us his personal code of honor, which easily unfolds into a code of national identity.

Esteban's personal growth frequently coincides with that of the nation. He clearly respects differences as part of a personal philosophy, in particular underscoring the syncretic Cuban culture and religious differences as worthy of respect: "Todas las religiones se han mezclado aquí en esta tierra. El africano trajo la suya, la más fuerte, y el español también trajo la suya, pero no tan fuerte. Hay que respetarlas todas. Esa es mi política" (129) [No person is one thing pure and simple in this country, because all the religions have got mixed together. The African brought his, which is the stronger one, and the Spaniard brought his, which isn't so strong, but you should respect them all. That is my way of thinking (142)]. Esteban is capable of painting a portrait of Cuban society focusing on racial, ethnic, religious differences and different pressures imposed by society on each group.[17] But more than a portrait of customs, Esteban's narrative demonstrates personal growth in relation to others in a fairly sophisticated fashion that enlists Blacks, Chinese, Gypsies, Spanish, whites born in Cuba, Catholics, and Santeros, in the metonymical potential of one representing a blended population. In essence, he is tracing the timeless story of nature and nation. The education Esteban receives forms him not in the sense of lessons learned but in a way of becoming and being-in-the-world, being his disclosure of world, which in effect encourages him to respect himself as well as others: "A mí me enseñaron muchas cosas sin saber leer ni escribir. Las costumbres, que son más importantes que los conocimientos. Ser educado, no meterse en problemas ajenos, hablar bajito, respetar, ser religioso, buen trabajador . . . todo eso me lo inculcaron a mí los africanos" (149) [They taught me many things without being able to read or write—customs, which are more important than knowledge: to be polite, not to meddle in other people's affairs, to speak softly, to be respectful and religious, to work hard (165)]. In a text dedicated to self-reflection Esteban communicates his becoming his culture and his absorbing his language through a hybrid, communal exchange. The existence of numerous traditions in Cuba opens the possibility that everything is absorbed as in Bildung, so a simultaneity of languages, or heteroglossia, and cultural codes reinforces the values of a newly formed cultural heritage.

With respect to cultural codes and testimony to suffering, Esteban's narrative of the War of Independence reveals in the beginning that no one really understands why they are fighting. They reason, however, that justice and liberty do not exist unilaterally and only a war can resolve this dilemma. Esteban submits to the battle completely and to a struggle in Mal Tiempo that brings out the worst in the cowardly Spanish and the brutal revolutionaries. Once again as testimonial narrative we observe the battle through Esteban's eyes as he fights for social justice. He principally fights for the preservation of values while others fight for personal glory. The battle of

Mal Tiempo gives the revolutionaries the courage to believe they can win against the Spanish. Esteban receives and follows orders there and in other battles to assure victory, but that which he will not support is the greed that permits some to assume an immoral position in the revolution. Once the line is crossed and his moral code is confronted, Esteban rejects even his superiors who are fighting for his rights as well. He leaves his superior Tajó, who is using the revolution for personal gain, to fight under Cayito, discovering unfortunately that he has left one criminal and assassin to fight for another. Esteban, however, excuses his own excesses and petty thievery with which morally he could live because, after all, the food he steals keeps many alive to serve during the War of Independence: "Creo que lo que más hice en la guerra fue eso: atrapar ganado. Como no se podía sembrar, atrapábamos ganado. De alguna forma había que buscarse la comida, al que hacía ese trabajo lo consideraban mucho" (172) [I think that stealing animals was what I did most of during the war. We had to do it because there was no way of growing crops, and we had to eat somehow or other. The people who carried out these exploits were highly thought of (193)]. The fact that he rises in the estimation of others and aids their survival assuages his guilt and permits a deviation from his moral code, which is the reason why he includes this justification of his actions in his self-reflection.

Unconscionable acts notwithstanding, Esteban continues to fight for honor rather than personal gain, which underscores a goal of self-cultivation through the many diverse stages of personal development. Esteban awakens us to a gripping tale of a nation through his self-realization because even after the abolition of slavery in 1886, the tales of bravery of black liberators during the War of Independence, and the Resolution of 1912 prohibiting racist political parties, racism continues to force blacks in Cuba into a marginal position.[18] This statement goes beyond Barnet's original desire for "identity, a sincere confession" that would ground the narrative in the personal need of the author.[19] Similarly, it goes beyond the goals of an anthropological examination to explore the truth about Afro-Cuban religions and their importance in Cuban society.[20] Esteban's journey of self-knowledge uncovers the painful birth of the Cuban nation that continues its Bildung process searching for transcendence, the self beyond the self, and survival, because as Esteban concludes: "[la] verdad no se puede callar" (199) [truth cannot be silenced (223)].

Las memorias de Mamá Blanca (1928), [*Mamá Blanca's Memoirs* 1993] is a foundational fiction of the growth and development of protagonist and nation, in this case a female protagonist in another Caribbean nation, Venezuela. The novel intends two oppositional structures and goals: to recapture the innocence of youth and to pit it against a social consciousness that elaborates the struggles inherent in the birth and founding of a nation. Blanca Nieves's demystification of this world is aided by her relationship with the new mother as discussed in chapter 1, but her being-in-the-world, that is her conception of essence as rooted in her possibilities, is also enlivened by her relationship with male figures either through parody or inspired imitation, as the heroic, foundational, national figures are usually male. For example, the narrator informs us that Primo Juancho's efforts on the girls' behalf assured that: "nos iniciáramos ya en algo de la sana mentalidad y del indispensable idioma inglés" (58) [[we] should receive early notions of the sound mentality and the indispensable language of the English (57)]. His influence over Carmen María inspires her to hire Evelyn, a Trinidadian nanny to tutor the girls in English, the language of progress. Ironically, the girls' disdain for Evelyn's oppressive nature encourages them to appreciate the Spanish of their mother even more. Blanca Nieves's cultural identity develops as she parodies the male text of Primo Juancho. Her admiration grows in direct proportion to the insults hurled by Primo Juancho at their native country, Venezuela, and the entire southern continent. Significantly, Bildung consists of learning to allow what is different from oneself and to find universal viewpoints from which one can grasp the thing.[21] Primo Juancho's position of the other, mirroring de la Parra's study of her native Venezuela from Europe, provides a rich, nuanced view of race, gender, cultural, social and human relations in Venezuela that makes the text memorable. By parodying Primo Juancho, who is often given to broad-stroked descriptions of misguided political passions and somber morning coats, Blanca Nieves is able to release her own passionate impulses, admiration for the literature of her native language (nostalgia for the poem of the Cid, intimacy with the protagonists of *Don Quijote*), and appreciation of difference.

Another aide to the demystification of the world is found in Blanca's relationship with Vicente Cochocho. Denigrated and reviled by Evelyn for his physical appearance, which produces a racial tension that goes beyond his impoverished semblance, Vicente becomes, nevertheless, a model of nature and its purity. Cochocho does not take offense at his nickname, meaning louse, and suggests only delightful memories inscribed in Blanca's mind. But Vicente, who in his person joins black and Indian, embodies the racial tension and hatred that arises from a protracted struggle for the abolition of slavery and a national struggle for independence. Historically, Afro-Creoles play an important role in the nineteenth century but do not participate in the modernization of Latin America. This result gives the debasing effect of slavery, pauperism, and isolation to the Afro-Creole worker, even after the abolition of slavery.[22] It is an effect that opposes white hacienda owners and Afro-Creole workers in an economic struggle, which, at times, neither side wins. It is also an effect that embattles a highly mixed race. At first we understand this tension through an aporia. The protagonist slips out of a historical narrative of memories to signal her Bildung process to us, which includes arriving at intellectual and moral maturity with respect to race and equality: "En el fondo, *hoy lo comprendo*, la guerra a muerte que Evelyn declaraba diariamente a nuestro querido Cochocho tenía por base un complicado y personal odio de raza. Por eso era encarnizada y sin tregua. Evelyn, que tenía tres cuartos de sangre blanca, maldecía con ellos su cuarto de sangre negra. Como no le era posible maltratar su negro en ella, le pasaba poderes a Vicente y lo maltrataba en él" (70, *my emphasis*) [At bottom—*I understand it now*—the war to the death that Evelyn carried on daily against our beloved Cochocho had its origin in a complex, personal race hatred. For that reason it was relentless and without quarter. Evelyn's three-quarters of white blood cursed her quarter of Negro blood. As she was unable to bedevil the Negro in herself, she took it out on Vicente (64, *my emphasis*)]. Perhaps we could conclude that Teresa de la Parra forms a part of a group of nationalist writers who in the 1920s discovers that "race matters". In support of the theory that previously ignored racial sectors contribute to the formation of national identity, José Vasconcelos and Gilberto Freyre, among others, celebrated mestizaje as a positive force in national identity that develops a Spanish-American identity in positive terms. The personal development and self-realization process that continues into Mamá Blanca's mature years ("hoy lo comprendo"), mirrors the development of national identity in de la Parra's native Venezuela. The author's exploration of national identity significantly also extends to class and cultural issues, language being an indicator of and key to both.

Blanca Nieves frequently praises Vicente's use of language, which is rooted in the Spanish of the Golden Age, a "gift" from Spain to the New World. In spite of his simplicity and unsociable habits, the girls admire Vicente and praise him for his keen mind:

El trato con Vicente Cochocho nos iba instruyendo en filosofía y en ciencias naturales como ningún libro o profesor hubiera podido hacerlo.

Su espíritu hermano por la sencillez, fuerte por la experiencia, estaba adornado de conocimientos amenos que corrían fácilmente de su inteligencia hacia las nuestras con la naturalidad de un arroyo regocijado y claro. (73)

[Our association with Vicente Cochocho gave us a better training in philosophy and the natural sciences than any textbook could have done. His spirit, one with ours in its simplicity, strong with the wisdom of experience, held a fund of pleasant information which followed from his mind to ours with the ease of a limpid, running brook (73–74).]

Once again, as is the case with Primo Juancho, it is in parodying Vicente Cochocho's life and comparing it to that of the mother, that Blanca Nieves is compelled to give herself her existence in the world through language and self-articulation. Furthermore, her exploration of language enables her to "become" more Venezuelan and Spanish American. In this manner, she is able by employing language to work from the inside out, to exteriorize what is in herself and give it life through speech even as she seeks to understand her national identity. As in all hybrid cultures, she is privileging orality. Blanca Nieves encounters the liberating and at once grounding qualities of articulation when she asks a rhetorical question with reference to Vicente's rhythmical speech: "¿Qué es una frase sin tono ni ritmo? Una muerta, una momia. ¡Ah, hermosa voz humana, alma de las palabras, madre del idioma, qué rica, qué infinita eres! Cuantas veces he tratado de explicarles aquí cómo hablaba Vicente y cómo hablaba Mamá, aquellos dos polos: el extremo de la rusticidad y el extremo de la exquisitez o "preciosismo", uno más ritmado que melodioso, otro más melodioso que ritmado, he tenido que contemplar con tristeza la miseria realizada por mi buena intención. La palabra escrita, lo repito, es un cadáver" (75) [What is a phrase without tone or rhythm? A corpse, a mummy. Oh beautiful human voice, the soul of words, the mother of language, how rich, how infinite thou art! As many times as I have attempted to explain to you how Vicente talked and how Mama talked, those two opposed poles, one the essence of rusticity and the other of refinement or preciosity, one in which the rhythm predominated, the other, the melody, I have sadly realized the uselessness of my endeavor. The written word, I repeat, is a corpse (75)]. Orality is a cultural sphere that is most relevant to a blended society. The key to Vicente's speech, for example, is in the rhythm, the accenting of meaning that lends it emphasis. It is loyal to the speech of the sixteenth century and the colony that the "masters" had long abandoned. His speech gives life to his thoughts, raising a humble figure to the sublime, while empowering the subaltern text and making it memorable. Vicente is never disrespectful to Juan Manuel or Carmen María, his employers, yet his intentionality in the subaltern discourse, like the feminist discourse, reveals a rebellious nature under agreeable speech and an affable exterior. His speech is an example of his everyday acts of rebellion. It entitles him to do his own bidding regardless of the anger and frustration felt by others when he disregards orders and supplications to stop practicing medicine, marry one of his two lovers, or abandon the revolution for the work he has given his word to complete.

Vicente's sense of loyalty to his military and medical vocations take precedence over his duties at the hacienda, because his strategic brilliance shines in the military and his trust in God rules in the field of medicine. This overturning of class and social order confuses Juan Manuel's sense of order and produces a rebellion against all hacendados [landowners] who stand idly by as groups of men from each hacienda leave to fight periodically for their cause in the revolution. Vicente's speech causes frustration for some even as it reserves for itself a special place in the soul of Blanca Nieves, because for her it conceals an idealistic and romantic soul. Most importantly, its rhythms register the obligation of the new nation to continue its debate on social justice.

Vicente's manner of speech encourages the girls to respect him, his lifestyle choices, his unusual looks and his mixed race, and admire his code of honor from the treatment of women to participation in the revolution. Blanca may choose to confront social injustice through relationships rather than through revolution, but, importantly, her relationship with Vicente and Evelyn and many others at Piedra Azul inspires her to challenge the revolutionary process as an identifying force of societal change. Her challenge to hierarchical society, like most of the narrative, is subtle, and seen in delightful description that goes right to the heart of a social problem. For example, if Piedra Azul is their cosmos and world, then the sugar mill is their club, theater, and city—but it exists exclusively for the daughters of the owners. The daughters of the hacendado alone are allowed to interrupt work, make imprints in cane sap, ask questions, and demand that the peons release the water and cut sugar cane upon their request and for their pleasure. Nothing is hidden in the mill and everyone knows why things happen there as the protagonist explains, which is why the contrasting portrayal of workers' children begging for scraps or broken pieces is particularly effective.

This challenge to society is clearly understood when one returns to the foreword after reading the conclusion. Mamá Blanca is "a character who may be a first in Spanish-American literature—a woman who is simultaneously convincing and joyful."[23] Her ability to convince and negotiate a consensus while maintaining a pleasant relationship with all is valuable. Her relationships with others and the land compel us to see life, society, and morality as the stories she tells. As a mature person, Mamá Blanca's open door is: "una muestra natural de su amor a los humildes" (6) [an outward sign of her love for the humble (4)], her friendship is "como la oración en labios de los místicos" (7) [like prayer on the lips of mystics (6)]. Her generosity is endless to those in need even as she slips into poverty. Blanca's relationship with Vicente uncovers the strong, traditional values of respect, honesty and humility, which serve as counterpoint to the father's and mother's equally strong values, of loyalty and beneficence with respect to the father, and morality, care and concern, with respect to the mother. Mama Blanca's victory turns on her transformation from mirrored image of society to agent, however modest, of social change.

Hijo de hombre (1960), the first novel of Paraguayan author Augusto Roa Basto, is a collection of memories and motifs and the final testimony and foundational fiction to be examined in this chapter. As Bildungsroman it represents a testimonial discourse, foundational narrative, linguistic clash of cultures, and precursor to the postmodern hybrid text. It alternates between the anguished, impossible life journey of protagonist Miguel Vera, who has a tenuous relationship with his own cultural and social community, and a tale of collective urgency of an impoverished people who are victims of violent social and political injustices. Rosa Monzón ends her letter as the novel ends with the following justification of the publication of Miguel Vera's manuscript: "Acaso su publicidad ayuda, aunque sea en mínima parte, a comprender, más que a un hombre, a este pueblo tan calumniado de América, que durante siglos ha oscilado sin descanso entre la rebeldía y la opresión, entre el oprobio de sus escarnecedores y la profecía de sus mártires . . ."[24] [Perhaps their publication will help, in however small a degree, to make people understand the much-slandered Paraguayan race, which for centuries has swung between oppression and rebellion, between the ignominy of its tyrants and the glory of its martyrs . . ."[25]]. The biblical quality evidenced in the struggles of a people between oppression and martyrdom brings the narration full circle in linking the ending to the epigraphs taken from the biblical chapter of Ezekiel and the "Himno de los muertos de los guaraníes" [Hymn of the Dead of the Guaraní People]. These competing voices, similar to those in Arguedas's *Los ríos profundos* and Vargas Llosa's *El hablador*, register the heteroglossia Bakhtin addresses as they demand space in the debate over what it means to give voice out of marginality to America and be Latin American.

The fact that these simultaneous voices form so completely the cultural history of Paraguay makes this at once a journey toward potentiality of the individual, the nation, and Latin America, including more universal viewpoints that battle the attack on the human spirit. The relationship that establishes itself between languages and cultures is seamless, one tradition flowing into the other so that the process of acculturation is mutually effective. It explains the powerful mutual acculturation that Rubén Bareiro Saguier refers to as the infiltration of indigenous values into the formulation of the strict "true faith."[26] Of particular note is the collective voice. The process of growth and development unpacks a molding and formation of the self not only in relation to others but also as a representative group. What distinguishes this novel as representative of the formational Bildungsroman is its collective Bildung process and relational quality. The protagonists of this novel set out on the journey of self-realization in spite of the fact that history has beaten them back, and deprived them of the freedom and justice many would believe essential to a journey of discovery.

Roa Bastos privileges the voice of the vanquished and marginalized members of society interweaving the singular, narrative voice of Miguel Vera from his position of power, and the collective voice of the guaraní. The blending itself does not reveal a power struggle but a survival of the strongest elements from the Bildung process of both. For example, upon describing the Catholic rite of Good Friday the narrator underscores: "Era un cielo áspero, rebelde, primitivo, fermentado en un reniego de insurgencia colectiva, como si el espíritu de la gente se encrespara al olor de la sangre del sacrificio y estallase en ese clamor que no se sabía si era de angustia o de esperanza o de resentimiento a la hora nona del Viernes de la Pasión" (13) [It was a harsh, primitive rite, an expression of the villagers' rebellious spirit which, as though roused by the smell of sacrificial blood, broke out on Passion Friday in this demonstration of fear and hope and anger (17)]. The cyclical ritual of the birth and death of Christ permits an acceptable outpouring of grief and anger, which revolves on a rebellious, primitive core affirming itself in a collective movement. The narrator tells us that this is what has given the itapeños the nickname of fanatics and heretics, but what he is also communicating is that the history of the town of Itapé transforms itself into the history of Paraguay, which looks to locate itself in the history of America.

In effect, the superficial calm or prosperity of a town or nation that bargains its future with the Spanish conquerors in a less violent encounter than the one their neighbors suffer, belies a rebellious spirit feeding on the misery and hopelessness of its people. Not only is this the story of a person in search of his identity and a people in search of social justice, but a nation in search of an independent status that is emblematic of Latin America. "Algo tiene que cambiar. No se puede seguir oprimiendo a un pueblo indefinidamente" (274) [Things must change. It is impossible to go on oppressing a nation indefinitely (256)] becomes the individual's and the collective's struggle for recognition and expression. Miguel Vera's need to atone for his memories of the itapeños and by analogy the true Paraguay, suggests a rite of passage toward self-actualization rooted in the many life stages by which he is formed.[27] His memories are an opportunity to revive the past and develop a new cultural relationship with it. That is, having chosen the side of power against the marginalized (slaves, lepers, defenseless women, the impoverished, etc.), his attempt to dislocate the social history of slavery and violation forms itself, ironically, in a maturing praise of the strength of Paraguay's cultural roots. For example, Vera speaks of the lilt of Guaraní, the indigenous language that is capable of rendering horrible images in calming tones. Significantly, the poetry of Roa Bastos's text encourages the reader to prefer the charm of Guaraní over the horrors of truth, but it does not dissolve the disconnect. That is, the way to speak of the struggle is through the language of symbols it produces, passed on by the oral tradition but in the framework of a narrative. The author privileges the "authentic" voice of the people over "literature", while at the same time being forced to resort to literature to preserve that authenticity.[28]

The structuring of the novel presents a multi-voiced tejido or weaving that blends opposing forces, languages, cultures, roles, and time periods, giving the appearance of a dialogue across time rooted in a hybrid culture. The element that unites disparate components is the journey toward potentiality and identity, which focuses at once on individuals and then on collective groups. It is a continuous, seamless revelation of dreams and aspirations for a more complete life on the one hand, and for social justice in the complex practice of national identity, on the other. While one could think of Chapter IV "Exodo" [Exodus] with its Biblical implications as an independent novel within a novel and one of the most compelling stories of the discovery of the self in relation to the other, it cannot easily be extricated from the threads of the narration in which Casiano, Natí, and their son, Cristóbal, are protagonists. There is an important synergy in evidence of presentation, relationship, and recovery. The numbers that divide the sections, furthermore, could be viewed as developmental threads that weave the self with others in a process of growth and development that extends beyond self-revelation to the creation of a nation and the exploration of its role in Latin American reality. Essentially, it represents a globalization of human values on the part of Roa Bastos.[29]

The Bildung process under these conditions redefine self-cultivation to mean the search for the most divine, superhuman qualities in the self and the strengthening of the image of God in one through a relationship with others. By definition, therefore, it moves beyond coming-of-age and the search for happy endings. The rites of passage explored here are similar to those we see in all novels of the making and molding of the self: birth, sexual awakening, the passage into manhood or womanhood, the testing of courage, religious beliefs and honor, and finally death. The desperation and extreme suffering that accompanies most of the narrative turns these ordinary rites of passage into extraordinary events. One example is when Natí tells Casiano she is going to have a child: "Casiano no sabe si alegrarse o ponerse más triste. Encuentra al fin una cara alegre para su tristeza. Bueno . . .—dice solamente. Ha olvidado que puede tener un hijo. ¡A buena hora le daban la noticia! Sin embargo, debe de ser bueno tener un hijo. La sangre se lo dice con ese nudo en la garganta que no le deja hablar" (90) [Casiano did not know whether to be glad or sad. In the end he managed to hide his sadness under a cheerful face. "Good," was all he said. He had forgotten that it was possible to have a child. What a time to hear such news! All the same it must be a good thing to have a child. He felt in his bones that it was a good thing; the thought of it brought a lump to his throat (89)]. The joy of a new life, a mandate to grow and cultivate the self through giving to another is tantamount to Roa Bastos's description of the hispano/guaraní discourse, which is a text the author does not create but rather that creates him.[30] In effect, the engendering of a new life molds and creates its author. The text is figuratively written on the body, as the "poética de las variaciones" instills the author, according to Roa Bastos, with the power to vary a text indefinitely without having it lose its original nature.[31] In this manner the text subordinates itself to orality.

The question of orality is perhaps the evidence that most strongly links this strategy to a hybrid pastiche of voices, and anchors it to a relationship because it implies a dialogue and an openness to others. Clearly this hybrid structure suggests an interweaving of Guaraní and Spanish, and in this context I would propose reading the Guaraní text as one would read a mwwassha of medieval Spain, a refrain almost always found at the end of a section that summarizes or moralizes in the oral language of the dyglossia. The mixing of cultures, furthermore, is also evident in cultural markers such as in a variety of religious rites. For example, the symbolic wooden statue of Christ carved by Gaspar Mora is honored and blessed by the descendents of the Guaraní but feared and rejected by the official, Spanish Catholic church. The blending of rites in the Guaraní promotes Macario's formation and development in relation to those who look to him, a beggar, as leader. Macario stations the statue of Christ on a hill by his shack after the village priest refuses to allow it in the church, claiming it will contaminate the house of God: "Durante esos días, el viejo mendigo fue el verdadero patriarca del pueblo. Un patriarca cismático y rebelde, acatado por todos (37) [The old pauper became the real patriarch of the village. A schismatic and rebellious patriarch, revered by all (39)]. Here the rebellion and schism Macario works toward reinforce his personal growth and rebellion against society's values and pressures brought to bear in this case by the Catholic Church. Religion, a powerful cultural and social influence, permits an indigenous, relational blending within a Catholic, hierarchical structure. It also produces a new, respected model for development grounded in a need to appease each other and arrive at consensus for the purpose of moving forward. That is to say, personal development and self-cultivation without the corresponding formation of others is without value and promise for further growth. It is for this reason that the curia moves to authorize and impose the Church's blessing on the statue and Macario reluctantly accepts knowing that the one depends on the other for meaning.

At times the relationships exemplifying the making and forming of the self appear to be of the most natural variety, that is between husband, wife, and child, as in the case of Casiano, Natí, and Cristóbal, but at other times they reveal uneasy alliances between those of opposing interests, such as Miguel Vera and Cristóbal Jara or Damiana Dávalos. Ironically, it is through these oppositional relationships that significant personal growth takes place, each side indebted to the other. Alone, Miguel Vera criticizes his personal development, his inability to transform grandiose dreams of battle into reality: "Rechacé irritado contra mí mismo ese pensamiento sentimental, digno de una solterona. ¡Siempre esa dualidad de cinismo y de inmadurez turnándose en los más insignificantes actos de mi vida!" (132) [Irritated with myself, I rejected this sentimental thought as worthy only of an old maid. There was always this duality, this alternation of cynicism and immaturity in the most insignificant acts of my life (127)]. The irony of being a military man confined to exile or police guard and unable to serve presents Vera with the opportunity to become involved in the development of revolutionary forces and ultimately to commit to his own personal development: "Pero ya sabía en ese momento que tarde o temprano iba a aceptar. El ciclo recomenzaba y de nuevo me incluía. Lo adivinaba oscuramente, en una especie de anticipada resignación. ¿No era posible, pues, quedar al margen?" (133) [But I knew at that moment that sooner of later I would agree. The cycle was beginning again and again I was included in it. I foresaw this, and was resigned to it in advance. Was it not possible, then, to stay on the sidelines? (129)]. Just as orality and writing oppose each other from contrasting socio-cultural worlds, the world of the guaraní and Spanish descendents oppose each other but also blend as the theoretical Bildung process of each is advanced by what is absorbed from the other. In this manner it exposes, critiques, and attempts to heal Paraguayan socio-cultural history.

This foundational narrative also relies on the testimony of the suffering of the collective to demand social justice. The story of growth and development of Miguel Vera and Cristóbal Jara is the story of the making of Paraguay. Vera pushes himself to his next level by dismantling his own actions giving the impression that he truly does not understand why he is doing what he is doing or that he had any other choice in the matter. His death, like his life, is ambiguous and unresolved.[32] When Teresa Méndez Faith describes the cemetery and leper's village as concrete cases of no-exit, she reflects on a reality of everyone held captive, including Miguel Vera who is confined to quarters and held prisoner, who search within themselves for a solution because outside forces only confer misery and despair.[33]

Questions of identity resurface from those connected through relationships such as blood relationships, and those that unite the barefoot peasants against those who loyally represent the patria and their version of government and America. Differences tend to blur in this version of Paraguay and America, and what separates groups at times are pure symbols rather than ideologies or genuine distinctions. The foundational impulse in this narrative is to demonstrate the complexities inherent in government by distinctions that are even less understood by those who must enforce them: "'¿Servir a

la patria entonces quiere decir matarnos los unos a los otros?'
'Estos se quisieron levantar contra el gobierno.'—'Porque el
gobierno aprieta desde arriba.' 'Para eso es gobierno.' —'Pero no
aprieta a sus correligionarios' (146) ['Serving our country means
killing our fellow-countrymen, then, does it?' 'These men were
going to rebel against the government.'—'Because the government
was grinding them down.' 'That's what the government's for.'—
'But they don't grind down people of their own party' (140)] Even
the symbols cause doubt and do not convince their defenders:
"'¿Pero por qué vinimos a matarlos nosotros? Somos descalzos
como ellos . . .'—'Ahora no—le interrumpió Luchí—. Llevamos
los reyunos del ejército . . .' (147) [But why did we come here to
kill them? We're barefoot like them . . .'—'Not any more,' Luchí
put in. We're got army boots . . .' (141)].

One clear symbol that is woven throughout the novel is water as
a metaphor for life understood as the human heart. Frequently Roa
Bastos associates women with this metaphor, not that he is privileging the role of women over men, but is reinforcing rather a mythical
quality and ability to exemplify the liquid, be that mother's milk,
aloja, or water, that nourishes the body as well as the soul. One need
only think of Natí, María Regalada, Damiana Dávalos, or the aloja
and chipá vendor at the train station to be convinced of this image.
Water as a metaphor for life grounds this foundational novel, and is
vividly described in Vera's diary, which recreates a national history. It is a powerful image throughout the novel because of its absence. It can relieve the pain of poverty, desolation and war, but as
metaphor tragically folds back upon itself to inspire another disas-
trous cycle of internecine struggle.

The water for which everyone thirsts is a metaphor for the human
heart that unites those with others even in the most inhumane conditions. Roa Bastos gives the reader the key to this metaphor so as
to underscore the mechanism of survival, which governs the developmental process of the protagonists of this novel. Roa Bastos suggests this mechanism to be brotherhood, the relationship of one to
another under God from whichever source of religion they choose,
which is why the two epitaphs convey messages of humanity from
indigenous and Christian traditions. Even the protagonist Miguel
Vera, who does not believe he possesses the devouring passion for
life he sees in his compatriots, is an essential part of this weaving
of brotherhood. In effect, his guidance in teaching those from his
town to defend themselves in battle has advanced their Bildung
process, even while he claims not to understand why he is helping
them. The sense of brotherhood that unites begins within the human

heart, which once untapped is like finding water in the dessert: "La aguja de la sed marca para ellos la dirección del agua en el desierto, el más misterioso, sediento e ilimitado de todos: el corazón humano. La fuerza de su indestructible fraternidad es su Dios. La aplastan, la desmenuzan, pero vuelve a recomponerse de los fragmentos, cada vez más viva y pujante y sus ciclos se expanden en espiral" (274) [These men's thirst for life acts as a compass through the thirstiest, most mysterious and most boundless desert of all: the human heart. The strength of the fellow-feeling between them is their God. They may crush it, break it, shatter it, but the pieces join together again, and it is livelier and stronger than ever. And it moves in an ever-widening spiral (256)]. This fraternity is broad in nature and excludes neither man nor woman, those barefoot nor those wearing shoes, those in opposition to nor those in support of the government. It becomes evident in the novel that the exploration of what it means to be Paraguayan (witness the insertion of Guaraní and a nationalistic use of language that separates it from the common usage of Spanish in other countries), reflects on what it means to be a part of something larger as in Latin America or America. The "hermosa guerra" enlightens solely through its reinforcement of brotherhood: "Uniformes kakis y verdeolivos confundidos, hilvanados por cuajarones carmesíes, cosidos a una indestructible fraternidad" (191) [Khaki and olive-green uniforms were jumbled together, joined by scarlet blood-stains, in an indestructible fraternity (181)]. Enmity turns into fraternal support as a civil war turns into the war of the Gran Chaco against Bolivia and dissolves into enmity again as the war ends and wounded soldiers are discarded from the social fabric. The strategy for reading this foundational fiction contextualizing the history of Paraguay and giving testimony to the struggle for social justice is found in the relational quality of the Bildung process. It explains the superhuman qualities of all protagonists woven together both communally and relationally to seek social justice through the collective battle cry "algo tiene que cambiar" [something must change]. Through this effort Augusto Roa Bastos succeeds in writing a very human, Paraguayan, and American story.

6

The Bildungsroman in a Global Cultural Economy: Relationships and the Postmodern World

> In a global cultural economy all constructions are exportable and importable: recipes, slogans, and gender roles are all reproduced as intrinsically theatrical significations.
> —Marjorie Garber, *Vested Interests*

THIS CHAPTER SUGGESTS A FINAL STRATEGY THAT EXPLORES SELF-identity through associations, relationships and aesthetics. The final strategy mixes myth and pieces as pastiche from different sources—sociological, psychological, aesthetic, mythical, and so on—to create, in a disguised or ambiguous form, a self-actualized hero with a purely hybrid, inventive, Latin American identity. This strategy is the site par excellence for experimentation with culture and gender. The identity in question is the reality Octavio Paz envisioned blossoming from the imagination: "la literatura hispanoamericana es una empresa de la imaginación. Nos proponemos inventar nuestra propia realidad"[1] [Latin American literature is a work of the imagination. We suggest inventing our own reality, *my translation*]. The inventive Spanish-American reality, imagined as a grounding of identity, owes much to hybrid cultures and the picaresque. In rewriting the social text, the disenfranchised hero establishes new categories of success to define her/himself as independent of the "normative human model" created of the white male formational process. This final strategy suggests *who* can create her/himself as the self-actualized hero either a) relationally and/or communally, or b) through cultural exchanges in the form of parody or pastiche. This chapter focuses on self-realization and self-identity promoted by relationships and community, while the final chapter, chapter 7, emphasizes self-realization through cultural exchanges informed by pastiche and parody.

169

With respect to relationships, this chapter evaluates development in terms of who takes responsibility for the cohesive self and who successfully, and often, ironically, combines gender and culture to make the journey toward self-realization. The Bildungsromane examined relationally have made enormous strides in rewriting the social text by relying on newly developed relationships of care, support, and consent. In this manner they explore the complexities of marriage, love, gender, family, friendship, and work. Thus, the central metaphor for identity formation Gilligan asserts becomes dialogue rather than mirroring; the self defined by gaining voice and knowledge in the experience of engagement with others.[2] As stated earlier, what in other strategies might be seen as a turning point in the hero's Bildung, that is, acceptance of self-sacrifice or death in order to be considered an adult, here debates the question of responsibility, choice, and alternative forms. Ultimately, these portraits of development are grounded in sexual, political, and dialogical relationships. Seen in this manner, the questions of sexual identity to be explored for their behavioral and relational traits point toward dynamic national identities in service of interpolation and social transformation.

Examples of the Bildungsromane to be examined in this chapter that focus on relational growth are: Manuel Puig's *El beso de la mujer araña* (1976), Reinaldo Arenas's *El palacio de las blanquísimas mofetas* (1980) and *Arturo, la estrella más brillante* (1984), José Agustín's *Ciudades desiertas* (1982), Rosamaría Roffiel's *Amora* (1989), Sara Levi Calderón's *Dos mujeres* (1990), Marcela Serrano's *Antigua vida mía* (1995), and *Hijo de hombre, Teresa la limeña, Las memorias de Mamá Blanca, La casa de los espíritus, Abel Rodríguez y sus hermanos, Biografía de un cimarrón, Conversación al sur, Oficio de Angel,* and *Hasta no verte, Jesús mío,* mentioned earlier.

Through the works of Puig and Arenas, the myths of homosexuality and the implications of queer theory defy an interpretation of gay contestatory writing as emblematic of Latin America's failure to register strength and vision contextually. Essentially, the Latin American foundational fiction or family romance is based on heterosexual love and the ability to reproduce a nation, thereby barring gays and lesbians legally and socially from its plot. Underscoring Doris Sommer's important designation of family romance as within the heterosexual variety that restricts homosexual military, family, and marriage opportunities, Brad Epps further registers a common phobia of the homosexual as susceptible to seduction and therefore a threat to national integrity.[3] The opposite stance, or that of the homosexual's ability to contribute to the greater goals of society, is made patently obvious in Puig's *El beso de la mujer araña*. Concurrently, the path of everyday resistance followed by the protagonists of Arenas's *El palacio de las blanquísimas mofetas* and *Arturo, la estrella más brillante*, illuminates a vital journey toward self-discovery that privileges human relational values. Goals are achieved in the novels mentioned through relationships of an amorous, exemplary, imaginative, spiritual, or familial nature. They are constructive and destructive, enabling and stultifying, enlightening and injurious, in essence, displaying the qualities of all relationships. They do not represent a greater pathos or possess a greater truth nor should they be admitted to an exploration of the Bildungsroman because, following Katha Pollitt's argument, they might wield a moral superiority. They should be admitted, nevertheless, drawing once again on Pollitt's logic, because they have a right to be there.

It could be said that *El palacio de las blanquísimas mofetas* (1980) belongs to the category of "don't ask, don't tell" literature.[4] That is, homosexuality is not here the unique space of enactment that explores the tension between individual and the collective. This could be due to the fact that, as Paul Julian Smith observes, Castro's treatment of homosexuals has proved to be a unique point of contention that surprises given the prevalence of homophobia throughout Latin America and elsewhere.[5] Correspondingly, it could be due to the desire to emphasize homoerotic acts over homosexual actions that Foster recognizes as Arenas's contribution to the hermeneutic strategy of gay writing. For example, little reference, if any, is made to the status of the young male protagonist, Fortunato, which may go beyond gratuitous descriptions of his relationships with women. His Bildung process as an act of becoming takes him through many sites of experimentation both insular and communal. He seeks release in behavioral transfigurations to undo the self in order to become that which he would become, "deshaciéndose para poder hacer" [coming undone, being undone, undoing himself, in order to do something],[6] not only for his own personal journey of growth and development but for all those whose lives he touches. At every stage of his Bildung process he is acting out and performing his potential self, a work in progress that is not confident of the final product but aware of its potentiality. If the reader still needs to be disavowed of the theory of Bildungsroman as happy ending, a reading of *El palacio de las blanquísimas mofetas* should prove enlightening.

Fortunato's everyday resistance is located in his self-designed

explosion ("estallar") where his particles and liquids will contaminate the earth. That is, his apparently non-critical acceptance of social codes and behaviors prescribes first a path toward uniformity
(a "stupid" acceptance of the traditional, white male normative
process of growth), that later doubles back and slides toward inter-
pretative theatricality, and finally secures for him his union with the
Other. Arenas's life work critiques pre-revolutionary Cuban bourgeois values in addition to ultimately restrictive, revolutionary
models that almost always create a more coercive state apparatus
after gaining power. His literature forcefully, quietly, and at times
humorously drags its feet, sabotages, and dissimulates. The success
of these everyday forms of resistance, James C. Scott concludes,
lies in the power to present struggle without establishing any direct
symbolic confrontation with authority or with elite norms. In this
context Scott draws a parallel to feminist literature on peasant rebellions and notes that "women, it is occasionally argued, can exercise considerable power to the extent that they do not openly
challenge the formal myth of male dominance. 'Real' gains are possible, in other words, so long as the larger symbolic order is not
questioned."[7] When we generalize this statement to reflect gay literature—that is, *gays* can exercise considerable power to the extent
they do not challenge the formal myth of male dominance—we understand Arenas's self-portrayal as passive, in collusion with fiction
and real life. Homophobia as another form of oppression was best
confronted obliquely, by depriving guidance as to the sexual identi-
ties/orientations of the protagonists in *El palacio de las blanquísimas mofetas* and *Arturo, la estrella más brillante*, as well as in the
filmic model of "Conducta impropia" [Improper Conduct, 1984],
in which Arenas and Néstor Almendros appeared.

   Ultimately, it persists and is inventive. For example, by disarticu-
lating erroneous Cuban social values, Fortunato achieves his victory over hypocrisy. Curiously, the apparently "simple" Fortunato,
whose past rivals his future for lack of ambition, aggressively puts
into question and reformulates gender and cultural models: "Fue
entonces cuando comenzó a enamorar a todas las muchachas del
barrio, y llegó a tener una novia en cada cuadra, y llegó a ser el Don
Juan del reparto, y llegó a aborrecer a todo hombre que le sonriese a
otro hombre, y llegó varias veces a la casa con las ropas deshechas
y la nariz sangrante, luego de haber sostenido, a causa de una
mujer, una gran bronca en el Parque Infantil, círculo de reunión de
toda la juventud del barrio de Vista Alegre" (117) [That was when
all the girls in the neighborhood began falling in love with him, and
at one point he had a girlfriend on every block, he was the Don Juan

of that whole part of town, and he began to detest any man who smiled at another man, and he came home several times with his clothes ripped to pieces and his nose bloodied from a fight he had had, over a girl, in the Parque Infantil where all the young people from Vista Alegre (his neighborhood) congregated (103)]. The sliding from the actions of a Don Juan and a loathing of overt homosexual acts to numerous homoerotic moments celebrated alone suggests an awakening to improper conduct in its inception and perhaps its initial rejection.

It is curiously at the point when Fortunato's acceptance by others is achieved owing to his pursuit of members of the opposite sex, that he rejects this definition of himself and withdraws into self-exile. His critique of a society that imposes its version of decency on individuals, who must forego their individual rights to ironically uphold a morally decaying social structure, is powerful. Significantly, Fortunato is eager to be productive, to work to relieve the boredom of a day-to-day intergenerational and eccentric family life, even where there is no money to be made. His enterprises rarely yield success from box to homemade alcohol production, and ironically, his inability to deceive his boss and co-workers (an unmacho-like stance) or sustain the monotony of assembly work without injuring his hands, encourages his boss to think he lacks initiative. Paradoxically, blemished hands from having carelessly hammered his fingers or stuck himself with a nail contrast with the white, delicate hands of a woman that Fortunato's tortured body reveals when it is discovered hanging from a tree. Viewed together, his everyday forms of resistance, his refusal to move from object of the family resources to a labor-intensive product of the family, his un[re]productive sexuality or political stance as insurgent, and so forth, serve to undermine a hypocritical society.

In sum, Fortunato rejects the self by dissolving the present self and becoming/interpreting through his relationships with them, the other members of his family:

Y fue entonces (cuando ya todos lo aceptaban, cuando ya se había ganado con su astucia, con su aparente estupidez, la consideración y el afecto de todos), cuando comprendió que no podía más, que era imposible, que nunca había podido, y que ahora más que nunca tenía que desaparecer. Y fue entonces cuando comenzó a interpretar a toda su familia, y padeció más que todos ellos sus propias tragedias . . . Fue entonces cuando se pegó candela, cuando se exiló voluntariamente, cuando se convirtió en un viejo gruñón, cuando enloqueció, cuando, transformado en una solterona, se lanzó a la calle en busca de un hombre. (117)

And then came the time (for now he was accepted by everyone, he had won them all over by his willingness, his apparent stupidity, everyone liked and even loved him) when he realized that he couldn't go on anymore, that it was impossible, that he had never been able to stand all this, and that now more than ever before he had to disappear. And that was when he started to look at, and to try to understand, his family, and he began to suffer for their tragedies even more than they themselves did . . . That was when he set himself afire, when he went voluntarily into exile, when he became a grouchy old coot, when he went mad, when, transformed into an old maid, he ran out into the streets to try to find a man . . . (103–4)

Fortunato's communal relationships with family and friends depict a society on the verge of collapse, reform, and reinterpretation, characterized by a lack of memory or interest in the past ("Pero, ¿cuándo fue eso? ¿Cuándo Machado? ¿Cuándo Batista? ¿Cuándo Prío? . . . Qué importaba. En la memoria confluían todas las desgracias" (174) [But when was all this? During Machado's time? Batista's? Prío's? What difference did it make? Bad times all ran together in his memory (157)]) as well as a clear ideology for the future ("La mayoría de los rebeldes no tenía una idea determinada sobre el futuro, ni principios filosóficos estáticos. Cuando triunfó la Revolución muchos de ellos—que no conocían más que el resto del pueblo la verdadera situación—fueron, lógicamente los más sorprendidos" (325) [Most of the men fighting with the rebels had no very clear idea about the future, no fixed philosophy or principles by which they lived their lives. They were simple men, fighting against a dictator, and so when the Revolution triumphed (as the phrase unavoidably had it), many of them—who knew no more than anybody else in the country what the real story was—were more surprised than anyone at the way things turned out" (291)]). The agonies by which the novel is divided serve to move the narrative further along its journey and are the crux that propel the Bildung process from one level to another, absorbing good and bad in the effort.

Fortunato's everyday forms of resistance, the acts that brand him stupid in the eyes of family, employers, and co-workers, reveal a great sensitivity to life and the plight of others. His ability to become the others—the intransigent and speechless grandfather Polo, the imperfect and inexperienced Aunt Adolfina, the long-suffering grandmother Jacinta (the coincidence of Fortunato y Jacinta reinforces the Spanish family romance that is rewritten in a late twentieth-century, Cuban version), his careless mother who suffers in foreign circumstances so she would not have to suffer within the family, unite to transform him also into the suicidal cousin Esther who enables the reader to share life after death. Death in this novel is a time–space that coexists alongside that of the living, Francisco Soto concludes, but the narrative does not favor one over the other.[8] A conceptualization of death as present to life affords one further level of the Bildung process of rites of passage and dissolve the barriers to individual potentiality. Fortunato's marginal sexual experiences reinforce the rites of passage (masturbation as Fortunato, abstention as Aldofina) and underscore the historic cleaving to the Colonial dogma of the Catholic Church and the Counterreformation as a plan for domestic government. Carlos Monsiváis insightfully demonstrates how the Inquisition in the New World dominated the public sphere of politics and the private sphere of thoughts and the bedroom, wherein private conduct (orthodox sexual conduct as opposed to certain heterodox, indigenous practices) determined one's conservation of goods.[9] Orthodoxy, of course, was modified by issues of gender, that is, in the clear division of sexes and sexual mores. But by opening up normative formulas to bolder interpretations of life, that is, gender is something one becomes and the Bildung process places one on a journey toward becoming, we can appreciate these concepts as being more ambiguous than the conquerors could have imagined.

Fortunato becomes the mute grandfather who refuses to speak about his nature. He also becomes his Aunt Adolfina who is betrayed by island morality and does not know what to do with her life. Fortunato becomes the abandoned and betrayed Aunt Digna who lives the dream but fails at it. He ultimately becomes his cousin Esther who lives life after death, after she commits suicide, an act he contemplates but concludes all of the other family members should perform instead. Consistently, however, it is Fortunato's ability to rebel against everything they represent as a family on the verge of moral and emotional decay that saves him from the same aimless fate: "Qué se puede esperar de una familia de isleños. Qué se puede esperar de quien vive entre las bestias. Nada, nada se puede esperar. Todo, todo se puede esperar" (12) [What can you expect from a family of island country hicks? What can you expect from people that live with beasts? Nothing. You can't expect a thing. Everything. You can expect just about everything (6)]. His everyday acts of rebellion anchored in the pleasures of the flesh and an ideologically empty political stance enable him to be through his relationships with the others the only family member to leave and risk his life for something greater or simply different than what he had. In this rebellion Fortunato counteracts as David Foster terms it, "society's violent assault on the individual [which] is specified by a homoerotic conduct that derives as much from the individual's assumed marginal status as from an identity imposed on him because the social dynamic requires, in a process of semiological differentiation, a category of sexual outlaws in order to pride itself for its decency."[10] The brilliant posture and theatricality exposed here is that Arenas has exported a homoerotic model that is a non-threatening counterpoint to machismo, which does not disrupt the official balance of decency, or, in other words, directly challenge the formal myth of male dominance.

Through his relationships Fortunato chooses his finale, not to underscore a political goal but rather to give voice to the silenced voices of those individuals who differentiate themselves from others. His testimony of an oppressive morality that punishes difference mines a critique of society that Arenas will repeat in *Arturo, la estrella más brillante* and his autobiography *Antes que anochezca* [*Before Night Falls*, also made into an internationally recognized film]. By design, as Arenas is writing his life and rewriting his death in all his literary creations, his making and molding of the self is practiced through Fortunato and Arturo so that the final lines of Arenas's letter received by a Spanish newspaper in Miami after his death, make imminent sense: "My message is not a message of failure, but rather one of struggle and hope. Cuba will be free, I already am."[11] As is evident in the choices Fortunato and Arturo make, the act of dying becomes one more emancipatory step in the developmental process toward fulfillment, hence the incorporation of death within life. It is a liberating strategy he hopes will free emotionally and intellectually all of Cuba.

Arturo of *Arturo, la estrella más brillante* (1984) performs the theatricality of Severo Sarduy's "teatro lírico de las muñecas" from *Cobra* and the solitude of Barnet's Esteban Montejo from *Biografía de un cimarrón*. The division in Arturo between public and private holds the narrative to a monologue of memories and dreams without pauses. The novel is a testimonial narrative portraying the marginalized and dispossessed whose dreams are forbidden and whose desired lifestyles and lives are in danger of extinction. Arturo, perhaps the voice of Nelson Rodríguez Leyva to whom the novel is dedicated, is interred for re-education in one of the concentration camps, or UMAP (Unidades Militares de Ayuda a la Producción), in use in Cuba during the 1960s, until international pressure in 1967 closed them. Many of those interred there for their sexual deviancies and "mental illnesses" succumb to the symbolism expected of them, homogenizing homosexual experience as social code in order to seek social inclusion. Politically, this stance expedites inclusion because they do not pose a threat to male hierarchical dominance, as exemplified in this hybrid of two incontrovertible symbols of power—the military and the prison regime.

Arturo, it may be said, defies transformation into the Other who is easy to despise and resist. Through his everyday, commonplace acts of resistance, a cultural opposition is born that refuses to respond to the common homosexual experience that safely sets itself up as the other to society's norm. James C. Scott, in his study of everyday forms of resistance in Asia, contends that these commonplace forms require little or no coordination or planning, represent a form of individual self-help, and, as stated earlier, typically avoid any direct symbolic confrontation with authority or with elite norms.[12] Arturo contributes to this definition at first through his experiments of a sexual nature becoming that which the others within the homosexual or military structure desire in their relationship with him. His development through the process of self-realization and self-help is to become the best at whatever he attempts purely for personal gains. Therefore, he is acknowledged "la Reina de las Locas Cautivas," the star or queen of the homosexual prisoners who perform at night for their own entertainment. But Arturo must learn to escape the oppression of a homosexual "sisterhood" that does not tolerate individualism, as well as struggle against also being objectified by a hypocritical military whose guards desire him and for whom he performs to perfection. By not confronting authority on any level, he is able to conceal an ironic core of resistance, in addition to a self-expression and formation that are more fulfilling than any imposed by society.

First, and foremost, no one can control Arturo's thought processes despite efforts to make a man out of him through forced labor. The solitude and harassment characterized by his relationships with the military, other homosexuals, endless hours of brutal labor cutting sugarcane, and ferocious humiliation at the hands of all who surround him inspire Arturo to undertake two courses of action: 1) dreamlike flights of imagination and 2) the ironic glossing of official texts. The dreamlike flights of imagination are interesting because they suppose an ideal lover, the corresponding side of ourselves for whom one would like to perfect the self. The glossing or writing, however, is an extraordinary action, an everyday act of resistance that combines a common exercise with great courage, while at the same time avoiding direct confrontation with authority. These efforts should be seen as exemplary; that is, not solely heroic acts to save the self from death but to encourage the rebellion of others for the same goal of self-realization.

Since the soldiers do not permit him to keep a diary because diaries are "cosas de maricas" [13], ["pansy-ass bullshit"[14]] that is, holdovers from a decadent, self-absorbed period, Arturo chooses to gloss the margins and blank pages of prime, revolutionary propaganda, that is, economic books, Marxist-Leninist manuals and political posters. His scratchy, almost indecipherable writing has been termed graffiti by some critics, but I view it as enigmatic and political with respect to the process of self-evolution. There are several points to be made here: first is that no one realizes or suspects that these very *public* materials have been altered in any fashion until Arturo's death, when, obviously, the writing ceases. Curiously, his captors and companions are powerless to notice that he is stealing time from work, sleep, eating, and so on, in order to accomplish this task. Second, his oppressors are incapable of deciphering his writing, not simply for the difficulty of such but because it speaks to a self they do not comprehend. That is to say, the writing is invisible to those who lack a commitment to individuality and self-realization. As in our discussion of *La ciudad y los perros*, the narrative suggests that only by making the "weak" of the private sphere a negative force can the military of the public sphere retain its positive identity. Consequently, the theory follows that anything created by the weak could never threaten a power structure. It has been demonstrated, however, that the behaviors and cultural practices of subordinate groups, which contest hegemonic social formations, do unravel the strategies of domination and unsettle power. The final point to be made here is that the enigma does not have to be decipherable in order to create a powerful image that confounds the power structure; its meaning perpetually delayed in the process of becoming suffices.

What is curious in this case is that the soldiers are unable to "read", that is, comprehend certain seemingly harmless and poetic images, and so they label them counter-revolutionary: "jacintos, turquesas, ónix, ópalos, calcedonias, jades . . . un aterido lo-fo-ro-ro, ¿lofororo? ¡qué coño es esto! Qué cantidad de sandeces y boberías, qué verborrea, qué palabras tan raras . . . (76) [jacinths, turquoise, onyx, opals, chalcedony, agate, jade . . . a half-frozen pter-o-dac-tyl – "Pterodactyl! What the fuck is that! Have you ever heard such nonsense, such gobbledygook, can you believe the gibberish! I never saw such words . . . (94)]. Some critics have attempted to decipher the term *lofororo*, but as an enigmatic call to action it underscores the ironic core of writing. It could be said that

Arturo, like a word on a page, requires more than a contextual reading. Robert Richmond Ellis notes that the soldiers are unable to see the *lofororo* or understand its name when written. Therefore, something eludes the overarching hegemony, if only in potential.[15] Potentiality, the process of realizing the potential self, is the tool that eludes the power structure. Only in opening the self to the other will the self return fulfilled and enhanced through contact with the other. Arturo's creation of the mind has become his only escape from the horrors of a concentration camp, and it is the only thing that others cannot possess.

By uniting with the ideal self, Arturo will reach his potentiality so that his death in the end should once again be read as a triumph, teasing victory away from death and frustrating even the most sinister agent, who in this case turns out not to be soldiers but his mother pointing a rifle at him. Her bellicose "maricón, ahora sí que no te me vas a escapar" (91) [Faggot, faggot faggot, you won't get away from me this time (103)], strikes terror as she is dressed in the military uniform and commands obedient soldiers in the deathly chase. But in truth, he *will* get away from her and complete himself in another domain, and there is nothing she as mother or symbol can do to prevent this from occurring. Brad Epps suggests that rage, suffering, and terror are crucial for both Arturo's and Arena's conception of individual freedom and creativity, what I would term self-realization in the making and molding of the self. This conception of individual freedom clashes, Epps concludes, not only with the collectivity of communism but with the solidarity of gay identity as well.[16]

In another important study, "Estados de deseo," Epps identifies the homosexual as the "ab-yecto del pro-yecto revolucionario" [abject of the revolutionary pro-ject]. But if we understand the abject as Kristeva does as the violence of mourning for an "object" that has always already been lost, as a resurrection that has gone through death (of the ego), as an alchemy that transforms death drive into a start of life, of new significance,[17] we can understand the contemporary significance of the impending loss of the revolution, and the start of a new life. The clash between individuation and the solidarity of gay identity leaves Arturo and Arenas little space within which to construct the ideal sensuality. Carefully, the space is broached, however, through positive and negative relationships that guide toward fulfillment in completing the ideal self. Arturo's relationships with his mother and former lovers as revealed in memories, as well as his relationships with the oppressor and other homosexual prisoners suggest to him only one path to escape: the castle, or body, as formidable metaphor for the formed, inviolable being.

Dos mujeres (1990) by Sara Levi Calderón focuses insistently on the potentiality of intimate relationships and in so doing contrasts with the homoerotic experimentations of Arenas's novels and Puig's *El beso de la mujer araña*. In this effort it joins the novels of José Agustín, *Ciudades desiertas* (1982) and Marcela Serrano, *Antigua vida mía* (1995), in probing the battles of exploring and developing the self through the intimacy of relationships. In her autobiographical Bildungsroman, Levi Calderón writes about a protagonist, Valeria, who is writing a novel about her forming and development through relationships. *Dos mujeres* attempts to come to terms with hypocritical social and cultural codes of Mexican bourgeois society that impugn her conduct and force her into self-exile. The pressures of a wealthy immigrant Jewish family fuse with a passion for acceptance occasioned by distinct goals depending on generational, social values. Viewed ultimately as a testimony of lesbian life, Valeria's self-realization process is informed by anger and must respond to the additional social, economic, and gender expectations and pressures to conform placed on those who defy the normative model, that is, not even within the prescribed zone of marginality of the heterosexual female narrative. Elena Martínez recognizes *Dos Mujeres* for its power as a testimony of lesbian lives and the conditions of dependency and submission under which women live (27). The narrative plot affords an exploration of the Bildung process of Valeria, one of the two protagonists of the novel, from childhood, when social and cultural codes determine a tense relationship with her strong-willed mother, hatred for her jealous and insensitive brother, and love for her rigid and powerful father, which predetermine the route of her journey toward adulthood. As testimony she speaks out against the abuses of women and for social justice for all women to choose their lifestyle according to their potentialities.

After a variety of rites of passage—learning to smoke, drink, have sexual intercourse, enter society, and so forth—Valeria falls in love with a man from the wrong social class. Incapable of rebelling against her family's values to elope and marry her lover, Valeria's sexual and emotional frustration is funneled into the role of obedient, socially responsible daughter, whose intelligence is admired as long as it does not interfere with reality, that is, her role as subordinate figure. Her forays into university life in theater and art are without implied goals for her future. She enters into a marriage, another rite of passage, with a man whom she discovers she does not love and who is not in love with her but her wealth. She immediately has two sons and is the pride of her father but still incurs the wrath of her husband who beats her even during her pregnancies. Her everyday acts of resistance are to demonstrate pride in herself and to perform an exaggerated role of "perennial supplicant,"[18] seeking compassion from her parents and in-laws before she seeks a legal solution. When the former is not forthcoming, Valeria faces the scorn of society and determines to be independent and divorce her husband or any man who cannot fulfill her image of ideal love. Her emotional, moral, spiritual, and intellectual growth proceeds erratically, progressing and retreating depending on her rage and the relationship she as woman is subject to, from which not even her mother will release her.

The transformative steps toward freedom Valeria takes to make sense of her life inspire a completely fulfilling love relationship with another woman, Genovesa. Their lesbian relationship is revealed in an oppositional moral stance to the values of Valeria's family and the Judeo-Christian tradition. That is, a conscious decision to further marginalize a culturally marginalized family whose religion sets them apart even though it appears more culturally than spirtually contextualized, is an alienating force that implies strong will, determination and ego-centeredness. Carlos Monsiváis perceptively encodes Mexican society's violent reaction to the marginalized who seek the center, in a hierarchy reinforcing "cómo se atreve a atreverse?" [How dare he/she?].[19] The question may be further aggravated by the nature of a lesbian lifestyle that demands equality. The relative absence of lesbian texts historically may reflect the overall difficulty of women in centering the ego owing to their role of dependency in a phallocentric society. Therefore, it is not surprising that Valeria is not eager to reveal her relationship or proclaim publicly her love for the woman she professes to adore in private. David William Foster categorizes the work as a novel of liberation foregrounded by a critical price paid:

Dos mujeres is a novel of feminine rage in the face of a constellation of abusive forces, which engage in every physical and psychological strategy possible to coerce the protagonist into submission and subservience. Not surprisingly, and in response to an imperative to break with the (essentially gay male) prototype of homosexual tragedy, Levi Calderón's novel is the chronicle of triumphant liberation. But the cost is a tremendous one, as layers of conventionally successful feminine identity are stripped away: the protagonist's identity as a good Jewish daughter, her identity as a loyal wife, as an omnipresent and balsamic mother, and, most generally, as a dedicated guardian of the patriarchal order . . .[20]

Valeria fears the debilitating rage that envelops her public life and fears losing whatever it is that anchors her life in private at that point.

The joy she feels of motherhood when her sons are small is what sustains her through a difficult, violent marriage, so she is unable to completely sever ties with her sons even when they despise her for not living up to the sacrificing model of Mexican motherhood inspired by the Virgin de Guadalupe. To her sons and her family alike, she represents more the betrayal of la Malinche, doubly felt by these "conversos" [converts] to Mexican culture. Every effort is made by Valeria and her family to have her relationship remain a private affair, behind closed doors or on trips away from her home. Her joy may be shared only with a few close friends, and is never used to betray her family. The use, furthermore, of guilt is particularly effective in women and inscribes forces in Valeria of two competing women: "la que me permitía gozar plenamente de la vida y la otra que me lo impedía" [21], [The one who lets me fully enjoy life and the other one who forbids me to[22]]. Most of all she never wants to hurt her father, whom she loves in spite of his obstinate demand that she remarry and come home to her family and obligations.

Valeria's life traditionally has been tied to her family's values. Her rites of passage including her coming out into society, marriage, the birth of her children, and her education all reinforce those values without rebelling against their intent. Even her chosen field of study, sociology, leaves her wondering what she will do with it and returns this woman, who above all desires her independence, to the values of her family:

Evidentemente era tiempo de salir del encierro. Agarré el álbum de familia. Siempre había tenido necesidad de volver una y otra vez a reconocer mis lazos de parentesco. . . . Yo, que toda la vida huí conscientemente de las taras de mi estirpe femenina tratando de convertirme en una mujer pensante, autosuficiente: para no volverme una de esas mujeres ridículas que no pueden envejecer con dignidad. Estaba por cumplir los treinta y nueve años y la dorada juventud iba a desaparecer: mi poderío de mujer guapa quedaría como un recuerdo para el álbum . . . (14)

[Obviously, I had confined myself inside the study for too long and needed some fresh air. I looked for the family album that I kept in one of the desk drawers. I often had the need to go back and search into my

blood ties. . . . During my entire life I'd consciously tried to avoid wor-
rying about aging; I tried to be different, to become a self-sufficient,
thinking woman. But now that I was about to turn thirty-nine, I couldn't
help feeling that the golden age of my youth was ending. The power
conferred by beauty would only be a memory for the album. (8)]

The disjuncture between declaring the need to leave the enclosed
space of her life and returning to her family ties reinforces the difficulty for women of even raising everyday acts of resistance in defiance of a paternalistic society supported, ultimately, by many
women also. Valeria's anger transformed into acts of resistance
such as her refusal to be a subservient wife and accept her punishment, or accept her father's bribes and answer his questions, or attend her son's wedding, or comply with the social obligations of
her class, in effect, to deny the death of that valueless persona, is
critically tied to her past. The framing of her rebellion is visual,
furthermore, because the reflections and the recording of images
with the symbol of her rebellion, Genovesa, in the forefront reinforce her presentness and point the journey toward the future. Instead of confronting her life directly, which is a confrontation with
a genetic tradition that predates her and one that is extremely difficult to surmount, ("lo nuestro significa romper con los símbolos
más antiguos: símbolos aprendidos desde antes de nacer" [59–60]
["What we are doing means that the oldest symbols, the ones we
were given even before birth, have to be replaced . . . and we must
find new ones" (48)]), she rebels against traditional values through
someone else's life. Valeria projects her Bildung process on the
clean slate of Genovesa's being, a much younger woman without
the "mistakes" of marriage, children, or unsatisfying career. Not
only can she learn the lessons of Genovesa, she can have the freedom to experiment with self-cultivation and self-actualization
through her.

Valeria's relationship with the painter Genovesa is the most personally liberating of her life. Claudia Schaefer-Rodríguez views
Genovesa as a catalytic figure onto which Valeria projects her fanta-
sies and through which she attempts to construct her own identity
as an independent woman.[23] Schaefer-Rodríguez underscores the
visual quality of this relationship: "The center of contact between
Valeria and Genovesa is the visual perception of the other, each acting as a mirror for the other's actions and relentlessly observing
the other to possess her—and, through this procedure, to possess
herself—by means of this reciprocal gaze" (229). Valeria's inner
process of cultivation and formation must work toward forming

rather than consuming a thing or giving in to the excessive satisfaction of needs. So the struggle against giving in to particularity, in this case blind desire, and remaining unformed is ironically and unforgivingly linked to Valeria's search for the ideal. Valeria's search in her soul for the image of God after whom she is fashioned ironically takes her to a much younger, freer, uninhibited, self-directed woman than she could ever claim to be. So it is through a lens or through multiple reflections that this reality is softened and made mutually reinforceable. The reflections permit an explosion of emotions that reality cannot absorb directly: "Intuitivamente encontró los reflejos en los espejos. Fijó su mirada en mí, sentí una descarga eléctrica que comenzó en mi cráneo y bajó por toda la columna vertebral hasta llegar a mi sexo" (20) [Instinctively, her gaze drifted to the reflection in the mirrors. She fixed her eyes on me and an electric surge, starting in my skull, rushed down my spine until it reached my sex, (13)]. One's stare also has to be mediated by a feeling for or an observation of the other that interprets what it is seeing: La sentí mirarme con un deseo que no lograba controlar . . . En la recámara, a un lado de la cortina, la observé sin que ella pudiera verme. Su mirada era como un estado de ánimo (55–56) [I could sense she was looking at me with desire she couldn't control . . . I peeped out from the edge of the bedroom curtains and watched her. The way she looked at things was like a state of mind; a mood (45)]. From the first moment of surrender "nos perdimos en el espejo frente a la cama" (59) [We lost ourselves in the mirror that faced the bed (48)] to moments of discovery of the self through the other "los espejos devolvían nuestras imágenes desnudas" (63) [The mirrors reflected our naked bodies (52)] and "el espejo nos reflejaba. . . . Se me quedó mirando, y, como si un rayo fulminante la alcanzara, se tapó la cara—Tenemos la mirada idéntica—dijo alarmada. —A través de mi mirada descubro tu deseo—le dije (76) [the mirror cast back our reflections . . . She glanced at me and covered her eyes as if struck by lightening. "Our eyes look exactly the same," she uttered, alarmed. "Your desire reflects in my eyes, that's why" (65)], the self is mediated through the reflection of the Other. The mirror, like a photograph, reflects back the image of herself with Genovesa that Valeria desires to see, and not the common self-doubts or insecurities her lover occasions with a categorization of their relationship as a phase through which true artists must pass, or Genovesa's irresolvable desire to sustain the biological function of motherhood.

The steps Valeria needs to take in order to make herself independent of her family and the role of woman in traditional Mexican society, "mi papá se arregló el saco de su traje y ordenó que nos fuéramos inmediatamente de esa casa, incluyéndome a mí. 'Cómo me las voy a arreglar con dos hijos', sin padre, pensaba preocupada" (154) [my father adjusted his jacket and told my mother and me that the three of us were leaving immediately. How am I going to raise two children without a father? I worried as we came down in the elevator (132)], are measures that appear beyond her consumerist appetite or strength of character. Valeria, unwilling to exchange her personal comforts for freedom and offend her family for fear of being banished and further marginalized "no era posible que mi adorado padre hubiese tomado medidas tan terribles en contra mía" (217) [After all, how was it possible that my dearest father could take such terrible measures against me? (192)] wonders if she has taken the right measures to achieve her goals: "me preguntaba si eso era la libertad que tanto anhelaba y comencé a detestarla" (217) [I kept asking myself if this were the freedom that I so longed for. And I began to hate it (192)]. The answer to that question is complex because her growth and formation through her relationship and alliance with Genovesa forces her outside the boundaries of a national, heterosexual identity. Preferring not to hurt her family, she desires, nevertheless, to rebel against all they represent including their demands of submission and subservience without having to fear the consequences. Ultimately, she is incapable of resisting the person she is becoming through her relationship with Genovesa.

This choice leaves her outside the values her parents uphold, but the disjuncture is that Valeria initially is incapable of abandoning those values completely. That is, she recognizes she and Sandra, a childhood friend, wanted to be liberated as adults, "ambas estábamos buscando cómo protestar" (163) [Both of us have been looking for a way to go against the grain (141)] but the desired goal of freedom leaves Valeria feeling abandoned and exhiled from those who were supposed to love her, "yo lloraba deshecha por el abandono en que me tenían los míos" (229) [I was crying. I was suddenly shattered by the realization that my family had forsaken me as I had forsaken her {Valeria's grandmother} (203–4)]. Her inability to break off relations with her family and the anguish she feels when they attempt to punish her economically and with their indifference to her pain produces a reaction only when she is uprooted by the death of her father. This decisive moment and her family's need to blame her for his death provide the impetus to complete her access to personhood through self-exile in Paris. Rather than assigning a happy or failed ending to this coming-of-age narrative, we appreciate how Valeria creates herself through her relationship with Genovesa as a self-actualized hero. Ultimately, it is in the state of self-exile that she achieves peace and self-awareness, learning to live without Genovesa and with herself.

Amora (1989) by Rosamaría Roffiel precedes *Dos mujeres* in publication and as testimony reinforces to a greater extent the collective urgency with which the marginalized attempt to manipulate their surroundings. The concept of self-awareness and development through community is symbolic of the woman's approach to the Bildung process as discussed earlier. For Roffiel, the goal of survival through connectedness affords women the space to articulate new concepts of career, family, and love. The novel builds on the strength of these groups, Grupo de Ayuda a Personas Violadas (GRAPAV), Movimiento de Liberación de la Mujer, Movimiento de Liberación Homosexual en México, the magazine *fem*, and various other loose associations of women such as the group with whom the narrator shares an apartment, meals, chores, homestyle psychoanalysis, hopes, and dreams. These new communities of being converge historically in a moment and place that empower the individual to reach potentiality under imperfect and at times impossible, living conditions for the disenfranchised. The everyday acts of resistance that supporting these groups justifies, that is, simply listening to the horrors of others, cooking and dancing together, and refusing to live in fear in order to transform resistance into change, single out the failure of the disconnected—those judges, bureaucrats, police, and aggressors who refuse to see the whole of human reality. Part political manual for a new regimen of social crusaders, part autobiographical journey toward the making and the molding of the self, *Amora* registers the fulfillment of the self through community and solidarity: "Las tres hemos formado una familia y hemos hecho de nuestro espacio un templo. Le hablamos, le prendemos incienso, le ponemos música, le compramos flores. Lo llenamos constantemente de buena energía, de olores, de risa" [We three formed a family, and we have made our space a temple. We talk to it, we burn incense, put on music, and buy flowers for it. We fill it constantly with positive energy, good smells, and laughter].[24] It is no surprise, then, that this effort of creating and sustaining relationships is accomplished through dialogue and everyday conversations. Quite significant in *Amora* is the assumption, as David William Foster explains, that this is a plausible narrative pattern for a relationship that is both legitimate and realizable.[25] The female dialogic relationship reinforces the differences in the grand design: "Con el paso del tiempo he descubierto que con los hombres me relaciono de afuera hacia dentro y con las mujeres de dentro hacia afuera" (64) [With the passage of time I have discovered that I relate to men from the outside in and I relate to women from the inside out] in that conversation—the revealing, peeling of layers of meaning, and exploring emotions—is the cultural axis for women on which all else depends.[26]

In contrast, the confined space of a prison cell in *El beso de la mujer araña* (1976) does not produce the same type of open-ended conversation between two men but rather an occasion to recount formulaic traditions of movie plots and political theory. Relying on time honored codes of silence that inhibit spontaneity—for example, the fact that revolutionaries cannot reveal emotions for fear of betraying the cause, or that a homosexual and a heterosexual may not converse for fear of contaminating the other—the two male protagonists confront endless hours of silence by reverting to the retelling of plot summaries, half truths, and political theories. The relationship is based on an innate trusting of the other, rather than on spontaneous and revelatory conversation. The novel assumes, significantly, the exposing of prejudices and stereotypes to the point that a reversal of roles or a politicization through revolution of the homosexual figure and the feminization of the revolutionary figure takes place. The absorbing of the more admirable qualities of the other heightens awareness in the process of self-actualization. The relationship insinuates a homo-erotic quality, which opens homosexuality to a comprehensive, informative examination that undermines the stereotypes of the normative model. Introducing homosexuality as social practice, this groundbreaking novel of growth and development registers, ultimately, a moral consensus that advances the social experiment. *El beso de la mujer araña* purports a socio-political power struggle that skillfully inverts and stands on its head the theory of homosexual as threat to national identity. It accomplishes this through the silences of solidarity ("Callado es mejor . . . No hables . . . por un ratito" [It's better if it's quiet . . . Don't talk . . . for a little while][27] rather than through the filmic or political/psycho-analytical aspects of their dialogue. As the crux of human encounter, it points toward a much freer society where contradictions and individual differences are read as strengths. That is, the relationship becomes an empowering tool for the individualization of the modern period.

One final look at self-realization through relationships would have to include the adventures and difficulties of heterosexual marriage. José Agustín's *Ciudades desiertas* (1982) picks up where most traditional Bildungsromane leave off, that is after the rite of passage to career, marriage, and a steady future. The novel critiques conventionality and social customs through the picaresque relationship of wife and husband, the new Mexican couple. Elena Poniatowska reads this couple as an updated version of the myth of Orpheus and Eurydice,[28] and certainly the novel could also be read as development through a pastiche of mythology and modern-day industrialization. A modern, professional, Mexican couple, Susana and Eligio are separated when she accepts a grant for a writer's workshop in the United States and leaves without informing him of her plans. Susana's introduction into the American, midwestern academic scene provokes a critical assessment of North American way of life, the ironic world of writers in general, and the frenetic desire to reach one's potentiality through a loved one.[29] Susana's attraction to a Polish writer, who is her husband's physical and intellectual opposite, is problematic especially when Slawomir refuses to recognize her the morning after making love and throws her out of his room. But when confronted by her husband, Eligio, who has tracked her down, she refuses to offer explanations and enters into long, bitter battles with him about her behavior.

A novel that reproduces eroticism marked by the indifference and obsessive love of marriage, *Ciudades desiertas* opens the path toward individuation through the reflection of the Other, that is, the spouse of indigenous features who simultaneously keeps her from realizing, and aids her in reaching, her potentiality. A springboard for the debate on *machismo, malinchismo,* and the role of the indigenous in the elusive new Mexican identity, *Ciudades desiertas* obviates a discourse on Mexican cultural heritage that eschews social justice and the equality of men and women, while pointing simultaneously toward the tension inherent in the internal quality of being "foreign".[30] Susana's love obliges a suppression of Eligio's *machista* instincts and his love tempers her desire for a solitary emotional independence. The frenetic pace of abandonment, search, and recovery only to begin the process over and over again does in effect suggest the myth of Orpheus who has descended to the underworld, in this case clearly the culture-less United States, to rescue his wife Eurydice. Breaking the commandment not to look back at her as they leave the underworld, the equivalent of Eligio's attempting to mold Susana once more into the subservient object of a Mexican wife he desires, Eligio loses Susana for what appears to be a final time and returns to Mexico alone. The horrors, violent assaults, trivialization of feelings, psychological games, and buried desires of love inspire Susana to take what she needs from her marriage while she transforms it and herself: "¿por qué todo tiene que ser con tanta palabrería? ¿por qué no se puede estar juntos simplemente sin hablar tanto, tratando de establecer una comunicación profunda, menos obvia, menos banal y vulgar?" [why does everything have to be with so many words? Why can't we simply be together without talking so much, trying to establish a profound, less obvious, banal, and vulgar connection?].[31] Perhaps as a parody of post-modern love that searches for compelling meaning in every relationship, Susana and Eligio fall into an uncritical solution. Their solution is imperfect, but the egos are able to cede enough to the other so that in their surrendering to mutual love, Susana is confident of her potentiality in her process of becoming. Having confronted the Other, the freedom and open creativity available to her counterparts in academia in the United States, Susana is capable of returning to the self and demanding recognition of her personhood rather than the object status women had come to represent in Mexico.

7

Pastiche, Displacement, and the Recreation of Cultural Memory

> On close inspection, all literature is probably a version of the apocalypse that seems to be rooted, no matter what its socio-historical conditions might be, on the fragile border (borderline cases) where identities (subject/object, etc.) do not exist or only barely so—doubly, fuzzy, heterogeneous, animal, metamorphosed, altered, abject.
>
> —Julia Kristeva, *Powers of Horror*

THIS CHAPTER UNDERSCORES THE IRONY AND JOY OF LINKING SELF-realization to pastiche. The journey of self-realization and self-cultivation would appear to be at odds with pastiche, but pastiche serves as supplement to the past by rearticulating the goals of modernity and modernization in terms of pluralities. Pastiche goes a long way to recreate cultural memory. It assumes the process of becoming as an individual journey but then reinscribes individual expression within pluralities—that is, of hybrid cultures of peasants, women, and indigenous peoples—within ethnic, racial, homosexual, colonial and post-colonial political, and religious contexts. Pastiche provokes by seeking interpretive power through the art of supplementation, by locating the site of debate in identity, be it gender, national, or cultural, and building on what is assumed of the past. Following this framework, pastiche effects a multi-voiced cultural translation bridging continents, politics, and cultural markets. It incorporates and dismantles myth, canonical, historical, political, economic and religious texts, theatrical and artistic models, and gender practices to rearticulate inherited cultural scripts. With respect to the Bildungsroman, pastiche can be formulated as cultural performance, or, as George Yúdice terms it, cultural practice, which argues for or against enfranchisement, representation and recognition for all of its citizens.[1] By asking **who** can create themselves as self-actualized heroes in the Spanish-speaking Americas, pastiche

190

points toward hybrid forms. The Bildungsromane that exemplify this strategy and span the spectrum from picaresque to pastiche are: Severo Sarduy's *Cobra* (1972), *Colibrí* (1984), and *Cocuyo* (1990); Sylvia Molloy's *En breve cárcel*, (1981); Diamela Eltit's *El cuarto mundo* (1988) and *Vaca sagrada* (1991); Tununa Mercado's *En estado de memoria* (1990); Cristina García's *Dreaming in Cuban* (1992)/ *Soñar en cubano* (1993); Julia Alvarez's *In the Time of the Butterflies* (1994)/ *En el tiempo de las mariposas* (1995); Angeles Mastretta's *Mal de amores* (1995); and Esmeralda Santiago's *América's Dream* (1996)/*El sueño de América* (1996).

The strategy that defines the heroes/protagonists of Severo Sarduy's novels incorporates a structure that counters surface with submerged plots, linear development with weblike connections, totalities with pieces. Severo Sarduy's work embodies the relationship to another's speech that Jean Franco classifies as an "appropriation, expropriation, 'cannibalization' and celebration."[2] For example, in *Cobra* (1972) the ability to take possession of the other's speech signifies the ability to become transformed into a form of that person blending subject ("I", "he", "you"), gender (he/she) and national and cultural differences.[3] Significantly, the needs are those of the group. Their enfranchisement enables them to organize and demand satisfaction through transcendence of their present selves to a reality beyond. For example, Sarduy exposes the artificiality of gender by putting into question the notion of the duality of the sexes. This he accomplishes through a marginalized group of transvestites that destabilizes gender as a notion of binary categories. Transvestism here should be read as cultural performance. Transvestism, like parody, is an inversion, but unlike parody it should be read as itself. It does not interpret something else, be that heterosexuality or homosexuality, non-heterosexuality or non-homosexuality, but rather, it is "always undoing itself as part of its process of self-enactment."[4] Self-enactment is Cobra's developmental process, or Bildung process of self-realization through which the hero represents an alternative signifier to gender and culture.

Cobra's constitution is always complex because it is transmutable from reptile to person, from singular to plural, and back again. In the plural Cobra could represent Cuba, the lost signified, the language of exile, the object of the search, the always implied, alluded to and missing referent, the "toppled ideology of Cuban identity."[5] Sarduy, however, a student of Barthes, Buddhist theory, oriental tradition, Freud, Lacan, and Japanese iconography, is not purely a Cuban or Latin American author. Or perhaps it is because he is open to a hybrid Cuban and Latin American culture that he assumes other perspectives with ease. Clearly, his Cubanness is always implied in all of his books as well as in everything he does, as the author himself states.[6] But his postmodernist and post-structuralist play with language obliges participation in an autonomous game of writing beyond geography to a cultural pluralism of meaning. For example, what does it mean to approach a rite of passage to sexuality as neither strictly male or female, minority or majority? How does self-development proceed in a pluralistic context?

Transformation is key to interpreting *Cobra* as an enabling fantasy for development and cultivation. The reader could attribute Sarduy's playful transposition of human subject to self-parody, knowing completely the ironic irreverence of the author, but that would only tell part of the story. Through pastiche Sarduy confounds culture and gender, in addition to the need for category itself. From the first instance Cobra is both hero and heroine. Far from the juxtaposition of magic and/or marvelous realism associated with the writings of the Boom, Sarduy writes to reconfigure space—the space of writing and in particular the space of self. From his postmodernist displacement of center, the crisis of category of the self supplements and unsettles the interconnectedness to other forms. Pastiche effects the dissolution of the present form or the subject as we know it through a displacement of the hierarchy of authorial over cultural voices. *Cobra*'s cultural voices privilege context—gender, philosophic, social, geographic, historic—over text.[7] That is, the known categories of marginalization are further redefined and supplemented in an effort to dissolve the marginalized self and bring it back to itself. The subject is always a space of possibility.

Every "I" in *Cobra* is also a concealed he/she. A plot summary reveals an overt challenge to that which had been previously known and had been considered reliable. The protagonist begins life as a female "doll", pained by the only physical defect—unsightly feet—that wrests perfection from the queen of the Teatro Lírico de Muñecas. Numerous cures and sado-masochistic treatments do not transform this creature into the absolutely divine creature he/she feels is a birthright. The frustrated prima donna becomes obsessed with the shrinking of her feet, a phallic symbol that is studied by many critics in a variety of cogent articles.[8] The desire to shrink the feet is curious because what would have been privileged for its dimensions as a masculine attribute (ironically touted later with reference to Eustaquio el Sabrosón) is here perceived as an inflated appendage that devalues the owner. The hero's theatrically concealed space of the self, ironically hidden within the theatricality of the star of the show, points toward a disruption in the configuration of the subject. In an essay entitled "Escritura/Travestismo" [Writing/Travestism], Sarduy concludes, "todo él/ella es un encubrimiento; un yo latente lo amenaza, lo mina por dentro, lo resquebraja" [the entire *he/she* is a false front; a latent *I* threatens, undermines, cracks it].[9] This is true in Cobra, but an inversion of this model is simultaneously implied.

Significantly, the Muñecas as subject becomes an apt metaphor for identity. Historically, in the ritual, oriental theater (No and Kabuki) the muñecas are female impersonators, confounding the symbol of female, beauty, perfection, and subservience with an ironic masculine core. The identity of the muñeca or subject rests on an explosion of the myth of origin that could be traced back logically to a true center. Cobra's identity is necessarily hybrid. It displaces the unified self with a disruptive plurality that guides the development of the self. Upon asking "who" can create her/himself as a self-actualized hero, it becomes clear that Cobra's ambiguous form with its mixing of pieces leads to a unique cultivation of talents and humanity that is personhood.

The Teatro Lírico de Muñecas, or burlesque playhouse, where the process begins adds to the notion of joy or playfulness in the acting out of the self. The performance onstage becomes a disguise that seeks the impossible in the Bildung process—perfection rather than personhood in a harmonic molding of the self. Cobra seeks to mold him/herself both physically and spiritually, employing first societal values and standards of beauty. The adherence to these values has the effect of raising Cobra to a figure of fervent adoration, pursued by everyone from Dior to Sontag and an English importer of tea. But if, as Sarduy suggests in *Cobra*, "la escritura es el arte de la elipsis" [writing is the art of ellipsis] and "el arte de recrear la realidad" [writing is the art of recreating reality], so too the creation of the self by following this strategy can be read as an elliptical recreation.[10] The pieces that are intentionally missing or displaced by the author represent a reevaluation of subject and the rebellion of the protagonist against society's values, remaining ultimately and ironically outside those values while appearing to support them.[11] "La escritura es el arte de descomponer un orden y componer un desorden"(20) [Writing is the art of disorganizing an order and organizing a disorder (9)] clarifies the intentional disorder through which the self emerges in Sarduy's text. The disorder destabilizes subject, sex, and gender signs by defamiliarizing cultural signs. The cultural sign of the muñeca would suggest an oriental inversion, a man playing a woman's role, but in reality the protagonist's identity is hybrid, because Sarduy puts into question the dyad of representation. Judith Butler formalizes a prism through which to explore sex and gender: "If gender is not tied to sex, either causally or expressively, then gender is a kind of action that can potentially proliferate beyond the binary limits imposed by the apparent binary of sex. Indeed gender would be a kind of cultural/corporeal action that requires a new vocabulary that institutes and proliferates participles of various kinds, resignifiable and expansive categories that resist both the binary and substantializing grammatical restrictions on gender."[12]

Initially, the cures Cobra attempts to reduce her/his feet in terms of size and displeasure they give fail miserably and even have the reverse effect on the rest of the body: "Los dioses no escatiman su ironía: mientras más se deterioraban, mientras más se pudrían los cimientos de Cobra, más bello era el resto de su cuerpo" (35) [the gods do not skimp on irony: the more they deteriorated, the more Cobra's foundations rotted, the more beautiful was the rest of her body (17)]. In our interview entitled "La serpiente en la sinagoga," Sarduy speaks of the references to feet in his novels as claims to a foot fetish, but of course this irony is not lost on his readers.[13] His overwhelming centering of pain and displeasure on the feet is not only pertinent to Freudian interpretations and Chinese theories of pain and cures, but also to the establishment of the ungroundedness of identities on which social structures normally depend. The feet, therefore, are unformed, so large and grotesque as to lose their recourse to referentiality, that is, their masculine or feminine characteristics. The decision to appeal to a greater religious or philosophic power recalls the values of a traditional Bildungsroman. Sarduy's parody, however, of religious ritual brings to mind the comic ritual appropriation by the disenfranchised in a picaresque form: "En una tableta de bambú, que luego dividieron en dos, redactaron un contrato con los dioses: prometían respetar la gimnasia, la higiene sexual y la dietética: exigían en cambio la cura y reducción inmediatas. Con esa escritura como talismán, la Señora subiría a la montaña: parado sobre una tortuga y surgiendo entre jinjoleros, un Inmortal le entregaría en un cofre de laca el producto de la novena sublimación; éste, debidamente aplicado, operaría el milagro" (36–37) [On a bamboo tablet, which they divided in two, they wrote out a contract with the gods: they promised to respect gymnastics, sexual hygiene and dietetics; in return they demanded immediate cure and reduction. With this writing as a charm, the Madam would go up the mountain; standing on a tortoise and rising from the jujubes, an Immortal would hand her the product of the ninth sublimation in a lacquer case; this, duly applied, would produce the miracle (18)]. This dialogue with the gods is conceived in a truth bearing form— not in the authoritarian words of a higher being but in a discursive process that eventually arrives at the truth. Sarduy's parody or carnivalization of a covenant with the divine opposes official culture and produces laughter as a by-product. Laughter can be ambivalent, both salutary and mocking, but always remains outside the official strict forms of social relations. That is, the dialogues should only be interpreted as parody because the author had not intended them to be a representation of reality, and, very sadly, the truth of the pact is that the covenant is not upheld either in the novel or in the author's life. Laughter is also the challenge of the hybrid Bildung form to those that refuse to homogenize or assimilate the disenfranchised (transvestite, woman, minority, gay, etc.) into the majority culture.

The above example is part of a pattern developed throughout the novel. That is, a cultural crisis occurs (for example, the ritual performed does not produce the desired miracle) and this occasions a dramatic cultural counterpoint (in this instance the picaresque hero/ heroine sets out on an exotic journey toward enfranchisement and fulfillment). Each stage in Cobra's development has a value of its own, while establishing an interconnectedness of stages through the process of transformation. The theater is the first site of transformation. The herbs and potions tried as cures have the effect of reducing Cobra to a dwarf, known as Cobrita and then Pup, Cobra's reductive double, who remains in the theater. However, this figure folds back on itself producing a double, Cobra in the original size, who travels to India with Eustaquio el Sabrosón, in search of a cure and colors for their oriental burlesque. The experimentation with Cobra both in text and context, that is, the fact that there may be more than one version of the self—at least a double—operating at all times (depending on the context), is instrumental to self-realization.

Doubling for Freud meant castration or death. Carrying this image a step further, Freud reminded Jung that for many primitive peoples the placenta is the fetus's brother or twin that must also be fed and cared for, and which naturally does not last long. In other words, the child is born alongside a sibling double who cannot be kept alive.[14] This fact and inevitability are what make the Bildung drive of the surviving fetus/child so compelling. The surviving child is left to mourn, incorporate that other into the structure of the ego, and then compensate by leaving the familiar to seek her/his own in the world of a 'new' other so as to be able to return, ultimately, to him/herself. This is played out in *Cobra* when opposite processes are initiated: the Señora attempts to "expand" Pup so that in a normal size she/he could replace his/her double in the Theater, while Cobra travels through India searching for a cure. The self is then confronted with a portion of its personality, "cuando Cobra volvió de la India la encontró tan raquítica como de costumbre" (81) [When Cobra returned from India she found her as rickety as ever (45)], and decides to return to the theater to take up her/his place in the show.

Another transformation is signaled by a repetition through which Sarduy underscores, "la escritura es el arte de la elipsis" (85) [writing is the art of ellipsis (46)]. It takes place in Tangiers, where Cobra has gone in search of Dr. Ktazob, a surgeon famous for his sex-change operations for transvestites. Cobra undergoes the operation during which his/her pain is transferred to Pup. Cobra's journey through stages of development awakens the identity of the individual self to the possibility of multiplicity. Cobra's instructor enthuses: "Has aprendido a desviar el dolor" (114) [you have learned to deflect pain (64)], the signifier producing an effect in another area of the being or its double that allows the one form to remain without pain, egotistically overcome by the desire to be "fascinante como un fetiche" (116) [fascinating, like a fetish (65)]. Cobra once transformed is a combination of former and present selves.

The desire to be as fascinating as a fetish reminds the reader of Cobra's multiple representations as protagonist, prima donna, serpent, and phallic symbol. An example of the blending of the last two is evident in the following description, "Se recobra/ . . . Se yergue/ Sopla y silba/ . . . viscosas espirales lentas/ . . . la cabeza triangular que corona un arco de ventosas . . . (118–119) [she recovers/ . . . She raises herself/Blowing and whistling/ . . . Slow viscous spirals/ . . . crosses the triangular head crowned by an arch of suction cups (67)]. The deep sleep of the intermediate state that Cobra attempts to enter during the operation is an invitation to the serpent, namesake and impregnating incubus, to deliver the semen of the dead, that is, of the progenitor. In effect, after the operation Cobra's pillow is covered by "almidón límpido o semen" (118) [limpid starch or semen (67)], and the recipient is left "pregnant" with prophecy. While the Catholic and universal interpretation of the serpent in the Garden of Eden is that of a source of evil, gnostic literature tells the story of the Garden of Eden from the viewpoint of the serpent. Here the serpent appears as the principle of divine wisdom encouraging Adam and Eve to partake of knowledge.[15] The serpent acts as an access to spiritual understanding. I believe this interpretation is closer to the Oriental tradition and would have satisfied Sarduy. The author himself points to the hidden mysteries of the "serpiente en la sinagoga" in our interview and the coiling of the serpents around the gods in Asian temples (*Cobra*, 120). It is essential, of course, that Sarduy interpret this wisdom ironically. The prophecy, then, is tinged with black humor, "Cobra se contempló largamente: ¿Vio alguna vez 'La Dama de las Camelias?" (121) [Cobra contemplated herself at length: "Have you ever seen *Camille*?" (68)], which foreshadows the hero's death.

Everything has been absorbed in the process of becoming, both good and bad, which points to a closure in Bildung. The prefiguring of Cobra's death is made explicit first by another rite of passage— the ritual of initiation of Cobra into a gang of motorcyclists, initiated in Tantric Buddhism—through which the hero/heroine passes on the journey to self-cultivation. The selection of companions is a developmental stage in the Bildung process. This stage, however, signifies the protagonist's death. The protagonist in her/his hybrid form has rebelled against the voices of authority using drugs, potions, illicit sexual activity, and unorthodox operations, and has associated with irreverent companions in an effort to expand and perfect the self, in order to become the image he/she had of the self. Symbolically, Cobra's journey ends in death and Tantric ritual, codifying the extinguishing of duality and desire, for the purpose of detachment. But Cobra is very much the impulse and subject of the Tantric funeral rite and for that matter a guiding spirit for the rest of the novel. The last section, the "Diario Indio" reinforces with Buddhist doctrine and Koen exercises, the devastating freedom from individual passion achieved through death by Cobra and the acknowledgment of death as rite of passage toward potentiality. The negative "tu baile destructor ha extinguido la Tierra" (253) [your destructive dance has extinguished the Earth (143)] is counterposed with creation or renovation "bailarás otra vez" (253) [you will dance again (144)], as the extinction of desire leads to Enlightenment and rebirth. The selection of the dance as an activity for Cobra whose only source of suffering was the feet, is an example of ironic impermanence that blends Buddhism and Sarduy's experiments with subject.

Cobra "se recobra./se enrosca./ (la boca obra.)" (118) [She recovers./Curls around./ The mouth labors. (67)], blending "yo", "él", and "tú" as subjects capable of bringing the disenfranchised voice into the community through the telling of Cobra's story. Sarduy brings competing subjects, historical times, and varied geographies into a pastiche symbolizing the triumph of context over text in the identity of the self-actualized hero. The weblike connections and submerged plots depend on gender and cultural exchanges through which the self-cultivated hero creates hybrid forms. However, Sarduy writes of transvestites not so that the reader will mix categories, but rather so transvestism will be read as itself. Marjorie Garber concludes,

> . . . this is a directive to look *at* rather than through the transvestite; and it is worth noting that Sarduy does not need to disarticulate his fictive transvestites from their homosexuality in order to do so. He does not read or write transvestism as a figure for something else; for Sarduy, transvestism, like those other, supposedly 'exterior' elements . . . are the alternative signifiers waiting to be read . . . But, for Sarduy, what that face expresses, and what transvestism expresses, is itself—figure rather than ground, figure as ground, and as the calling into question of the possibility of ground.[16]

Once the figure is read, he/she can be understood as plural.[17] Cobra's perpetually evolving subject, gender, and cultural identities in addition to Sarduy's evolving concept of narrator/hero, is the basis for an evolving Bildung process that approaches personhood and harmony. It answers the question of "who" can become the self-actualized hero, even if the answer has an ambiguous, hybrid form.

If transvestism is the form written on the body that is an alternative signifier waiting to be read in *Cobra*, it is also the theatrical nexus that supports both postmodern culture and the process of political and social disintegration in two later Sarduy novels, *Colibrí* (1984) and *Cocuyo* (1990). In *Colibrí* transvestism represents authority and socio-political power, embodied by La Regente and la Casona, against which the hero rebels in an ambivalent movement that attracts and repels at the same time. In contrast to his earlier Bildungsroman, *Cobra*, *Colibrí* belongs to the traditional strategy and appears to be a copy of and fusion with the premises for growth and development of the classical Bildungsroman by Ricardo Güiraldes, *Don Segundo Sombra*.[18] For example, both Fabio Cáceres and Colibrí are unaware of their origins. They were abandoned at an early age and pass through similar rites of passage: abandonment of home and society to pursue personal development through education and apprenticeship (as a gaucho/as a painter of fleas), the initiation of the young man into the world (through alcohol/through drugs), the sentimental and sexual education of the young man (las chinitas/Paula//el tutor/el japonesón) and the acculturation in the end into the society they had previously rejected (owner of his father's large estancia and bearer of his name/owner of la Casona and an authoritarian lifestyle). In the end, Fabio claims his background and name previously unknown to him and exchanges his transient lifestyle for an authoritarian, patriarchal demeanor and family values. In the end, Colibrí is also the strictest convert, more addicted to traditional, social codes than the authority embodied in la Regente, whom he replaces. He punishes his Japanese "tutor," who had initiated him in the sexual act, for the immoral life he is living: "Se acabararon para siempre, ¿oyeron bien? . . . para siempre en esta casa el alcohol y la hierba. Se acabó todo lo que corrompe y debilita . . . Y además . . . déjate de mariconerías. El poder es cosa de machos" [That's the end of alcohol and marihuana for ever in this house, do you hear me? That's the end of everything that corrupts and weakens and besides that . . . forget the queer stuff. Power belongs to macho men].[19] Colibrí's developmental process folds back upon itself returning him to the social order he originally tries to escape, as he ironically concludes that power is the domain of machos.

One of the most powerful indications of Sarduy's turn toward a fusion with the traditional strategy is the recurring ironic image of the transvestite. The transvestite opens the space to other spaces and once everything original and artificial has been attempted, it opens the space to the traditional, which then becomes a recognizably innovative force.[20] The written word can experiment to a degree what reality cannot, so that the fictive self-realization, if not autobiographical, is achieved: "Ya tú eres un hombre y de los Sarduy, hasta ahora, no ha habido ningún pájaro" (129) [You are now a man and among the Sarduys, until now, there haven't been any gays]. There are many protagonists, including la Regente, la Enana, and El Gigantico, who are transvestites in *Colibrí*. La Enana, curiously, represents an acculturation to the traditional norms of society: "Pero, ver para creer: travestida en varón, con un trajecito de terciopelo blanco y un gran lazo punzó en el cuello, guante de cabritilla y un perrito personal, chiguagua para no romper las proporciones, y monísimo, hecha un verdadero príncipe arrogante y veleidoso, exigiendo un cambio completo de maquillaje y vestuario a la menor contrariedad, o a la substitución de todo el equipo técnico, hoy triunfa en Hollywood . . . Se ha casado tres veces, y sus mujeres, de talla normal, aseguran que es un amante excepcional. Aprendió a cocinar" (145–146) [But to see is to believe: transdressed as a man, with a white velvet suit and a big red bow at the neck, kidskin gloves and his own dog, a chihuahua to keep everything in proportion, and handsome, turned into a real arrogant, fickle prince demanding a complete change of makeup and clothing at the slightest provocation, or with a replacement of technical teams, today he's a huge success in Hollywood . . . He has been married three times, and his women, of normal size, insist that he is an exceptional lover. He learned to cook.] Sarduy insists on the transvestite form as a mode of articulating another space of possibilities.[21] The transvestite puts in doubt a single identity and self-knowledge. In *Colibrí* interpretation opens to a symbolic and semiotic questioning of literary genres and masculine and feminine genders, including other spaces of possibilities. It is a "guerra de escrituras" and a "robo del relato" where "nada . . . se ha dejado al azar" (60) ["war of writing" and a "stealing of narratives" where "nothing . . . has been left to chance"]. Ultimately, it is a self quest and self study from which the author cannot escape self-criticism, always presented with irony: "tu papel . . . es el más fácil: partir, cortar y no jugar" (175) [your role . . . is the easiest: divide in two, cut and refuse to play].

Sarduy's final Bildungsroman, *Cocuyo*, is the least ironic, and the most direct of the three works discussed in this chapter. The plot presents itself in a linear format, with a psychological development of protagonists that could be compared to those of a realist novel. It narrates the process of self-realization of the protagonist of the same name. It is an exploration of the initiation into the world of adults in Cuba with the traditional rites of passage that reflect a form that is very similar to the autobiography. Like all literature, it is written for a certain conversation and stage in life: "Creo . . . que lo escrito surge en un momento dado y para un interlocutor dado, que justifica lo efímero de un instante, que prolonga o amplía una conversación casual . . . y la proyecta en una noche sin bordes . . ."[22] [I do believe . . . that writing emanates from a given moment and is for a given interlocutor who justifies that ephemeral moment, prolonging or amplifying a casual conversation . . . projecting it upon a limitless night, an ink-dark night[23]]. *Cocuyo* dialogues with *Colibrí* and *Cobra* not only in the linguistic parodies, but also in the self-realization that impels the protagonist as author, to the next level of the Bildung process.

Ironically, *Cocuyo* exemplifies the traditional Bildungsroman of substitution, but it is linked also to the new relational and hybrid form. Cocuyo clearly rejects the values of his family when he tries to kill them, and searches for his development upon substituting the evidence for a simulacrum so that no one would realize how afraid he is and reject him for not being macho. As the first identification for the boy is with the father, his melancholy exists on the level of the lost object, his manhood, because he is instructed that "un machito no puede ablandarse" [a macho cannot go soft].[24] Cocuyo identifies with his loss and internalizes it, and justly laments its absence as he starts out on his journey of discovery and development. Cocuyo achieves various rites of passage of the sentimental variety: "Ella [Ada] se acercó más . . . Su perfume a naftalina y a violeta, el ritmo de su respiración, la tibieza de su aliento . . . lo estremecieron con la misma intensidad que el miedo" (95) [She got closer . . . Her naphthalene and violet perfume, the rhythm of her breathing, the lukewarmness of her breath . . . shook him with the same intensity as fear]. His sentimental education includes a sexual initiation into the heterosexual world: "Cocuyo esperaba la sorpresa del sexo" (133) [Cocuyo waited for the surprise of sex]. Throughout these various rites of passage, however, Cocuyo never loses his fear of not measuring up to others. For this reason, he opens his mouth to speak but frequently nothing comes out. Upon substituting writing for the symbolic castration imposed by the father, he rejects the father's power in order to take advantage of the mother's procreative power. Laurence Rickels observes the relationship between the mother and the child's fetal past: "The maternal body is the fetus's object . . . The mother thus emerges as full-fledged object for the child's psyche because she already embodies the child's fetal, objectless past."[25] The relational experiment of *Cocuyo* is the transvestite's metamorphosed form, which is foregrounded by the fetal, objectless past.

The protagonist, Cocuyo, is a child disguised as a male child. That is to say, with a masculine core he identifies for the first time with "masculine" desires, which are evidenced in his appearance and feelings. But the reader's obligation is to see him and understand him for what he is—a being who is afraid of death and even having others look at him. He presents himself as a being that is neither masculine nor feminine. Therefore, his process of self-realization reveals traditional elements such as sentimental and sexual rites of passage, the smoking of his first cigarette, getting drunk, and visiting a brothel for the first time in his life. But it also incorporates relational elements such as the awakening to new emotions with respect to Ada, his family, and the illicit side of life. His association of Ada with an almost completely naked boy dancing in a brothel, and his relationship with Ada and his sister are complex, owing to his understanding of the horrid rite of selling women as a symbol of their degradation in society. Cocuyo's response to these emotions is to become a transvestite: he dresses as a man but has neither masculine nor feminine qualities. He simply wants to be the Other. The theme of sexual exploitation of women does not represent a feminist or macho critique. It is rather an ambiguous signification that ultimately demands the reader direct his/her attention to it without weakening or looking away. Furthermore, the author will not offer an interpretation of what the reader sees. The different levels of development have combined to produce in Cocuyo a stage that is more complete both emotionally and psychologically. That is, the existential frustration that bewilders Cocuyo is the frustration of the marginalized being that does not encounter relief, completion, or personhood in the body or his native country. It is the performance that Sarduy offers to us in a given moment of his personal development toward self-realization, which unfortunately, was cut short too early in his life.

Personal development through challenges and performance that reverberate with elements of the author's life is also profoundly revisited in Sylvia Molloy's *En breve cárcel* (1981). The relationship created in this novel between the body and writing (the self, to be precise), writing as figure of the self, explores intellectually and intuitively the process of becoming. Writing initially reenacts an affair with Vera, exploring its pain and difficulties so as to continue the process of development.[26] Occurring simultaneously, the dialogue is with the self, with no one else, and with everyone else who is eavesdropping through the reading of the novel. Dialogue here creates a synergy between the private self and the outside world it privileges to comprehend the marginalization of the lesbian figure. Disenfranchised by a patriarchal society, the self explores how it has also become disengaged by its own making, permitting violence to anchor development. Formed through pastiche and rejecting linear plot development, *En breve cárcel* registers through musings, voices, recollections, mythology, dreams, musical pieces, and so forth, the confining, enclosed spaces of the room, dreamlike state, and childhood closet in which she seeks to make and mold herself. The internalized voices of the living and dead create a fragmentary mixture of places and sounds invoking Diana, Zeus, and Apollo, the "Meditation" from Thais, White Plains, Othello, Buffalo, Paris, Buenos Aires, and "Desdemona's willow song". Specifically, these are sites of aloneness that subvert, through pastiche, a simple exorcism of lifestyle. Clearly, a double task of demonstrating the harshness of exile by a socio-cultural structure that fears the woman's body for and of itself, and the next level of exploring a new lesbian space, dominates the strategy of Molloy's work.

Amy Kaminsky adds a geographic tension created between fictional and actual space to the analysis of *En breve cárcel*, which alternates between exposing and protecting the protagonist.[27] This tension is symbolic of another rite of passage: the naming of one's social and sexual self as lesbian. It evokes the anchored, actual self without the protection of the fictive self (career, social and marital status) just as surely as naming a geographic location does: "Sabe que nombrar es un rito, ni más ni menos importante que la inscripción de una frase trivial. Pero también sabe que los nombres, las iniciales que había escrito en una primera versión, han sido sustituidos; la máscara del nombre que recuerda, del nombre que dijo, con que creyó que decía, ha sido reemplazada por otra, más satisfactoria porque más lejana. Se pregunta por qué disimula nombres literalmente insignificantes cuando pretende transcribir, con saña, una realidad vivida"[28] [She knows that to name is a ritual, neither more nor less important than the recording of a trivial sentence. But she also knows that the names, the initials she had included in an earlier version of this story have been replaced by others; the mask of the name she remembers, of the name she uttered or thought she uttered, has been changed to another one, more satisfactory because more distant. She asks herself why she conceals names that are insignificant while at the same time trying furiously to transcribe a lived reality].[29]

Perhaps the answer to this is found in the borgesian strategy of transforming a space that multiplies itself like reflections in a mirror instead of reducing itself to the one. It is designed to become the self by staying open to all possible versions of the self. Through this release we are able to comprehend a sequence of the dream when the narrator and the father are seated at a table in the closet in front of an unidentified woman. The father gestures to her as if to give his permission for her action: "Algo, un gesto de su padre, hace que ella, a la vez que está leyendo en voz alta un texto que la aburre, se levante la pollera, aparte el calzón y se toque el sexo. En ese momento, es ese instante de su sueño, encuentra un placer que pocas veces ha alcanzado" (147) [As she sits reading aloud from some text she finds tedious, something, perhaps a gesture from her father, makes her lift up her skirt, push down her underpants, and touch herself. At that moment in the dream, she experiences a pleasure such as she will seldom reach again (118)]. The equation of the patriarchal figure with permission for sexual pleasure is a difficult interpretation for female readers but perhaps it argues the complicity of women within the hierarchical structure. In essence, the dream father gives permission to continue to her next stage of development, liberate herself sexually, and escape the patriarchal demands on women. *En breve cárcel* is political in the sense that it attempts to open this space and choice to all. In essence, this novel makes more sense as a process of becoming (Bildungsroman) than a retrospective detailing of life (autobiography), in that it attempts to work out its being-in-the-world through writing. I would argue, ultimately, that it is a work enriched by self-realization that is representational in its desire to fight for a creative, intellectual and physical, even if frightening, space for all women.

A more ironic battle for woman's space occurs in Angeles Mastretta's *Mal de amores* (1995), which intentionally misguides the reader with a romantic title suggesting failure or dis[ease]. In truth, Emilia, the liberated daughter of Josefa and Diego enters her Bildung process guided by her Aunt, Milagros Veytia, as her tutor through the distinct rites of passage and levels of development. In the performance of self-realization, Emilia by natural selection chooses Milagros, the new mother, to guide her rather than her own mother who lives a traditional existence. Emilia will have other tutors on her journey—her father who teaches her the wonders of pharmacy and the preparation of medicines for healing, her husband who instructs and inspires her in the curing of disease as a doctor, and an old woman who teaches her acupuncture, but Milagros as her madrina, godmother, takes her to the beginning of her journey where she must search for God's grace, that is the search for God that completes us in the ancient mystical tradition of the Bildung process. After Emilia's birth, Milagros delivers an incantation designed to inspire and empower:

Niña—dijo Milagros con la solemnidad de una sacerdotisa—, yo te deseo la locura, el valor, los anhelos, la impaciencia. Te deseo la fortuna de los amores y el delirio de la soledad. Te deseo la inteligencia y el ingenio. Te deseo una mirada curiosa, una nariz con memoria, una boca que sonría y maldiga con precisión divina, unas piernas que no envejez-can, un llanto que te devuelva la entereza. Te deseo el sentido del tiempo que tienen las estrellas, el temple de las hormigas, la duda de los tem-plos. Te deseo la fe en los augurios, en la voz de los muertos, en la boca de los aventureros, en la paz de los hombres que olvidan su destino, en la fuerza de tus recuerdos y en el futuro como la promesa donde caba todo lo que aún no te sucede. Amén.[30]

"Child," said Milagros, with the solemnity of a priestess, "for you I wish madness, valor, yearning, impatience. May you have the good for-tune of love and the delirium of solitude. A taste for comets, water, and men. Intelligence and wit. Curious eyes, a nose that remembers, a mouth that smiles and curses with godly precision, legs that never grow old, tears that restore wholeness. For you I wish the sense of time of the stars, the temperament of the ants, and the doubt of temples. And may you have faith in auguries, the voices of the dead, the lips of the adventurous, the peace of men who forget their destinies, the strength of your memories and of the future as a promise that holds all you have yet to experience. Amen."[31]

Importantly, all women find what they want and need in the narrative, and generally attain their potentiality with the support of the men in their lives. Even Milagros, the older, politically committed but non-castrating female tutor, is supported by a lover whom she refuses to marry but who, nevertheless, gives her the space needed for the making and molding of the self.

Milagros never feels shy about denouncing arbitrariness or inequalities because she is always clear about her role in society.[32] Milagro's personal development is meant to mirror the potentiality of a reformed Mexican socio-political system and economy. It is a call for a social system in which all participate as equal partners. Milagros imparts this passion to her niece and her 'son' Daniel, Emilia's lover, whom Milagros raises for the first few years of his life after her friend's death. Social codes and moral conventions are flaunted to permit a greater freedom of expression for women than men in this novel but significantly with the support of their fathers, husbands and lovers. This is not a denial of history but a rescuing of the voice of the marginalized whose contributions had slid into the obscure. Occupying the space in which only men resided before during a period of both political and religious oppression and upheaval in Mexican history, both Milagros and Emilia are admired and respected for their accomplishments toward social, political and economic empowerment of the marginalized. Confident in their roles fighting the patriarchal structure with everyday acts of resistance, these women work side by side with the men who help them escape the ancestral demands on women in order to reach their potentiality.

Diamela Eltit's novels, *El cuarto mundo* (1988) and *Vaca sagrada* (1991), deconstruct gender and social beings, and experiment with language in a manner that suggests the influence on her work of the Tel Quel group, to which Severo Sarduy belonged. The sites of performance that both novels probe in an opening of language to new cultural interpretations are far from the academic and social traditions that preserve dominant cultural thought. They are grounded, rather, in the tension between the exterior/city/house/public space and the interior/family/womb/private space in *El cuarto mundo*, and the city (public) and Manuel's memories of the South (private) in *Vaca sagrada,* to demonstrate the complexity of social discourse that is evolving in Latin America according to Eltit. In effect, Eltit juxtaposes subservience to and rebellion against metropolitan paradigms. In both novels rites of passage are explored, absorbed and remodeled in an effort to reconstruct potentiality in the face of the postmodern world and the tactics of terror and violence of the Chilean dictatorship. *El cuarto mundo* rewrites the biblical family romance of Adam and Eve in a bold recreation of family thrust out of paradise into a new world, in this case, *el cuarto mundo*. This belongs to a class of literature that is metafictionally self-reflective but reveals, as Linda Hutcheon suggests, real political and historical realities.[33] Genetically related (having been formed of the same rib), the post-modern version of the original family is enacted by twins whose performances of rites are sacred and enduring, even if stood on their head, and which reinstate rite as the nucleus of aesthetic experience in the postmodern.[34] These performances recreate the ancient objective of rites to ensure survival and harmony, the modern objective to encourage self-realization, and the post-modern objective to deconstruct for the sake of the experience. Rites as performance serve to transform the disruptive conflict of the community into a collaborative, social act, even if the social act turns out to be disruptive also.

Deconstructing the first part of the story of creation, Eltit writes the first half of the novel from the male twin/protagonist point of view. Serving as counterpoint to Teresa de la Parra's portrayal of family as social model, Julio Ortega characterizes Eltit's family as a model of de-socialization. The author creates the model by subverting accepted codes and myths, such as the myth of the national family and the codes of matriarchy, patriarchy, socialization, and sexuality.[35] It is an effort to destroy in order to create whatever may come later. In contrast to the Bildung process explored in the reaching of potentiality through the lives of the older protagonists of *La viuda* and *Las memorias de Mamá Blanca*, *El cuarto mundo* launches the performance of development from before the beginning of life. That is, breaking the boundaries for rites of passage that ignore the pre-life stage, the narrative voice of the fetus in *El cuarto mundo* dedicates the beginning of the novel to the beginning of life from a space before conception: "Un 7 de abril mi madre amaneció afiebrada. . . . Mi padre, de manera inexplicable y sin el menor escrúpulo, la tomó, obligándola a secundarlo en sus caprichos. . . . Ese 7 de abril fui engendrado en medio de la fiebre de mi madre y debí compartir su sueño [On April 7 my mother woke up with a fever. . . . Inexplicably and without compunction, my father possessed her, forcing her to submit to his desires . . . On that April 7, enshrouded in my mother's fever, I not only was conceived, but also must have shared her dream because I suffered the horrible feminine attack of dread[36]]. The male protagonist retraces life to pre-conception, conception (the male twin is conceived the seventh of April), and doubling (the female twin is conceived on the eighth: ". . . ese 8 de abril mi padre había engendrado en ella a mi hermana melliza" (12) [On that April 8, my father engendered my twin sister" (4)]). The first half of the novel explores the male twin's individuation through rebellion against both the fear of being forgotten in the external mother's world and the male's desire for autonomy through competition with his sibling with respect to their physical, emotional, and intellectual developments (the sister is the first to speak and walk inspiring a violent reaction of deception in the father).

While their closeness in the womb provides protection against the mother's nightmarish existence, "En esas ocasiones el estar cerca permitía paliar en parte nuestro desatado miedo a la ceguera" (20) [On those occasions, to be close to each other would partially alleviate our perpetual fear of oblivion (9)], their closeness transforms into a movement toward individuation at the first year mark: "Después del primer año, mi hermana y yo nos alejamos visiblemente" (39) [After that first year my sister and I became noticeably detached (21)]. Let us remember that doubling for Freud meant castration or death, and that the twin could be understood as being like the placenta, which naturally does not last long. Eltit mirrors this belief engendering a child born alongside a sibling double who cannot be kept "alive", allowing in this case the male twin to be transformed for lack of dominance. The space of performance after birth initially opens up an exchange and interchange of personalities: "Jugábamos, también, al intercambio. Si yo era la esposa, mi hermana era el esposo y, felices, nos mirábamos volar sobre nuestra suprema condición (43) [We also exchanged roles: if I was the wife, my sister would play the husband while we watched the other rise blissfully to our ideal condition (24)]. Exchange enacts and rewrites other rites of passage such as the sister's entrance into womanhood through the first menstrual cycle, the brother's first sexual act, and the discovery of the imperfectability of the mother through her adultery. Ultimately, exchange evolves into experimentation with transvestism signaled by the mother at the child's birth as the path to the feminization of the male twin: "Mi madre, solapadamente, me miró y dijo que yo era igual a María Chipia, que yo era ella. Su mano afilada recorrió mi cara y dijo: "Tú eres María Chipia" (29) [My mother, looking at me deviously, said I was the same as María Chipia, that I was she. Running her slender hand over me, she said: 'You are María Chipia' (14)]. That is, the female figure survives and is enacted in both twins.[37]

After having been mocked by and cast out of the city, the family moves into the house in the second half of the novel, which the twin sister narrates. The site of performance has been transformed from Adam and Eve of the original family to the proclamation of a virginal figure: "Mi hermano mellizo adoptó el nombre de María Chipia y se travistió en virgen. Como una virgen me anunció la escena del parto. Me la anunció. Me la anunció. La proclamó" (109) [My twin brother adopted the name María Chipia and, like a transvestite, became a virgin, for a virgin could predict the birth. He predicted it. He predicted it for me. He proclaimed it (69)]. Having put into crisis the categories of truth and "real" in the landscape of the sudaca wasteland throughout the first half, Eltit declares all truths to be exchangeable through performance in the second. The grand narratives of creation, Adam and Eve, the fall from grace, conception, and even the founding of a nation have been suspended, as Lyotard would conclude, because they have lost their credibility. In its place the performance as rite becomes the aesthetic of the postmodern experience. The brother transformed into a virgin announces, proclaims, that is, demands the reader look at the hybrid act of fertilization. The city or exterior world has collapsed yielding to a rampant market economy where in the exchange everything is bought and sold including the salespeople. Adultery, which yielded to personal passions in the first half as the figure and myth of the mother is stripped away, is controlled by the city that exchanges it for anything at any price, in the much shorter second half. What is at stake here is that knowledge moves away from truth and approaches experience, which eschews values such as social justice: "La transacción está a punto de concluir, y en el dinero caído del cielo está impresa, nítidamente, una sonrisa de menosprecio a la raza sudaca" (159) [The transaction is about to conclude and the contempt for the sudaca race is clearly printed on the money falling from the sky (114)]. Not even the house can protect the twins or their offspring from the incursions of the devastated, shortsighted city, as the novel concludes: "La niña sudaca irá a la venta" (159) [The sudaca baby will go up for sale (114)]. In effect, the values needed to anchor a high velocity, lightweight culture have also been put up for sale.

As Diamela Eltit physically took the act of reading her novel to a brothel in Santiago to juxtapose literature's marginality to that of prostitutes, facing head on the intractability of class and racial strat-ification,[38] she "goes public" in *El cuarto mundo* shattering the in-violability of creation, language, and gender and social category. Read as performance, the world of the female is being played out in the womb and from incest to adultery in order to cast and critique roles and values put upon women by the seemingly orderly male world. For example, working against the easy readability of roles and rituals the sister through pastiche demonstrates to her brother logically and geometrically that "un padre no se rompe, ¿ves? (49) [Don't you understand that a father never veers off track (28)] while the brother reports that the mother's vice is to cling to highly dan-gerous circumstances "para lograr rehacerse a sí misma" (49) [in order to reconstruct herself (28)]. The indestructibility of the father choreographed by the geometric progression of the sister's steps in relation to the brother's axis contradicts the reality of the father's demise as tutor figure. In contrast, the marginal, ambivalent mother figure achieves independence by way of unspeakably risky, fever-ous, adulterous acts through which she continues to remake and mold herself. The "linguistic incest" of the linguistic family in El-tit's work is the unresolved contradiction between the masculine and feminine discourse, according to Raymond Williams.[39] Going beyond unresolved in this novel, language is purposefully ambigu-ous or "androgynous" to unsettle the method of reading on the body for gender identification. Consequently, *el cuarto mundo*, or fourth world, is the world that escapes paradise and the second world of male dominance or the third world of pure female domi-nance. It is the world of globalization (that is much more than a nod to first and third world economies and a point to which I will return later) and it is the world of pure potential emboldened by the Bil-dung process that rewrites gender and social contexts.

For example, the first half of the novel details a chronological progression of the twins, and mirrors Plato's design of the androgy-nous that possessed simultaneously male and female natures and searched nostalgically for their other half split off by the gods.[40] It is the female half that perfects the male twin in Eltit's novel ("con el mundo partido en dos, mi única posibilidad de reconstrucción era mi hermana melliza. Junto a ella, solamente, podía alcanzar de nuevo la unidad" 48) [With the world severed in two, my only path to reconstruction was my twin sister: being next to her would allow me to achieve wholeness once again (27)]. The brother who had once vowed to annihilate his twin (81), therefore, participates in a hybrid, compromising, and incestuous act that engenders offspring in the second half of the book (109). Sylvia Tafra concludes that incest as taboo "permite redimir y purificar las culpas de una familia, de un país, y de un continente" [permits a redeeming and purifying of the sins of a family, a country and a continent][41] because it confronts boundaries of reason, logic, and morality. In ritualistic fashion similar to the koen exercise in performance of the extinction of opposites through simulation, the incestuous act performed by the ambiguous and bisexual male twin and the dominant female twin, diamela eltit, purges the entire Chilean nation and gives life to writing a new social and gender order.

If gender roles are compromised in *El cuarto mundo*, social and cultural identities are similarly jeopardized. In the second half the incestuous relationship between María Chipia and his twin sister turns this very competitive relationship into a fight for the survival of the sudaca family. Sudaca is a pejorative adjective used by the Spanish to refer to certain Latin Americans. I believe Eltit registers with the sudaca family metaphor the anguish many critics and scholars such as Nelly Richard and Sonia Montecino in their respective studies commented on with the return of the policy of "blanqueamiento" in Chile. Read as performance on an allegorical level, the sudaca can be understood as the marginalized in Chile who play out the values of the Judeo-Christian tradition while the political and military powers employ ironically the same values against them for their destruction ("Sin cansarse, [María Chipia] repite obsesivamente 'soy un digno sudaca, soy un digno sudaca', mientras las sílabas se trizan contra los muros de contención de la casa" 113) [Obsessed, he repeats untiringly, 'I am an honorable sudaca, I am an honorable sudaca,' while the syllables split apart against the walls of the house (73)]. The sudaca family of twins performs its rites of incest nightly in view of their parents (read patriarchy and alienated matriarchy) until María Chipia asks his twin sister to violate her secret. "Quiero hacer una obra sudaca terrible y molesta" (114) [I want to create a creature that is terribly and scandalously sudaca (74)] she responds. The hyper-real declaration by the author Diamela Eltit, that diamela eltit assisted by her twin brother gives birth to a girl, reveals that terrible work that is an awakening. Eltit's critique goes beyond the devastating effects of the Chilean economy on the poor and disenfranchised by an oppressive military regime. It calls into question globalization (the fourth world and space of possibility), the system shaping the domestic politics and foreign relations of virtually every country. Within this context, the challenge for countries and individuals is to find a healthy balance between preserving a sense of identity, home, and community and doing what it takes to survive within the globalization system, the Chilean miracle notwithstanding.[42] Eltit's conclusion that the child will go up for sale, does not hold much hope for relieving the tension between globalization and cultural integrity, when left unchecked by the people that inhabit it.

Eltit's later novel, *Vaca sagrada* (1991), approaches the process of growth and development in the postmodern through an appropriation of politically and culturally charged images of the city (economic, political, social) that ground the female subject's self-development and self-construction. Its goal through linguistic dissection is subject to Eltit's goal of preparing the marginal to step out of that condition. In contrast to the Bildungsroman that synecdochically programs the constitution of a Latin-American national identity (e.g., *En el tiempo de las mariposas, Los ríos profundos, Las memorias de Mamá Blanca, Biografía de un cimarrón*, etc.), *Vaca sagrada* proceeds from a hyper-real identification with the city as strategy for a self-conscious, self-contradictory, and self-undermining examination. While appearing again as pastiche to be at odds with a determined Bildung process, its subversive nature ironically nudges through self-reflexivity a stronger subject toward personhood. That is, to undo and undermine the given conventions and presuppositions of city causes us to question in the same parodic light the portrayal of women in anything but their social and cultural categories.[43] *Vaca sagrada* narrates the construction of the subject of Francisca. Even if, as Roland Barthes asserted, the chronological linearity or the causality of the Bildungsroman is rejected, there is still the story of a self, a construction of a subject, however 'deconstructed' it may be.[44] The female self, mediated by the city, undoes the truth of presuppositions about women. To this end Jo Labanyi signals the relationship between the female body and political terror, and the disquieting self-identification of women with horror in the abjection process. Upon going against dominant trends and underscoring the political nature of the postmodern, Linda Hutcheon appears to anticipate the ideological foregrounding of city in *Vaca sagrada* as site for violence and horror as written on the female body: "postmodern art cannot but be political, at least in the sense that its representations—its images and stories—are anything but neutral, however 'aestheticized' they may appear to be in their parodic self-reflexivity."[45] Francisca spews lies and vomit, and secretes blood and tears for the abjection of horror that is a prelude to death. This abjection as she gives birth to herself amid the violence of vomiting and bleeding (menstruation, or purifying the body of unused and unusable life) interferes ironically, Julia Kristeva concludes, with what is supposed to save one from death, such as, I contend, childhood, or the assurance of growth and development.[46] Menstrual blood reinforces the danger to society from within the identity ("dijo que no quería nada conmigo si yo estaba con sangre. Que no soportaba ver las sábanas manchadas. ¿Estás con sangre?—me preguntó.—No—le contesté[47] [He said he didn't want anything to do with me if I was bleeding, that he couldn't bear the sight of stained sheets. 'Are you bleeding?' he asked me. 'No' I answered[48]]), threatening, as Kristeva concludes, the relationship between sexes and the identity of each sex in the face of sexual difference (71). Eltit achieves her goal of making this novel a penetrating study of the nature of blood: "Yo quise, intenté en esta novela hacer una estética de la sangre. Ampliar por ejemplo el concepto de sangre menstrual en tanto rito, porque es cíclico, y hacerla circular por un cuerpo. El cuerpo de la mujer es un cuerpo que sangra . . ."[49] [I wanted to, I tried in this novel to create an aesthetic of blood. To enlarge for example the concept of menstrual blood as rite, because it is cyclical, and make it circulate through the body. The body of a woman is a body that bleeds . . .]. Not appearing to support or dissect sexual difference, Eltit returns to menstrual blood as a rite of passage that is inhibiting, liberating, and proved continuously as developmental process that simultaneously supports and threatens life for the male and female bodies.

The female body mediated by the city stands in contrast to the return to nature in the utopia of the South that Manuel represents. The city in *Vaca sagrada* is the site of self-critical analysis that portends a recovery of the self: "Pensé que alejándome de Manuel iba a encontrar una parte perdida de mí misma" (30) [I thought that by getting away from Manuel I would rediscover a part of myself I had lost (10)]. Sergio, on the other hand, obliges her to feel the sensation of death that invades the city (31) and search for something that would erase the perversity of those times and place. The disjuncture between the historical city and her seduction by the male image of her interiority that Sergio comes to symbolize (even in school he claims to captivate her when they meet [57]), conjugates a truth that Labanyi views in context of the unboundedness of the female body. That is, the unboundedness of the female body makes it a threat to all forms of control because the more it becomes identified with horror, and the more this identification becomes self-conscious, the more it is able to provide a kind of salvation, as a "zone of resistance to political terror."[50] Upon retracing her steps in the Bildung process, Francisca recalls that the city was always [already] threatening her even in her youth. When Sergio achieves their union through violence, ". . . la golpeó con su brazo activo. La golpeó con el puño cerrado en uno de sus ojos, y sólo entonces ella se aferró a él para lograr la unión más perfecta que tuvieron" (73) [he punched her with his good arm. He punched her in the eye with his clenched fist, and only then did she cling to him to make love more perfectly than they had ever done before (36)] the equation that Labanyi identifies of horror with the female body makes this an uncomfortable message for women readers she concludes and men, I would add, who refuse to victimize. The reader's dis[ease] reflects Kristeva's question of who would agree to call himself abject, subject of or subject to abjection? (209) knowing that the victims of the abject are its willing ones because of its violent and painful association with joy ("one joys in it" Kristeva asserts).[51]

This unsettling of categories politicizes the hierarchy of urban structures (phallic to a fault), and redefines obsession in which women are co-conspirators: "[Ana] Quería apoderarse de mi mundo, pretendía tomar todo lo que yo tocaba. Hasta la más compleja y sutil sensación debía compartirla con ella, y lo más insoportable fue su fijación en el recuerdo de Manuel. Fascinada con mi particular fascinación se acercó a mi obsesión, intentando el hurto personal de mi relato" (79–80) [She wanted to take over my world, she tried to take everything I touched. She demanded that I share with her even the most complicated or most evanescent of my feelings, and the worst thing was her fixation on my memories of Manuel. She was fascinated by my fascination and wormed her way into my obsession, trying to steal my personal history (40)]. The complexity of Francisca's love for Ana, Juan, Manuel, and Sergio is that with each there is a mark of defilement, a violence or a scar like blindness that replaces the invisible abjection constituted of rites of passage and layers of abjection. These marks of defilement transform the novel's characters into scapegoats that are ejected/rejected from the city, in an effort to free the city finally from defilement.

The further association with female workers rests on the fragile border of the city as leveling site: "El mundo del trabajo desfila ante mis ojos. Las trabajadoras caminan en línea recta y sangran por las narices. Quiero sangrar, desfilando con el puño en alto, gritando por la restitución de nuestros derechos, conmovida por una energía semejante a la histeria" (115) [The world of work marches past before my eyes. The workers are walking in a straight line and their noses are bleeding. I want to bleed, to file past with my fist in the air, yelling for the restitution of our rights, seized by an energy close to hysteria (63)]. Relating blood to power in her association with the workers, this act of performance does not relieve Francisca of her powerlessness, joblessness, ritelessness even in the face of the restitutive power of blood: "La sangre se había transformado en un líquido neutro que sólo me hacía cumplir una molesta rutina que arruinaba algunos de mis días. Ya no sangraba" (178) [Blood had become transformed into a neutral liquid that caused me only routine annoyance and ruined a few of my days. I was no longer bleeding (99)], and ultimately betrays the defilement of the female workers whose minds are conquered by the images of the city. Violence is political and economic, in the justification of terrorism and the disqualifying of social values by the free play of the market. The violence that political conflict takes to the most intimate of subjectivity equates as its alter ego the external history of the city with the individual female story, as Luz Angela Martínez concludes.[52] Eltit's strategy is to have the alter ego reject market images to offer images whose mark is pain, wanting, and marginalization.[53] It becomes clear, furthermore, that violence is the sacred cow, protected against all logic, in performance of ritualistic renewal, cathartic release, joy, and passion.

In the Time of the Butterflies (1994)/*En el tiempo de las mariposas* (1995) is a historical novel and foundational Bildungsroman that tells the story of the struggle for the foundation of a free nation from the female perspective, placing it in a fairly unique position with *Las memorias de Mamá Blanca* and select others. An example of Latina literature, written first in English by Julia Alvarez who was born in the Dominican Republic but who spends most of her cultural life in the United States, the novel is a pastiche of rites of passage, memories, recipes, diary entries, diagrams of bombs and fashions, and so on, of the lives of the four Mirabal sisters. Similar to the other examples of Latina literature to be analyzed here, Alvarez is aware of the double voicing of her text written in English with some Spanish words, to open the Anglo world to this process of being and privilege text over context. When it is translated into Spanish, the translation bears political consequences unlike translations made in a host of other languages.

In the Time of the Butterflies explores the transformation of four young sisters who unsettle social, religious, and political pressures to conform, which traditionally truncate the Bildung process of women. Their rites of passage from education, on the insistence of the mother, to courting, marriage, children, and religious, political, and social awakenings duplicate the potentiality of a nation held dormant through years of dictatorship. That is, their childhood and journeys of growth and development reflect the developmental stages of a nation in transition. For example, Dedé, the surviving sister, is left to use memory to communicate the individual and collective struggles for identity and articulation. Patria, the most religiously conservative of the four, who is married with three children, at first concentrates on her own development but then learns to appreciate her sisters' contrasting ways, "my sisters were so different! They built their homes on sand and called the slip and slide adventure"[54] [Mis hermanas eran tan diferentes! Ellas construyeron su casa sobre la arena, y dijeron que era una aventura de deslizamientos"[55]]. The dominant paradigms and predefined concepts that exist as unquestionable and unchallengeable are transmitted to us through culture Gloria Anzaldúa proclaims,[56] and it is possible even within the same family, as demonstrated here and in *Abel Rodríguez*, that family members react differently to the collusion of culture and power. Patria inevitably succumbs to the pull of the battle for social justice when she understands her religious beliefs to call her to defend the values of a free nation as opposed to the violence of the Dictator Trujillo and his sham democracy, "things had gotten so bad, even people like me who didn't want anything to do with politics were thinking about it all the time" (149) [las cosas estaban tan mal que hasta las personas como yo, que no queríamos tener nada que ver con la política, no hacíamos más que pensar en un cambio (152)]. Without sacrificing her spiritual beliefs, Patria uses her rite of mourning for the young person killed by Trujillo's men as a rite of defiance and political commitment to countermand the male political culture and the culture of the Church with its subservient roles for women.

For Minerva and María Teresa, on the other hand, the journey to political commitment is undeviating, Minerva being the one who confronts Trujillo directly, not wishing to have her rite of passage to adulthood violated by the dictator who seemingly rapes the nation and its women with impunity. Minerva, not committed to the value system of men, wants love and revolution, and is capable of standing up equally to her father when he attempts to control her life, "I don't owe you a thing . . . you've lost my respect" (89) [No te debo nada . . . Has perdido mi respeto (97)] and to the President of the Republic who makes his intentions clear at a dance to which Minerva and her family are invited, "He yanks me by the wrist, thrusting his pelvis at me in a vulgar way, and I can see my hand in an endless slow motion rise—a mind all its own—and come down on the astonished, made-up face (100) [Me tira de una muñeca, haciendo un movimiento vulgar con la pelvis, y veo que mi mano se levanta, como con una mente propia, y descarga una bofetada sobre la alelada, maquillada cara (107)].

Within the personal stories are interspersed informative pieces about disappeared persons, illiteracy, poverty, torture, young friends seduced and abandoned by Trujillo, friends turned over to the police, brothers and fathers murdered, and extreme poverty. Minerva decides to fight everyone's fight declaring it to be the same fight (108), reinforcing her struggle for the collective will of the people to contest the patriarchal system and its models of cultural legitimacy that exclude the subaltern voice. Alvarez enlists the sympathetic listener/collaborator to the orality of the woman's text in this testimony of self-realization that seeks social justice and ethical choices from the dominant culture. *In the Time of the Butterflies* portrays the Mirabal sisters as subjects in a growth process aligned with the marginalized and the oppressed, and shatters common stereotypes of low-income Latin American women as politically passive, voiceless, and submissive.[57] In essence, it facilitates an identification by readers worldwide who have experienced similar growth and cultural patterning and who sympathize with the struggle for justice. The double-voiced narrative seeking an English audience (to acknowledge suffering and complicity) and a Hispanic audience (for solidarity and self-awareness), inspires a nation described as "one big rotten family of cowards" (317) to move toward free elections, free economic zones, and education for women, mirroring through the Bildung process of the Mirabal sisters the development of the Dominican Republic.

Two final Bildungsromane by Latina authors, *América's Dream* (1996)/*El sueño de América* (1996) and *Dreaming in Cuban* (1992)/*Soñar en cubano* (1993), explore growth and development through gender and cultural patterning that links Puerto Rican and Cuban cultures to Westchester County, New York, Brooklyn, and Miami. América's Dream is the performance of América González of the island of Vieques in her effort to break the cycle of poverty and submission to a machista, Latin culture and have her daughter, Rosalinda, escape through education a morally and economically bankrupt pattern of being. When Rosalinda chooses to run away with a young man at age fourteen and possibly bear his child, it becomes obvious that América's submission to Rosalinda's brutal father is the pattern Rosalinda has chosen to emulate. What follows is América's escape from Correa, the man who controls her life, to the inhospitable North as a nanny and her cultural clashes with a white, well-to-do, Anglo-Saxon community. Her formation through confronting the Other, permits an appreciation of Hispanic cultural patterning (music, foods, art, values) that she had undervalued in her familial relationships before.

Perhaps because her relations with the Anglo world are primarily with another woman, her employer Karen, rather than with Karen's husband, Charlie, América is afforded the space to grow in her self-awareness and self-esteem by raising Karen and Charlie's children, "Isn't is strange, she smiles to herself as she pulls into traffic. They're learning so much from me. Karen and Charlie hardly ever see them, between their jobs and the kids' weekend play dates. Frida, Mercedes, Liana, and Adela are teaching the children they watch. All these *Americanitos* are learning about life from us"[58] ['Verdad que es extraño' se sonríe, entrando en el tráfico. 'Están aprendiendo tanto de mí. Karen y Charlie casi no los ven, entre sus trabajos y las actividades de los niños los fines de semana. Frida, Mercedes, Liana y Adela también les están enseñando a los niños que cuidan. Todos estos americanitos aprendiendo lo que es la vida de nosotras'[59]] A pastiche of popular Spanish talk shows, cultural critiques, foods, and economic systems, Santiago reconstructs the portrait of childhood by unsettling the authorized, traditional version (as represented by the Westchester County model of childhood), contaminating her portrait with the humanity lost along the way (perhaps at MacDonald's) through the voices of all the Latin American nannies hired to substitute for the parents. América's everyday acts of resistance that release her from an abusive lover and unappreciative employers, inspire her growth toward potentiality as she chooses independence, a new job, a new apartment for herself and her daughter, and a life free from abuse, the convenient, melodramatic end to Correa notwithstanding. "It is, after all, her life, and she's the one in the middle of it" (325) [Es después de todo su vida, y es ella quien la vive (370)].

Dreaming in Cuban (1992)/*Soñar en cubano* (1993) portrays three generations of a Cuban family that symbolize a battle for the Cuban soul, how Cuba will be reconceived and remembered. In effect, Cuba is the metaphor for the evolution of the Bildung process of the three female protagonists and the Cuban collective. This work centers the female process of development from Celia del Pino, who, like the island, was seduced and conquered by Spain in the person of her Spanish lover Gustavo, to her Cuban-American daughter, Lourdes, and granddaughter, Pilar, who recreate Cuba through memories. Celia transforms her obsession with Spain (father) into one with Cuba (son), a political seduction (although she fantasizes a physical seduction) by El Líder, Fidel Castro, and the Revolution. In between those events Celia marries Jorge del Pino and unsettles the role of mother and wife in Cuban society against all odds, because of the anguish of the privileging space reserved for boys and men in this culture. When she discovers she is about to embark on another rite of passage, motherhood, she greets the news with resolve—she will abandon her husband and Cuba if she has a boy or stay in Cuba if she has a girl: "If she had a girl, Celia decided, she would stay. She would not abandon a daughter to this life, but train her to read the columns of blood and numbers in men's eyes, to understand the morphology of survival. Her daughter, too, would outlast the hard flames"[60] [Si tiene una niña, Celia se quedará. No dejará a su hija inerme ante la vida, sino que la entrenará para que pueda leer en los ojos de los hombres su bagaje genético familiar y sus verdaderas intenciones, para que comprenda la morfología de la supervivencia. Su hija también logrará sobrevivir a las fuertes llamas[61]]. The act of "dreaming in Cuban" is a license to reach potentiality through unformed cultural markers that ground the Cuban and Cuban-American being-in-the-world. Celia, for example, personifies rites of resistance through correspondence with her Spanish lover that she never mails, and through vowing not to remember her daughter's name (the idea being that if she is not recognized, she will not suffer the same indignities). Her husband attempts to curtail this dreamlike state that sends her to the piano to play Debussy whenever he leaves town on a business trip. Jorge commits Celia to an insane asylum and in effect declares her development an anti-Bildung process of growing down rather than growing up. These failed portraits of coming of age, frequently ascribed to non-conforming women as mental illness, essentially characterize cultural impotence and political castration. With our goal of unpacking the Bildung process of the marginalized, however, they can be assumed to present themselves more effectively as enabling inspiration that constructs a way of life out of marginality.[62] Celia subsumes strength in her self-realization and affirmation process, which empowers her. She volunteers to guard the coast of Cuba against American invaders and participate in a People's Court in her neighborhood. The fact is, Ruth Behar asserts, that Cuba and its diaspora are always defined within a U.S. framework, on the right and the left.[63] In effect, the Revolution permits Lourdes to rise above self-interest and take on non-traditional female roles of defense in the public sphere. And as an outlet for her cries for social justice, the revolution satisfies for the same reasons it stifles her entrepreneurial, "yankee" daughter Lourdes. Her inner fortitude and desire for strength she will bequeath to her daughter Lourdes.

Lourdes, a businesswoman devoted to the free market system, leaves Cuba with her husband and baby daughter, Pilar, for Brooklyn, New York, in an effort to freeze out the contagion of madness and revolution that Communism represents for her.[64] Lourdes is the owner of two branches of the Yankee Doodle Bakery and she is happy with her new life: "Lourdes considers herself lucky. Immigration has redefined her, and she is grateful. Unlike her husband, she welcomes her adopted language, its possibilities for reinvention. . . . She wants no part of Cuba, no part of its wretched carnival floats creaking with lies, no part of Cuba at all, which Lourdes claims never possessed her" (73) [Lourdes se considera afortunada. La inmigración la ha redefinido y ella se siente muy agradecida. A diferencia de su marido, ella da la bienvenida a su lengua de adopción, a sus posibilidades para la reinvención . . . No quiere ni la más mínima parte de Cuba, ni una sola de esas carrozas de carnaval chirriantes de mentiras, nada de esa Cuba a la que Lourdes afirma no haber pertenecido nunca (105–106)]. But what does reinvention mean and can double voicing ever overcome her cultural impulses such as her sensuality and predilection for sugar that ground her cubanness? Lourdes's Bildung process mimics her father's ordered and predictable life and transforms her mother's passion guarding the coast of Cuba and infatuation with El Líder to guarding her neighborhood in a Brooklyn block watch and a democracy that permits her daughter Pilar's irreverent artistic depiction of the Statue of Liberty.

Pilar's Bildung process is perhaps the most balanced perspective of all because she can be critical but appreciate its mysterious qualities at the same time, "Cuba is a peculiar exile, I think, an island-colony. We can reach it by a thirty-minute charter flight from Miami; yet never reach it all (219) [Cuba es un exilio muy peculiar, pienso yo, una isla-colonia. Podemos llegar hasta ella en un vuelo *charter* desde Miami en treinta minutos, o bien podemos elegir no ir nunca (289)].[65] Pilar is tied to Cuba by a romantic version of her grandmother and the sea but visually reads Cuba as a version of "an earlier America" (220). Cuba is her cultural aesthetic, belonging to her memory and imagination, but it does not center her growth process as does New York where she feels she belongs not "instead of" but "more" than in Cuba (236). Through her Bildung process Pilar discovers a language that obliterates clichés, taking from her abuela Celia and mother Lourdes a sense of identity in spite of, or owing to, their differences. Dreaming in Cuban is what unites the three generations because the personal aesthetic of the dream permits its mutation to fulfill their needs. If the adolescent rebellions of Celia's children parallel Castro's rise to power, then the return of Pilar and Cristina García to New York impels a final seizing of this dreamlike period before the next stage of Cuba's growth and development in civil society for the new millennium.

Conclusion

I. THE BILDUNGSROMAN: JOURNEY, PROCESS, AND PASSAGE

RECONSTRUCTING CHILDHOOD IS AN INTERDISCIPLINARY STUDY that explores growth, coming of age, self-realization, and actualization in Spanish America as a way of remapping and rethinking human development. The study's theoretical, historical, and socio-cultural foundation gives the reader the sense of a powerful process of self-awareness that complements the equally powerful social movements of discovery taking place in Spanish America, particularly from the period of Independence to the present. The point it makes as a critique of the grand narrative of coming of age is that the unique journey of self-realization in the making and molding of the self invites an examination of intersections where ethnic identities and hybrid cultures merge. It redefines growth and development, confronting the privileged purview of youth, and expanding through cultural and gender patterning the stages of performance to explore greater socio-economic, ethnic, generational, racial and sexual differences.

The strategies developed and exercised are meant to be representational, with the hope that they will be applied in the future to many other fine Bildungsromane that could not be included because of the nature of inclusivity. It is my expectation that through close textual analysis many intercultural, interdisciplinary, and exportable models of self-realization may emerge in this study that will appeal to a wide range of diverse interests and suggest further study.

II. BILDUNG'S STRUGGLE FOR ORIGINAL IDENTITY, OR THE FUTURE OF THE BILDUNGSROMAN

If literature is the site of our dreams, then the Bildungsroman, which encourages self-examination and realization, is the cathartic location of our being-in-the-world, explored through the life processes of others. What, then, is the future of the Bildungsroman in Spanish America? Perhaps it will point, to paraphrase Diamela Eltit, to the way out of marginality, or explore, to quote Néstor García Canclini, further strategies for leaving modernity. Operating in a pluralistic mode, nothing in acquired Bildung is thrust out, rejected, or abandoned; rather, everything is absorbed. But once the cultural capital has been spent, will the Bildung process be overtaken by something more technologically advanced and programmable? This is not likely since it presents a hybrid consciousness that has a tolerance for contradictions and ambiguity, resolving the Beautiful Soul into the collective. It is the stage after this that is not yet clear.

The cultural shift in the post-modern novel foregrounds uncertainty and the consumption of differences, which works against the desire for expressions of original identity. Bildung is, if nothing else, a desire for the pleasure of original identity. We find ourselves in the post-modern in a collective (for example the collective groups representing indigenous migratory workers, feminist theorists, ecologists, religious fundamentalists, or the marginalized), which pits itself against dominant cultural forces and in doing so brings us closer to simulations of ourselves as we work out our being-in-the-world. At times there appear to be more legitimate, self-referential members of these groups than members of the dominant culture, but even as "pleasure" (i.e., authentication, recognition, affirmation) is secured in simulated events (the recognition of mass subaltern rights of working women or for land in Chiapas, for example), one despairs more and more at the loss of original identity. Similar to commodified images in the cultural market, events too become commodified and devoured as images. As groups we relate to these images. For instance, the images of Rigoberta Menchú, Che Guevara, or Comandante Marcos simulate an original and construct a recognizable cultural meaning. But the absence of the original does not satisfy. Furthermore, as Ian Angus concludes, through duplication we become fractional audiences of ourselves searching for a new original to authenticate our choices from the promiscuity of simulations. Thereby we regard the self as an "Other" to be searched for and authenticated.[1]

Post-modern culture opens a distance from modernity in that simulations oppose the desire for the pleasure of original identity. The search for the reappropriation of origins returns us to the reconciliation of the authentic self with difference. Perhaps this explains (beyond the obvious reasons) the furor and desire for the collapsing of "I, Rigoberta" with the story of the Maya-quiché, whereby a recognition of collective struggles still begs for the reconciliation of self with difference. This is a tension understood by Stephen Greenblatt as the representation of the concrete individual who only exists by virtue of forces that pull against spontaneous singularity and draw any given life toward communal norms.[2] Modernity failed to produce free and equal autonomous subjects, but the post-modern reliance on identity as a relationship between self and others still has to do battle with the desire for the authentic self. It is on this battleground where the future of the Bildungsroman will be determined.

Notes

INTRODUCTION

1. See the works of Steinecke (in *Reflection and Action,* James Hardin, ed.), Rosowski (in *A Voyage In* Abel, Hirsch, Langland, eds.), Shaffner, Aizenberg, Pratt, Steele, Masiello, Lagos-Pope, Fraiman, and Ferreira Pinto for a full discussion of terminology to enhance or replace the concept of Bildungsroman.

2. Significantly, Hans-Georg Gadamer's examination of Bildung recognizes its intellectual and spiritual challenges, which contemporize the concept for us. Gadamer concludes, "The concept of *Bildung* most clearly indicates the profound intellectual change that still causes us to experience the century of Goethe as contemporary" *Truth and Method,* 10.

3. I alternate in this study between the use of "Spanish American" solely to connote those works written in Spanish in Spanish America, and "Latin American" to convey the larger and more conflictive sense of identity. Similarly, a clarification of my usage of the term development as human development unless otherwise stated, is important.

4. Smith, *A Poetics of Women's Autobiography: Marginality and the Fictions of Self-Representation,* 12.

5. Fritz Martini (in *Reflection and Action*) credits Karl Morgenstern (1770–1852) of Dorpat with the first references to Bildungsroman in the years 1819 and 1820. Morgenstern allowed that the Enlightenment principle of harmony through aesthetic, moral, rational, and scientific education had become the driving impulse behind the cultivation of Bildung. One compelling reason for its creation may be seen in a desire for a total growth process, which grew out of the fear of specialization and narrowness that overtakes societies at times. The German response was to legitimize a popular literary form but distinguish it with social, intellectual, psychological, and cultural concerns. Morgenstern supported a harmonious form of cultivation, to the extent that he viewed inaccurately every good novel as a Bildungsroman.

6. Various studies support this as Gadamer points to the origins of Bildung in medieval mysticism (11), Robert Proctor provides a model that looks to the forming or shaping of the individual self through the study of the Greeks of classical antiquity (*Education's Great Amnesia,* 104), and Jeffrey Sammons speaks of the early bourgeois, humanistic concept as a shaping of the individual self from its innate potentialities through acculturation and social experience to the threshold of maturity: "It does not much matter whether the process of Bildung succeeds or fails, whether the protagonist achieves an accommodation with life and society or not" (41, in *Reflection and Action*).

7. Bildung, an early bourgeois, humanistic concept, embodies human development, the making and molding of the self, and has its roots in Ancient Mysticism, that is, in the search for the divine in us all. There are many valued critics, how-

ever, who continue to associate it essentially with the happy-ending novel or an account of middle- or upper-class status.

8. See Edward Wynne's study "The Great Tradition in Education: Transmitting Moral Values," 6, and William Bennett's popular *The Book of Virtues*, 12–13, for a defense of character education. One important critic who challenges the constructs of character education is Alfie Kohn who suggests, "Children must be invited to reflect on complex issues, to recast them in light of their own experiences and questions, to figure out for themselves—and with each other—what kind of person one ought to be, which traditions are worth keeping, and how to proceed when two basic values seem to conflict. In this sense, *reinvention* is necessary if we want to help children become moral people, as opposed to people who merely do what they are told—or reflexively rebel against what they are told" (*my emphasis*, "The Trouble with Character Education," 159–60).

9. The work of critics Abel, Hirsh, Langland, and Jameson are important exceptions. Jameson concludes that many Third World cultures are beginning a significant renovation of literature with the appropriation of the Bildungsroman, and more specifically with the stories of childhood development, "On Literary and Cultural Import-Substitution in the Third World. The Case of *Testimonio*," 183.

10. Gail Sheehy, adapting the research of psychologist Erik Erikson and cultural anthropologist Margaret Mead, has long argued in her studies (*Passages*, 1976; *Understanding Men's Passages*, 1998) that adulthood is also a series of developmental stages, and not the safe harbor reached after adolescence that many believed.

11. My usage of the term hybrid reflects the concept suggested by Nestor García Canclini in his foundational work *Culturas Híbridas. Estrategias para entrar y salir de la modernidad*, because it encompasses not only racial but cultural mixes and because it goes beyond the religious and symbolic fusion evident in the term "syncretism" to emphasize modern forms of hybridization, 14–15.

12. Alonso, *The Burden of Modernity*, 3–15.

13. Aníbal González's argument links modernist textual advances to the assimilation of philology, which is blessed by the past and a materiality in the present:

Esta quiebra de ideologías—sobre todo de la ideología literaria que servía de base al modernismo—que ocurre al amparo de los grandes cambios sociopolíticos, económicos y tecnológicos que se dan en Hispanoamérica a principios del siglo XX, mueve a muchos escritores, inicialmente, no a abrazar las nuevas nociones de la literatura propuestas por la vanguardia, sino a indagar acerca de los orígenes de la cultura hispanoamericana, con el fin de entender y superar la crisis. De esta forma, el gesto filológico de búsqueda de orígenes que formaba parte, desde un principio, de la escritura modernista, se vuelve todavía más obvio, más autoconsciente. En medio de la crisis de valores de principios de siglo, los modernistas, asumiendo cada vez más deliberadamente su función como intelectuales, se dedican a buscar en la historia los orígenes más remotos de los problemas de su tiempo. (*La novela modernista hispanoamericana*, 41)

[This breach in ideologies, above all of literary ideology that served as the basis for modernism, which occurs with the protection of the great socio-political, economic, and technological changes that occur in Spanish America at the beginning of the twentieth century, move many writers, initially, not to embrace the new notions of literature proposed by the Vanguard, but to investigate the origins of Spanish American culture, with the goal of understanding and overcoming the crisis. In this manner, the philological gesture of the search for origins that formed from the beginning of modernist writing, becomes even more obvious, more self-conscious. In the middle of the crisis of values of the beginning of the century, the modernists, assuming each time more deliberately their function as intellectuals, dedicate themselves to search through history for the most remote sources of the problems of their times] (*my translation*)

14. Alonso, *The Burden of Modernity*, 26.
15. Sommer concludes, "Romantic novels . . . fueled a desire for domestic happiness that runs over into dreams of national prosperity; and nation-building projects invested private passions with public purpose," *Foundational Fictions*, 6.
16. Masiello, *Between Civilization & Barbarism*, 8,11.
17. See Romano's "Authorial Identity and National Disintegration," for a discussion of the tensions inherent in the author's role of cultural ambassador, on the one hand, and witness to the nation's cultural disintegration, on the other.
18. This literature embodies what Gloria Anzaldúa terms "a consciousness of Borderlands," which arises from a racial, ideological, cultural, and biological cross-pollination (Anzaldúa, *Borderlands*, 77).
19. Quoted in Swales, "Irony and the Novel," 50.
20. See Hernán Vidal's examination of new social movements in "Postmodernism, Postleftism and Neo-Avant-Gardism" in *The Postmodernism Debate in Latin America*, Beverley, Aronna, and Oviedo, eds.
21. See Nelly Richard's examination of Dávila's work under a discussion of diverse themes including carnival identities, *Residuos y metáforas*, 179–98. I would suggest viewing the first cover of the political magazine, *George*, edited by the late John F. Kennedy, Jr., for a corresponding transgression of a North American national portrait of George Washington.
22. In her essay in *La sartén por el mango*, Gabriela Mora points to the particularly Latin American characteristics of the Bildungsroman such as childhood memories linked to the family's political affiliation, which separates the Latin American from the classical English or German model (72).
23. Tu Wei-ming, "Mustering Conceptual Resources to Grasp a World in Flux," 4, in *International Studies in the Next Millennium*, Julia A. Kushigian, ed., and Martha Nussbaum, *Cultivating Humanity*.
24. Nussbaum, *Cultivating Humanity*, 11.
25. Durán's farewell address, Yale University, November 1996.
26. See González Echevarría's illuminating study *Myth and Archive* for a comprehensive discussion of the picaresque in Hispanic literature, foregrounded by a theory linking literary narrative to legal text.
27. Yúdice, "Testimonio and Postmodernism," 17.
28. See Gugelberger and Kearney, "Voices for the Voiceless," 3–12.
29. Beverley, *Del Lazarillo al sandinismo*, 160. Beverley also reinforces its anchoring in marginality with the following: "Testimonio represents an affirmation of the individual subject, even of individual growth and transformation, but in connection with a group or class situation marked by marginalization, oppression, and struggle. If it loses this connection, it ceases to be *testimonio* and becomes autobiography, that is, an account of, and also a means of access to, middle- or upper-class status, a sort of documentary *Bildungsroman*." ("The Margin at the Center: On *Testimonio*," 103). I argue a reading of testimonio as Bildungsroman because their edges of cultural performance overlap and encourage a new reading of Latin America.
30. Elzbieta Sklodowska focuses on the unique perspective of the editor in the prologue, where the authority of the text is established in a contract for reading that predetermines the narrative's interpretation. For a thoughtful reflection on mutually reinforced developments and personal journeys see Burgos's prologue to *Yo me*

llamo Rigoberta and Elena Poniatowska's essay "*Hasta no verte Jesús mío*: Jesusa Palancares".

31. With respect to Argueda's view of Peru and Latin America George Yúdice concludes: ". . . culture seems to be the only hope, modern politics and leftist revolution having failed" (10), in *On Edge*, Flores, Franco, and Yúdice, eds.

32. Dilthey states: "A certain lawful development is considered in the individual's life; each stage has a value of its own, while at the same time it forms the basis for a higher stage. The dissonances and conflicts of life appear as necessary transitions in the individual's progression toward maturity and harmony. And the 'highest happiness' of the 'children of the earth' is 'personhood' as the unified and firm form of human existence" (quoted in Von Mücke, *Virtue and the Veil of Illusion*, 230).

33. Frances Rothstein bases her research on a variety of historical studies to arrive at the conclusion that changes in childhood and child-rearing in this period were related to the development of wage labor and proletarianization. Furthermore, anthropological studies also hinted that children in dependent capitalist countries of the Third World were also becoming "a labor-intensive, capital-intensive product of the family" (Minge-Kalman quoted in Rothstein, "Capitalist Industrialization and the Increasing Cost of Children," 38). Society and labor gained because of a uniform socialization that taught skills and discipline. What men, women and children hoped to gain from their sacrifices and a shift in work ethic was self-realization through mobility. Rothstein suggests that many studies explicitly or implicitly conclude that education is the means to mobility in both the advanced and dependent capitalist countries (38). Education is one significant element of the Bildung process that should by understood as contributing to self-development rather than simply registering lessons to be learned, as in the *Erziehungsroman*.

34. Statistics compiled by the Pan American Health Organization for 1991, for example, confirm a high percentage of deaths per 1000 live births from the poorer countries (Bolivia 83; Dominican Republic 54; Ecuador 42; Paraguay 35; Peru 54) to the wealthier nations in Latin America (Argentina 25; Chile 17; Costa Rica 23; Mexico 36; Venezuela 34) when compared to the United States (9) and Europe (France 7; Germany 7; Sweden 6; and United Kingdom 7). Another contributing element is the result of child-centeredness, which caused a shift from children being the object of much of the family's resources, to increasing the family's resources through their labor (Rothstein, in *Women and Change in Latin America*, Nash and Safa, eds., 43).

35. Hegel, *Phenomenology of Spirit*, 406–7.

36. Rickels, *Aberrations of Mourning*, 23.

37. Norton, *The Beautiful Soul*, 281. Norton's engaging study suggests the qualities of the Beautiful Soul may be used to solve contemporary moral dilemmas: "By contemplating the rise and fall of the beautiful soul, which was originally conceived in response to a widespread perception of moral instability and social drift, we might be better able to measure the efficacy of any similarly inspired 'aesthetics of existence' at a time when far fewer certainties exist" (8).

38. Rickels, *Aberrations of Mourning*, 22–23.

39. Gadamer, *Truth and Method*, 12.

40. Hirsch, "Spiritual Bildung: The Beautiful Soul as Paradigm," 29.

41. I offer three contemporary examples from real life of the triumph of the Beautiful Soul through an examination of the Bildung process of those who led very public lives: Princess Diana, John F. Kennedy, Jr., and Eva Perón. We have read over the years many explanations for the uncanny outpouring of public grief

over and worship of these public figures. Still there are those who suggest it is not easy to explain this outburst of emotion, and books written specifically on the subject aspire to but cannot explain its source ("Diana," *New York Times Book Review*, 22 August 1999). I offer one other theory. The very public lives of figures already designated Beautiful Souls shadowed by death because of very public tragedies in life, play on the guilt that the public endures for not being able to save them from their suffering. Princess Diana's failed marriage and loss of the father who raised her, John F. Kennedy, Jr.'s tragic loss of his father and uncle at a young age, Evita's political enemies and debilitating illness at a relatively young age make the public's sin, the fact that they could not save them, unbearable. There is one measure that enables the public to forgive themselves and move on, and that is the acknowledgment that the Beautiful Soul is not gone when it is not forgotten. That by which it is formed is preserved and will not disappear. Their formation allows these figures to reach full potential in death by inspiring others to seek their own potentiality. These Beautiful Souls, while normally the first to go, do not vanish because their stories written in the public sphere become "the blank slate for other people's dreams" (*U.S. News & World Report*, 2 August 1999).

42. In the *Origins of Totalitarianism* Hannah Arendt unpacks the seeming paradox of assimilation for the Jewish people—they were accepted because they did not behave like ordinary Jews, but they were accepted only because they were Jews, because of their foreign, exotic appeal. Arendt finds the root of this quest for assimilation in the new humanism of the eighteenth century, the culture of Bildung, which looked for "new species of humanity" to demonstrate the possibility of intercourse with all types of mankind.

43. Fraiman, *Unbecoming Women*, 131.

44. Kristeva, *Powers of Horror*, 208.

45. Hoover Braendlin, "Bildung in Ethnic Women Writers," 76–77.

46. Felman, *What Does a Woman Want? Reading and Sexual Difference*, 4,8.

47. Mackinnon, *Feminism Unmodified*, 56.

48. Butler, *Gender Trouble*, 112.

49. Clearly the traditions are different, but frequently and ironically literary critics, according to the editors of *A Voyage In*, have described "human" development in exclusively male terms (7). This is seen in the "anti" or "failed" approaches to the Bildungsroman examined by respected critics Aizenberg, Masiello and Mora, where they focus on the heroine's total failure or death. Cynthia Steele points to this perspective as one of the salient differences between literature by men and literature by women (327). Cristina Ferreira Pinto notes that the "failed" or "truncated" terms surface in a socio-historical and cultural context that permit an indirect method of protest from a feminist perspective (16–17). I believe this to be nevertheless a question of focus—a woman's Bildung process does not rely on the success of her efforts but on the journey she maps to potentiality. These are highly personal measures because the goal in self-realization is specifically the forming of the self. This model can be used to reinvest Annis Pratt's model of the male hero who "grows up" and the female hero who "grows down" (14, 41) with an underscoring of female resistance in the text.

50. Franco, *Plotting Women*, xxii–xxiii.

51. Edwards, *Psyche as Hero*, 14.

52. I am influenced by James Clifford's lucid interpretation of identity: "I argue that identity, considered ethnographically, must always be mixed, relational, and inventive" (*The Predicament of Culture*, 10), and by Néstor García Canclini's powerful study of hybrid cultures: "Postmodernism is not a style but the tumultu-

ous copresence of all styles, the place where the chapters in the history of art and folklore are crossed with each other and with the new cultural technologies" (*Hybrid Cultures*), 244.

53. Gilligan, *In a Different Voice*, 170.

54. Bannet, "Rewriting the Social Text," 213, in *Reflection and Action*, James Hardin, ed.

55. Chodorow, *Feminism and Psychoanalytic Theory*, 186.

56. Pollitt, "Are Women Morally Superior to Men?" 806.

57. Foster, *Sexual Textualities*, 9.

58. Foster, *Cultural Diversity*, 58.

59. See Daniel Balderston, "Poetry, Revolution, Homophobia: Polemics from the Mexican Revolution," 57.

60. See Renato Prada Oropeza's article: "De lo testimonial al testimonio" in *Testimonio y literatura* , Jara and Vidal, eds., for a further discussion of Díaz del Castillo, Las Casas, and Portillo.

61. Pratt, *Archetypal Patterns in Women's Fiction*, 14–15.

62. Tomás Ybarra-Frausto notes, "The practices of the 'underdog' are the tactics of parody, pastiche, and ironic refiguring, which make up a whole panoply of commentaries on the master discourse" (214, in *On Edge*, Flores, Franco, and Yúdice, eds).

63. Julio Ortega insightfully views the traits of Postmodernism in Spanish as turning the practice of self reflexiveness into a textuality open to other cultures and to the "other" specifically, which subverts institutionalized values allowing for solutions from the periphery, "Postmodernism in Latin America," 197–98. Related to the concepts in discussion here, it is the self-reflexiveness of the Bildung process that demonstrates its potentiality most conclusively as it moves toward hybrid relations with others.

CHAPTER 1. THE NEW MOTHER

1. Montecino, *Madres y huachos*, 39–51. Montecino summarizes: "Cada madre, mestiza, india y española dirigió el hogar y bordó laboriosamente un **ethos** en donde su imagen se extendió poderosa," 50. [Each mother, mestiza, Indian and Spaniard, managed the home and embroidered laboriously an ethos where her powerful image unfolded]. All translations are my own unless otherwise noted.

2. Showalter, "Feminist Criticism in the Wilderness," 203.

3. Moretti, *The Way of the World*, 24.

4. Bannet, "Rewriting the Social Text," 213, in *Reflection and Action*, James Hardin, ed.

5. See Mario Rojas, "*La casa de los espíritus*, de Isabel Allende: Un caleidoscopio de espejos desordenados," 920, and Peter Earle, "Literature as Survival: Allende's *The House of the Spirits*," 551.

6. Marjorie Agosín, "Isabel Allende: *La casa de los espíritus*," 450.

7. Julia Kristeva, *Powers of Horror*, 168.

8. This conclusion is drawn by Jean Baker Miller in a general effort to explore "normal human relationships" through the division of groups into dominant and subordinate entities (*Toward a New Psychology of Women*), 10.

9. See Doris Meyer's "'Parenting the Text': Female Creativity and Dialogic Relationships in Isabel Allende's *La casa de los espíritus*", 360–61.

10. Allende, *La casa de los espíritus*, 117. Future references will appear in the text.

11. Allende, *The House of the Spirits*, trans. 109–10. Future references will appear in the text.

12. Flora Schiminovich concludes, "Her novel effectively exemplifies one of the directions that feminist writing has taken in our century showing a woman inserting herself into history, making a place for herself in the cultural and political life of her time" ("Two modes of Writing the Female Self: Isabel Allende's *The House of the Spirits* and Clarice Lispector's *The Stream of Life,*" 109).

13. Correlatively, it may be suggested that writing advances the Bildung of the author herself. Isabel Allende's words would seem to support this theory: "Escribí *La casa de los espíritus* como un exorcismo, una forma de sacarme del alma los fantasmas que llevaba por dentro, que se me habían amotinado y no me dejaban en paz. Pensé que si lograba ponerlos por escrito les daría forma para que vivieran sus vidas, pero también los haría prisioneros y los obligaría a cumplir mis leyes. De manera muy primitiva, le atribuí a la palabra el poder de resucitar a los muertos, reunir a los desaparecidos, reconstruir el mundo perdido," "La magia de las palabras", 448. [I wrote *The House of the Spirits* as an exorcism, a way of getting out of my soul the ghosts that I was carrying around inside, that had piled up on me and wouldn't leave me alone. I thought that if I was successful in writing them down I would be giving them form so that they might live their lives, but also I would make them prisoners and I would oblige them to follow my rules. In a very primitive way, I attributed to writing the power to resurrect the dead, reunite the disappeared ones, reconstruct the lost world].

14. Gadamer, *Truth and Method*, 16.

15. Marjorie Agosín lucidly speaks of the upheaval in women's lives that oblige them to take action,"we observe that women are moved to political activity by problems of a personal nature, by personal concern for the family, by the maternal instinct to nurture and protect, at all costs" (*Scraps of Life*, 10).

16. Richard, *Residuos y metáforas*, 188.

17. Hoover Braendlin concurs: ". . . the focus of the Bildungsroman upon the interaction between individual and environment encourages women to expose and to condemn pre- and proscriptive patriarchal social customs and values" (*"Bildung* in Ethnic Women Writers," 77).

18. See Sharon Magnarelli's review of Allende's *The House of the Spirits*, 103.

19. Miller, *Latin American Women and the Search for Social Justice*, 74.

20. Sarlo concludes, "Si, en el pasado, la pertenencia a una cultura aseguraba bienes simbólicos que constituían la base de identidades fuertes, hoy la exclusión del consumo vuelve inseguras todas las identidades. Esto, precisamente en la cultura juvenil, es bien evidente: el deseo de la marca, marca socialmente" (*Escenas de la vida posmoderna*, 116–17) [If, in the past, belonging to a culture assured a symbolic wealth that constituted the basis for strong identities, today the exclusion from consumerism makes those identities unstable. This, precisely in the youth culture, is truly evident: the desire for brand names, brands one socially, *my translation*].

21. de la Parra, *Las Memorias de Mamá Blanca*, 17. Future references will appear in the text.

22. de la Parra, *Mama Blanca's Souvenirs*, trans. Harriet De Onis, 15. Future references will appear in the text.

23. Rich, *Of Woman Born*, 250.

24. Referenced in Elsa Krieger Gambarini, "The Male Critic and the Woman Writer: Reading Teresa de la Parra's Critics," 179.

25. Hoover Braendlin concludes, "Although women often select the subjective lyric to express strong personal feelings, the objectivity of the Bildungsroman offers female authors distancing devices, such as irony and retrospective point of view, which convey the complexity of the female quest for selfhood and confirm its universality," "*Bildung* in Ethnic Women Writers", 77.

26. See Nancy Chodorow, *Feminism and Psychoanalytic Theory*, 62, for a discussion of mother–child identification.

27. José Carlos González Boixó, "Feminismo e ideología conservadora," 224, 235.

28. Jacque Lacan states, "The mirror stage is a drama whose internal thrust is precipitated from insufficiency to anticipation—and which manufactures the subject, caught up in the lure of spatial identification, the succession of phantasies that extends from a fragmented body-image to a form of its totality . . ." Lacan, *Écrits*, trans. Alan Sheridan, 4.

29. Lacan, *Écrits*, 1–7.

30. Sommer declares this creation an "incitation to play with possible miscombinations. In other words, thanks to our disobedience and our deterriorialization, we already remark on the arbitrariness of authority" (*Foundational Fictions*, 314).

31. Puga, *La viuda*, 97.

CHAPTER 2. PRIVATE LIVES/PUBLIC SPHERES

1. Habermas, *The Structural Transformation of the Public Sphere: An Inquiry into a Category of Bourgeois Society*, 8.

2. Catharine MacKinnon adds, "The private sphere, which confines and separates women, is therefore a political sphere, a common ground of women's inequality," *Toward a Femininst Theory of the State*, 192.

3. Magnarelli, *The Lost Rib*, 108.

4. A popular, contemporary example of this would be the outspoken demands made by the public on the British royal family to demonstrate more openly their sorrow and be more like them following the untimely death of Princess Diana.

5. Vargas Llosa, *La ciudad y los perros*, 20. Future references will appear in the text.

6. Vargas Llosa, *The Time of the Hero*, trans. Lysander Kemp, 19. Future references will appear in the text.

7. Habermas, *The Structural Transformation of the Public Sphere*, 89–92.

8. Roy Boland suggests that Alberto's resentment and hostility toward his father conforms to a pattern of the Oedipus complex demonstrated through an ambivalence toward the father (*Mario Vargas Llosa*, 42).

9. Magnarelli states, ". . . all boys' actions are designed to prove them MALE and, therefore, NOT FEMALE; their acts endeavor to separate SELF from OTHER, but one soon discovers that there are two types of OTHER: the female and the other male. Thus, this separation from the OTHER becomes a double-edged, bidirectional endeavor. There must be total separation from and negation of the female OTHER in order to define masculinity, since the SELF is identifiable insofar as it recognizes, separates itself from, and stands in contrast to the OTHER. At the same time, and in relationship to other males, the SELF must demarcate itself only partially from that OTHER. Each male seeks individuality and identification, but the uniqueness must not be total; the overall personality must evidence common traits, shared and approved by the other men" (*The Lost Rib*, 110). The

approval of others speaks to a collective, social context that Vargas Llosa in our interview terms indispensable for the development of the novel, "Entrevista," 36.

10. Garber, *Vested Interests*, 32.

11. Ibid., 223.

12. Habermas, *The Structural Transformation of the Public Sphere*, 48.

13. José Miguel Oviedo confirms that there is a reinitiation with Alberto and a restitution with Jaguar to society made evident in the novel's epilogue (*Mario Vargas Llosa: La invención de una realidad*, 84).

14. Swales, *The German Bildungsroman from Wieland to Hesse*, 34.

15. Buckley, *Season of Youth*, 23.

16. See Román Soto's interpretation of *La ciudad y los perros* ("Fracaso y desengaño") in which he concludes that the novel should be understood as a parody of the Bildungsroman. Soto bases this approach on theories that support the Bildungsroman as an optimistic genre that possesses an open ending. This theory illuminates the complexity of the debate over the Bildungsroman as I define it in the Introduction.

17. Soto, "Fracaso y desengaño," 69.

18. Magnarelli, *The Lost Rib*, 105.

19. Interview with Piña, 240.

20. Elena Poniatowska, *Hasta no verte, Jesús mío*, 10. Future references will appear in the text.

21. Poniatowska, *Here's To You, Jesusa*, trans. Deanna Heikkinen, 4. All translations are from this edition unless otherwise noted. Future references will appear in the text.

22. In my unpublished interview with Elena Poniatowska (October 1991), the author concludes the following: ". . . se da a lo largo de toda la novela [*Hasta no verte*] una poderosa manera de ser que es tan definitiva cuando es niña como cuando es grande. Creo que la Jesusa, cuando es niña, tiene ya todos los alimentos de la Jesusa que va a ser en la Revolución, que va a estar en la Revolución" [the entire novel gives a powerful way of being that is as definitive when she is a young girl as when she grows up. I think that Jesusa, when she is a girl, already has all the seeds of the Jesusa she is going to be in the Revolution, of the one who is going to participate in the Revolution, *my translation*].

23. For a discussion of the metaphor of hunger see my article, "Transgresión de la autobiografía y el *Bildungsroman* en *Hasta no verte, Jesús mío*" in *Revista Iberoamericana* July–Sept, 1987.

24. *Hasta no verte* achieves what Mabel Moraña identifies as the social function of literature and its capacity to return to national culture the patrimony of its heritage re-elaborated, re-interpreted, and made complex, "Historicismo y legitimación del poder en *El Gesticulador* de Rodolfo Usigli," 1265. *El Gesticulador* is, of course, a classic example of the division of public and private for men in Mexican society through the use of masks.

25. Octavio Paz, *Posdata*, 76.

26. Franco, *Plotting Women*, 179.

27. See Lucille Kerr's treatment of Jesusa Palancares in her study *Reclaiming the Author*.

28. Monsiváis, "No con un sollozo, sino entre disparos," 731.

29. This is particularly true upon examining foundational Bildungsromane such as Poniatowska's *Hasta no verte, Jesús mío*, Allende's *La casa de los espíritus*, de la Parra's *Las memorias de Mamá Blanca* and Alvarez's *In the Time of the Butterflies*.

30. Franco, *Plotting Women*, 181.

31. McGee, *Telling the Other*, 122. The appropriation of the other in Western tradition is an act that singularly and ironically guarantees Jesusa's position in literary history. This is true because literature, to paraphrase García Canclini, is a social art that changes the rules, creates not only an aesthetic issue, a defiance, but also a disjuncture in the relationship that the work holds with its readers, *Culturas híbridas*, 39.

32. Sidonie Smith, "Who's Talking/Who's Talking Back?" 404. Smith provides an important discussion here of the fascination with personal narrative that centers responsibility in collaborative projects.

33. Castillo, *Talking Back*, 29.

34. Poniatowska, "Testimonios de una escritora: Elena Poniatowska en micrófono,"160, in *La sartén por el mango*, González and Ortega, eds.

35. See Spivak's "Imperialism and Sexual Difference," 319–37.

36. See García Canclini, "Cultural Reconversion," 31.

CHAPTER 3. THE LOGIC OF IDENTITY

1. See Auerbach's "Philology and Weltliteratur," (*Centennial Review* 1 Winter 1969) and Gadamer's "The Problem of Historical Consciousness," in *Interpretive Social Science,* Paul Rabinow and William M. Sullivan, eds. for important discussions of the triumph of the hermeneutical and philological methods in understanding the relation between the self and the other. With respect to the texts of Miguel Barnet, Juan Ramón Duchesne believes that this fusion with the language and vision of the other exemplifies Barnet's access to integral knowledge, "Miguel Barnet y el testimonio como humanismo," 158–59.

2. González Echevarría, *"Biografía de un cimarrón* and the Novel of the Cuban Revolution," 250.

3. See Luis's *Literary Bondage: Slavery in the Cuban Narrative* and Sklodowska's "La forma testimonial y la novelística de Miguel Barnet," *Revista/Review Interamericana* and "Miguel Barnet," *DLB*.

4. Eckstein points to the drive to rein in the markets during this period in a variety of areas including the housing and farmers' markets, as well as the service sector where many informal economies thrived. Labor, which to this point had manipulated work rules to their own advantage at enterprises' and the government's expense, had their prerogatives attacked, losing, in some cases, what had been believed to be guaranteed basic wages. The support of minibrigades, *Sociedades Anónimas,* farm cooperatives, and "parallel markets" was deemed necessary to thwart those individuals and enterprises that benefited at the state's expense. Ultimately, through "rectification" the government failed to regulate effectively its employees. Illegal activity persisted and people took advantage of their positions for their own ends. See Susan Eckstein, *Back From the Future,* 60–87.

5. Carmelo Mesa-Lago charges that the RP launched economic policies that resemble those applied in the idealistic anitmarket period of 1966–70. Decision making was recentralized under Castro and his inner group, some institutions that were discredited in the 1970s were reintroduced (e.g., construction minibrigades) along with excessively optimistic economic strategies and goals (*Cuba After the Cold War,* 137).

6. See González Echevarría's *"Biografía de un cimarrón* and the Novel of the

Cuban Revolution" for an important discussion of Cuban literature of the Revolution in general.

7. Barnet, quoted in González Echevarría, *"Biografía de un cimarrón,"* 260.

8. Barnet, *Oficio de ángel*, 14. Future references will appear in the text.

9. All translations are my own unless stated otherwise.

10. Leslie Bethell, ed., *Cuba. A Short History*, 68–85.

11. Eckstein, *Back From the Future*, 136.

12. Ibid., 42–59, 145.

13. Helg demonstrates that Cuba tends to show a two-tier racial system similar to that of the United States—with a significant difference, however: in Cuba, the line separating blacks and mulattoes from whites was based on "visible" African ancestry, not on the "one drop rule." Moreover, Cuba's racial system was not a product of U.S. influence (*Our Rightful Share*, 3).

14. Helg, 17–18.

15. González Echevarría, *"Biografía de un cimarrón,"* 249–263.

16. See George Yúdice, "Testimonio and Postmodernism," for an important discussion of common features of testimonial writing and postmodern texts that will also be invaluable to our examination of Sarduy's novels *Cobra, Colibrí,* and *Cocuyo.*

17. Elzbieta Sklodowska informs the discussion of value in testimonial literature with the following: "Lo que sí constituye su valor en el contexto latinoamericano y cubano es que Barnet les deje hablar a aquéllos que no han podido crear modos de su propia expresión o, más aún, divulgarlos" [What constitutes its value in the Latin American and Cuban context is that Barnet lets those talk who have not been able to create modes of self expression or, furthermore, disclose them and get them out there, *my translation*], 383, in "La forma testimonial y la novelística de Miguel Barnet."

18. The editors of *Contesting Power*, Douglas Haynes and Gyan Prakash, focus in their collection on those everyday forms of resistance that may be individual and unorganized, which as practice transform domination.

19. James C. Scott in *Weapons of the Weak*, xvi–xvii.

20. See Carlos Moore, *Castro, The Blacks, and Africa*, 2, 46.

21. Ibid., 14.

22. In an interview with Emilio Bejel, Barnet says that growing up in the Americanized Cuban middle-class before the revolution was "an internal exile," (*Hispamérica* 10 [August 1981] 49,45). This sense of internal exile, making one a stranger in one's own country, is evident in the cultural wars of *Oficio de ángel.*

23. Romano, "Authorial Identity and National Disintegration in Latin America," 171.

24. Moulian, *Chile Actual*, 258–59.

25. Helena Araujo makes reference to the linear nature of Vásquez's narrative and suggests that it is the author's fictional conscience that imposes a self-censure on her writing with resepect to subjectivity, "Las huellas del 'Propio camino' en los relatos de Ana Vásquez," 10.

26. Ana Vásquez, "Escribir en el exilio," 2, quoted in Judith Morganroth Schneider "Ana Vásquez: Interrogantes sobre el exilio y la identidad," 229.

27. Ana Vásquez, *Abel Rodríguez y sus hermanos*. Barcelona: La Gaya Ciencia, 1981, 39. Future references will appear in the text. All translations are my own unless otherwise stated.

28. See Lucía Guerra Cunningham, "Vigilancia y confusión en *Abel Rodríguez y sus hermanos*," 7–8.

29. See Sarkar, "The Conditions and Nature of Subaltern Militancy: Bengal from Swadeshi to Non-cooperation, c. 1905–1922," *Subaltern Studies III*, Delhi: Oxford University Press, 1982–1986, pp. 273–74.

30. Camilo Marks in his review of the novel ("Otra casa de campo" *La Epoca*, 3) suggests that Solita is punished by the rest for being poor and a foreigner. He concludes that this is curious since Chile has never been known for its xenophobia. It would seem, however, that this is the tension to which the author dedicates the novel. It is clear in Marks's reading that he is analyzing *El paraíso* as a traditional Bildungsroman, and that the strategy of action and progress for the traditional form cannot be applied satisfactorily to one in which relationships inform the process of self realization.

31. Elena Castedo, *El paraíso*, 67. Future references will appear in the text.

32. Elena Castedo. *Paradise*, 57. Future references will appear in the text.

33. Butler, *Gender Trouble*, 16.

34. Oldenburg in *Contesting Power*, 51.

35. See Marta Traba's interview in García Pinto's *Women Writers of Latin America*, 188–89.

36. See Elia Kantaris's excellent study, "The Politics of Desire," for a discussion of the process of marginalization that the patriarchal system employs against women in order to aid its own efforts toward self-identity and self-preservation.

37. Nancy Kason speaks of an evolution of candor between the protagonist which lends a confidential and confessional character to the conversation, "La conciencia del exilio en *Conversación al sur* de Marta Traba," 222–23. Frances Fukuyama concludes in his groundbreaking study, *Trust: The Social Virtues and the Creation of Prosperity*: ". . . a nation's well-being, as well as its ability to compete, is conditioned by a single, pervasive cultural characteristic: the level of trust inherent in the society" (7), and in the final instance, its customs, morals and habits "cannot be divorced from culture" (13). Ultimately, an examination of Argentina's Dirty Little War must include a cultural study of the breakdown of the norms of trust socially, economically, politically, and philosophically.

38. Jonathan Tittler, *Narrative Irony in the Contemporary Spanish-American Novel*, 18.

39. Marta Traba, *Conversación al sur*, 18. Future references will appear in the text.

40. Marta Traba, *Mothers and Shadows*, trans. Jo Labanyi, 13. Future references will appear in the text.

41. Marjorie Agosín makes the point that women are moved to the point of political activity by problems of a personal nature, by personal concern for the family, by the maternal instinct to nurture and protect, at all costs (*Scraps of Life*, 10).

42. Marguerite Guzmán Bouvard in *Revolutionizing Motherhood: The Mothers of the Plaza de Mayo*, explains that Chilean women accepted the term "crazy" and turned it back on the military by charging the military had made them crazy from the grief of not knowing where their children and loved ones were. It was a charge that enlisted the sympathy of the world and brought international recognition to their struggles for justice and truth that continue today.

43. The space between anguish and hope is the metaphor employed by Nobel laureate, Adolfo Pérez Esquivel, in his address at Connecticut College November 1996, to communicate movement beyond polarization.

44. María Solá, "*Conversación al sur*, novela para no olvidar," 68.

CHAPTER 4. THE TRANSITIONAL STATE OF TRUTH AND MORAL MATURITY

1. MacIntyre, *After Virtue*, 8.
2. Vargas Llosa, "The Power of Lies," 28.
3. See the Introductory chapter of Alonso's *The Spanish American Regional Novel: Modernity and Autochthony,* as well as the preface to his more recent text *The Burden of Modernity.*
4. *Soledad Acosta de Samper*, intro. by Montserrat Ordóñez, 21.
5. Bethke Elshtain, "Cultural Conundrums and Gender," 123, in *Cultural Politics*, Ian Angus, ed.
6. Méndez Rodenas concludes, "Women's memoirs were as concerned with the affairs of state and the governing of the new countries as were the public texts of male political leaders. The difference lies, however, in their reception, for women's histories are excluded from most traditional accounts of Latin American nationalism," *Gender and Nationalism in Colonial Cuba*, 5.
7. Molloy, "Too Wilde for Comfort," 191.
8. In fact, *El corazon*'s translation of woman's [dis]ease both physical and psychological through a rich tapestry of narrations, puts into question the goal of supreme sacrifice. In effect, the narrative appears to conclude that married women who espouse family duty are destined to a traumatic end while those who remain single experience a somewhat neutral ending. Gómez Ocampo suggests that the novel appears to criticize the self-sacrificing, joyless life of the angelic woman at home, *Entre María y La vorágine*, 140.
9. Gómez Ocampo concludes that family obligation is also the motivation that serves as subtext to the Acosta de Samper Bildungsroman, *El corazón de la mujer*, because it is understood as the duty whose satisfaction should surpass its cost, *Entre María y La vorágine*, 131–32.
10. Soledad Acosta de Samper, *Soledad Acosta de Samper,* 108. Future references will appear in the text.
11. All translations are my own unless otherwise stated.
12. Butler, *Gender Trouble*, 121.
13. In my unpublished interview with Carlos Fuentes he discusses his own Bildung culture and the break that was necessary from his family and his social world in order to write.
14. Fuentes, *Las buenas conciencias*, 14. Future references will appear in the text.
15. Fuentes, *The Good Conscience*, 3. Future references will appear in the text.
16. Owing to a denial of racism in Mexico, unresolved racial tensions exist today and even after centuries of intermarriage, "nearly all Mexicans are considered part Indian" ("Racism? Mexico's in Denial" *NY Times* 11 June 1995).
17. Ortega, "Texto, comunicación y cultura en *Los ríos profundos* de José María Arguedas," 52.
18. Felicitously, Ernesto's self-development is grounded in "the result of *Bildung* . . . [that] grows out of the inner process of formation and cultivation and therefore remains in a constant state of further continued *Bildung*" (Gadamer, *Truth and Method*, 12).
19. José María Arguedas, *Los ríos profundos*, 7. Future references will appear in the text.

20. Arguedas, *Deep Rivers*, trans. Frances Horning Barraclough, 3. Future references will appear in the text.

21. John Murra, Introduction to *Deep Rivers*, xi.

22. Ibid., xi.

23. González Echevarría, *Myth and Archive*, 160.

24. Felman, *What Does a Woman Want?*, 21–22.

25. Vargas Llosa explains, "Su obra, en la medida en que es literatura, constituye una negación radical del mundo que la inspira: una hermosa mentira. Simplemente . . . su visión de ese mundo, su mentira, fue más persuasiva y se impuso como verdad artística . . . La literatura expresa una verdad que no es histórica, ni sociológica, ni etnológica, que no se determina por su semejanza con un modelo pre-existente. Es una escurridiza verdad hecha de falsedades: modificaciones profundas de la realidad, desacatos subjetivos ante el mundo, correcciones de lo real que fingen ser su representación. Discreta hecatombe, contrabando audaz, una ficción lograda destruye la realidad real y la suplanta por otra cuyos elementos han sido nombrados, ordenados y movidos de tal modo que traicionan esencialmente lo que pretenden recrear. No se trata de una operación caprichosa: el desordenador verbal rehace, corrige, desobedece lo existente a partir de experiencias claves que estimulan su vocación y alimenta su trabajo," *José María Arguedas*, 27. [His work, in as much as it is considered literature, constitutes a radical negation of the world that inspires it: a beautiful lie. Simply stated . . . his vision of that world, his lie, was more persuasive and imposed itself as artistic truth . . . Literature expresses a truth that is not historic, or sociological, or ethnological, that is not determined by its similarity with a pre-existing model. It is a slippery truth based on falsehoods: profound modifications of reality, irreverent subjectives facing the world, corrections of real things, which pretend to be their representation. Discrete disaster, audacious contraband, well-crafted fiction destroys a real reality and supplants it with others whose elements have been named, ordered and moved in such a way that they essentially betray what they pretend to recreate. This is not a capricious operation: the verbal disorganizer remakes, corrects, disobeys that which exists through key experiences that stimulate his vocation and nourish his work].

26. María Victoria Reyzábal concludes that Arguedas uses memory in order that his characters may be capable of generating a new cultural synthesis and a different history ("Los ríos iniciáticos de José María Arguedas," 58).

27. Mario Vargas Llosa, Afterword, "Dreams and Magic in José María Arguedas," 239.

CHAPTER 5. THE FORMING OF THE SELF AND NATION

1. As stated earlier, Fredric Jameson not only signals the fact that many cultures of the Third World are beginning a renovation of their cultures through the appropriation of the Bildungsroman, he dwells in his study on the Bildungsroman as "the very epitome of an ideologically charged technical apparatus or technological innovation (which can then be exported from the West in all directions)," "On Literary and Cultural Import-Substitution in the Third World," 183.

2. We realize how global the appeal for self development is when we read in the Merck & Co., Inc. Annual Report of their status as one of the top ten companies to work for in Fortune Magazine's survey (1997) and their strategy for the growth of their company. One building block in their strategy is the following, "Know and Develop Yourself."

3. See John Beverley's study "Del Lazarillo al sandinismo," pages 157–68 in particular, for an excellent discussion of the characteristics of testimonial narratives.

4. Kadir, *Questing Fictions*, 3–4.

5. Barnet, *Biografía de un cimarrón*, 7. Future references will appear in the text.

6. All translations are my own unless otherwise noted.

7. Sklodowska, *Testimonio hispanoamericano*, 13.

8. Carlos Alonso, *Burden of Modernity*, 17

9. See Carlos Moore's *Castro, The Blacks, and Africa*, 15, 17–19. Castro's own Bildung process is grounded in the ideology of a first-generation Cuban. Of middle class, Catholic, Euro-Mediterranean background, he would belong to the first strategy in that as a traditional "hero" he rebels against the social, economic, political and ethical values of his social class and father, the Spaniard Angel Castro. Like many other Spanish soldiers, Angel Castro was enticed to Cuba after the war by the blanqueamiento (whitening) policy of Cuba's new rulers, which offered land and facilities to any foreigner who was white. Fidel Castro's father, an affluent landowner who built an estate that employed several hundred laborers, was reputedly an inveterate hater of the Blacks and a severe disciplinarian. But Fidel ethically (even if not substantially) opposed discrimination, moral duplicity, and the aristocratic goals of his father's generation. Some would say his coming of age is marred by the irony of a revolution grounded in the brutally paternalistic, aristocratic goals of protecting the less fortunate. That is, true to the first strategy, he reinserts himself in the goals and values of his social class, family, and Euro-Mediterranean tradition. What makes Castro's making and molding of the self interesting, is that he is the product of absorbing all experiences, which inspires a fight within the Cuban psyche: ". . . [these are] problems in which we have to find ourselves not only confronting a series of interests and of privileges that gravitated to our nation and our people, but also problems which imply that we have to struggle against ourselves. We have to struggle very strongly against our own selves" (*Revolución* 26 March 1959, 2).

10. See González Echevarría, "*Biografía de un cimarrón* and the Novel of the Cuban Revolution," 249–63.

11. Miguel Barnet, *The Autobiography of a Runaway Slave*, edited by Miguel Barnet, trans. Jocasta Innes, 17.

12. González-Echevarría, "*Biografía de un cimarrón*," 259.

13. If we look to the charters of the Afro-Cuban cabildos and societies of color during the nineteenth century, we can understand the importance of the role of elder that Esteban, himself an elder of over one hundred years of age when he tells his story, describes with great affection: "After arriving in Cuba, Africans, particularly those in the principal cities and towns of the island, established mutual aid societies known as *cabildos de naciones de afrocubanos*. As early as the middle of the sixteenth century, these voluntary associations were created in order to mitigate the psychological and cultural shock of transplantation from the familiar context of traditional African societies to the uncertainties of life in the Americas as slave laborers. In the countryside, plantation owners, with government approval, even permitted their slaves to gather on days of rest or holidays to allay their sense of alienation. These reunions were spontaneous affairs without structure, however, and consisted only of recreational activities. But in the towns and cities of the island, individuals who spoke the same or related languages—such as Yoruba, Mandinga, Arará, and Carabalí—came to form and employ their mutual aid societies

to promote the maintenance of African languages, customs, and heritage. The associations also provided assistance to sick members and assured them a decent funeral and burial when they died. Thus, these language—and group-based associations—not only provided a sense of community to members and cushioned them from the blow of cultural dislocation, but they also provided a forum for the transmission of African cultures in Cuba," Howard, *Changing History*, xviii–xxiv.

14. In a discussion of homosexuality and the term effeminate, Esteban rationalizes the term's origins: "Después de la esclavitud fue que vino esa palabra de afeminado, porque ese asunto siguió. Para mí que no vino de Africa; a los viejos no les gustaba nada" (39) [It was after Abolition that the term 'effeminate' came into use, for the practice persisted. I don't think it can have come from Africa, because the old men hated it (41)].

15. González Echevarría, "*Biografía de un cimarrón* and the Novel of the Cuban Revolution," 261.

16. While this is obviously a true statement, there are reported cases of *cimarrones* (runaway slaves), rebels, and free blacks aiding each other: "The urban *cimarrones* (runaway slaves) used numerous methods to evade their masters and the authorities, some of which were known to the slaveholders. For example, in many escaped-slave notices owners commented that fugitives had used false identification cards to make their escape. A warning might also state that a *cimarrón* was probably being concealed in the house of a free black. In fact, innumerable fugitive slave notices printed in newspapers reported the help that slaves received from free blacks, principally those of the villages outside the city walls. The cooperation of the free Afro-Cuban population in this illegal act grew out of the commonly felt struggle of the oppressed to survive, and to this experience of commonality, linguistic and cultural ties going back to Africa may well have contributed," 15; "Many *cimarrones* who were longtime residents of the mountains of Oriente joined the revolutionaries. The rebels took advantage of the struggle of the *cimarrones* against enslavement. Not only did the *palenques* (the hidden mountain villages of the runaway slaves) serve as rebel camps and hospitals; but the cimarrones also allowed their secret trade with Jamaica, Haiti, and Santo Domingo to be converted by the rebels into a channel for obtaining weapons and war materiel," Howard, *Changing History*, 112.

17. In this sense Monika Walter sees the work as related to a "performance juglaresca" where a democratic representation of the masses creates culture, "El cimarrón en una cimarronada," 205.

18. The outside world witnesses this in brief glimpses over the last two decades through pictures of black Cuban forces defending against the United States invasion of Grenada on the one hand, and poor, mixed race children playing near garbage and a poster announcing the Pope's visit, on the other. But Barnet, the individual, as Elzbiea Sklodowska recognizes, remains silent on the racial question ("La forma testimonial de Miguel Barnet," 383), letting the text speak for itself. As Hugo Achugar points out, testimonial discourse does signal the elimination of distance between writing and praxis, "Notas sobre el discurso testimonial latinoamericano," 286.

19. Barnet, "La novela testimonio. Socio-literatura," in *La fuente viva* 297.

20. Rossana Nofal sees Barnet's abundant use of archival facts as a way to legitimize a discourse based in truth not fiction, "*Biografía de un cimarrón* de Barnet," 35–39.

21. Hegel cited in Gadamer, *Truth and Method*, 14.

22. Davis, Darién, ed. *Slavery and Beyond: The African Impact on Latin America and the Caribbean*, xviii.

23. Nance, "Pied Beauty: Juxtaposition and Irony in Teresa de la Parra's *Las memorias de Mamá Blanca,*" 49.

24. Roa Bastos, *Hijo de hombre*, 281. Future references will appear in the text.

25. Roa Bastos, *Son of Man*, trans. Rachel Caffyn, 263. Future references will appear in the text.

26. Bareiro Saguier, "La cara oculta del mito guaraní en *Hijo de hombre* de Augusto Roa Bastos," 296.

27. Josefina Ludmer speaks of the stages of Vera's life that would suggest a Bildung process that continues throughout his life: childhood, presence of the mother and father, journey of self discovery and coming of age, education, rebellion against society's values, punishment, military service during the war, and finally access to power. "Las vidas de los héroes de Roa Bastos," 115–16.

28. Jean Franco, Afterword to *Son of Man*, 278.

29. Manuel Quiroga Clérigo notes this globalizing tendency in Roa Bastos: ". . . nos hace compaginar el espíritu indígena del autor con su proyección universal en un ánimo de globalizar esa historia de hombres y miserias que han configurado excepcional visión de ese pueblo acosado desde siempre, y hasta ahora, por unos enemigos tan crueles como han sido y siguen siendo la más feroz incultura, la más grave injusticia social y, también, la incomprensión amplia de sus países cercanos, como Argentina, Brasil y el otro enemigo militar, Bolivia, de donde contemplamos a Paraguay en el centro inhóspito de un hemisferio militarizado y empobrecido por los desgobiernos de despóticos generales y viviendo con la esperanza de una redención que no parece acabar de tocarle en suerte" "Un pueblo en busca de su libertad" (226) [It makes us fit the Indigenous spirit of the author's in with his universal projection, in a spirit of globalizing the story of men and miseries that have formed an exceptional vision of a people that has been harassed since the beginning, and even now, by those who have been and continue to be the cruelest of enemies demonstrating the most ferocious lack of culture, the gravest social injustice and, also, the complete lack of comprehension on the part of the closest countries like Argentina, Brazil and the other military enemy, Bolivia, from where we contemplate Paraguay in an inhospitable center of the hemisphere made poor and militarized by the disorder of despotic generals and living with the hope of redemption that does not ever seem to come to them].

30. Roa Bastos, *Hijo de hombre*, 7.

31. Ibid., 8.

32. Carlos Pacheco believes Vera's life to be a testimony to the clash of cultures: "Su vida, trágica, sin llegar a ser heroica, permanece como testimonio del choque de culturas, de dominados y dominadores y de los ámbitos en conflicto de la oralidad y la escritura" "*Hijo de hombre*: El escritor entre la voz y la escritura," 413 [His life, tragic, without approaching heroic, becomes a testimony of the clash of cultures, of the dominated and dominators and the conflicting boundaries of orality and writing].

33. Méndez Faith, "Dictadura y 'espacios cárceles': Doble reflejo de una misma realidad en *Hijo de hombre* y *Yo el Supremo,*" 241.

CHAPTER 6. THE BILDUNGSROMAN IN A GLOBAL CULTURAL ECONOMY

1. Paz, *Puertas al campo*, 16.

2. Ward, and Taylor, eds., *Mapping the Moral Domain*, 17.

240 NOTES

3. Epps, "Estados de deseo: Homosexualidad y nacionalidad (Juan Goytisolo y Reinaldo Arenas a Vuelapluma)," 808–809.

4. Ex-president Clinton's policy of "don't ask, don't tell" for military service has been debated as perhaps the greatest contributing factor to an opening of public debate to gay and lesbian principles globally. This is not to suggest the military policy has been a success, because Clinton himself reported that the policy as implemented in 1993 does not work (*The New York Times*, 12 December 1999), but it rescues the debate from obscurity and has inspired an openness that is evident in our popular culture of television, the internet, and advertising. With respect to Cuba, the combination of Catholicism as a fortress of homophobia and Marxist dogma that views homosexuality as part of a corrupt market system, gives rise to one of the grimmest homophobic campaigns in all of Latin America from the 1960s through the 1980s [See David Foster, *Sexual Textualities*, 88–89]. In 1993, however, the international release of the film "Fresa y chocolate," based on a narrative by Senel Paz, made significant inroads in the debate of a once historically and politically taboo subject, even though it leaves room for a critique of "aesthetic timidity." See Paul Julian Smith's *Vision Machines*, 81–98.

5. Smith, "Cuban Homosexualities," 250, in *Hispanisms and Homosexualities*, Sylvia Molloy and Robert McKee Irwin, eds.

6. Arenas, *El palacio de las blanquísimas mofetas*, 391; *The Palace of the White Skunks*, trans. Andrew Hurley, 352. Future references will appear in the text.

7. Scott, *Weapons of the Weak*, 29, and note, 33.

8. Soto concludes, "The binary opposition of life and death is not exploited, but in true carnivalesque spirit both terms of the antithesis are embraced and united, intermixed and confused," *The Pentagonía*, 94.

9. Monsiváis, "Ortodoxia y heterodoxia en las alcobas," 184.

10. Foster, *Cultural Diversity in Latin American Literature*, 45.

11. Quoted in Foster, *Latin American Writers on Gay and Lesbian Themes*, 25.

12. See James C. Scott, *Weapons of the Weak*, 29.

13. Arenas, *Arturo, la estrella más brillante*, 44.

14. Arenas, *Old Rosa. A Novel in Two Stories*, trans. Andrew Hurley, 72.

15. Ellis, "The Queer Birds of Juan Goytisolo and Reinaldo Arenas," 57.

16. Epps, "Grotesque Identities," 49; "Estados de deseo," *Revista Iberoamericana*, 813.

17. Kristeva, *Powers of Horror*, 15.

18. M. Jacqui Alexander couches her term "perennial supplicant" in the context of patriarchal violence: "To the extent that the state as ideal typical patriarch chides women for wanting more (in light of the entanglements around implementing the law), or dismisses their demands for the transformation of the mechanisms of punishment (even as women's demands are being misnamed in the service of disciplining and criminalizing womanhood while authorizing patriarchal violence), women are forced publicly to remain focused on the court system and its skewed, narrow definitions of violence in order to legitimize their broader claims. The gesture works to place women in the role of perennial supplicant, the permanently grateful, and otherwise, as guardian of the minimal" "Erotic Autonomy as a Politics of Decolonization," 77–78, in *Feminist Genealogies, Colonial Legacies, Democratic Futures*, Alexander and Talpade Mohanty, eds.

19. Monsiváis explores society's avowed hatred of the other through an ironic example of the institution of the idol Juan Gabriel: "En el encono contra Juan Gabriel actúa el odio a lo distinto, a lo prohibido por la ética judeo-cristiana, pero también se manifiesta el rencor por el éxito de quien, en otra generación, bajo otra

moral social, hubiese sido un paria, un invisible socialmente. '¿Cómo se atreve a atreverse?' Toda proporción guardada, el caso de Juan Gabriel es semejante al del escritor Salvador Novo. A los dos, una sociedad los eligió para encumbrarlos a través del linchamiento verbal y la admiración. Las víctimas consagradas. Los marginados en el centro," *Escenas de pudor y liviandad*, 282. [In the rancor against Juan Gabriel at play is the hatred of that which is different, of that which is prohibited by the Judeo-Christian ethic, but the animosity also manifests itself in the success of someone who, in another generation, under other social ethics, would have been a pariah, a socially invisible man. 'How dare he [sic]?' All proportion aside, the case of Juan Gabriel is similar to that of the writer Salvador Novo. Society chose those two to exalt them through a verbal lynching and admiration. The consummate victims. The marginalized in the center].

20. Foster, *Sexual Textualities*, 11.

21. Sara Levi Calderón, *Dos mujeres*, 30. Future references will appear in the text.

22. Sara Levi Calderón, *The Two Mujeres*, trans. Gina Kaufer, 22. Future references will appear in the text.

23. Schaefer-Rodríguez, "Monobodies, Antibodies, and the Body Politic: Sara Levi Calderón's *Dos mujeres*," in *Bodies and Biases*, David William Foster and Roberto Reis, eds., 1996.

24. Roffiel, *Amora*, 24, my translation. Future references will appear in the text.

25. Foster, *Gay and Lesbian Themes in Latin American Writing*, 118.

26. Another important work grounded in development through dialogue and relationships is Marcela Serrano's *Antigua vida mía*. This novel gives testimony to the power of dialogue as creative axis that enables growth, and without which the protagonist's self-realization process is stunted. Through dialogue the other reflects back the self, its oppositional quality serving to unfold previously uncontested truths: "Me abracé a él [tapiz], llorando a las mujeres—ciertas mujeres—incapacitadas para encontrar solas su interioridad. Porque, lamentablemente, yo soy una de ellas, de las que no lo logran sino en el reflejo de otra. Porque no he sabido mirarme de frente, porque he necesitado de otra femineidad—aunque fuese mi opuesta—para hacer mi propio relato" (368) [I hugged it, crying for those women—certain women—who are incapable of exploring their interiority on their own. Because, sadly, I am one of those who do not achieve interiority except in the reflection of another. Because I have not known how to see myself for who I am, because I have needed other women—even though they were my direct opposites, to create my own story].

27. Puig, *El beso de la mujer araña*, 221. Puig, *Kiss of the Spider Woman*, trans. Thomas Colchie, 218–219.

28. See Mario Rojas' review "Vagando por ciudades desiertas," 51–52, for a discussion of myth and the origin of the novel's title.

29. For his part, Raymundo reads Agustín's novel as a turn about/fair play critique of life in the United States after many respected American works painted Mexico as the land of corruption, violence, and death. He credits the United States, however, with providing the protagonist Susana with the freedom and creative space she could not have enjoyed in Mexico, which permit her in the end to return to Mexico to be treated and loved as a woman and not an object. See L. Raymundo's review in *La palabra y el hombre*, 136.

30. See Miguel González Abellás' "Ciudades desiertas: El México profundo de José Agustín," 101, 104.

31. Agustín, *Ciudades desiertas*, 192, my translation.

CHAPTER 7. PASTICHE, DISPLACEMENT, AND THE RECREATION OF CULTURAL MEMORY

1. Yúdice, *On Edge*, 24.

2. Franco, "Pastiche in Contemporary Latin American Literature," 97.

3. Earlier versions of portions of this chapter appeared in "Gender and Culture Reconsidered: The Transformation of *Cobra* into *Bildungsroman*," in *Between the Self and the Void: Essays in Honor of Severo Sarduy*, Alicia Rivero-Potter, ed.; and in "Severo Sarduy, orientalista posmodernista en camino hacia la autorrealización: Une ménagerie à trois—*Cobra, Colibrí* y *Cocuyo*," in *Severo Sarduy Obra Completa*, Gustavo Guerrero y François Wahl, coord.

4. Garber, *Vested Interests*, 149.

5. For an important discussion of the origin of *Cobra* see Roberto Gonzaléz Echevarría's "Plain Song," 457.

6. Sarduy, "¿Por qué el oriente?" *Quimera*, 102 (1991): 41. In *Escrito sobre un cuerpo*, Sarduy further explains "Cuba no es una síntesis, una cultura sincrética, sino una superposición" (69) [Cuba is not a synthesis, a syncretic culture, but a superposition" (56)] Sarduy, *Written on a Body*, trans. Carol Maier. Future references will appear in the text.

7. Roberto González Echevarría clarifies the use of culture, history and *bricolage* in Cobra in the following manner: "El presente en *Cobra* no es transparente, es un tiempo caído, del exilio, en el que se rehacen, se recobran, los símbolos después del golpe devastador de la historia. Es un *bricolage*, como el que vimos en *De donde son los cantantes*, cuyo modelo podría ser aquí la era imaginaria lezamiana, que se hace a base de los fragmentos de diversas épocas y culturas, es decir, con girones de textos que adquieren mayor sentido en la mezcla actual que en los originales de donde fueron arrancados," (*La ruta de Severo Sarduy*, 165) [The present in *Cobra* is not transparent, it is a fallen period, of exile, in that which symbols are remade and recovered after the devastating blow of history. It is a *bricolage*, like that we saw in *De donde son los cantantes*, whose model could be Lezama's imaginary era, that comes into being based on fragments of diverse epochs and cultures, that is, with shreds of texts that acquire greater meaning in the present mix than in the original from which they were taken].

8. See Alicia Rivero-Potter's "Algunas metáforas somáticas—erótico—escripturales—en *De donde son los cantantes* y *Cobra*"; Enrique Márquez's "*Cobra*: De aquel oscuro objeto del deseo"; and René Prieto's "La ambivolencia en la obra de Severo Sarduy."

9. Sarduy, *Escrito sobre un cuerpo*, 45, *Written on a Body*, 35.

10. Sarduy, *Cobra*, 15, 17. Buenos Aires: Editorial Sudamericana, 1969. Sarduy, *Cobra and Maitreya*, trans. Suzanne Jill Levine, 5, 7. Future references will appear in the text.

11. Alicia Rivero-Potter speaks to the complexity of subjects in *Cobra* concluding that "El ludismo textual de Sarduy hace enigmática la identidad del que habla. Tampoco es claro siempre a quién se dirige el narrador con 'tú' o con la tercera persona singular" "Iconografía oriental," 14. [Sarduy's textual playfulness makes enigmatic the identity of the speaker. Neither is it always clear to whom the narrator is speaking when he says "you", second or third person singular, familiar or formal.

12. Butler, *Gender Trouble*, 112.

13. "La serpiente en la sinagoga," Sarduy and Kushigian, Vuelta, 14–20.

14. Laurence Rickels, *Aberrations of Mourning*, 50.

15. Pagels, The *Gnostic Gospels*, xvii.

16. Garber, *Vested Interests*, 150.

17. As René Prieto concludes, "reading is an ongoing process and the pleasure it provides is not only contingent upon enlightenment or clarification but also, and just as much, on fluctuation and variety," "Mimetic Stratagems," 71. Patrick McGee clarifies that there is not one sexuality that would be normative for either or any sex, and concludes that if sexuality is something that is written, then it can be rewritten, *Telling the Other*, 68.

18. I am endebted to Adriana Méndez Rodenas's reading of *Colibrí* in which she concludes that *Colibrí* is a copy/similacrum of the novelas de la tierra such as *Doña Bárbara* and *La Vorágine*, and the foundational, Latin American texts of Rubén Darío and Lezama Lima. Her analysis understands Colibrí to fuse with its parody, a movement toward capitulation to the "texto enemigo," "Reseña", *Revista Iberoamericana*, 400–401, and could be expanded further if one were to underscore the homo-erotic nature of these male relationships, the occluded sexual energy, the phallic surrogates and violent, erotic interaction in *Don Segundo Sombra* as explored in Christopher Leland's study, *The Last Happy Men*.

19. Sarduy, *Colibrí*, 177. Future references will appear in the text. All translations are my own unless otherwise stated.

20. Roberto González Echevarría insightfully concludes: "La fijación en el tránsito de la adolescencia a la madurez refleja un proceso de arqueo, de balance en la obra de Sarduy; el paso de una postura de escritor joven, que practica la novedad como terrorismo y emblema propio, a la del escritor maduro, que ya ha consolidado una posición, y cuya novedad se ha convertido en un discurso reconocible, en una especie de facticidad," *La ruta de Severo Sarduy*, (228–29) [The fixation in the passage from adolescence to maturity reflects an arching process, a balance in the work of Sarduy; the movement from the posture of a young writer, who practices novelty like terrorism and like his own emblem, to that of a mature writer, who has already consolidated a position and whose novelty has been converted into a recognizable discourse, into a kind of factitiousness] .

21. Upon studying the onomastic used by the author, Leonor and Justo Ulloa underscore an interpretation of the Enanota as an anamorphosis of el Gigantico. The anamorphosis, they conclude, permits a variety of readings of the protagonists at any one specific moment, "La función del fragmento en Colibrí de Sarduy," *MLN* 109, (March 1994) 2: 268–82.

22. Sarduy, *El Cristo de la Rue Jacob*, 99.

23. Sarduy, *Christ on the Rue Jacob*, trans. Suzanne Jill Levine and Carol Maier, 125.

24. Sarduy, *Cocuyo*, 26. Future references will appear in the text. All translations are my own unless otherwise noted.

25. Rickels, *Aberrations of Mourning*, 334–35.

26. David William Foster recognizes the empowering effect of the relationship: "Despite all of the pain and sense of loss, it is obvious that her relationship with Vera has given the protagonist a compelling point of reference for her life, one that is magnified through the complex undertaking of (con)textualizing it in life and in writing," *Gay and Lesbian Themes in Latin American Writing*, 112. This compelling element of reference for her life is one of the points by which the narrator/author is able to resist blind desire and see life through more universal points of view.

27. Kaminsky, *Reading the Body Politic*, 108–9.

28. Molloy, *En breve cárcel* (Buenos Aires: Ediciones Simurg, 1998), 19.

29. Molloy, *Certificate of Absence*, Daniel Balderston, trans., 8.

30. Angeles Mastretta. *Mal de amores*, 22–23.

31. Mastretta, *Lovesick*, trans. Margaret Sayers Peden, 15.

32. See Trinidad Barrera, "Tácticas, estrategias y utopías de Angeles Mastretta," 34.

33. Hutcheon, *A Poetics of Postmodernism*, 5.

34. García Canclini, *Culturas híbridas*, 46.

35. Ortega, "Diez novelas hispanoamericanas del XX," 51.

36. Diamela Eltit, *El cuarto mundo*, 11; Eltit, *The Fourth World*, trans. Dick Gerdes, 3. Future references will appear in the text. Carlos Fuentes's postmodern novel *Cristóbal Nonato* shares this innovative quality of the making and molding of the self from the perspective of the fetus and is studied comparatively in Gisela Norat's article "Diálogo fraternal: *El cuarto mundo* y *Cristóbal Nonato*."

37. Nelly Richard signals a "travestismo femenino-literario" in the Latin American postmodern narrative of the end of the century, ". . . que nos habla de las torsiones y contorsiones de una palabra de fin de época: una palabra llena de arabescos capaz de actuar su sospecha—desde la estética—hacia racionalidades sistematizantes, entre ellas, la de las ciencias sociales y políticas que mantienen su posición de querer resguardar la tradición del pensamiento cultural de América Latina," [that speaks to us of the twisting and contortion of a word at the end of the epoch: a word that is filled with arabesques capable of acting on its suspicion—from aesthetics—toward systemizing rationalities, among them the social and political sciences that maintain their position of wanting to defend the tradition of cultural thought in Latin America]. "Bordes, diseminación, postmodernismo: una metáfora latinoamericana de fin de siglo" in *Las culturas de fin de siglo en América Latina*, Josefina Ludmer, ed., 244–45. This travestismo femenino-literario becomes a key to deconstructing the power of the hegemonic word.

38. Jean Franco, "Going Public," in *On Edge*, 70.

39. Williams, *The Postmodern Novel in Latin America*, 75.

40. Ricardo Krauel reads *El cuarto mundo* as an illustration of this Platonic myth with some significant reversions based on the anxious and competitive nature of the twins, "Lectura mítica y ambigüedad genérica," *Inti*, 256–57.

41. Tafra, *Diamela Eltit: El rito de pasaje como estrategia textual*, 81, *my translation*.

42. Thomas Friedman, *The Lexus and the Olive Tree*, 3–24.

43. Hutcheon, *The Politics of Postmodernism*, 3.

44. Barthes, *Roland Barthes*, trans. Richard Howard, 56.

45. Hutcheon, *The Politics of Postmodernism*, 3.

46. Kristeva, *The Powers of Horror*, 4.

47. Diamela Eltit, *Vaca sagrada*, 97. Future references will appear in the text.

48. Diamela Eltit, *Sacred Cow*, trans. Amanda Hopkinson, 50. Future references will appear in the text.

49. Diamela Eltit, "El cuerpo femenino es un territorio moral." *El Mercurio*, 4–5.

50. Labanyi, "Topologies of Catastrophe. Horror and Abjection in Diamela Eltit's *Vaca sagrada*,"86, 102, in *Latin American Women's Writing*, Anny Brooksbank Jones and Catherine Davies, eds.

51. Bernard Schulz Cruz underscores this dangerous aspect of *Vaca sagrada* when he asserts the use of bodily obsessions in a writing that is almost pure, carefully crafted and loaded, like a firearm, "*Vaca sagrada*: El cuerpo a borbotones de escritura," 68.

52. See Luz Martínez, "La dimensión espacial en 'Vaca Sagrada' de Diamela Eltit: La urbe narrativa," *Revista chilena de literatura*, 1996.

53. Sandra Garabano, "*Vaca sagrada* de Diamela Eltit," *Hispamérica*, 127.

54. Alvarez, *In the Time of the Butterflies*, 148. Future references will appear in the text.

55. Alvarez, *En el tiempo de las mariposas*, trans. Rolando Costa Picazo, 151. Future references will appear in the text.

56. Anzaldúa, *Borderlands*, 16.

57. See Concepción Bados Ciria's article "In the Time of the Butterflies," 414–15.

58. Santiago, *América's Dream*, 228. Future references will appear in the text.

59. Santiago, *El sueño de América*, 265. Future references will appear in the text.

60. García, *Dreaming in Cuban*, 42. Future references will appear in the text.

61. García, *Soñar en cubano*, 67. Future references will appear in the text.

62. Contrast the non-productive image of castration and impotence with an ironic image of mental health/illness or the psychological state of mind and one derives the essence of self-realization and development through the exploration of memory in Tununa Mercado's *En estado de memoria* (1990). The protagonist ironically equates a profound analytical cure as something thousands and thousands of Argentines have had a right to for the last thirty years (15), that is, we assume, framing the period of violence and dirty wars that occasions these memories. Patrick O'Connell draws attention to the association in this novel of the narrator's psychological intricacies [self-identity] with the writer's overarching social and historical issues, "Individual and Collective Identity Through Memory in Three Novels of Argentina's 'El Proceso,'"36. That is, personhood and wholeness reflect individual and collective goals. Because the sixteen chapters of memories and remembrances are not revealed chronologically, the narrator is able to revive and reenact her self-identity and search for self-actualization as a reconversion of social and political goals for the collective as well. Drawing as does *Dos mujeres* on writing as catharsis, *En estado de memoria* ultimately also reinforces the cathartic nature of the Bildungsroman for the individual as well as the collective, not because "healing" has been achieved in the end but because it obliges a reconciling of the marginal position to history.

63. Behar, *Bridges to Cuba/Puentes a Cuba*, 2.

64. See Kimberle López's article "Women on the Verge of a Revolution", Mary Vásquez's "Cuba as Text and Context in Cristina García's *Dreaming in Cuban*", and Joseph M. Viera's "Matriarchy and Mayhem" for a thorough discussion of the oppositional worlds of Cuban/Cuban-American and their fusion in Pilar.

65. This is one instance where for political reasons I believe the Spanish translation offers a different meaning than the English version conveys.

CONCLUSION

1. Angus, "Circumscribing Postmodern Culture," 102, in *Cultural Politics in Contemporary America* Angus and Jhally, eds.

2. Greenblatt, "Fiction and Friction," 34, in *Reconstructing Individualism*, Thomas Heller et al.

Appendix

Table 1.1
INFANT MORTALITY RATES, 19 LC, 1960–96[a]
(Deaths PT Live Births)[1]

Country	Code	1960	1965	1970	1975	1980	1985	1988	1989	1990	1991	1992	1993	1994	1995	1996
A. ARGENTINA[2]	C	62.4	56.9	58.9	—	33.2	26.2	25.8	25.7	25.6	24.7	23.9	22.9	22.0	22.2	—
B. BOLIVIA[2]	**	—	76.5	—	—	138.2‡	124.4‡	98.0ᶠ	—	—	—	—	75.0ᵍ	—	—	—
C. BRAZIL[2,3]	U	—	—	—	—	78.8‡	70.6†	63.0ᶠ	—	—	—	—	47.0ᵍ	—	—	—
D. CHILE[2,4]	C	125.1	107.1	78.8	56.4	33.0	19.5	18.9	17.1	16.0	14.6	14.3	13.1	12.0	11.1	—
E. COLOMBIA[2,3,5,6]		99.8	82.4	—	46.7	55.0‡	50.0‡	40.0ᶠ	—	—	—	—	28.0ᵍ	—	—	—
F. COSTA RICA[7]	C	70.8	71.8	61.5	38.2	20.2	—	14.7	13.9	15.3	13.8	13.7	—	13.0	13.2	—
G. CUBA[3,8,9]	C	35.4ᵈ	38.4	35.9	27.3	19.6	16.5	11.9	11.1	10.7	10.7	10.2‡	9.4	—	—	8.0‡
H. DOMINICAN REP.[2]	U	100.6ᵈ	72.7	50.1	43.5	84.3‡	74.5‡	55.0ᵍ	—	—	—	—	42.0ᵍ	—	—	—
I. ECUADOR[2,7,10]	U	100.0	93.0	76.6	65.8	82.4‡	69.5‡	63.0ᶠ	—	—	—	—	50.0ᵍ	—	—	—
J. EL SALVADOR[2]	C	76.3	70.6	66.6	58.1	42.0	—	54ᶠ	—	—	—	—	44.0ᵍ	—	—	—
K. GUATEMALA[2]	C	91.9	92.6	87.1	81.4	65.5	56.0	46.6	43.6	—	47.6	46.6	46.2	—	—	—
M. HONDURAS[2,3]	U	52.0	41.2	33.2	33.7	94.7‡	81.5‡	53.0ᶠ	68.0ᶠ	—	—	—	43.0ᵍ	—	—	—
N. MEXICO[2,3,11]	U	74.2ᵇ	60.7	68.5	52.8	60.0‡	53.0‡	40.0ᶠ	—	—	—	—	34.0ᵍ	—	—	—
O. NICARAGUA[2,3]	U	70.2	51.6ᵈ	—	—	93.0‡	76.4‡	65.0ᶠ	—	—	—	—	52.0ᵍ	—	—	—
P. PANAMA[2,12]	U	56.9	44.7	40.5	31.6	31.6‡	25.6‡	28.0ᶠ	—	—	—	—	25.0ᵍ	—	—	—
Q. PARAGUAY[2,3]	U	—	41.5	33.3	—	48.6‡	45.0‡	47.0ᶠ	—	—	—	—	43.0ᵍ	—	—	—
R. PERU[2,13]	C	92.1	90.7	—	—	104.9‡	100.5	107.5	129.2	124.2	79.5	77.0	74.9	73.0	81.0	77.8‡
S. URUGUAY	C	47.4‡,ᶜ	49.8	42.6	48.8ᵈ	37.6	29.4	21.0	21.2	20.6	21.1	18.6	20.1	—	—	—
T. VENEZUELA[2,10]	U	53.9	47.7	49.3	43.7ᵈ	43.3‡	26.1	21.5	23.3	24.2	20.2	21.1	22.0	23.5	21.0	16.8‡
UNITED STATES	C	26.0	24.7	20.0	16.1	12.6	10.6	10.0	9.8	9.2‡	8.9‡	8.4	8.4	8.0	7.5	—

Code: C = Data estimated to be virtually complete, representing at least 90% of the events occuring each year.
U = Data estimated to be virtually incomplete, representing less than 90% of the events occurring each year.

1. Infants: less than 1 year.
2. Estimates for 1975–85 prepared by the Population Division of the United Nations.
3. Data tabulated by year of registration rather than of occurrence.
4. Prior to 1968 rates computed on live births with an upward adjustment for underenumeration.
5. Prior to 1951 tabulated by year of registration rather than of occurrence.
6. Rates computed on number of baptisms recorded in Roman Catholic Church registers, for years 1960, 1965, and 1970 while 1975 data are based on burial permits.
7. Rates for 1960 and 1965 were computed on live births registered during the period 1951–65 tabulated by year of occurrence.
8. Prior to 1957 rates excluded those dying within 24 hours of birth. Beginning in 1957 rates computed on births which are in turn estimates based on analysis of 1943 and 1953 census and the application of an assumed rate of growth.
9. Rates for 1965–85 computed on live births recorded in the National Register of Consumers established December 31, 1964.

10. Excludes tropical forest Amerindians.
11. Rates computed by date of occurrence for years 1975–85.
12. Excludes the former Canal Zone, prior to 1980.
13. Excludes Indian population in remote areas estimated at 100,830 in 1961.

a. For 1930–59, see SALA, 23–705.
b. Data considered complete.
c. Data considered incomplete.
d. Data tabulated by year of occurrence.
e. Estimate for 1980–85 prepared by the Population Division of the United Nations.
f. Estimate for 1985–90 prepared by the Population Division of the United Nations.
g. Estimate for 1990–95 prepared by Population Division of the United Nations.

SOURCE: UN-DY, 1966, table 14; 1974, table 20; 1980, 1985, table 20; 1986, table 9; 1992, table 18; 1993–95, table 15; 1996, table 20.

Table 1.2
CRUDE BIRTH RATES, 20 LC, 1960–96[a] (PT1)[1]

Country	Code	1960	1965	1970	1975	1980	1981	1982	1983	1985	1986	1987	1988	1989	1990	1991	1992	1993	1994	1995	1996
A. ARGENTINA	C	22.8‡	21.7	22.7	—	24.7	23.7	22.8	22.1	21.5	22.0	21.5	21.6	20.8	20.9	21.1	20.3	19.7	19.6	18.9	—
B. BOLIVIA	**	25.6‡c	46.1	45.6	45.4e	44.8f	—	—	39.4	—	42.8h	—	36.6h	—	—	—	—	35.7i	—	—	—
C. BRAZIL[2]	U		42.1	38.3	33.6e	32.0f	—	—	30.6g	—	28.6h	—	26.7h	—	—	—	—	21.6i	—	—	—
D. CHILE[3]	C	35.7	33.2	27.6	24.2	22.2	23.4	23.8	22.2	21.6	22.1	22.3	23.3	23.4	23.3	22.4	21.6	21.1	20.6	19.7	—
E. COLOMBIA[4]	**	42.4c,d	44.6	39.6	33.3e	32.1f	—	—	31.0g	—	29.2h	—	25.9	—	—	—	—	26.0i	—	—	—
F. COSTA RICA[4]	C	48.4	42.3	33.4	29.5	29.4	29.8	30.7	30.0	33.9	—	28.9	28.5	28.6	27.4	28.2	27.3	—	24.6	24.1	—
G. CUBA[5,6]	U	29.8	33.8	27.6	20.7	14.1	14.0	16.3	16.7	18.0	16.3	17.4	18.0	17.6	17.6	16.2	14.5	14.0	—	—	13.5‡
H. DOMINICAN REP.[4]	U	36.8c	42.7	35.8	41.9e	34.6f	—	—	33.6g	—	31.3h	—	—	31.3h	—	—	25.5	24.1	21.6	—	19.1‡
I. ECUADOR[7]	U	47.7c	46.1	44.2	41.2e	38.2f	—	—	36.8g	—	35.4h	—	32.3h	—	—	—	—	28.3i	—	—	—
J. EL SALVADOR	U	46.5	46.9	40.0	39.9	37.7	35.6	33.6	38.0	—	36.3h	—	34.6h	—	—	—	—	29.9i	—	—	—
K. GUATEMALA	C	49.5	45.3	40.3	41.4	43.9	43.4	42.7	40.8	41.0	39.0	37.8	39.3	—	38.0	38.0	37.3	36.9	—	—	—
L. HAITI[6]	**		44.4	43.7	42.7e	41.8f	—	—	35.4g	—	34.3h	—	36.2h	—	—	—	—	35.3i	—	—	—
M. HONDURAS[4]	U	44.7c,d	50.9	50.0	48.6e	47.1f	—	—	38.7g	—	39.8h	—	39.8h	—	—	—	—	37.1i	—	—	—
N. MEXICO[4]	U	46.0c,d	44.6	43.9	42.7e	37.6f	—	—	32.6g	—	29.0h	—	30.0h	—	—	—	—	27.0i	—	—	—
O. NICARAGUA[4]	**	45.2c,d	50.0	48.6	46.8e	45.6f	—	—	45.0g	—	41.8h	—	43.5h	—	—	—	—	35.8	—	—	—
P. PANAMA[8]	C	40.8	38.4	36.4	31.6	26.9	26.9	26.7	26.4	26.6	25.9	25.3	25.2	24.9	24.8	24.6	24.1	23.3	21.7	23.5	22.4‡
Q. PARAGUAY	U		42.2	40.4	37.5e	36.7f	—	—	35.8g	10.8	9.7	9.6	34.8h	—	—	—	—	34.1	—	—	—
R. PERU[2,9]	**	38.9c,d	46.4	44.5	40.5	38.0	41.5	35.7	33.2	32.6	31.9	31.4	31.0	30.5	30.1	29.7	29.3‡	28.9‡	28.7	28.2‡	25.7‡
S. URUGUAY[4]	C	21.4g,c,d	22.4	19.5	20.9	18.5	18.4	18.5	18.0	17.9	17.9	17.5	18.2	18.0	18.1	17.6	17.3	17.8	17.7	17.8	—
T. VENEZUELA[10]	U	45.9c,d	45.2	37.0	35.2	32.8	32.1	32.0	31.4	29.0	28.8	28.8	28.4	28.0	29.9	30.4	27.4	25.1	25.6	24.1	26.2‡
UNITED STATES	C	23.7	19.4	18.2	14.6	15.9	15.8	15.8	15.5	15.7	15.6	15.7	16.0	16.3	16.6	16.3‡	16.0‡	15.5	15.2	14.8	—

Code: C = Data estimated to be virtually complete, representing at least 90% of the events occuring each year.
U = Data estimated to be virtually incomplete, representing less than 90% of the events occurring each year.

1. Crude birth rates are determined by the number of live births per thousand, mid-year population.
2. Excludes Indian population in remote areas.
3. For 1960, data are births tabulated by year of occurrence.
4. Data tabulated by year of registration rather than year of occurrence.
5. For 1960, data estimates based on analysis of 1943 and 1953 census returns plus an assumed rate of growth.
6. Based on births registered in National Consumer Register.
7. Excludes nomadic Amerindians
8. Excludes Canal Zone.
9. Includes an upward adjustment for under-registration.
10. Excludes Indian population in remote areas estimated at 31,800 in 1961.

a. 1930–59 data, see SALA, 21–705.
b. Data considered complete.
c. Data considered incomplete.
d. Data tabulated by year of registration.
e. Estimate for 1970–75 prepared by the Population Division of the United Nations.
f. Estimate for 1975–80 prepared by the Population Division of the United Nations.
g. Estimate for 1980–85 prepared by the Population Division of the United Nations.
h. Estimate for 1985–90 prepared by the Population Division of the United Nations.
i. Estimate for 1990–95 prepared by the Population Division of the United Nations.

SOURCE: UN-DY, 1975, 1981, table 21; 1984–85, table 9; 1986, table 21; 1992, table 15; 1993–96, table 9.

Bibliography

Abel, Elizabeth, Marianne Hirsh and Elizabeth Langland, eds. *The Voyage In: Fictions of Female Development.* Hanover, NH: University Press of New England, 1983.

Aching, Gerard. "On the Creation of Unsung National Heroes: Barnet's Esteban Montejo and Armas's Julián del Casal." *Latin American Literary Review* 22(43) (January–June 1994): 31–50.

Achugar, Hugo. "Notas sobre el discurso testimonial latinoamericano." In *La historia en la literatura iberoamericana*, edition and prologue by Raquel Chang-Rodríguez and Gabriella de Beer. Hanover, NH: Ediciones del Norte, 1989.

Acosta de Samper, Soledad. *Novelas y cuadros de la Vida Sur-Americana (Teresa la limeña).* Gante: Imprenta de Eug. Vanderhaeghen, 1869.

———. *Soledad Acosta de Samper. Una nueva lecutra.* Montserrat Ordóñez, intro. Bogotá: Ediciones fondo cultural cafetero, 1988.

Agosín, Marjorie. *Scraps of Life. Chilean Arpilleras. Chilean Women and the Pinochet Dictatorship.* Translated by Cola Franzen. Trenton, NJ: The Red Sea Press, 1987.

———. "Isabel Allende: *La casa de los espíritus.*" *Revista Interamericana de Bibliografía/Inter-American Review of Bibliography* 35 (1985): 448–58.

Agustín, José. *Ciudades desiertas.* México: Alfaguara, 1995.

Aizenberg, Edna. "El *Bildungsroman* fracasado en Latinoamérica: El caso de Ifigenia, de Teresa de la Parra." *Revista Iberoamericana* 51(132–33) (July–December 1985): 539–46.

Alden, Patricia. *Social Mobility in the English Bildungsroman: Gissing, Hardy, Bennett, and Lawrence.* Ann Arbor: University of Michigan Research Press, 1986.

Alexander, M. Jacqui. "Erotic Autonomy as a Politics of Decolonization." In *Feminist Genealogies, Colonial Legacies, Democratic Futures*, edited by Jacqui Alexander and Chandra Talpade Mohanty. New York: Routledge, 1997.

Allende, Isabel. *La casa de los espíritus.* Barcelona: Plaza & Janés, 1982.

———. *The House of the Spirits.* Translated by Magda Bogin. New York: A. A. Knopf, 1985.

———. "La magia de las palabras." *Revista Iberoamericana* 51(132–33), (July–December 1985): 447–52.

Alonso, Carlos. *The Burden of Modernity. The Rhetoric of Cultural Discourse in Spanish America.* New York: Oxford University Press, 1998.

———. *The Spanish American Regional Novel: Modernity and Autochthony.* New York: Cambridge University Press, 1990.

Alvarez, Julia. *En el tiempo de las mariposas*. Translated by Rolando Costa Picazo. Buenos Aires: Editorial Atlántida, 1995.

———. *In the Time of the Butterflies*. Chapel Hill, NC: Algonquin Books, 1994.

Angus, Ian. "Circumscribing Postmodern Culture." In *Cultural Politics in Contemporary America*, edited by Ian Angus and Sut Jhally. New York: Routledge, 1989.

Anzaldúa, Gloria. *Borderlands: La Frontera The New Mestiza*. San Francisco: Aunt Lute Books, 1987.

Araujo, Helena. "Las huellas del 'propio camino' en los relatos de Ana Vásquez." *Escritura* 16 (31–32) (January–December 1991): 9–16.

Arenas, Reinaldo. *Arturo, la estrella más brillante,*. Barcelona: Montesinos, 1984.

———. *Old Rosa. A Novel in Two Stories*. Translated by Ann Tashi Slater (*Old Rosa*) and Andrew Hurley (*The Brightest Star*). New York: Grove Press, 1989.

———. *El palacio de las blanquísimas mofetas*. Caracas: Monte Avila editores, 1980.

———. *The Palace of the White Skunks*. Translated by Andrew Hurley. New York: Viking Press, 1990.

Arendt, Hannah. *The Origins of Totalitarianism*. New York: Harcourt, Brace & World, Inc., 1951.

Arguedas, José María. *Los ríos profundos*. Madrid: Alianza Editorial, 1981.

———. Arguedas, *Deep Rivers*. Translated by Frances Horning Barraclough, introduction John Murra, afterword Mario Vargas Llosa. Austin: University of Texas Press, 1978.

Auerbach, Eric. "Philology and *Weltliteratur*." *Centennial Review* 13 (Winter 1969): 1–17.

Bados Ciria, Concepción. "*In the Time of the Butterflies*, By Julia Alvarez. History, Fiction, Testimonio and the Dominican Republic." *Monographic Review/ Revista Monográfica* 13 (1997): 406–16.

Balderston, Daniel. "Poetry, Revolution, Homophobia: Polemics from the Mexican Revolution." In *Hispanisms and Homosexualities*, edited by Sylvia Molloy and Robert McKee Irwin. Durham, NC: Duke University Press, 1998.

Bannet, Eve Tavor. "Rewriting the Social Text: The Female *Bildungsroman* in Eighteenth-Century England." In *Reflection and Action: Essays on the Bildungsroman*, edited by James Hardin. Columbia: University of South Carolina Press, 1991.

Bareiro Saguier, Rubén. "La cara oculta del mito guaraní en *Hijo de hombre* de Augusto Roa Bastos." *Escritura* 15 (30) (July–December 1990): 295–311.

Barnet, Miguel. *Biografía de un cimarrón*. México: Siglo Veintiuno Editores, 1968.

———. *The Autobiography of a Runaway Slave*, edited by Miguel Barnet, translated by Jocasta Innes. New York: Pantheon Books, 1968.

———. *Oficio de ángel*. Madrid: Alfaguara, 1989.

———. *La fuente viva*. La Havana: Editorial Letras Cubanas, 1983.

Barrera, Trinidad. "Tácticas, estrategias y utopías de Angeles Mastretta." *Insula* 618–619 (June–July 1998): 33–35.

Barthes, Roland. *Roland Barthes*. Translated by Richard Howard. New York: Hill & Wang, 1977.

Behar, Ruth. *Bridges to Cuba/Puentes a Cuba*. Ann Arbor: University of Michigan Press, 1995.

Bejel, Emilio. "Miguel Barnet." *Hispamérica* 10(29) (August 1981): 41–52.

Bennett, William J., ed. *The Book of Virtues: A Treasury of Great Moral Stories*. New York: Simon & Schuster, 1993.

Bethell, Leslie, ed. *Cuba. A Short History*. New York: Cambridge University Press, 1993.

Beverley, John. *Del Lazarillo al sandinismo: Estudios sobre la función ideológica de la literatura española e hispanoamericana*. Minneapolis, MN: Prisma Institute, 1987.

———. "The Margin at the Center: On *Testimonio*." In *De/Colonizing the Subject. The Politics of Gender in Women's Autobiography*, edited by Sidonie Smith and Julia Watson. Minneapolis: University of Minnesota Press, 1992.

Boixó, José Carlos González. "Feminismo e ideología conservadora." In Teresa de la Parra, *Las memorias de Mamá Blanca*. Velia Bosch, coordinator. México: Colección Archivos, 1988.

Boland, Roy. *Mario Vargas Llosa. Oedipus and the "Papa" State: A Study of Individual and Social Psychology in Mario Vargas Llosa's Novels of Peruvian Reality: From La ciudad y los perros to Historia de Mayta*. Madrid: Voz, 1988.

Buckley, Jerome H. *Season of Youth: The Bildungsroman from Dickens to Golding*. Cambridge: Harvard University Press, 1974.

Butler, Judith. *Gender Trouble: Feminism and the Subversion of Identity*. New York: Routledge, Chapman & Hall, Inc., 1990.

Calderón, Sara Levi. *Dos mujeres*. Mexico: Editorial Diana, 1990.

———. *The Two Mujeres*. Translated by Gina Kaufer. San Francisco: Aunt Lute Books, 1991.

Cardoso, Eliana and Ann Helwege. *Cuba After Communism*. Cambridge: The MIT Press, 1992.

Castedo, Elena. *Paradise*. New York: Grove Weidenfeld, 1990.

———. *El paraíso*. Santiago: Editorial Zeta, 1990.

Castillo, Debra. *Talking Back: Toward a Latin American Feminist Literary Criticism*. Ithaca: Cornell University Press, 1992.

Chodorow, Nancy J. *Feminism and Psychoanalytic Theory*. New Haven: Yale University Press, 1989.

Clifford, James. *The Predicament of Culture: Twentieth-Century Ethnography, Literature and Art*. Cambridge: Harvard University Press, 1988.

Davis, Darién J., ed. *Slavery and Beyond. The African Impact on Latin America and the Caribbean*. Wilmington, DE: Scholarly Resources Inc., 1995.

Duchesne, Juan Ramón. "Miguel Barnet y el testimonio como humanismo." *Revista de Crítica Literaria Latinoamericana* 13(26) (1987): 155–60.

Earle, Peter. "Literature as Survival: Allende's *The House of the Spirits*." *Contemporary Literature* 28(4) (Winter 1987): 543–54.

Eckstein, Susan Eva. *Back From the Future. Cuba under Castro*. Princeton: Princeton University Press, 1994.

Edwards, Lee R. *Psyche as Hero: Female Heroism and Fictional Form*. Middletown, CT: Wesleyan University Press, 1984.

Ellis, Robert Richmond. "The Queer Birds of Juan Goytisolo and Reinaldo Arenas." *Romance Quarterly* 42(1) (Winter 1995): 47–60.

Elshtain, Jean Bethke. "Cultural Conundrums and Gender." In *Cultural Politics in Contemporary America*, edited by Ian Angus and Sut Jhally. New York: Routledge, 1989.

Eltit, Diamela. *El cuarto mundo*. Barcelona: Editorial Seix Barral, 1996.

———. "El cuerpo femenino es un territorio moral." *El Mercurio*, "Revista de libros" 5 January 1992, 1, 4–5.

———. *The Fourth World*. Translated by Dick Gerdes. Lincoln: University of Nebraska Press, 1995.

———. *Sacred Cow*. Translated by Amanda Hopkinson. London: Serpent's Tail, 1995.

———. *Vaca sagrada*. Buenos Aires: Editorial Planeta, 1991.

Epps, Brad. "Estados de deseo: Homosexualidad y nacionalidad (Juan Goytisolo y Reinaldo Arenas a Vuelapluma)." *Revista Iberoamericana* (July–Dec 1996) 62 (176–177): 799–820.

———. "Grotesque Identities: Writing, Death, and the Space of the Subject (Between Michel de Montaigne and Reinaldo Arenas)." *Journal of the Midwest Modern Language Association* 28(1) (1995): 38–55.

Felman, Shoshana. *What Does a Woman Want? Reading and Sexual Difference*. Baltimore: The Johns Hopkins University Press, 1993.

Ferreira Pinto, Cristina. *O Bildungsroman Feminino: Quatro Exemplos Brasileiros*. São Paulo, Brasil: Editora Pespectiva, 1990.

Flores, Juan, Jean Franco and George Yúdice, eds. *On Edge. The Crisis of Contemporary Latin American Culture*. Minneapolis: University of Minnesota Press, 1992.

Foster, David W. *Bodies and Biases. Sexualities in Hispanic Cultures and Literatures*. Minneapolis: University of Minnesota Press, 1996.

———. *Cultural diversity in Latin American Literature*. Albuquerque: University of New Mexico Press, 1994.

———. *Gay and Lesbian Themes in Latin American Writing*. Austin: University of Texas Press, 1991.

———, ed. *Latin American Writers on Gay and Lesbian Themes. A Bio-critical Sourcebook*. Westport, CT: Greenwood Press, 1994.

———. *Sexual Textualities. Essays on Queer/ing Latin American Writing*. Austin: University of Texas Press, 1997.

Fraiman, Susan. *Unbecoming Women: British Women Writers and the Novel of Development*. New York: Columbia University Press, 1993.

Franco, Jean. "Going Public: Reinhabiting the Private." In *On Edge. The Crisis of Contemporary Latin American Culture*, edited by Juan Flores, Jean Franco, and George Yúdice. Minneapolis: University of Minnesota Press, 1992.

———. "Pastiche in Contemporary Latin American Literature." In *Studies in 20th Century Literature* 14(1) (Winter 1990): 95–107.

———. *Plotting Women: Gender and Representation in Mexico*. New York: Columbia University Press, 1989.

Freud, Sigmund. "Mourning and Melancholia." In *Essential Papers on Object Loss*, edited by Rita Frankiel. New York: University Press, 1994.

Friedan, Betty. *The Fountain of Age*. New York: Simon & Schuster, 1993.

Friedman, Thomas L. *The Lexus and the Olive Tree. Understanding Globalization*. New York: Farrar, Straus and Giroux, 1999.

Fuentes, Carlos. *Las buenas conciencias*. México: Fondo de Cultura Económica, 1959.

———. *The Good Conscience*. New York: Farrar, Straus and Giroux, 1961.

Fukuyama, Frances. *Trust: The Social Virtues and the Creation of Prosperity*. New York: Free Press, 1995.

Gadamer, Hans-Georg. "The Problem of Historical Consciousness." In *Interpretive Social Science: A Reader*. Berkeley: University of California Press, 1979.

———. *Truth and Method*. New York: The Seabury Press, 1975.

Gambarini, Elsa Krieger. "The Male Critic and the Woman Writer: Reading Teresa de la Parra's Critics." In *In the Feminine Mode. Essays on Hispanic Women Writers*, edited by Noël Valis and Carol Maier. Lewisburg, PA: Bucknell University Press, 1990.

Garabano, Sandra. "*Vaca sagrada* de Diamela Eltit." *Hispamérica* 25(73) (April 1996): 121–27.

Garber, Marjorie. *Vested Interests: Cross-Dressing & Cultural Anxiety*. London: Routledge, Chapman and Hall, Inc. 1992.

García, Cristina. *Dreaming in Cuban*. New York: Ballantine Books, 1992.

———. *Soñar en cubano*. Translated by Marisol Palés Castro. Santiago: Editorial Planeta, 1994.

García Canclini, Néstor. *Culturas híbridas: Estrategias para entrar y salir de la modernidad*. México: Editorial Grijalbo, 1990.

———. "Cultural Reconversion." In *On Edge. The Crisis of Contemporary Latin American Culture*, edited by Juan Flores, Jean Franco, and George Yúdice. Minneapolis: University of Minnesota Press, 1992.

———. Hybrid Cultures: Strategies for Entering and Leaving Modernity. Translated by Christopher L. Chiappari and Sylvia L. López. Minneapolis: University of Minnesota Press, 1995.

García Pinto, Magdalena. *Women Writers of Latin America*. Translated by Trudy Balch and Magdalena García Pinto. Austin: University of Texas Press, 1991.

Gilbert, Sandra M. and Gubar, Susan. *The Madwoman in the Attic*. New Haven: Yale University Press, 1984.

Gilligan, Carol. *In a Different Voice. Psychological Theory and Women's Development*. Cambridge: Harvard University Press, 1982.

———, Janie Victoria Ward and Jill McLean Taylor, eds. *Mapping the Moral Domain: A Contribution of Women's Thinking to Psychological Theory and Education*. Cambridge: Harvard University Press, 1988.

Gohlman, Susan Ashley. *Starting Over: The Task of Protagonist in the Contemporary Bildungsroman*. New York: Garland Publishing, 1990.

Gómez Ocampo, Gilberto. *Entre María y La vorágine: La literatura colombiana finisecular (1886–1903)*. Bogotá: Ediciones fondo cultural cafetero, 1988.

González, Aníbal. *La novela modernista hispanoamericana*. Madrid: Editorial Gredos, 1987.

González, Patricia Elena and Eliana Ortega, eds. *La sartén por el mango: Encuen-*

tro de escritoras latinoamericanas. Río Piedras, Puerto Rico: Ediciones Huracán, 1985.

González Abellás, Miguel. "Ciudades desiertas: El México profundo de José Agustín." In *Visión de la narrativa hispánica,* edited by Juan Cruz Mendizábal and Juan Fernández Jiménez. Indiana, PA: Department of Spanish and Classical Languages, Indiana University of Pennsylvania, 1999.

González Echevarría, Roberto. *"Biografía de un cimarrón* and the Novel of the Cuban Revolution." In *Novel—A Forum on Fiction,* 13 (3) (1980): 249–63.

———. *La ruta de Severo Sarduy.* Hanover, NH: Ediciones del Norte, 1987.

———. *Myth and Archive. A Theory of Latin American Narrative.* Cambridge: Cambridge University Press, 1990.

———. "Plain Song: Sarduy's *Cobra." Contemporary Literature* 28(4) (Winter 1987): 437–59.

Greenblatt, Stephen. "Fiction and Friction." In *Reconstructing Individualism,* edited by Heller, Thomas C., Morton Sorna and David E. Wellberg. Stanford, CA: Stanford University Press, 1986.

Guerra Cunningham, Lucía. "Vigilancia y confesión en *Abel Rodríguez y sus hermanos* de Ana Vásquez." *PCCLAS Proceedings* 14(1) (Spring 1987): 129–34.

Gugelberger, Georg and Michael Kearney. "Voices for the Voiceless: Testimonial Literature in Latin America." *Latin American Perspectives* 18(3) (1991): 3–14.

Guha, Ranajit, ed. *Subaltern Studies: Writings on South Asian History and Society.* Delhi: Oxford University Press, 1982–86.

Guillén, Claudio. "Luis Sánchez, Ginés de Pasamonte y los inventores del género picaresco." In *Homenaje a Rodríguez Moñino, I.* Madrid: Editorial Castalia, 1966.

Guzmán Bouvard, Marguerite. *Revolutionizing Motherhood: The Mothers of the Plaza de Mayo.* Wilmington, DE: Scholarly Resources, Inc., 1994.

Habermas, Jürgen. *The Structural Transformation of the Public Sphere: An Inquiry into a Category of Bourgeois Society.* Translated by Thomas Burger and Frederick Lawrence. Cambridge: The MIT Press, 1989.

Haynes, Douglas and Gyan Prakash, eds. *Contesting Power. Resistance and Everyday Social Relations in South Asia.* Berkeley: University of California Press, 1992.

Hegel, G. W. F. *Phenomenology of Spirit.* Translated by A.V. Miller. Oxford: Oxford University Press, 1977.

Helg, Aline. *Our Rightful Share. The Afro-Cuban Struggle for Equality, 1886–1912.* Chapel Hill: The University of North Carolina Press, 1995.

Hirsch, Marianne. "Spiritual *Bildung*: The Beautiful Soul as Paradigm." In *The Voyage In: Fictions of Female Development,* edited by Abel, Elizabeth, Marianne Hirsh and Elizabeth Langland. Hanover, NH: University Press of New England, 1983.

Hoover Braendlin, Bonnie. "Bildung in Ethnic Women Writers." *Denver Quarterly,* 17(4) (1983): 75–87.

Howard, Philip A. *Changing History. Afro-Cuban Cabildos and Societies of Color in the Nineteenth Century.* Baton Rouge: Louisiana State University Press, 1998.

Hutcheon, Linda. A Poetics of Postmodernism: History, Theory, Fiction. London: Routledge, 1988.

Jameson, Fredric. "On Literary and Cultural Import-Substitution in the Third

World. The Case of *Testimonio*," in *The Real Thing. Testimonial Discourse and Latin America*, edited by Georg M. Gugelberger. Durham, NC: Duke University Press, 1996.

———. "Postmodernism and Consumer Society." In *The Anti-Aesthetic: Essays on Postmodern Culture,* edited by Hal Foster. Port Townsend, WA: Bay Press, 1983.

Jara, René and Hernán Vidal, eds. *Testimonio y literatura.* Minneapolis, MN: Ideologies & Literature, 1986.

Kadir, Djelal. *Questing Fictions: Latin America's Family Romance.* Minneapolis: University of Minnesota, 1986.

Kaminsky, Amy. *Reading the Body Politic. Feminist Criticism and Latin American Women Writers.* Minneapolis: University of Minnesota Press, 1993.

Kantaris, Elia. "The Politics of Desire: Alienation and Identity in the Work of Marta Traba." *Forum for Modern Language Studies* 25(3) (1989): 248–64.

Kason, Nancy. "La conciencia del exilio en *Conversación al sur* de Marta Traba." *Alba de América* 8(14–15) (July 1990): 221–27.

Kerr, Lucille. *Reclaiming the Author: Figures and Fictions from Spanish America.* Durham, NC: Duke University Press, 1992.

Kleinbord Labovitz, Esther. *The Myth of the Heroine: The Female Bildungsroman in the Twentieth Century.* New York: Peter Lang, 1986.

Kohn, Alfie. "The Trouble with Character Education." In *The Construction of Children's Character*, edited by Alex Molnar, Ninety-sixth Yearbook of the National Society for the Study of Education, Part II. Chicago: University of Chicago Press, 1997.

Kontje, Todd. *Private Lives in the Public Sphere: The German Bildungsroman as Metafiction.* University Park: Pennsylvania State University Press, 1992.

Krauel Ricardo. "Lectura mítica y ambigüedad genérica: *El cuarto mundo* de Diamela Eltit y *Diana o la cazadora solitaria* de Carlos Fuentes." *Inti,* 45 (primavera 1997): 255–65.

Kristeva, Julia. *Powers of Horror. An Essay on Abjection.* New York: Columbia University Press, 1982.

Kushigian, Julia. "Gender and Culture Reconsidered: The Transformation of *Cobra* into *Bildungsroman.*" In *Between the Self and the Void: Essays in Honor of Severo Sarduy,* edited by Alicia Rivero-Potter. Boulder, CO: Society of Spanish and Spanish-American Studies, 1998.

——— and Severo Sarduy. "La serpiete en la sinagoga." *Vuelta* 89 (8) (April 1984): 14–20.

———. "Severo Sarduy, orientalista posmodernista en camino hacia la autorrealización: Une ménagerie à trois—*Cobra, Colibrí y Cocuyo.*" In *Severo Sarduy Obra Completa*, Gustavo Guerrero y François Wahl, coordinators. Paris: Archivos, 1999.

———. "Transgresión de la autobiografía y el *Bildungsroman* en *Hasta no verte, Jesús mío.*" *Revista Iberoamericana* 53(140) (July–September 1987): 667–77.

Labanyi, Jo. "Topologies of Catastrophe. Horror and Abjection in Diamela Eltit's *Vaca sagrada.*" In *Latin American Women's Writing. Feminist Readings in Theory and Crisis,* edited by Anny Brooksbank Jones and Catherine Davies. Oxford: Clarendon Press, 1996.

Lacan, Jacques. *Écrits. A Selection*. Translated by Alan Sheridan. New York: W. W. Norton Co., 1977.

Lagos-Pope, María Inés. *En tono mayor: Relatos de formación de protagonista femenina en Hispanoamérica*. Santiago: Editorial Cuarto Propio, 1996.

Leland, Christopher Towne. *The Last Happy Men. The Generation of 1922, Fiction and the Argentine Reality*. Syracuse, NY: Syracuse University Press, 1986.

Lértora, Juan Carlos. *Una poética de literatura menor: la narrativa de Diamela Eltit*. Santiago, Chile: Editorial Cuarto Propio, 1993.

López, Kimberle S. "Women on the Verge of a Revolution: Madness and Resistance in Cristina García's *Dreaming in Cuban*." *Letras Femeninas* 22(1–2) (Spring–Fall 1996): 33–49.

Ludmer, Josefina. "Las vidas de los héroes de Roa Bastos." *Cuadernos Hispanoamericanos* 493/94 (July–August 1991): 113–18.

Luis, William. *Literary Bondage. Slavery in Cuban Narrative*. Austin: University of Texas Press, 1990.

MacIntyre, Alastair. *After Virtue: A Study in Moral Theory*. Notre Dame, IN: University of Notre Dame Press, 1984.

MacKinnon, Catharine A. *Feminism Unmodified: Discourses on Life and Law*. Cambridge: Harvard University Press, 1987.

———. *Toward a Feminist Theory of the State*. Cambridge: Harvard University Press, 1989.

Magnarelli, Sharon. *The Lost Rib. Female Characters in the Spanish American Novel*. Lewisburg, PA: Bucknell University Press; London: Associated University Presses, 1985.

———. Review of Allende's *La casa de los espíritus*. *Latin American Literary Review* 14(28) (July–December 1986): 101–04.

Mahoney, Dennis F. "The Apprenticeship of the Reader: The *Bildungsroman* of the 'Age of Goethe.'" In *Reflection and Action: Essays on the Bildungsroman*, edited by James Hardin. Columbia: University of South Carolina Press, 1991.

Marks, Camilo. "Otra casa de campo." Review of *El paraíso* by Elena Castedo. *La Epoca* 141 23 December 1990: 3.

Márquez, Enrique. "*Cobra*: De aquel oscuro objeto del deseo." *Revista Iberoamericana* 57(154) (January–March 1991): 301–7.

Martínez, Luz Angela. "La dimensión espacial en 'Vaca Sagrada' de Diamela Eltit: La urbe narrativa." *Revista Chilena de Literatura* 49 (1996): 65–82.

Martini, Fritz, "Bildungsroman—Term and Theory." In *Reflection and Action: Essays on the Bildungsroman*, edited by James Hardin. Columbia: University of South Carolina Press, 1991.

Masiello, Francine. *Between Civilization & Barbarism. Women, Nation, and Literary Culture in Modern Argentina*. Lincoln: University of Nebraska Press, 1992.

———. "Texto, ley, transgresión: especulación sobre la novela (feminista) de vanguardia." *Revista Iberoamericana* 51(132–33) (July–December 1985): 807–22.

Mastreta, Angeles. *Mal de amores*. Buenos Aires: Seix Barral, 1996.

———. *Lovesick*. Translated by Margaret Sayers Peden. New York: Riverhead Books, 1997.

McGee, Patrick. *Telling the Other. The Question of Values in Modern and Postcolonial Writing*. Ithaca: Cornell University Press, 1992.

Menchú, Rigoberta and Elizabeth Burgos. *Yo me llamo Rigoberta y así me nació la conciencia.* México: Siglo Veintiuno, 1985.

Méndez Faith, Teresa. "Dictadura y 'espacios cárceles': Doble reflejo de una misma realidad en *Hijo de hombre* y *Yo el Supremo.*" *Cuadernos hispanoamericanos* 493/94 (July–August 1991): 239–45.

Méndez Rodenas, Adriana. *Gender and Nationalism in Colonial Cuba. The Travels of Santa Cruz y Montalvo, Condesa de Merlin.* Nashville, TN: Vanderbilt University Press, 1998.

———. Review of *Colibrí. Revista Iberoamericana* 51(130–31) (1985): 400–1.

Mercado, Tununa. *En estado de memoria.* Buenos Aires: Ada Korn Editora, 1990.

Mesa-Lagos, Carmelo, ed. *Cuba After the Cold War.* Pittsburgh, PA: University of Pittsburgh Press, 1993.

Meyer, Doris. "'Parenting the Text': Female Creativity and Dialogic Relationships in Isabel Allende's *La casa de los espíritus.*" *Hispania* 73(2) (May 1990): 360–65.

Meyer Spacks, Patricia. *The Adolescent Idea: Myths of Youth and the Adult Imagination.* New York: Basic Books, 1981.

Miller, Francesca. *Latin American Women and the Search for Social Justice.* Hanover, NH: University Press of New England, 1991.

Miller, Jean Baker. *Toward a New Psychology of Women.* Boston: Beacon Press, 1976.

Molloy, Sylvia. *En breve cárcel.* Buenos Aires: Ediciones Simurg, 1998.

———. *Certificate of Absence.* Translated by Daniel Balderston with Sylvia Molloy. Austin: University of Texas, 1989.

———. "Too Wilde for Comfort: Desire and Ideology in Fin-de-Siècle Spanish America." *Social Text* 2–3(31–32) (1992): 187–201.

Molloy, Sylvia and Robert McKee Irwin, editors. *Hispanisms and Homosexualities.* Durham, NC: Duke University Press, 1998.

Monsiváis, Carlos. *Escenas de pudor y liviandad.* México: Editorial Grijalbo, 1981.

———. "No con un sollozo, sino entre disparos. (Notas sobre cultura mexicana 1910–1968)." *Revista Iberoamericana* 55(148–49) (July–December 1989): 715–35.

———. "Ortodoxia y heterodoxia en las alcobas. (Hacia una crónica de costumbres y creencias sexuales en México." *Debate feminista* 6(11) (1995): 183–212.

Montecino, Sonia. *Madres y huachos. Alegorías del mestizaje chileno.* Santiago: Editorial Sudamericana, 1991.

Moore, Carlos. *Castro, The Blacks, and Africa.* Los Angeles: Center for Afro-American Studies, University of California, Los Angeles, 1988.

Mora, Gabriela, "El *Bildungsroman* y la experiencia latinoamericana: 'La pájara pinta' de Albalucía Angel." In *La sartén por el mango. Encuentros de escritoras latinoamericanas*, edited by Patricia Elena González and Eliana Ortega. Río Piedras, Puerto Rico: Ediciones Huracán, Inc., 1985.

Moraña, Mabel. "Historicismo y legitimación del poder en *El gesticulador* de Rodolfo Usigli." *Revista Iberoamericana* 148–49 (July–December 1989): 1261–75.

Moretti, Franco. *The Way of the World: The Bildungsroman in European Culture.* London: Verso, 1987.

Moulian, Tomás. *Chile Actual: Anatomía de un mito.* Santiago: LOM-ARCIS, 1997.

Nance, Kimberly A. "Pied Beauty: Juxtaposition and Irony in Teresa de la Parra's *Las memorias de Mamá Blanca.*" *Letras Femeninas* 16(1–2) (Spring–Fall 1990): 45–49.

Nofal, Rossana. "*Biografía de un cimarrón* de Barnet: La construcción de una voz." *Revista Chilena de Literatura* 40 (November 1992): 35–39.

Norat, Gisela. "Diálogo fraternal: *El cuarto mundo* de Diamela Eltit y *Cristóbal Nonato* de Carlos Fuentes." *Chasqui* 23(2) (1994): 74–85.

Norton, Robert E. *The Beautiful Soul. Aesthetic Morality in the Eighteenth Century.* Ithaca: Cornell University Press, 1995.

Nussbaum, Martha. *Cultivating Humanity. A Classical Defense of Reform in Liberal Education.* Cambridge: Harvard University Press, 1997.

O'Connell, Patrick L. "Individual and Collective Identity Through Memory in Three Novels of Argentina's 'El Proceso.'" *Hispania* 81(1) (March 1998): 31–41.

Oldenburg, Veena Talwar "Lifestyle as Resistance: The Case of the Courtesans of Lucknow." In *Contesting Power. Resistance and Everyday Social Relations in South Asia*, edited by Douglas Haynes and Gyan Prakash. Berkeley: University of California Press, 1992.

Ortega, Julio. "Postmodernism in Latin America." In *Postmodern Fiction in Europe and the Americas*, edited by Theo D'haen and Hans Bertens. Amsterdam: Rodopi, 1988: 193–208.

———. "Diez novelas hispanoamericanas del XX." *Inti* 48 (Fall 1998): 47–52.

———. "Texto, comunicación y cultura en *Los ríos profundos* de José María Arguedas." *Nueva Revista de Fiología Hispánica* 31(1) (1982): 44–82.

Oviedo, José Miguel. *Mario Vargas Llosa: La invención de una realidad.* Barcelona: Barral Editores, 1970.

Pacheco, Carlos. "*Hijo de hombre*: El escritor entre la voz y la escritura." *Escritura*, 15(30) (July–December 1990): 401–19.

Pagels, Elaine. *The Gnostic Gospels.* New York: Vintage Books, 1989.

Parra, Teresa de la. *Las memorias de Mamá Blanca.* México: Colección Archivos, 1988.

———. *Mama Blanca's Souvenirs.* Translated by Harriet de Onis. Washington: General Secretariat, Organization of American States, 1959.

Paz, Octavio. *Posdata.* Mexico: Siglo Veintiuno Editores, 1979.

———. *Puertas al campo.* Mexico City: UNAM, 1966.

Piña, Juan Andrés. "Diamela Eltit: Escritos sobre un cuerpo" quoted in Jo Labanyi "Topologies of Catastrophe. Horror and Abjection in Diamela Eltit's *Vaca sagrada.*" In *Latin American Women's Writing*, edited by Anny Brooksbank Jones and Catherine Davies. New York: Oxford University Press, 1996.

Pollitt, Katha. "Are Women Morally Superior to Men?" *The Nation* 255/22 (28 December 1992): 799–807.

Poniatowksa, Elena. *Hasta no verte Jesús mío.* México: Ediciones Era, 1969.

————. *Here's To You, Jesusa!* Translated by Deanna Heikkinen. New York: Farrar, Straus and Giroux, 2001.

————. *"Hasta no verte Jesús mío*: Jesusa Palancares.*"Vuelta* 24 (1978): 5–11.

————. "Testimonios de una escritora: Elena Poniatowska en micrófono." In *La sartén por el mango. Encuentros de escritoras latinoamericanas,* edited by Patricia Elena González and Eliana Ortega. Río Piedras, Puerto Rico: Ediciones Huracán, Inc., 1985.

Prada Oropeza, Renato. "De lo testimonial al testimonio." In *Testimonio y literatura,* edited by René Jara and Hernán Vidal. Minneapolis, MN: Ideologies & Literature, 1986.

Pratt, Annis with Barbara White, Andrea Loewenstein, and Mary Wyer. *Archetypal Patterns in Women's Fiction.* Bloomington: Indiana University Press, 1981.

Prieto, René. "La ambivolencia en la obra de Severo Sarduy." *Cuadernos Americanos,* 1 (CCLVIII) (January–February 1985): 241–53.

————. "Mimetic Stratagems: The Unreliable Narrator in Latin America Literature." *Revista de Estudios Hispánicos* 19(3) (October 1985): 61–73.

Proctor, Robert. *Education's Great Amnesia: Reconsidering the Humanities from Petrach to Freud.* Bloomington: Indiana University Press, 1988.

Puga, María Luisa. *La viuda.* México: Editorial Grijalbo, 1994.

Puig, Manuel. *El beso de la mujer araña,* Barcelona: Seix Barral, 1976.

————. *Kiss of the Spider Woman.* Translated by Thomas Colchie. New York: Alfred A. Knopf, 1979.

Quiroga Clérigo, Manuel. "Un pueblo en busca de su libertad. Relectura de *Hijo de hombre.*" *Cuadernos Hispanoamericanos* 493–494 (July–August 1991): 225–238.

Rabinow, Paul and William M. Sullivan, eds. *Interpretive Social Science: A Second Look.* Berkeley: University of California Press, 1979.

Raymundo, L. Review of Agustín's *Ciudades desiertas. La palabra y el hombre* 63 (July–September 1987): 136.

Reyzábal, María Victoria. "Los ríos iniciáticos de José María Arguedas." *Anthropos* 128 (1992): 57–60.

Rich, Adrienne. *Of Woman Born.* New York: Norton, 1976.

Richard, Nelly. "Bordes, diseminación, postmodernismo: una metáfora latinoamericana de fin de siglo." In *Las culturas de fin de siglo en América Latina,* compiled by Josefina Ludmer. Rosario, Argentina: Beatriz Viterbo, 1994.

————. *Residuos y metáforas. (Ensayos de crítica cultural sobre el Chile de la transición).* Santiago: Editorial Cuarto Propio, 1998.

Rickels, Laurence A. *Aberrations of Mourning: Writing on German Crypts.* Detroit, MI: Wayne State University Press, 1988.

Rivero-Potter, Alicia. "Algunas metáforas somáticas—erótico—escripturales—en *De donde son los cantantes* y *Cobra.*" *Revista Iberoamericana* 49(123–24) (April–September 1983): 497–507.

————. "Iconografía oriental y la leyenda del futuro Buda parodiadas en *Cobra* y *Maitreya.*" *Revista de la Universidad Autónoma de México* June 1986: 14–19.

Roa Bastos, Augusto. *Hijo de hombre.* Buenos Aires: Editorial Losada, 1960.

————. *Son of Man.* Translated by Rachel Caffyn. Afterword, Jean Franco. New York: Monthly Review Press, 1988.

Roffiel, Rosamaría. *Amora.* Mexico: Colección Fábula, 1990.

Rojas, Mario. "*La casa de los espíritus,* de Isabel Allende: Un caleidoscopio de espejos desordenados." *Revista Iberoamericana* 51(132–133) (July–December 1985): 917–25.

————. "Vagando por ciudades desiertas." Review of *Ciudades desiertas* by José Agustín. *Revista de la Universidad de México* April 1983: 51–52.

Romano, James V. "Authorial Identity and National Disintegration in Latin America." *Ideologies & Literature* 4(1) (Spring 1989): 167–98.

Rosowski, Susan. "The Novel of Awakening." In *The Voyage In: Fictions of Female Development,* edited by Elizabeth Abel, Marianne Hirsh and Elizabeth Langland. Hanover, NH: University Press of New England, 1983.

Rothstein, Frances. "Capitalist Industrialization and the Increasing Cost of Children." In *Women and Change in Latin America,* June Nash and Helen Safa and contributors. South Hadley, MA: Bergin & Garvey Publishers, Inc., 1985.

Sammons, Jeffrey. "The *Bildungsroman* for Nonspecialists: An Attempt at a Clarification." In *Reflection and Action: Essays on the Bildungsroman,* edited by James Hardin. Columbia: University of South Carolina Press, 1991.

Santiago, Esmeralda. *América's Dream.* New York: Harper Collins, 1996.

————. *El sueño de América.* Editorial Grijalbo, 1996.

Sarduy, Severo. *Christ on the Rue Jacob.* Translated by Suzanne Jill Levine and Carol Maier. San Francisco: Mercury House, 1995.

————. *Cobra.* Buenos Aires: Editorial Sudamericana, 1972.

————. *Cobra and Maitreya.* Translated by Suzanne Jill Levine. Normal, IL: Dalkey Archive Press, 1995.

————. *Cocuyo.* Barcelona: Editorial Tusquets, 1990.

————. *Colibrí.* Barcelona: Editorial Argos Vergara, 1984.

————. *El Cristo de la Rue Jacob.* Barcelona: Edicions del Mall, 1987.

————. *Escrito sobre un cuerpo.* Buenos Aires: Editorial Sudamericana, 1969.

————. "¿Por qué el oriente? " *Quimera* 102 (1991): 39–41.

————. *Written on a Body.* Translated by Carol Maier. New York: Lumen Books, 1989.

———— and Julia A. Kushigian, "La serpiente en la sinagoga." *Vuelta* 89(8) (April 1984): 14–20.

Sarkar, Sumit. "The Conditions and Nature of Subaltern Militancy: Bengal from Swadeshi to Non-cooperation, c. 1905–1922." In *Subaltern Studies: Writings on South Asian History and Society* , edited by Ranajit Guha. Delhi: Oxford University Press, 1982–86.

Sarlo, Beatriz. *Escenas de la vida posmoderna: Intelectuales, arte y videocultura en la Argentina.* Buenos Aires: Espasa Calpe Argentina S.A./Ariel, 1994.

Sax, Benjamin. *Images of Identity: Goethe and the Problem of Self-Conception in the Nineteenth Century.* New York: Peter Lang, 1987.

Schaefer-Rodríguez, Claudia. "Monobodies, Antibodies, and the Body Politic: Sara Levi Calderón's Dos mujeres." In *Bodies and Biases. Sexualities in Hispanic Cultures and Literatures,* edited by David William Foster and Roberto Reis. Minneapolis: University of Minnesota Press, 1996.

Schiminovich, Flora. "Two modes of Writing the Female Self: Isabel Allende's *The House of the Spirits* and Clarice Lispector's *The Stream of Life*." In *Redefining Autobiography in Twentieth-Century Women's Fiction. An Essay Collection*, edited by Janice Morgan and Colette T. Hall. New York: Garland Publishing, 1991.

Schneider, Judith Morganroth. "Ana Vásquez: Interrogantes sobre el exilio y la identidad." *Alba de América* 6(10–11) (July 1988): 225–34.

Schulz Cruz, Bernard. "*Vaca sagrada*: El cuerpo a borbotones de escritura." *Hispanófila* 123 (1998): 67–72.

Scott, James C. *Weapons of the Weak. Everyday Forms of Peasant Resistance*. New Haven: Yale University Press, 1985.

Serrano, Marcela. *Antigua vida mía*. Mexico: Alfaguara, 1995.

Shaffner, Randolph. *The Apprenticeship Novel. A Study of the Bildungsroman as a Regulative Type in Western Literature with a Focus on Three Classic Representatives by Goethe, Maugham, and Mann*. New York: Peter Lang, 1984.

Sheehy, Gail. *Passages: Predictable Crises of Adult Life*. New York: Dutton, 1976.

———. *Understanding Men's Passages: Discovering the New Map of Men's Lives*. New York: Random House, 1998.

Showalter, Elaine. *A Literature of Their Own: British Women Novelists From Brontë to Lessing*. Princeton: Princeton University Press, 1977.

———. "Feminist Criticism in the Wilderness." *Critical Inquiry* 8(2) (Winter 1981): 179–205.

Sklodowska, Elzbieta. "La forma testimonial y la novelística de Miguel Barnet." *Revista/Review Interamericana* 12(3) (Fall 1982): 375–84.

———. "Miguel Barnet." in *Dictionary of Literary Biography* 145: 57–65.

———. *Testimonio hispanoamericano: Historia, teoría, poética*. New York: Peter Lang, 1992.

Smith, Paul Julian. "Cuban Homosexualities: On the Beach with Néstor Almendros and Reinaldo Arenas," in *Hispanisms and Homosexualities*, edited by Sylvia Molloy and Robert McKee Irwin. Durham, NC: Duke University Press, 1998.

———. *Vision Machines. Cinema, Literature and Sexuality in Spain and Cuba, 1983–93*. London: Verso, 1996.

Smith, Sidonie and Julia Watson, eds. *De/Colonizing the Subject. The Politics of Gender in Women's Autobiography*. Minneapolis: University of Minnesota Press, 1992.

Smith, Sidonie. *A Poetics of Women's Autobiography: Marginality and the Fictions of Self-Representation*. Bloomington: Indiana University Press, 1987.

———. "Who's Talking/Who's Talking Back? The Subject of Personal Narrative." *Signs* 18(2) (Winter 1993): 392–407.

Solá, María. "*Conversación al sur*, novela para no olvidar." *Sin nombre* 12(4) (July–September 1982): 64–71.

Sommer, Doris. *Foundational Fictions. The National Romances of Latin America*. Berkeley: University of California Press, 1991.

Soto, Francisco. *The Pentagonía*. Gainesville: University Press of Florida, 1994.

Soto, Román. "Fracaso y desengaño: héroes, aprendizaje y confrontación en *La ciudad y los perros* y *Conversación en la catedral.*" *Chasqui* 19 (2) (1990): 67–74.

Spacks, Patricia Meyer. *The Adolescent Idea: Myths of Youth and the Adult Imagination*. New York: Basic Books, Inc., 1981.

Spivak, Gaytri. "Imperialism and Sexual Difference." *Oxford Literary Review* 8(1–2) (1986): 225–40.

Steele, Cynthia. "Toward a Socialist Feminist Criticism of Latin American Literature" *Ideologies & Literature* 4(16) (May–June 1983): 323–39.

Steinecke, Harmut. "The Novel and the Individual: The Significance of Goethe's Wilhelm Meister in the Debate about the *Bildungsroman.*" In *Reflection and Action: Essays on the Bildungsroman*, edited by James Hardin. Columbia: University of South Carolina Press, 1991.

Swales, Martin. *The German Bildungsroman from Wieland to Hesse*. Princeton: Princeton University Press, 1978.

———. "Irony and the Novel." In *Reflection and Action. Reflection and Action: Essays on the Bildungsroman*, edited by James Hardin. Columbia: University of South Carolina Press, 1991.

Tafra, Sylvia. *Diamela Eltit: El rito de pasaje como estrategia textual*. Santiago: Ril Editores, 1998.

Tittler, Jonathan. *Narrative Irony in the Contemporary Spanish-American Novel*. Ithaca: Cornell University Press, 1984.

Traba, Marta. *Conversación al sur*. México: Siglo Veintiuno editores, 1981.

———. *Mothers and Shadows*. Translated by Jo Labanyi. London: Readers International, Inc., 1985.

Tu, Wei-ming. "Mustering Conceptual Resources to Grasp a World in Flux." In *International Studies in the Next Millennium. Meeting the Challenge of Globalization*, edited by Julia A. Kushigian. Westport, CT: Greenwood Press, 1998.

Ulloa, Justo C. and Leonor A. de. "La función del fragmento en Colibrí de Sarduy." *MLN* 109(2) (March 1994): 268–82.

Vargas Llosa, Mario. *La ciudad y los perros*. Barcelona: Editorial Seix Barral, 1970.

——— and Julia A. Kushigian, "Entrevista," 63, Hispamérica 1992: 35–42.

———. *José María Arguedas, entre sapos y halcones*. Madrid: Ediciones Cultura Hispánica del Centro Iberoamericano de Cooperación, 1978.

———. "The Power of Lies." *Encounter* 69(5) (1987): 28–30.

———. "Questions of Conquest." *Harper's* (December 1990): 45–53.

———. *The Time of the Hero*. Translated by Lysander Kemp. New York: Farrar, Straus and Giroux, 1986.

Vásquez, Ana. *Abel Rodíguez y sus hermanos*. Barcelona: La Gaya Ciencia, 1981.

———. "En boca cerrada no entran moscas," quoted in "Las huellas del 'propio camino' en los relatos de Ana Vásquez," Helena Araujo. *Escritura* 16(31–32) (January–December 1991): 9–16.

———. "Escribir en el exilio," quoted in "Ana Vásquez: Interrogantes sobre el exilio y la identidad," Judith Morganroth Schneider. *Alba de América* 6(10–11) (1988): 225–34.

Vásquez, Mary. "Cuba as Text and Context in Cristina García's *Dreaming in*

Cuban." *The Bilingual Review/La Revista Bilingüe* 20(1) (January–April 1995): 22–27.

Vidal, Hernán. "Postmodernism, Postleftism and Neo-Avant-Gardism." In *The Postmodernism Debate in Latin America,* edited by John Beverley, Michael Aronna, and José Oviedo. Durham, NC: Duke University Press, 1995.

Viera, Joseph M. "Matriarchy and Mayhem: Awakenings in Cristina García's *Dreaming in Cuban.*" *Americas Review* 24(3–4) (Fall/Winter 1996): 231–42.

Von Mücke, Dorothea. *Virtue and the Veil of Illusion.* Stanford, CA: Stanford University Press, 1991.

Walter, Monika. "El cimarrón en una cimarronada: Nuevos motivos para rechazar un texto y de la forma como éste se nos impone." *Revista de Crítica Literaria Latinoamericana* 18(36) 1992: 201–5.

Weber, Max. *Economy and Society. An Outline of Interpretive Sociology,* 2 vols, edited by G. Roth and C. Wittich. Berkeley: University of California Press, 1978.

White, Barbara A. *Growing Up Female: Adolescent Girlhood in American Fiction.* Westport, CT: Greenwood Press, 1985.

Williams, Raymond L. *The Postmodern Novel in Latin America. Politics, Culture, and the Crisis of Truth.* New York: St. Martin's Press, 1995.

Wynne, Edward. "The Great Tradition in Education: Transmitting Moral Values." *Educational Leadership* 43 (December 1985/January 1986): 6.

Ybarra-Frausto, Tomás. "Interview with Tomás Ybarra-Frausto: The Chicano Movement in a Multicultural/Multinational Society." In *On Edge. The Crisis of Contemporary Latin American Culture,* edited by Juan Flores, Jean Franco, and George Yúdice. Minneapolis: University of Minnesota Press, 1992.

Yúdice, George, "Postmodernity and Transnational Capitalism." In *On Edge. The Crisis of Contemporary Latin American Culture,* edited by Juan Flores, Jean Franco, and George Yúdice. Minneapolis: University of Minnesota Press, 1992.

———. "Testimonio and Postmodernism." *Latin American Perspectives* 18(3) (Summer 1991): 115–31.

Index

Abel, Elizabeth, 224n.9
Achugar, Hugo, 238n.18
Acosta de Samper, Soledad, 32, 125–
26, 130–31; *El corazón de la mujer*,
126, 235n.8; *Teresa la limeña*, 17,
32, 34, 125–31, 170
Afro-Cuban, 176–77, 185
Agosín, Marjorie, 143, 229n.15,
234n.41
Agustín, José, 34, 170, 180, 187; *Ciu-
dades desiertas*, 34, 170, 180,
187–89
Aizenberg, Edna, 223n.1
Alexander, M. Jacqui, 240n.18
Allende, Isabel, 31, 40, 229n.13; *La
casa de los espíritus*, 17, 31, 34, 40–
50, 170
Almendros, Néstor, 172
Alonso, Carlos, 16–17, 125, 148
Alvarez, Julia, 35, 191, 214, 216; *In the
Time of the Butterflies* [*En el tiempo
de las mariposas*] 17, 35, 191, 211,
214–16
Amancebamiento, 38
Angus, Ian, 221
Animism, 138,
Anzaldúa, Gloria, 32, 215, 225n.18
Araujo, Helena, 143, 233n.25
Arenas, Reinaldo, 34, 170–72, 176,
179–80; *Antes que anochezca*, 176;
Arturo, la estrella más brillante, 34,
170–72, 176–80; *El palacio de las
blanquísimas mofetas* , 34, 170–76
Arendt, Hannah, 33, 227n.42
Arguedas, José María, 31, 38, 125, 136,
138, 141–43, 162; *Los ríos profun-
dos*, 31, 38, 125, 136–45, 162, 211
Auerbach, Eric, 94, 232n.1
Ayllu, 141

Bakhtin, Mikhail, 34, 162
Balderston, Daniel, 26

Bannet, Eve Tavor, 32
Bareiro Saguier, Rubén, 162
Barnet, Miguel, 34, 95–97, 102–3, 106,
147–49, 176, 233n.22; *Biografía de
un cimarrón*, 17, 34, 147–56, 170,
176, 211; *Oficio de ángel*, 34, 95–
106, 108, 170; *La sagrada familia*,
102
Barracones, 149
Barraganía, 38
Barthes, Roland, 191, 211
Batista, Fulgencio, 98, 104
Beautiful Soul, 13, 24–25, 100, 102,
108, 120, 122, 221, 226n.37, 227n.41
Behar, Ruth, 218
Being-in-the-world, 26, 37, 102, 106,
123, 155, 157, 204, 218, 220–21
Bejel, Emilio, 142
Betancourt, Juan René, 148
Beverley, John, 22, 32, 146, 225n.29
Bildung, 13–27, 64, 80, 94, 99, 111,
119, 135, 150–151, 155, 157, 170,
221, 223–24n.7
Bildung process, 13, 15–16, 22, 25–28,
30–31,36, 41–44, 46, 49, 50–51, 54,
60, 64–65, 68–69, 72–80, 86–89,
91–93, 98, 102, 106, 109, 113–14,
117, 120, 129, 131, 136, 138–39,
144, 146–47, 151–52, 156, 158, 162,
164, 167–68, 171, 174–75, 180, 183,
186, 191, 193, 197–98, 200, 204,
206, 209, 211–12, 214, 216–19, 221
Bildungsroman, 13–16, 20–21, 76–77,
91, 94, 102, 104, 111–12, 120, 124–
25, 128, 131, 135, 150, 161–62, 171,
180, 190, 194, 198, 200, 204, 211,
214, 220–21, 223n.1, 236n.1; bridging modernism and postmodernism,
16; classical, 28; female, 29–34, 111;
foundational, 97, 146–147, 214,
231n.29; goals of, 19; marginalized,

263